THE LIFE AND TIMES OF MENAHEM BEGIN

By the author

THUNDER OVER THE MEDITERRANEAN
ADOLF HITLER: A BIOGRAPHY
THE CASE FOR ISRAEL
THE REAL ROCKEFELLER: A BIOGRAPHY
TO WHOM PALESTINE?
BIG GOVERNMENT
BUT SOLDIERS WONDERED WHY
WAR HAS SEVEN FACES

NORTH LITTLE ROCK HIGH SCHOOL
WEST CAMPUS LIBRARY
101 West 22nd Street
North Little Rock, Arkansas 72114

DATE			

The life and times
of Menahem Begin

92   Gervasi, Frank
BEGIN   Henry, 1906-

31854

THE LIFE AND TIMES OF MENAHEM BEGIN

Rebel to Statesman

by Frank Gervasi

G. P. PUTNAM'S SONS, NEW YORK

Library of Congress Cataloging in Publication Data

Gervasi, Frank Henry, 1908-
   The life and times of Menahem Begin.

   Bibliography
   Includes index.
   1. Begin, Menahem, 1913-   2. Prime ministers—
Israel—Biography.   I. Title.
DS126.6.B33G47   956.94'05'0924 [B]   78-11555
ISBN 0-399-12299-0

Printed in the United States of America

This book is for
my sister
Clementine

Acknowledgments

Most helpful in obtaining the material for this book was my friend and former colleague, Harry Zinder, who long ago—the time was February, 1940—introduced me to Jerusalem and Zionism. He and his Sabra wife, Hemdah, instructed me in the struggle for nationhood of the Jewish people of what was then still Palestine and over the years nourished in me an understanding that eventually blossomed into a deep affection for Israel.

Of the nearly one hundred persons interviewed in the course of the research, a goodly number were interviewed on my behalf by Harry Zinder, who during World War II was a Time-Life Inc. correspondent in the Middle East, and shared with me a suite in Shepherd's Hotel when I was covering the area for *Collier's Weekly* back in the early 1940s. American-born, Harry Zinder now lives and works as an Israeli, but has retained his keen journalistic sense. His frequent memorandums and taped interviews with some of the personalities involved in this tale were immensely helpful. Herewith, Harry old friend, my warm thanks for keeping me up to date in an ever-changing situation, and kisses to the lovely Hemdah.

My thanks also to Menahem Begin's sister, Rachel, who gave me much valuable information, and my gratitude to the Prime Minister's aides, Yehiel Kadishai and Yehuda Avner. They told me many things about their boss I might not otherwise have learned, and made it possible for me to study Begin in action in Jerusalem, in London, whither I accompanied him early in December, and in New York, where I talked with the Prime Minister briefly after the Camp David summit conference.

Bouquets also to Sybil Wong, a professional researcher and an author in her own right; and to Arlene Gross, another experienced researcher. Between them, they "strip-mined" the writings and speeches of Menahem Begin for information about his adventures as leader of the Irgun's revolt against the British available nowhere else, thereby rendering valuable service hereby gratefully acknowledged.

For information about President Carter's "package deal" that provided the F-15s to Saudi Arabia and related military data concerning the altered balance of power in the Middle East, I am indebted to my son, Tom Gervasi, an authority on weaponry, and author of the highly successful "Arsenal of Democracy."

With all due respect to the aforementioned helpers, the one person who contributed most during nine months of arduous writing and rewriting, was my wife Georgia. She fed me regularly, saw to it I did not smoke too many cigarettes or drink too much coffee, and otherwise kept me mentally and physically fit throughout the ordeal. For her patience and supportive attitude I hereby confer upon her the DMS—the medal for Distinguished Matrimonial Service—with palms.

Lastly, but by no means leastly, my sincere thanks to Rochelle Mancini, who typed and retyped the manuscript, doubled as researcher when necessary, and was generally encouraging during the agony of creation and to my friend and fellow Baltimorean, Stanley Blumberg, who suggested the project in the first place.

FRANK GERVASI
New York, November 6, 1978

Contents

Prologue

Wherein thou judgest another,
thou condemnest thyself

—New Testament, Romans 2:1

When Menahem Begin assumed command of the Irgun Zvai Leumi in Palestine in 1943, I was a war correspondent based in Cairo. I was working for *Collier's Weekly* at the time and had been covering the fighting in the Middle East since early 1940.

I first heard Begin's name sometime in the late summer of 1944, shortly after he had started his revolutionary underground struggle against British rule in Palestine, the territory which His Britannic Majesty's Government had solemnly if somewhat ambiguously promised to the Jewish people—in the famous Balfour Declaration of 1917—as the site of their future national homeland.

Reports from Jerusalem reaching the gossip mill at the bar of Cairo's Shepherd's Hotel—a favorite watering place for thirsty reporters and British officers—were to the effect that Menahem Begin was a "deserter" from General Anders' Polish army and a "radical right wing trouble-maker" who would bear watching. A British major with whom I had struck up a friendship—he had been instrumental in facilitating my accreditation to the British army on my arrival in Cairo—confided that this "Begin fellow" had "thousands of armed men" at his disposal and would "raise hell in Palestine" unless he was found and arrested.

It seemed, however, that British counter-intelligence in the Mandated Territory had no clear idea of what Menahem Begin looked like, or where he might be hiding. "The blighter has undergone plastic surgery," the major said, "and probably doesn't resemble even remotely the pictures we have of him as a Polish soldier. Besides, we don't really know where to

11

look for him. Our information is that he sleeps in a different bed every night."

I had visited Jerusalem two or three times between battles in Egypt's Western Desert and Libya. The Holy City of the Jews fascinated me. Gleaming like a multi-faceted jewel set on the broad brow of pinkish-brown Judean hill it was then—as now—an incomparably beautiful city, and more evocative than any other on earth of the lives and times of those prophets whose ideas have influenced the moral attitudes and religious beliefs of at least half the human race.

Heavily garrisoned by the British, Jerusalem was a peaceful city in those days, and Cairo-based correspondents hurried to it whenever possible for the good food and drink to be had at the King David Hotel, and in the homes of friends. On long weekends in Jerusalem's embrace, one could forget the war that by the summer of 1944 had left the Middle East and North Africa but was still raging in Europe.

But while outwardly quiet, Jerusalem—indeed, the entire Holy Land— seethed with sub-surface animosity between Arabs and Jews. I came away each time fairly certain that a Jewish revolution was brewing there, and that it could only be averted if the British fulfilled their promise to grant the Jews national identity in their ancient homeland. But the Irgun's emergence—actually, I later learned, it was a reemergence—came as a surprise. The only "secret army" I had heard about in the Holy City was the Labor Zionists' Haganah, which had been organized mainly to protect Jewish pioneer settlements and population centers against marauding Arabs.

Back in Cairo, I sensed a big story in the making in Palestine, and having nothing to write about in the Egyptian capital after El Alamein and the American landings in North Africa—the Anglo-Americans had cleared the entire southern littoral of the Mediterranean of Axis forces—I cabled my editors in New York for permission to return to Palestine for the purpose of seeking out the mysterious Begin in Tel Aviv or wherever he might be hiding, interviewing him and discovering, if possible, what he was really up to. My message was never answered. I subsequently received instructions to accompany General Alexander Patch's army if and when it ever moved to attack the Germans in southern France. It eventually did, and I went with it. I forgot all about Begin, and it was only much later, on my return to the United States and reassignment to my magazine's Washington Bureau that I discovered the truth: my cable about Begin had not been received. It probably was stopped by the military censors in Cairo.

Incidentally, during most of the time that I was based in Cairo, an Egyptian army officer named Anwar el-Sadat was confined in a British prison camp after having been caught spying for the Nazis. His "drop" for communicating with the enemy was a lissome belly-dancer named Hekmet who performed nightly on the jasmine-scented rooftop garden of the Continental Hotel just up the road from Shepherd's. Hekmet herself was a double-agent, working for the British as well as the Germans, which was probably how Sadat came to grief.

After *Collier's* installed me in Washington toward the end of 1945, I started collecting newspaper clippings about Begin's exploits as commander of the Irgun in its relentless and often bloody campaign against the British in Palestine. Riffling through them almost thirty years later preparatory to writing the story of his life and times, I saw that Menahem Begin had not enjoyed a "good press" in the United States from about the end of 1945 until Israel actually achieved independence in the spring of 1948.

The Begin who materialized from the yellowing strips of newsprint was an outlaw, a "terrorist" allegedly responsible for a succession of atrocities committed by his Irgunists in the name of Jewish nationhood. Among the more notorious exploits attributed to him and his organization were the bombing of Jerusalem's King David Hotel in 1946—an incident in which nearly one hundred British officers and civil servants were killed—and the "massacre" of some two hundred and fifty Arabs, including women and children, at Deir Yassin in 1948 during Israel's War of Independence.

If one judges from the contents of their dispatches, few American correspondents seemed aware at the time that Begin's underground war against the British was hastening the dawn of Jewish sovereignty and independence in Palestine. For the most part, the reporters hewed to the party line of the Labor Zionists which characterized Menahem Begin as a "neo-fascist terrorist" whose activities were obstructing rather than helping the territory's Jewish community realize its long-cherished dream of national identity.

Begin, however, was not without friends and supporters in the United States. They included the lovely actress, Stella Adler, and the writer, the late Ben Hecht, a man of passion and deep convictions. From them, and from others with whom I came into contact in New York and Washington—notably Peter Bergson, the Irgun's unofficial "ambassador" and fund-raiser in the United States—I obtained a totally different view of Begin and the Irgun, and what they stood for.

The Menahem Begin they limned for me over luncheons and long postprandial "bull sessions" was not the bloody-handed terrorist he was being painted in the daily press but a sincere patriot fighting for the establishment of a Jewish state in the *whole* of Palestine in accordance with the teachings of his mentor, the late Vladimir Jabotinsky, founder of Revisionist Zionism. He vigorously opposed partition of the territory into Arab and Jewish states, a solution then being proposed at the newly created United Nations and favorably regarded by the Labor Zionists under the leadership of David Ben-Gurion. It was the solution eventually decreed by the United Nations in November 1947.

Meanwhile, in November 1946, I wrote a book in which I attempted, unsuccessfully, I fear, to bring Menahem Begin into proper focus as less terrorist than patriot—a revolutionary fighting for his people's freedom. By then, the dreadful arithmetic of the Holocaust that had destroyed six million of Europe's pre-war population of nine million Jews was well and widely known. American troops had liberated Belsen, Buchenwald and a dozen other death camps of Adolf Hitler's "final solution of the Jewish question," and the survivors were clamoring to be allowed to go to Palestine.

But the British had long since closed the Mandated Territory to Jewish immigration, and it was to open it to the pitiful remnants of European Jewry that Menahem Begin was pursuing his war against the British. I did not know, at the time, that he himself was in effect a survivor of the Holocaust in which he had lost his father, mother and an older brother.

Then, in the spring of 1948, Israel achieved statehood and Begin disappeared from the headlines and columns of the American press. Although over the years his name became a household word in Israel as that of the leader of the right wing opposition to a succession of ruling Labor governments, Menahem Begin and his activities rarely received more than passing mention in our newspapers. His face was seldom seen on television until he surfaced as Israel's new Prime Minister in the spring of 1977, when Begin's right wing *Likud* coalition roundly defeated the leftist Labor Alignment in national elections. Then came a veritable flood of vituperation and villification.

The Menahem Begin projected by our newspapers, newsweeklies and TV news programs was the same old Menahem Begin of his underground days as commander of the Irgun: an Arab-hating "terrorist," a "hyper-nationalist," a "fanatic" who was more likely to start another war with Israel's neighbors than negotiate with them the peace everyone was talking about at the time. To be sure, his entire career and his Revisionist ideology did suggest a militant nationalist rather than a statesman capable of making peace with Israel's enemies.

Not surprisingly, perhaps, Begin's rise to power in Jerusalem sent shock waves of apprehension through an oil-hungry Western world. Its governments feared he might precipitate a resumption of Arab-Israeli hostilities and a reprise of the disastrous oil embargo that followed the Yom Kippur War of 1973, the fourth major conflict between Israel and its Arab neighbors since the Jewish state was founded. Not even Washington, where Israel had many sympathizers in high places—everywhere, it seemed at the time, except the White House—was happy with Begin's nomination as Prime Minister. In fact, according to one prominent Senator, the gloom in the national capital was "thick enough to cut with a knife."

Nor was it surprising that Begin's emergence elicited hysterical responses in the Arab camp. The hysteria was self-serving and largely phony, but it deeply impressed those foreign observers who believed that the central issue in the Arab-Israeli conflict was not the establishment of "secure and recognized frontiers" for the Jewish state as envisioned by United Nations Resolution 242, but "statehood for the Palestinians."

The Palestinian Liberation Organization, meanwhile, its propaganda machinery liberally energized by the petro-dollars of the Arab oil states, officially characterized Menahem Begin as "a terrorist thug and murderer" who should be tried as a "war criminal." On radio and TV, and in the printed media, commentators were soon equating Begin with the PLO's Yassir Arafat, and the Irgun with Arafat's *Al Fatah*. This regardless of the fact that while the Irgun fought the British *army,* the PLO's hired "warriors" have never dared attack Israeli armed forces, their targets invariably being Israeli civilians at home or abroad, and innocent bystanders whoever they may be. Nonetheless, a prominent anchorman wondered aloud on a national TV network one evening how Menahem Begin, "himself a former terrorist chieftain," could possibly justify his refusal to negotiate with the PLO. The simple equations of Begin equals Arafat and Irgun equals *Al Fatah* were patently absurd as anyone sufficiently familiar with the history of the Arab-Israeli conflict would have known.

It was to attempt to bring Menahem Begin into focus that many months ago I started writing the story of his life and times. The project began as a straightforward biography of a right wing rebel who in the course of a tempestuous lifetime achieved the status of statesman. But in the midst of interviews with relatives, close friends—even opponents—who had known Begin intimately for many years, Egypt's President Sadat made his spectacular visit to Jerusalem, an event that changed the flow of history in the Middle East, and the narrative structure of my book.

It became necessary thereafter to explain not only much of Israel's history as well as Begin's origins and development, defeats and triumphs, but to attempt to capture between hard covers the meaning and scope of the episodes in the negotiating process that developed in the wake of Sadat's momentous encounter with Begin in the Israeli capital back in November 1977. What has resulted, I see now, is really a bio-history, at once the story of the man and of his country. I had hoped for a simpler task.

Book One:

Jerusalem 1977

Chapter 1

Begin Takes Charge

Menahem Begin, who became Israel's Prime Minister in the early summer of 1977, looks more like a high school principal than a statesman, and not at all like the formidable commander of the *Irgun Zvai Leumi,* the underground army that between 1943 and 1948 helped to blast the British out of Palestine to make way for the Jewish State. Nor does he possess any of the physical attributes of the Old Testament Prophet that his more idolatrous followers believe him to be, though not without reason, for ever since taking charge of his country's destiny he seems guided by a semi-mystical reliance on the power of his oratory, logic, and vision.

Menahem Begin (pronounced BAY-ghin) is of medium height, slight, bespectacled, with a prominent jaw, luminous blue-gray eyes and thinning, reddish-brown hair swept back from a broad brow, and is in many ways unique among Israeli Prime Ministers. He is the only national leader to emerge from the pre-state underground guerrilla movement and the first conservative to occupy an office that since Israel's establishment in the fateful spring of 1948 was held by a succession of socialist-oriented Laborites.

Begin rose to power in Jerusalem when his *Likud,* a coalition of centrist and rightist parties, confounded most experts in the springtime national elections by defeating the leftist Labor Alignment that had ruled Israel uninterruptedly for twenty-nine years. An analysis of how the astute Begin and his campaign manager, the handsome former commander of the Israeli Air Force, Ezer Weizman, engineered the *Likud's* victory, comes later. Weizman, who became Defense Minister in Begin's cabinet, apart from being widely known as a "hawk," is also one of Israel's cleverest politicians and a potential future Premier. In the campaign, Weizman used every television and radio technique known in the art of "image-making" and "sold the *Likud*," critics said, "like Americans sell Coca-Cola."

Begin was approaching his sixty-fourth birthday when he assumed the premiership, and looked so unwell at the time—he was recovering from a severe heart attack sustained during the campaign—that many Israelis were openly fearful of their new leader's physical ability to "stay the course," let alone deal effectively with the monumental economic, social, and political problems, internal and external, that the country faced. Politics in Israel is a rough business, as we shall see, possibly rougher than in any other parliamentary democracy except, perhaps, where Euro-Communism lately has been raising its divisive head. Even while Begin was assembling his cabinet there was widespread speculation as to who might succeed him, the name most frequently mentioned being, of course, that of the attractive Ezer Weizman.

Close associates more familiar with Begin's true clinical condition, however, were optimistic that *Adoni Hamefaked* (Mister Commander)—as oldtime colleagues of his underground days still address him—would survive the rigors of high office, even thrive on its daily diet of hard work. One of Begin's personal aides (an old friend of mine) put it this way. "It is a well-established fact that once in office our ailing Prime Ministers quickly develop what might be called psychosomatic health." He cited the example of Mrs. Golda Meir, who succeeded the late Levi Eshkol while suffering from a variety of ailments, then went on to serve out Eshkol's term and an entire term of her own during which she bore the enormous responsibilities attending Israel's conduct of the Yom Kippur War of 1973.

Menahem Begin may be frail-looking physically, but as an intellectual and as a politician he is undoubtedly the toughest leader Israel has known since the late David Ben-Gurion, the country's first Prime Minister, still revered by Laborites as one of the Jewish State's founders, but Begin's bitterest enemy. For years, during their frequent encounters in the Knesset, Israel's 120-member Parliament, Ben-Gurion refused to mention Begin by name, referring to him only as "the member sitting next to Dr. Bader."

In those days, the years of Begin's political Gethsemane between the birth of the state and the national emergency occasioned by the Six Day War of 1967, the leader of the opposition was considered a dangerous right-wing relic of the country's struggle for independence, a political pariah never to be trusted with power lest he demolish the nation's cherished democratic institutions. Begin's prognathous jaw gave his opponents a pretext for calling him "Duce," although he resembled Mussolini only as an orator. He is in fact, one of Israel's three or four best speakers. His speeches are impeccably composed and thoroughly rehearsed, which is why he often can deliver an address on a major subject as though he were speaking extemporaneously. But Begin's oratory sounded like demagoguery to his enemies back in the 1950s and early 1960s when some even stooped to calling him Hitler because he sported a small moustache, long since gone.

Nevertheless, despite Ben-Gurion's enmity, even overt hatred, Begin deeply respected "the Little Lion" of the Labor Party. It was Begin who, in the critical time of the approaching Six Day War in the spring of 1967, proposed to the then Prime Minister, Levi Eshkol, that Ben-Gurion be recalled from the retirement into which he had withdrawn in 1963, to make possible and strengthen a government of national unity. The touchy Eshkol refused, but took Begin into his cabinet as Minister Without Portfolio.

Excessive modesty, incidentally, is not one of Begin's more evident characteristics. He has confided to intimates that, in his opinion, "Jewish history in Israel came to a full stop when Ben-Gurion retired from politics and only resumed when I became Prime Minister." In the sense that Begin seems to have restored Israel's confidence in itself, badly shaken by the quasi-disastrous Yom Kippur War, and appears to have revived the dynamism that the country knew under Ben-Gurion, he may be right. The political methods of the two men are remarkably similar.

Like Ben-Gurion, Menahem Begin is autocratic, patriarchal and, some Israelis believe, fully as "charismatic." Many who saw in Ben-Gurion "the greatest Jewish leader since Moses" perceive in Begin the same qualities of firm leadership, eloquence, and personal magnetism, the bearer of a Messianic aura rare in the politics of modern Israel. Although on a personal level Begin is easier to talk to, more relaxed and affable where Ben-Gurion was tense and taciturn, his political behavior is every bit as authoritative, maybe even more so. There are no gray eminences around Begin as there were around Ben-Gurion, who in 1964 withdrew to his kibbutz at Sde Boker in his beloved Negev, where he died in 1973 at the age of 87.

But the differences between the two men are far more numerous than the similarities. Unlike Ben-Gurion, a secular socialist who couldn't remember when he was last inside a synagogue, Begin is an observant though not strictly Orthodox Jew. He scrupulously respects Judaism's dietary laws, wears a *yarmulkha* while reading the Bible—as he often does in the Knesset when interrupting a speech to quote from The Book—and observes all Jewish rites and traditions, particularly the sanctity of the Sabbath.

*   *   *

Although in frail health, Menahem Begin works hard at his job. He is at his desk daily, except Saturdays of course, between 7:45 and 8:00 A.M.; he spends an hour or more with his two aides: Yehiel Kadishai, his chef de bureau, and Yehuda Avner, a career diplomat who had served Yitzhak Rabin in a similar capacity. They are virtually the only members of his small staff who enjoy free access to him at all times. Incidentally, there have been remarkably few personnel changes since Begin took office, mainly because during his years in opposition he never developed a "shadow cabinet" and a cadre of professionals to help him run the government if and when he became Prime Minister.

Together, Begin and his aides go through the overnight cables from Israel's embassies throughout the world; the Prime Minister deals with each briskly, dictating brief replies when necessary or encharging one or the other of his aides to pass on the information to the appropriate functionary for action.

Avner, a longtime friend, told me Begin has a "photographic memory," reads entire paragraphs at a glance and remembers everything he has read. He is apt to interrupt the morning's work to say, "Yehuda, look on page five of yesterday's *Jerusalem Post,* and at the top of column three you'll find an item from London about this business," meaning a dispatch relevant to the matter at hand.

Begin, Avner told me, treats all problems, major or minor, in even-handed style. In a fifteen-minute period late in March—after Begin had hurled a large armored force into Lebanon in retaliation for the PLO's massacre of Israeli civilians on the Tel Aviv-Haifa road—the Prime Minister made three telephone calls in quick succession. The first was to his Defense Minister, Ezer Weizman, to discuss the latest news from the battlefront up north. The second was to the son of the late Rabbi Arieh Levin, the Irgun's chief rabbi during the revolt against the British, to assure him that his request for a donation for a yeshiva in Jerusalem would be honored. The third was to Foreign Minister Moshe Dayan requesting information on the latest developments in Israel's strained relations with the United States. To each call Begin devoted the same degree of intense concentration.

The Prime Minister breaks for lunch, which he invariably takes at home, at about 1:30 P.M. He eats sparingly, returning to the office between 4:00 and 4:30 after a mandatory rest and a nap. In the course of the afternoon, he may have a snack—usually bread and cheese with a glass of warm milk or hot, sugarless tea. He rarely has coffee, though he serves it to visitors if they prefer it to tea or fruit juice.

Begin's afternoons are devoted mainly to receiving visitors—cabinet members, job-seekers, his military aide or the Chief of Staff—but even in his office Begin is often the Jewish grandfather. Recently, his married daughter Hassia and her engineer husband went on holiday and left their three small children with their grandparents. Begin took the kids with him to the office and gave them the run of the place while consulting with politicians, diplomats, ministers, even, on one occasion, with the Belgian Minister of Foreign Affairs. Begin introduced the children all around, and took obvious pleasure in their presence while affairs of state were being discussed.

Officially, Begin's workday ends at about 8:30 P.M., when he goes home for supper, but he is rarely in bed much before eleven o'clock after the late radio news. Formal dinners are never held at the Prime Minister's residence, but in the Knesset dining room set aside for the purpose or in one of the major hotels, usually the historic King David. Cocktail parties and receptions are held down to a minimum, mainly because the Prime Minister's wife, Aliza, doesn't like them. All entertaining is done outside the home except when close friends have been invited. On such occasions, Aliza does the cooking and the baking with "one in help."

Life at the Prime Minister's residence is virtually as frugal as it was when the Begins lived in their simple flat in Tel Aviv during underground days. There has been a small rise in the family income since then, but the Prime Minister's monthly salary of 9,000 Israeli pounds—equivalent to roughly $643 at current rates of exchange and reduced to less than $250 after taxes and other deductions—leave little for "extras." Out of what is left, however, Begin and Aliza need buy only their clothing. Everything else—food, fuel, transportation, entertainment, travel—is paid for by the state. Fortunately for them, the couple's sartorial needs are simple; Aliza makes most of her own clothing herself.

Begin personally attaches no great importance to money. He is a zealous guardian of public funds, but carries no money on his person and knows little about managing the family income, which is handled by Aliza. She even buys most of Begin's apparel, except an occasional suit or pair of shoes. Since becoming Prime Minister, Begin has discovered that such purchases are no simple matter but must be "organized," with all the fuss and bother imposed by his security people. When he visited Comfort, his favorite shoe store in Ben Yehuda Street recently, the place had first to be cleared of customers, and checked, box by box, for hidden bombs. What should have been a routine transaction became a major quasi-military operation. Annoyed, the Prime Minister vowed it would be a long time before he bought another pair of shoes.

On the whole, however, Menahem Begin enjoys being Prime Minister, an office that allows him to play his favorite role, that of guardian of Israel's spiritual heritage as a Jewish state. This is most evident in his strict observance of the Sabbath.

The importance of the Sabbath in Jewish life, and in the life of Menahem Begin, cannot be overestimated. Among the holy days of the Jews, with the exception of Yom Kippur (Day of Atonement), the Sabbath—which starts shortly before sundown on Friday and ends just after sunset the following day—is revered as most sacred and inviolable. The very frequency of its occurrence and the many pleasurable associations it evokes in terms of the togetherness of families and friends have made it the most beloved institution in the Jewish religion. "More then the Jews have kept the Sabbath," said Achad Ha'am, the noted modern exponent of Jewish cultural nationalism, "the Sabbath has kept the Jews." The Sabbath is the eternal covenant between the Jews and God.

Once, when Menahem was a high school student in his native Brest-Litovsk, in Poland, he refused to write an examination paper in Latin because it was given on the Sabbath. He was only one of three Jewish boys in a large class of Gentiles. The *goyim* laughed uproariously when they heard Menahem tell their teacher that his religion forbade writing on the Holy Day. Menahem was flunked and a subsequent committee of inquiry demanded an explanation for his behavior. The boy's reply was at once a clue to his character and to the depth of his religiosity: "I might have broken the Sabbath and written out the answers to the questions, but my classmates laughed at my Jewish Sabbath. I wanted to demonstrate to them that the Sabbath is sacred to us Jews and therefore to me personally."

Begin still observes the Sabbath closely, though no longer as rigidly, perhaps, as when he was a schoolboy. He writes on the Sabbath now, and reads a great deal—newspapers, magazines, current books—and watches television. In fact, he is something of a TV addict, and has been known to spend two, even three hours watching news programs, documentaries, and such imports from the United States as *Starsky and Hutch, Hawaii Five-O,* and *Kojak,* three of Israel's favorite programs. (He is also inordinately fond of movies, especially Westerns.)

Begin and his wife Aliza—they've been married thirty-nine years—devote their Friday nights entirely to their family. Its members include their married children, Benjamin and Hassia and their respective spouses, an unmarried daughter, Leah, and a gaggle of grandchildren. Unless the Prime Minister is abroad on a mission, all gather at the Begin's home in leafy, residential Rehavia for the traditional Shabbat dinner which the housewifely Aliza has prepared before sundown and kept warm on an electric hotplate. The candles are lighted, Begin recites the Kiddush—the blessing on the bread and the wine—and the meal is eaten in the close, happy togetherness characteristic of Jewish family life.

On Saturdays, Begin spends most of his time reading the papers he has accumulated during the week for his Sabbath leisure hours, and, of course, the Bible, or the particular chapter due that week. Observant Jews divide the first five books of the Bible into fifty-two parts, beginning with Genesis and concluding with Deuteronomy. Tradition requires that the Holy Book be read from beginning to end in the course of the year, and Begin never misses his weekly reading. One of his favorites is the section entitled *Bamidbar*, meaning "in the desert," where, figuratively speaking, he spent much of his political life. Occasionally, after sundown, he discusses what he has read with close friends who come to visit.

A weekly event at the spacious Prime Minister's home on Saturday afternoons and evenings is "open house." When Begin first took office, this caused serious security problems. People came to "visit," not in tens or hundreds, but literally in the thousands, gathering outside the house and wandering through the residence in groups of fifty or seventy-five. The practice was stopped because it was impossible to control. Now, in the late Saturday afternoons, the house is open only to persons who are in a sense invited, for they have telephoned beforehand. The visitors have been reduced in number to a manageable one hundred or so. They enter in small groups of twenty-five or thirty, sit about on chairs or on the floor—in shirtsleeves if it is a warm day—and talk, sip fruit juices, sing folksongs, and for twenty minutes or half an hour make themselves at home with their leader, who listens to their problems and discusses solutions with them.

On such occasions, the usually formally attired Menahem Begin sheds jacket, necktie, and shoes, and may be seen in short-sleeved, open-collared shirt and bedroom slippers. Mrs. Begin is rarely in evidence during public "open house" time, preferring the solitude of the kitchen, where she goes about her chores, preparing the evening meal or the tea and cakes for family guests who will arrive later, after the public visitors leave.

Indirectly, Begin owes his high office to a violation of the Sabbath by his hapless predecessor, Yitzhak Rabin. The catalyst that precipitated the political crisis of early 1977 was a routine ceremony, apparently sanctioned by Rabin, for receiving five F-15 fighter-interceptors from the United States—on a Friday afternoon after sundown. The influential National Religious Party (NRP) was represented in Rabin's cabinet by several ministers who vigorously protested the "desecration of the

Sabbath," and subsequently voted against their own government in a vote of confidence. Incensed, the mercurial Rabin dismissed them and huffily tendered his own resignation.

Begin sternly refuses to receive official visitors or to transact official business of any kind on the Sabbath. Soon after Begin had taken office, for instance, the American Ambassador, Samuel Lewis, brought him a message from President Carter requiring immediate action. Begin politely informed Lewis that he would not be able to deal with the matter until after sundown Saturday and that thenceforth he would not accept any communications during the hours of the Sabbath. President Carter and other foreign statesmen quickly learned to respect Begin's wishes and have since timed their cables and telephone calls accordingly.

Although Carter and Begin could not be more different in personality and political style, or come from more widely diverse backgrounds, they do have in common a moral, highly principled, even puritanical stance and commitment. Like Carter, who makes no secret of his piety, Begin also has what an intimate collaborator of the Prime Minister described as "a personal relationship with God."

Otherwise, the two leaders, now major actors on the international scene, are as unlike as a square and a polygon. While the President is, comparatively speaking, a political newcomer, Begin is a seasoned politician with twenty-nine years of experience as leader of the parliamentary opposition to the dominant Labor Alignment. Both men may talk to God, but it has become abundantly evident that for some time God spoke to them in different tongues on the one subject of common interest: making peace between Israel and its Arab neighbors. The American President and the Israeli Prime Minister, whatever they might say to the contrary—and they often have—were for many months as far apart as the poles on the nature and structure of a final settlement of the long-standing Arab-Israeli conflict.

How to make peace between his country and its Arab neighbors was by far the biggest of the many tasks that confronted Menahem Begin when he took office early in June 1977. Peace had been Israel's paramount objective from the moment of its rebirth in a portion of the Palestine that once was Biblical Canaan, the ancient homeland of the Jewish people. In fact, so keen was the Israelis' desire for peaceful relations with their Arab neighbors that they made peace a fundamental precept of the Declaration of Independence:

We extend the hand of peace and good-neighborliness to all the states around us, and to their peoples, and we call upon them to cooperate in mutual helpfulness with the independent Jewish nation. The State of Israel is prepared to make its contribution in a concerted effort for the advancement of the entire Middle East.

This, even as Arab armies fell upon the newly created state to destroy it aborning.

Thereafter the official records abound with expressions of the Israelis' readiness to submit their differences with the Arabs to negotiation and with affirmations of their hopes for establishing normal political, commercial and social relations with their self-proclaimed enemies. Those records, however, are remarkable only for the frequency of Israeli peace overtures and the totality of Arab rejection. The Arab response to Israeli approaches was invariably the same: terrorism, boycott, maritime blockade, threats, anti-Semitic propaganda, arms-buildups and their inevitable consequence, wars costly to both sides in blood and treasure.

By the time Begin became Prime Minister, Israel had been obliged to fight four major wars in defense of its national existence—five, really, counting the 1969-1970 "War of Attrition" waged against the Jewish State by Egypt's late President Gamal Abdul Nasser—inflicting each time terrible punishment on its would-be destroyers, but each time to no avail. Historically, wars have always been followed by peace conferences and formal treaties, and the belligerents' return to normal political, social and commercial relations. But the Arabs steadfastly refused to make peace with Israel, or even to recognize the legitimacy of its existence.

Thus when Begin assumed the premiership, Israel remained in certain highly important respects much what it had been at birth: a small Jewish nation surrounded by Arab enemies bent on its destruction. It had no permanent frontiers, no friendly neighbors to visit or trade with, no memories of peace and only the vaguest prospects of ever achieving these things. True, over the years the infant state of '48 had matured. It had developed its industries, agriculture, and science to a remarkable extent; it had built half a dozen universities, and it had created the best-equipped and most highly motivated military force in the entire Middle East. In less than three decades the Jews had erected on the tiny portion of Mediterranean littoral allotted to them by the United Nations in November 1947 a vital, productive social-democracy with deep, ineradicable roots in its ancient homeland. But peace, the indispensable ingredient of future growth, economic stability and social progress continued to elude Israel.

As far back as July 1949, Israel offered to incorporate into its own meager territory the Palestinians who had abandoned or been driven from their homes during the first war in 1948–1949 and taken refuge in the already crowded Gaza Strip. But the offer was refused—not by the Palestinians, who had no real voice in their destiny at the time—but by the outside Arab powers whose armies had attempted to destroy Israel at birth.

Israel subsequently proposed making the problem of the displaced Palestinians the first item of business on the agenda of the peace negotiations called for in the 1949 Armistice, but that offer was also rejected. Israel then proposed to take back 100,000 Arab refugees, with no questions asked as to whether they had fled the country of their own free will or, as many claimed, had been ousted by the Israelis. This time, the Arabs did not even bother to respond.

In 1963, Israel announced at the United Nations its readiness to negotiate a comprehensive settlement of the refugee problem—for that was what the "Palestinian problem" was considered at the time—again with negative results.

In the years that followed, until the eve of the Six Day War of 1967, Israel repeatedly sought to settle the refugee question by offering compensation for landed property left behind by former Arab residents in Israeli territory, and, to this end, requested a United Nations body be created to appraise the properties involved. The Arab governments would have no part of such compensatory schemes because, as far as they were concerned, acceptance would have meant closing the books on the problem of the Palestinian refugees who had become collectively a useful pawn in the great game of Pan-Arabism being played by Egypt's Nasser. He dreamed of creating an "Arab World" reaching from the Atlantic coast of North Africa, across the Middle East to the western verges of Asia, a purely Moslem cosmos wherein there would be no place for the Israelis whom he repeatedly threatened to "push into the sea."

In the winter of 1966 and early spring of 1967, Nasser's threats materialized into actual preparations for a massive assault on Israel, then highly vulnerable, compressed as it was into a geographic hourglass shape which at its narrowest point—between Tulkarem on the West Bank and Netanya on the Mediterranean—could be traversed in a matter of minutes by an armored unit attacking from the east, cutting the country in half. It has since been established beyond reasonable doubt that Israel's preemptive strike of June 5, 1967, came in response to the threatened attack from Egypt in alliance with the new, radical *Ba'athist* regime in Syria and Jordan's King Hussein.

The Six Day War, the third in the dreary series that since 1948 has blackened the battlefields of the Middle East, resulted in a resounding victory for the Israelis. In the south, the Egyptians were driven out of the Gaza Strip and the Sinai Peninsula all the way to the Suez Canal; in the north, the Syrians were pushed off the strategic Golan Heights, and the

Jordanians, who entered the war reluctantly and only after Nasser had gulled Hussein into believing an Arab victory was imminent, lost everything west of the Jordan River—the West Bank, East Jerusalem and Jericho.

To Israel's offer to return the conquered territories in exchange for "genuine peace," the Arab leaders responded with their famous formula of the "three no's" drafted at a summit conference in Khartoum two months after the June war: *no* peace with Israel, *no* negotiations with Israel, *no* recognition of Israel's existence as a legitimate entity.

, Despite the adoption of Resolution 242 by the United Nations' Security Council in November, this formula governed the peace. Resolution 242 called upon Israel to "withdraw from territories occupied" in the Six Day War and exhorted the belligerents "to establish and maintain contacts . . . in order to promote agreement." Both sides ostensibly accepted Resolution 242, but disagreement developed over its meaning. The Arabs, seconded at the U.N. by their armorers and patrons, the Russians, maintained that the Resolution called for Israel to withdraw from *all* the conquered territories. Israel, supported at the U.N. by its only ally, the United States, disagreed with the Arab interpretation, pointing out that the Resolution deliberately avoided use of the word *all*. Result: deadlock.

Politically, the impasse worked to Begin's advantage. It would take him another decade to maneuver himself into the premiership, but it was in the wake of the Israeli victory in 1967 that Begin—the youngest and last of the generation of Diaspora-bred Zionist leaders—started assembling the center-right elements that eventually became the *Likud,* the vehicle of his stunning electoral triumph in the spring of 1977. The war' and its aftermath—the crystallization of what until then had been an amorphous and largely impotent Palestinian nationalism—served Begin's populist purposes admirably. To Palestinian irredentism, Begin opposed his own Zionist nationalism, stemming from his unshakable conviction that the whole of Palestine "on both sides of the River Jordan" is "historically and geographically an entity," and the patrimony of the Jewish people by "natural and eternal right."

Like-minded Israelis responded to his appeal, and Begin commenced gaining what until then he had lacked, political "respectability" in the eyes of an Israeli electorate long schooled to regard him with derision as a "terrorist," a "fascist," a "Nazi," or an *Andek,* a Polish chauvinist. Begin's following grew with nearly every election, and on his ninth try for the premiership he succeeded.

The Six Day War marked a crucial time in the common history of the Arabs and the Israelis. For the Israelis, the war's territorial gains meant defensible borders for the first time in their country's lifetime; they achieved what the generals call "strategic depth." But for the Arabs, the Israelis' swift, thorough victory was a wound to their pride as warriors. Their defeat further blockaded their minds behind walls of national egoism and vainglory, symptoms of collective paranoia. The psychological complexities that flowed from the war enormously complicated the job of peacemaking in the Middle East.

Over the years, no Arab statesman of the so-called "confrontation states"—Egypt, Jordan, Syria, Iraq—had ever come forward with an offer to talk peace with the Israelis, much less to recognize Israel's legitimacy. It had become a canon of Middle East politics that the Arab leader who dared suggest recognition of Israel or negotiations with the "Zionist entity," was automatically a candidate for assassination or, at the very least, political oblivion. Such infrequent meetings as did occur between Jordan's Hussein and various high-level Israeli officials were conducted in utmost secrecy and conveniently denied by both sides.

The Yom Kippur War in October of 1973, however, provided victories enough to salve the Arabs' wounded pride. Attacking simultaneously, with almost total strategic surprise and with nearly as much armored firepower as Hitler had used in the invasion of Russia in the summer of 1941, the Egyptians and the Syrians—the Jordanian participation this time was prudently minimal—scored impressively in the first seventy-two hours of fighting. Indeed, Israel survived only by the margin of massive infusions of airlifted American weapons, superior generalship and a higher level of motivation; every Israeli soldier, airman and sailor knows that to lose a war to the Arabs is to lose Israel. When a cease fire became effective on October 25, Israeli artillery was close enough to Damascus to shell the outskirts of the Syrian capital and Israeli tanks were less than fifty miles from Cairo at Kilometer 101, the site of subsequent Egyptian-Israeli negotiations leading to the withdrawal of Israeli troops from Egypt proper and their pullback from the Suez Canal.

The war was followed, thanks almost entirely to the then Secretary of State, the indefatigable Henry Kissinger, by the only peace conference ever held between Arabs and Israelis. It opened at Geneva on December 21 under the joint chairmanship of the United States and the Soviet Union, and was attended by Israel, Egypt and Jordan. Syria refused to participate. What developed, however, was far less a "peace conference" than confirmation of the Arabs' determination to dismember the Jewish State.

The first meeting was devoted to general policy speeches delivered by the foreign ministers of the participating countries. Kissinger pleaded for "a new relationship among the nations of the Middle East" and pledged, *inter alia,* America's good offices to obtain Israel's withdrawal from occupied territories as defined by the previously recognized borders; security arrangements; guarantees; settlement of "the Palestinian problem"; and, finally, recognition by Israel that Jerusalem "contains places holy to three great religions."

Russia's Foreign Minister, Andrei Gromyko, also sounded a plea for "peace," but expressed continued support for the Arab demand that Israel withdraw from *all* occupied territories. He attacked what he termed Israel's "policy of annexation" and the "trampling of the norms of international law and decisions of the United Nations," a truly remarkable statement coming from the representative of a Russia that had proved itself an all-time champion trampler of such norms since the birth of the United Nations. Not surprisingly, Egypt's Ismail Fahmy and Jordan's Zaid el-Rafi followed suit, stressing the need for an Israeli pullout from *all* Arab territories—including, especially, Jerusalem—as the basis for a settlement.

Israel's Abba Eban, on the other hand, saw the conference as "a new opportunity . . . to bring a halt to the spreading contagion of violence in the Middle East," and emphasized that his country was ready for a "territorial compromise." He pledged to help solve the "Palestinian refugee problem" with generous "compensation for abandoned lands," and indicated Israel's willingness to share responsibility for the administration of Jerusalem's holy places with Christendom and Islam. But he might as well have been talking to the dusty gray-brown stones of Cairo's cemetery, the City of the Dead.

Next day, December 22, after a perfunctory twenty-minute closed session, the Geneva conferees—never talking directly to each other but communicating through their chairman—issued a communique announcing that Israel and Egypt would enter into troop disengagement talks in Sinai and that committees would be established later to deal with other issues. Those committees never materialized.

Some time later, after the disengagement agreements negotiated in 1975 by Kissinger, vague hints began emanating from Cairo that Egypt, Israel's most populous and militarily most powerful enemy, was now ready to talk "real peace." The allusions almost invariably were made to visiting American Congressmen and correspondents, especially those representing the television networks, but were uttered strictly in the interest of influencing foreign opinion in favor of the Arab cause. Suggestions of Egyptian desires for peace with Israel rarely were published in Cairo's strictly controlled press, unless carefully phrased to sample public opinion and underscore Israeli "inflexibility."

One of Begin's first moves when he became Premier was to test the sincerity of the man who was dropping the hints: Egypt's President Mohammed Anwar el-Sadat. In August, less than two months after he had formed his new cabinet, Begin journeyed to Bucharest. During his five-day state visit, he conferred at some length with Romania's President Nicolae Ceausescu and indicated to him Israel's willingness to enter into direct talks with Sadat, "without preconditions of any kind." "I would be delighted to meet with President Sadat, or any Arab leader, anytime, anywhere," Begin said. President Ceausescu saw to it that Cairo was informed of Begin's desire for face-to-face talks.

Meanwhile, Moshe Dayan, a dissident Laborite of Ben Gurion's old breakaway *Rafi* faction, whom Begin had cleverly lured into becoming his Foreign Minister in the new government and had cast in the role of chief foreign policy advisor and negotiator, was making soundings of his own in hush-hush meetings with Arab diplomats—presumably Egyptian—in Geneva, Paris and London. Then, in September, on his way to the United States to "educate" President Carter in some of the realities of the Middle East situation, he interrupted his trip and flew to Tangier. There he conferred with Morocco's youthful King Hassan, one of two Arab leaders who have been consistently friendly toward Israel, the other being Tunisia's President, the aging Habib Bourguiba. (The latter long had urged the Arabs to "recognize Israel's existence" and "stop talking about wiping it off the map.")

King Hassan began making overtures to Israel by inviting Moroccan-born Israelis to visit Rabat. He informed a former deputy mayor of Jerusalem, Andre Chouraqui, and a labor union leader, Shaul Ben-Simchon, that for humanitarian reasons he fervently desired to play a peacemaker's role in the Arab-Israeli conflict. It was reportedly at the Moroccan King's suggestion that on or about September 16 Dayan went to Tangier, where he persuaded Hassan that Premier Begin was not only keenly interested in a settlement of Israel's dispute with the Arabs, but had the political power in the Parliament to negotiate a comprehensive peace.

The following month, in October, Sadat himself traveled to Bucharest. Subsequent intelligence reports reaching Jerusalem indicated that the Egyptian President had shown special interest not only in negotiations with Israel, but in Menahem Begin as a leader. What sort of man was he? Was Begin as inflexible as he had been painted? Did he have the political clout needed to persuade his fellow countrymen to make concessions? Whatever the replies to his questions, they were apparently sufficiently reassuring to cause him to make a "historic decision." It came to him, Sadat later confided, "like some divine inspiration, while flying from Bucharest to Iran."

The curtain was soon to rise on the Great Peace Drama of 1977-1978. It would unfold scene after dazzling scene before a worldwide television audience counted in the tens of millions. The main actors would be the handsome, eloquent Mohammed Anwar el-Sadat of Egypt and the plain-looking, but not so plain-spoken Menahem Begin of Israel—with President Jimmy Carter standing in the wings, coming on stage from time to time, and oftener than not confusing the action rather than developing it.

Unfortunately, the scenario was improvised, and at this writing it was not clear yet whether the drama would have a happy ending, whether, in fact, what the TV viewers saw in the making last November and December 1977, and at Camp David in the late summer of 1978, was a miracle or a mirage. Both, of course, are phenomena common to the Middle East.

Chapter 2

Before the Curtain Rose

During the first nine and a half months of the year 1977 B.S.—Before Sadat—the traditionally friendly relations between Washington and Jerusalem deteriorated rapidly. The United States suddenly became less supportive of the faraway, politically lonely democracy which the Jews had built on a sliver of Palestinian territory in the eastern crescent of the Mediterranean and began leaning the other way, in support of Arab objectives that were clearly inimical to Israel's continued existence as a sovereign Jewish state.

The deterioration was not entirely unexpected. It was foreseeable that Israel would be subjected to intense pressures during 1977 by the convergence of multiple interests—on the one hand the politics of the Soviet Union, of Arab nationalists and of the Third World, and on the other hand the policies of the governments of the United States and the Common Market countries. The Labor government, then still in power in Jerusalem, expected that pressure would be brought to bear on Israel with the aim of installing an independent Palestinian state in the Gaza Strip, the West Bank and Jerusalem, with Washington playing the leading role in the scenario.

The situation as it was looming back in the autumn of 1976, was summed up by the astute Shimon Peres, then Defense Minister in Rabin's already shaky government, as follows: "The powers will soon begin to make their demands on us. They will be prepared to grant us very little and will require us to give very much." As often in the past, Peres proved to be right. I have it on excellent authority, incidentally, that had the

Laborite Peres and not the conservative Begin emerged victorious in Israel's elections, Sadat would have made his dramatic peace bid much sooner than he did. That, in any case, is what the Egyptian President told Chancellor Bruno Kreisky of Austria.

Peres based his view on the future on the knowledge that American policy since the Six Day War of 1967 has been to urge Israel to trade territory for peace. President Gerald Ford exhorted Israel to "dare the exchange of the tangible for the intangible," as did Kissinger and others before him. Western governments more interested in ensuring themselves adequate supplies of oil for their industries than in Israel's destiny have traditionally implored Israel to be "daring," "forthcoming" and "flexible" where they themselves rarely were. It has become a bitter joke in Jerusalem that, "The Christian world is always asking us to be more Christian than the Christians."

The friction between Washington and Jerusalem started at the beginning of the year when the United States entered a new era under Jimmy Carter. Apparently anxious to resume America's mediatory role in the Middle East, he gave peacemaking in the area top priority, along with his energy program with which, it would seem, Carter's concepts of peace were indirectly linked. If Carter could achieve what he repeatedly called a "comprehensive" settlement of the Arab-Israeli conflict, there would not be another disastrous oil embargo such as the one that accompanied the Yom Kippur War of 1973. The policy was transparent enough but no one dared state it in those terms.

Immediately the Carter Administration was installed in the White House, high-ranking officials, including the President and Vice President Walter Mondale, showed little reticence in defining what they thought the terms of an Arab-Israeli peace should be. Oftener than not the specifics were simplistic, even ingenuous and at variance with ideas Carter had propounded during his election campaign.

While running for office, Jimmy Carter promised "unequivocally" to continue supplying Israel with economic and military aid at least as generously as in the past. He even criticized President Ford and Henry Kissinger for having withheld assistance to Israel in 1975 in order to push the Israelis into the Sinai troop disengagement agreements with Egypt after the Yom Kippur War. He denounced the militant PLO terrorists as "unrepresentative" of the Palestinian Arabs and pledged support for Israel's insistence on "secure and defensible borders," which in the language of Middle East diplomacy meant that he sympathized with Israel's claim to a reasonable fraction of the territories Israel conquered during the Six Day War. All of which was music in the ears of Israel's supporters, Jewish and Gentile.

Throughout the Presidential campaign, Carter, who had visited Israel only once—in 1974 as Governor of Georgia in one of those journeys to Jerusalem deemed mandatory by politicians with aspirations to high office—was obviously mainly concerned with winning Jewish votes in such key states as California, Illinois and New York. Whenever he touched on the Middle East in those heady months before he became President, his speeches reflected a clearly discernible pro-Israel stance. Indeed, they sounded as though they might have been based on material supplied by the American-Israel Public Affairs Committee, the influential pro-Israel lobby in Washington.

Once in office, however, President Carter's public statements on the Middle East began sounding to Israelis more and more as though they were inspired by Arab leaders resolved to seek a political showdown by inducing the United States to press the Jewish State into making massive withdrawals from the occupied territories as a pre-requisite of "real peace." The President seemed increasingly less interested in Israel's ultimate fate than in forestalling another Arab-Israeli war and its probable concomitant: another disastrous oil embargo.

Early on, the American "peace offensive" took the form of a plan to hustle the belligerents to Geneva for a resumption of the interrupted conference held there in December 1973 after the Yom Kippur War. "Geneva by Christmas" became a slogan announced by Secretary of State Vance. President Carter committed himself to it, and the Secretary General of the United Nations, Kurt Waldheim, solemnly warned the world of the catastrophic consequences if it did not take place. The sudden rush to Geneva, whether the Israelis were ready or not, reflected the warnings by several Arab spokesmen that 1977, marking the tenth anniversary of the Six Day War, would be the "year of decision" for peace, war, or even worse, a renewed oil embargo against the energy-hungry West.

It soon became apparent that Carter's "peace plan" derived from a twenty-three-page booklet entitled *Toward Peace in the Middle East* prepared for the "think tank" known as Brookings Institution by a panel of Middle East specialists in 1975. The document represented a consensus of widely divergent views, but, broadly speaking, put forward ideas that subsequently became the essence of President Carter's strategy. One of the sixteen members of the study group that produced the Brookings Report, as it came to be known, was Dr. Zbigniew Brzezinski, later Carter's National Security Advisor. The Columbia professor was not a Middle East expert, having done his graduate work at Harvard in East European studies. Nevertheless, his name appeared as one of the authors of the report along with those of such recognized authorities in the field as

Rita Hauser, Malcolm Kerr, Fred Khouri, Nadav Safran and others.

The report urged a "comprehensive approach" to a solution of the Arab-Israeli conflict instead of the step-by-step method employed by Kissinger in promoting the Egyptian-Israeli deal in Sinai. It warned that unless diplomatic momentum resumed, the Middle East's more "moderate" leaders might be ousted by radical rivals who, presumably, would opt for war rather than an overall settlement. Another war, it said, would, among other things, disrupt the flow of Arab oil to Western Europe, the United States and Japan.

The "comprehensive settlement" suggested by the report was to be built abound three main points:

First, an undertaking by Israel to "withdraw by agreed stages to the June 5, 1967 lines with only such modifications as are mutually accepted," the resultant boundaries to be safeguarded by demilitarized zones supervised by U.N. forces.

Second, a commitment by all parties concerned "to respect the sovereignty and territorial integrity of others," with the Arabs further committed to "giving evidence of progress toward the development of normal international and regional political and economic relations," i.e., substantial and immediate movement toward "real peace."

Third, "provision for Palestinian self-determination, subject to Palestinian acceptance of the sovereignty and integrity of Israel within agreed boundaries." This, the report said, might take the form of either an "independent Palestinian state accepting the . . . peace agreements," or of "a Palestinian entity voluntarily federated with Jordan, but exercising extensive political autonomy."

No specific solution was suggested to solve the "Jerusalem problem," which the report's authors regarded as "particularly difficult." They recommended, however, that some minimal requirements be met in any eventual solution. These were: "umimpeded access to all holy places," each of which "should be under the custodianship of its own faith." Finally, regarding Jerusalem, the report stressed there should be no barriers dividing the city—in other words, it should remain united as it is.

The report avoided endorsement of the PLO by sidestepping the question of how the Palestinians would be represented at an eventual peace conference. However, it called for Soviet participation and admonished the United States against attempting to "lay down a detailed blueprint of what it believes a settlement should be," sound advice that would be ignored by Jimmy Carter with controversial and often embarrassing consequences.

In the summer of 1976, Brzezinski, who had been chosen by Carter as a foreign-policy adviser and promised a high-level job in his Administration if he won, visited Israel. He came away with a clearer perception of

Israel's geographic vulnerability and the impression that any future Palestinian entity on the West Bank ought to be linked with Jordan—the prevailing Israeli-Laborite view at the time—and kept under Israeli military protection until such time as the area could be safely demilitarized.

Among other political leaders, Brzezinski met Menahem Begin while in Israel and reportedly was much impressed by him as "a statesman who has had the unique privilege of struggling for the ideals of his people." [1] Begin, according to my sources, however, was not equally impressed. When Brzezinski attempted to communicate in their common native language, Polish, Begin responded in English. He refuses to speak Polish because it reminds him of the Warsaw ghetto, just as he refrains from using German because it recalls the horrors of the Holocaust.

Informed persons in Jerusalem became alarmed in early March—while the Israeli national elections were in full cry and a caretaker government under Rabin was in charge—when Carter first broached the idea of a "homeland for the Palestinian refugees." The "homeland" Carter was suggesting could only be erected on the Gaza Strip and the West Bank, territories from which, before 1967, Palestinian terrorists launched innumerable raids into Israeli territory, killing and maiming hundreds of Israeli civilians, including women and children, and destroying millions of dollars worth of property.

Begin's electoral victory in mid-May resulted from many factors, as we shall see, but Carter undoubtedly influenced the outcome in his favor. If the President's purpose had been to defeat the Laborites instead of peacemaking, he did everything right by harping on the theme of a Palestinian "homeland," a *leit motif* to which he returned over and over again with and without variations. Israelis, who had grown uncomfortable with the dovish views being expressed by various Labor Party leaders since the 1967 war, left the party in droves and flocked to Begin's Likudist nationalist banner, when Carter proposed steps that, in the voters' view, threatened Israel's national security.

A pro-Arab tilt was visible from the start of Carter's campaign in Washington's (1) rejection of Israel's requests for concussion bombs, (2) denial of permission to export Israel-made *Kfir* jets merely because they were constructed with American engines, and (3) refusal of licenses to coproduce with the United States sophisticated weapons and communications systems. While these actions on the part of the new Administration did not unduly alarm the Israelis, Carter's speeches about Wilsonian-style "self-determination" for the Palestinian Arabs were another matter.

Now the Israelis felt they were being asked to make concessions in the

name of peace that would jeopardize their national existence, to ac-
quiesce, in effect, in their own destruction. They were duly grateful for
the generous financial and military help they had received from America
over the years, but they deeply resented being pressured by Washington
into making territorial restitutions which inevitably would return their
country to its highly vulnerable "hourglass" contours of 1967, with
frontiers that were, after all, merely the armistice lines of 1949. There was
no Israeli occupation of a West Bank then, but the Arabs attacked
anyhow.

In his zealous pursuit of a Middle East settlement, Carter made some
memorable boo-boos. One of the worst came on May 26, shortly after
Begin's electoral victory. At a news conference, the President returned to
his Palestinians' "right" to a "homeland" theme with a further proposal
that the "homeless" ones be compensated for their losses. He said these
"rights" had been "spelled out" in past Security Council resolutions
endorsed by "every Administration since they were passed."

Actually, the only resolution in favor of a Palestinian state that the
United States had ever approved was the resolution of the General
Assembly of 1947 that divided what was left of Palestine—Britain already
had lopped off the eastern two-thirds to create Transjordan in 1922—
between Arabs and Jews, a solution the latter accepted but the Arabs did
not. The slip caused the Israelis to wonder whether President Carter knew
what he was talking about when he discussed the Middle East.

President Carter seemed unaware of the fact that the overwhelming
majority of Palestinian Arabs are neither "homeless" nor "stateless."
Most are citizens of various countries, including Jordan. About four
hundred thousand Palestinian Arabs are citizens of Israel proper, with all
the rights of Israeli citizenship save one—the right to kill fellow Arabs by
serving in Israel's armed forces. The roughly one million Palestinian
Arabs residing in the West Bank still retain Jordanian citizenship and
move freely across the "open bridges" into Jordan and about Israel itself.
The few hundred thousand who are bona-fide refugees could easily be
absorbed in their host countries, most of which, except Egypt, are
underpopulated.

Of the tens of millions of refugees—the figure varies between 35 and 40
million—created since 1945 in Eastern Europe, Africa, the Indian
subcontinent and Southeast Asia only 472,000,[2] created by Israel's War of
Independence, are expected to be repatriated, compensated and/or
rewarded with a state of their own in an Arab World that already numbers
twenty-one independent nations covering a total of more than 4½ million
square miles of territory. The Arab-Israeli wars also produced approximately 875,000 *Jewish* refugees who were obliged to flee intolerable
conditions in the Arab countries. Of these, some 600,000 were absorbed
in Israel.

In passing, the temptation is irresistible to point out that the much talked-about Palestinian "homeland" already exists: it is called Jordan. This territory covers approximately two-thirds of historical Palestine. Here the Palestinians not only constitute a majority of the population but most members of King Hussein's government are of Palestinian origin. Hussein could contribute handsomely to resolving the matter of Palestinian "homelessness" by changing his country's name back to what it once was: Palestine.

Carter's misconception of the Palestinian problem was the most serious flaw in his Middle East strategy. Late in June, on the eve of Begin's expected arrival in Washington to confer with the President, Carter decided to caution his visitor in advance with a firmly worded statement of his administration's policy. It omitted the usual official phraseology about America's enduring friendship and support for Israel, and stressed the need for a Palestinian homeland, without reference to any Jordanian link, and bluntly declared that "no territories, including the West Bank, are automatically excluded from the items to be negotiated."

The statement, though issued by the State Department, was obviously the work of Zbigniew Brzezinski. In an article Dr. Brzezinski had written for the quarterly review, *Foreign Policy*,[3] he had called on Israel to face up "squarely" to the fact that, "essentially, Israeli policy should aim at trading the occupied territories for Arab acceptance of the partition of the old Palestine mandate territory between Israel and what would probably be the PLO-dominated state on the West Bank and Gaza Strip."[4]

This view was clearly reflected in the State Department's statement of June 27. It required Israel to withdraw from all three fronts, but particularly stressed the necessity of a pullback from the West Bank. But while the statement was aggressively specific on the nature of the concessions to be made by Israel, it was vague on reciprocal Arab concessions, merely stating that the Arabs would have to agree to implement "a kind of peace" involving steps toward "normalization of relations with Israel."

Obviously, the President and the Prime Minister were on a collision course even before they met. To Menahem Begin, the West Bank is composed of Biblical Judea and Samaria, which, he says, were not "conquered" by the Israelis in the Six Day War of 1967, but were "liberated" from its illegal occupants, the Jordanians. To him, Judea and Samaria are not merely historical abstractions, but living realities, something outsiders in general and the Arabs in particular would have difficulty understanding.

In their hearts, most Israelis, including Begin, I have found, are "doves"; they are "hawks" only out of despair. Theirs is a highly complicated, pluralistic social-democracy wherein mingle diverse secular and religious strains, a variety of people of many different national origins and cultures and a multitude of political affiliations, ranging from extreme left to extreme right. However, Israel's most striking characteristic, perhaps, is its hereditary fear that what happened to their distant ancestors in A.D. 70 at the hands of the Roman conqueror Titus—he razed Jerusalem and the Second Temple, killed an estimated one million Jewish defenders of the Kingdom of Judah, and dispersed those survivors whom he did not cart away in chains as slaves—might happen again at the hands of a surrounding multitude of well-armed Arabs, whose adjacent Moslem allies sit on most of the world's oil and through it wield almost incalculable politico-economic power.

Burned into their collective psyche is also the far more recent memory of the Hitlerian Holocaust that barely a generation ago took the lives of six million European Jews. The idea of allowing the creation in their midst of a Palestinian state that might readily become a base for the PLO to carry out those terms of its charter promising the destruction of the Jewish State is understandably abhorrent to the overwhelming majority of Israelis.

The notion is particularly repugnant to the man whom the Israelis chose to lead them at a critical juncture in Israel's history, Menahem Begin, himself a survivor of the Holocaust. He and an older sister, Rachel, barely escaped the fate that overtook their Polish parents and a brother. Begin almost literally vibrates with outrage when anyone mentions the tragedy that befell the Jewish people during World War II. "The Jews," I have heard him say on several occasions, "were not merely *decimated*, for that means only one in ten of the world's Jews were killed by the Nazis, but *tertiated*. One in every three were slaughtered."

Carter's tough stand on the West Bank as outlined in the State Department's policy announcement of June 25, which Brzezinski obviously had helped to draft, alarmed the American Jewish community. If, as some experts believed, the State Department's unpropitious pronouncement was intended to summon support for the President's strategy among those liberal American Jews who harbored misgivings at the unexpected emergence in Israel of the conservative Begin, it failed to achieve its purpose. Leading American Jews read in the statement clear and evident danger to Israel's national security, for it virtually demanded Israel's return to the uncertain frontiers prevalent at the time of the country's establishment in 1948. The White House and the State Department were swamped by a flood of angry letters and telegrams.

With the controversial Begin about to arrive, Rabbi Arthur Hertzberg, president of the American Jewish Congress (AJC), realizing or suspecting Brzezinski to be the policy's principal architect, wrote him a personal letter, saying, "I am fearful that present policy may lead needlessly to

confrontation with Israel and with its friends in the United States."
Similar warnings came from Rabbi Alexander Schindler, Chairman of the
Conference of Presidents of the Major Jewish Organizations, and others.

Carter invited a delegation of about forty American-Jewish leaders to
the White House to hear what they had to say and to explain his policy.
From the Jewish leadership, the President learned that Begin was not
nearly as "inflexible" and "fanatic" as he had been painted, and from the
President, the visitors learned that the United States would never
abandon Israel.

Outwardly at least, the subsequent meeting between Begin and Carter
went smoothly. The Israeli Premier arrived, armed with detailed maps
illustrating Israel's geographic and military vulnerability if it were obliged
to withdraw to its pre-1967 borders and a Palestinian state were erected
on the West Bank and Gaza. Begin went out of his way to appear
"flexible" and "cooperative" and succeeded in bolstering the President's
hopes for a speedy resumption of a Geneva conference, possibly in
October. Begin remained unmovable, however, on the question of PLO
representation in any form, reiterating in his usually eloquent manner that
the organization's aim as stated in its charter still demanded "destruction
of our country and destruction of our people."

According to all reports, "a warm personal relationship" was established between Carter and Begin. The latter came away with "a good
impression of Mr. Carter, a sincere man, a good man who also believes in
God."

Shortly after the two-day meeting, the Carter Administration officially
approved a $250 million arms package for Israel, including about $107
million in military assistance to produce Israel's new, powerful, battle
tank, the *Merkava*. Also included in the deal were a number of Corba
attack helicopters and two advanced Hydrofoil naval patrol boats, with
permission for Israel to produce them in quantity jointly with the United
States.

Altogether, from Begin's standpoint, it was not a bad two days' work.
He had won acceptance as Carter's partner in peacemaking and obtained
a substantial amount of military hardware.

But Carter's troubles with his Middle East policy were far from over.
Indeed, they had only begun. The mood throughout the always unstable
area was darkening, especially in Cairo, where President Sadat struggled
with heavy internal political and economic pressures. Israeli intelligence
reported several high-level Egyptian military alerts.

Among Sadat's problems was one rarely mentioned by foreign correspondents based in the Egyptian capital, namely the ongoing friction

between Egypt's masses of Moslems and its Copts, a large minority representing the continuity of Christian pre-Islamic society and culture. Several Coptic churches were burned in the revival of Islamic orthodoxy inspired mainly by Sadat's capricious Lybian neighbor, Colonel Mu'ammar el-Qadhafi. The Copts who represent approximately ten percent of Egypt's population, clamored for greater representation in the People's Assembly, where they hold only 10 seats out of 360. *Shari'a*, the Islamic Law, ascribes second-class status to all non-Moslems.

But Sadat's biggest problems were economic. The country verged on bankruptcy. Student riots early in the year underscored Egypt's rapidly deteriorating capacity to meet the basic needs of the people: jobs, food, housing, education and health services. Western investments in the Egyptian economy, which Sadat had anticipated as a result of his rapid switch from Nasserian socialism to a free enterprise system after expelling the Russians in 1972, had failed to materialize. The country was living on substantial, but nevertheless insufficient, subsidies from Saudi Arabia and other oil fiefdoms. The per capita income still would buy only a few rounds of ammunition for a tank's gun, and social services were steadily buckling under the strain of population growth.

Having closely observed the results of the Begin visit, the Arabs started raising serious objections to Carter's haste to reconvene Geneva. They refused to go along unless Israel agreed to total withdrawal from the occupied territories, at least in principle, and to the establishment of a Palestinian state. Furthermore, they insisted that the PLO be invited to the proposed talks. Secretary Vance, during a swing through the Middle East in August, found the Arab leaders immovable on this particular point. Vance also discovered a growing consensus everywhere, including Israel, for a pre-Geneva understanding on substantive questions to avoid serious snags and obstacles at the eventual conference.

Then, chatting informally with reporters in Plains, Georgia, Carter let it drop that the PLO "might participate" at Geneva, if it accepted U.N. Resolution 242—if, in other words, the PLO "recognized" Israel. However conditional, it was the President's first public endorsement of the terrorist organization as a peacemaking partner. It was prompted by a message from Vance, who was still touring the Middle East's capitals at the time, that the Saudi Arabians had indicated to him a burgeoning change in attitude on the part of the PLO. Its leadership, the Saudis hinted, was seriously considering modifying its opposition to Israel's right to exist.

In Jerusalem, Vance found Begin utterly opposed to doing business with "genocidists who should be treated like pirates and outlaws" and not as negotiating partners. The Secretary of State returned to Washington convinced that the Israelis, rather than the Arabs, were obstructing progress toward resumption of the Geneva conference. Carter, evidently sharing Vance's view, gave it public expression. Without mentioning Israel by name, he told a White House gathering of editors and publishers that, "Any nation in the Middle East that proved to be intransigeant would suffer . . . the condemnation of the rest of the world." He came as close as he could come to using American aid to pressure Israel into acquiescence, although he had promised Rabbi Schindler and other American Jewish leaders that he never would do so.

Tension between Washington and Jerusalem mounted when the Administration goaded Israel into assenting to Palestinian representation at Geneva as part of an all-Arab delegation. The Israelis went so far as to agree, however reluctantly to be sure, "not to scrutinize too carefully the credentials" of the attending Palestinians to determine whether or not they were in fact PLO sympathizers. Although accepted by Jerusalem, the formula caused an uproar in the American Jewish community whose leaders accused Carter of "betrayal." A showdown was narrowly averted, but worse was to come.

On October 1, the Soviet Union and the United States issued a joint declaration urging the convocation of the Geneva conference. The statement stemmed from a series of secret meetings between Russian Foreign Minister Andrei Gromyko and President Carter and Secretary Vance. To call it a "political surprise" would be gross understatement: it was a diplomatic bombshell. Seasoned observers saw it as heralding a major departure from traditional American attitudes towards the Middle East conflict.

One phrase in the statement attracted particular attention: it was a reference to the need to resolve "the Palestinian question, including the ensuring of the legitimate rights of the Palestinian people" This was the first time the United States had subscribed to a formula mentioning Palestinian "legitimate *rights*"; past references had been to the "legitimate *interests*" of the Palestinians. According to the Soviet concept, "legitimate rights" include the right to establish a Palestinian state but could be interpreted in Arab political jargon as the liquidation of the Jewish state. Thus the United States appeared to be aligning itself with the Soviet view on this point.

Another major point in the statement was the call for "withdrawal of Israeli armed forces from territories occupied in . . . 1967." Significantly, the statement did not use the wording: "withdrawal from *the* territories"—the standard Soviet and Arab reading of U.N. Resolution 242.

Another choice of wording in the joint statement which attracted particular attention was that circumstances pervailing in the Middle East *"dictate* the necessity of achieving, *as soon as possible,* a just and lasting settlement" and the great powers have a *"vital* interest" in this regard. It went on to name December 1977 as the latest acceptable date for renewing the Geneva conference, and added that the co-Chairmen, the United States and the Soviet Union, would "facilitate in every way the resumption" of the conference.

In short, the whole tenor of the joint statement could not fail to impress upon all concerned that the two Superpowers were preparing the ground for an imposed solution of the Middle East conflict according to a plan agreed to by both and prearranged between them. This impression was reinforced by what the statement actually left unsaid—primarily, the absence of any reference whatsoever to Security Council Resolution 242.

For the Russians, the statement was a diplomatic success of the first magnitude. It signaled its readmission, as an equal partner with the United States, into the center of Middle East affairs on terms under which Washington met Soviet attitudes more than halfway. With a single stroke of the pen, past American successes in minimizing Soviet influence over major developments in the Middle East seemed to have been wiped out.

Within a day or two of its signature and publication, the joint statement turned into a liability for Carter. Not only did it provoke adverse reactions among the American public, but it also cast doubt on Carter's ability to persuade Begin and Dayan that American policy in the Middle East was in Israel's best interest.

Carter proclaimed the document "an achievement of unprecedented significance," but it was evident to longtime Middle East watchers that Russia's reentry into the peacemaking process was a regression. The President's explanation—that by signing the joint declaration the Russians had for the first time recognized Israel's right to exist—turned out to be another *gaffe.* The Soviet Union was among those early United Nations members who had voted for Israel's creation in 1948 and had maintained diplomatic relations with the Jewish state until the 1967 war.

When the statement was published, Prime Minister Begin was in Tel Aviv's Ichilov Hospital for a checkup. There was no sign of the heart trouble that had stricken him earlier, severely during the springtime elections and again, but less seriously, later. Begin was suffering from acute exhaustion following two days of intensive activity. The day before entering the hospital, he had spent five or six hours in the hot desert sun touring Jewish settlements in northern Sinai. The morning of the day he was admitted, he had what his doctor described as "a very tough session" with U. S. Ambassador Samuel Lewis concerning the Soviet-American joint declaration.

A measure of how seriously Jerusalem regarded the situation created by the statement was the announcement by Finance Minister Simha Ehrlich, one of the senior members of Begin's closely knit family of advisors, that Israel might call for formation of a government of national unity to meet the looming emergency.

Begin's indisposition, however, did not prevent him from pronouncing the Soviet-American agreement "totally unacceptable." He objected strenuously to the document's reference to the Palestinians' "legitimate rights," of course, and was upset by its seemingly studied absence of any reference to "secure and recognized borders" for Israel. To Begin and Dayan, the document read as though it had been drafted in Moscow, not Washington.

The Prime Minister sent Dayan to Washington to attempt to resolve the newly created difficulties.

The reaction of American Jews as well as Gentile supporters of Israel was equally hostile. Again, thousands of letters, telegrams and telephone calls poured into the White House, where there was an obvious lack of coordination between foreign and domestic policy makers.

In an attempt to repair the damage, Carter inserted into his October 4 speech before the United Nations General Assembly a number of elements that had been missing in the Russo-American statement. He spoke of Israel's need for "recognized and secure borders," and reiterated America's "unquestionable" commitment to Israel's security. The speech also supplied the necessary references to Security Council Resolution 242, which the statement had omitted to make, and emphasized the "establishment of normal diplomatic relations (and) economic and cultural exchanges" between Israel and the Arab countries as cardinal objectives of the Geneva negotiations.

Meeting with a worried Dayan in New York, Carter agreed that Israel would not be bound by the Soviet-American declaration or compelled to negotiate with the PLO. Later, in Washington, he called a White House meeting with a large delegation of members of the House of Representatives, most of them Jewish, and told them he would "rather commit suicide than hurt Israel." The legislators left the White House sobered and pleased. None had ever heard such melodramatic language from a President, not even from Lyndon Johnson.

Carter had greater difficulty, however, regaining the confidence of the rank and file of Jewish Americans. A meeting of seventy leaders of American Jewry called by Vance at the State Department for a "dialogue" designed to clarify "misunderstandings" between the Administration and the Jewish community produced a storm of criticism. One of the group's spokesmen accused the Administration of having "pointed a dagger at the heart of every Jew in the world" by joining the Russians in a move to create a "PLO state" on the West Bank that spelled Israel's doom.

Soothing statements by Brzezinski and Vance followed, but the really substantive American retreat from the shambles created by the joint statement was incorporated in a subsequent American-Israeli so-called Working Paper. This new document, hammered out on October 5 as an eleventh-hour compromise by Carter and Vance with Moshe Dayan, established at least a "tentative formula" for reconvening the Geneva conference. It included the following points: (1) reaffirmation of Security Council Resolution 242 as the agreed basis of the Geneva negotiations. (2) exclusion from the negotiations of all subjects not previously included in the agenda or not stemming from Resolution 242, (3) inclusion of Palestinian representatives in a united Arab delegation, (4) discussions on refugees would apply equally to Jewish refugees forced out of Arab countries as well as Arab refugees created in 1949, (5) discussion of topics relating to the West Bank and Gaza Strip to be discussed in a working group composed of Israel, Jordan, Egypt and Palestinian Arabs, and (6) *peace settlements between Israel and each of its neighbors—Egypt, Jordan, Syria and Lebanon (if it participated)—to be negotiated in bilateral talks between Israel and representatives of each Arab country concerned.*

Approval of the Working Paper by the Israeli cabinet put the ball in the Arab court. First reactions on the part of the Arab countries were evasive and noncommittal. The only country to indicate tentative approval of the Working Paper in the days prior to the Israeli action was Egypt.

Sadat convened the Egyptian National Security Council on September 30, and ordered the Egyptian media to give rather dramatic sounding coverage to its session. Vice President Husni Mubarak left immediately for a whirlwind tour of Arab capitals as well as Teheran. Neither Syria nor Jordan (let alone Iraq) agreed with the favorable Egyptian line as presented to them by Mubarak.

In the Egyptian media, the Working Paper received lukewarm but encouraging approval which, to quote Foreign Minister Ismail Fahmi, set "things moving." By contrast, the Russo-American statement was described by a veteran Egyptian journalist as "a disaster." On the inter-Arab plane, the main thrust of Egyptian activity was to try to persuade the PLO to exploit the Working Paper as a lever for its entry into Geneva—perhaps even without the "PLO" label attached to its representatives. Yassir Arafat arrived in Cairo for talks on the subject on three separate occasions in early October. But, mindful of the divisions within his organization, he did not let himself be persuaded.

In Cairo, President Sadat had been brooding all year long. His policy of qualified de-Nasserization was bringing him increasingly under fire from all sides. On the one hand, it provided an opportunity to radical opposition forces—from the Marxists to the Qadhafi-inspired Neo-Nasserists—to raise the banner of Nasserism and denounce Sadat's policies as deviations from the "true revolution." On the other hand, it encouraged those political elements that had opposed the Nasserite revolution in the first place to demand a complete reversal of Nasserism, which would amount to a liquidation of Sadat's regime. Sadat had been oscillating between these two challenges to his regime for some time, turning his attention from one opposition group to the other, according to the magnitude of their potential threat. Thus, following the January food riots, he cracked down on the Egyptian leftists. Then the outburst of Islamic terrorism against the Copts directed his attention to the reactionary challenge.

The condition of the Egyptian economy deteriorated almost daily. Egypt's finances were in worse shape than at any time since Nasser's death in 1970. Sadat needed massive infusions of Western, particularly American, economic aid. Most of all, he realized, he needed peace so that Egypt's huge military expenditures could be reduced. Finally, he burned with an inner desire to assert his leadership in the so-called Arab World as President of its militarily most powerful member.

Like the Israelis, Sadat had felt all along that President Carter was making a dangerous mistake in pushing for a Geneva Peace Conference without proper preparation. When he had visited Carter in Washington in the spring, the President had assured him that the United States saw Geneva as a "ratifying," not a "negotiating," conference.[5] Geneva, Carter had told him, would merely ratify agreements reached beforehand through quiet diplomacy.

However, Sadat had noted with dismay the summertime shift in Carter's position. The indications coming out of Washington were that Geneva would be a "negotiating" conference after all. Sadat saw at once that this change, linked as it was to Carter's simultaneous advocacy of a Palestinian homeland, would doom a "negotiating" conference in Geneva through an inevitable open confrontation. He resolved to break the deadlock.

Throughout the summer, Sadat tried to persuade the PLO to alter its charter by dropping the clauses calling for Israel's destruction. The PLO refused. War talk began filling the air. In Riyadh, Crown Prince Fahd, Saudi Arabia's *de facto* ruler, was warning that a new Middle East war could lead to global warfare. There were rumors—utterly unfounded—that Israel was planning a preemptive strike.

It was at about this time and in this frame of mind that Sadat visited Romania's Ceausescu in Bucharest, where the idea for a direct meeting between himself and Menahem Begin was born. Late in October, Sadat confided to two or three trusted advisers that he had decided to make a major diplomatic overture in an effort to end the impasse, because the alternative was a war he neither wanted nor was sure he could win. The time had come to break with the past and face the substantive issues directly with Israel despite the enormous, indeed, potentially catastrophic, personal and political risks involved.

NOTES

1. Stanley Karnow, *The New York Times Magazine,* January 15, 1978.

2. This was the figure fixed on October 18, 1948, by the late Dr. Ralph Bunche when he was the U.N. Mediator in the Palestine dispute.

3. "Peace in an International Framework," in *Foreign Policy,* 19 (Summer, 1975): 3-17.

4. Ibid., p. 10.

5. Tad Szulc, *New York Magazine,* December 26, 1977.

Chapter 3

Sadat's Peace Offensive

For nearly three decades Israel had waited patiently for two things to occur to make possible fulfillment of its most ardent desire—a full and lasting peace. These two things were the emergence of an Arab leader disposed to talk to Israel and the acknowledgement by a major Arab statethat Jewish Israel was in fact a sovereign nation with its own permanent place in the geography of the Middle East. After living under unrelenting tension for twenty-nine years, rare indeed was the mature Israeli who believed he or she would live long enough to see either of those things happen. The future seemed to hold only more of what they had experienced in the past—continued stresses and strains, deprivation, isolation in an increasingly hostile environment and, quite probably, more war.

Then, suddenly, on November 9, 1977, the leader and the state materialized simultaneously in the person of President Mohammed Anwar el-Sadat of Egypt, the selfsame Sadat who almost exactly four years before had hurled at Israel the considerable might of his armed forces, ostensibly to regain territory lost by the Egyptians in the 1967 war, but in reality—in collusion with Syria, Jordan and Iraq—to expunge the Jewish state from the map of the preponderantly Moslem Middle East.

On that memorable day, speaking from the rostrum of the ornate chamber of the Egyptian People's Assembly in Cairo, Sadat declared he was ready to travel to Geneva or anywhere else, "to the end of the world, if necessary," to achieve peace in the Middle East and prevent the shedding of the blood of one more Egyptian soldier, "even to the Knesset in Jerusalem itself" to accomplish his purpose. The Egyptian legislators, the visitors in the packed balconies, even the Egyptian reporters in the press gallery—some of whom I would meet later in Jerusalem—burst into cheers and prolonged applause when Sadat made his momentous announcement. History was being made, and those present responded enthusiastically with one notable exception. A guest, Yassir Arafat, in town to discuss PLO business with the President, sat immobile, arms folded, expressionless.¹

Predictably enough, Sadat's declared willingness to go "even to . . . Jerusalem" in search of peace stunned his counterparts in the so-called Arab World; he had not consulted them before making his announcement. They would react soon enough, nearly all with violent denunciations, for they understood that Sadat's proposed visit would confer de facto recognition on the Israeli state and on Jerusalem as its capital. At first, however, they remained remarkably silent.

Incredibly, the historic implications of Sadat's proposal were lost on the Carter Administration, which evidently could not believe the Egyptian leader would break with the Arabs' "rejectionist front" by recognizing the Jewish state; there was no immediate reaction from Washington. President Carter spent the morning meeting with Robert Muldoon, New Zealand's Prime Minister, and entertaining him at lunch. At a State Department press conference, spokesman John Trattner fielded routine questions concerning an Israeli retaliatory air strike against PLO bases in southwestern Lebanon—which he studiedly refused to condemn—and regarding Israel's request to enter into co-production of American F-16 fighter planes—about which he said "no final action" had been taken.

In Jerusalem, Sadat's speech made front page news, but analysts and commentators were inclined to dismiss it as "just another propaganda ploy." The big story in the morning newspapers of November 10 was the Israeli air force's attack on PLO bases, encampments and training centers just across the frontier in Lebanon in retaliation for an earlier terrorist rocket attack on Nahariya, a seacoast resort town, that had claimed three Israeli lives, injured five and caused extensive damage.

While Sadat was talking peace in Cairo, Premier Begin was telling the Variety Club of Israel in Jerusalem that the days are over "when terrorists of the so-called PLO can launch deadly assaults upon us and we stand idly by." He accused the Soviet Union of supplying the PLO with "sophisticated weapons with which to kill innocent men, women and children." None of which was really news.

At the Prime Minister's office, a staff was arranging the details of Begin's forthcoming four-day state visit to Great Britain for meetings with Premier James Callahan and with British Jewish leaders. The visit had been postponed once, and would be postponed again, for it gradually dawned on everyone concerned that Sadat meant what he had said on November 9, although on the next day, the significance of the Egyptian President's proposal still had not yet been fully understood where, perhaps, it mattered most: Washington. The Carter Administration remained mesmerized by the prospect of a Geneva conference and continued pressing for a December 21 opening. At the State Department briefing for correspondents on November 10, a reporter asked for a comment on Sadat's speech, and Trattner replied, "We welcome his strong support for just what we are trying to do—reconvene a Geneva conference to get on with the business of peace . . ."

To Menahem Begin, however, must go the credit for being first among national leaders to react intelligently to Sadat's overture. Forty-eight hours after Sadat had spoken to his People's Assembly, the Israeli Premier broadcast a statement in English and Arabic, beamed by radio and television to Egypt, welcoming Sadat's initiative and assuring the Egyptian people that their President would be received "with the traditional hospitality you and we have inherited from our common father, Abraham," adding: "Let us say to one another, and let it be a silent oath between both peoples, of Egypt and Israel: no more wars, no more bloodshed, no more threats . . ."

Next day, Begin said to a delegation of visiting French dignitaries, "I hereby invite President Sadat of Egypt to come to Jerusalem to conduct talks about permanent peace between Israel and Egypt. This is an invitation."

It is not unimaginable, though highly improbable, that what had suddenly become an Arab-Israeli dialogue instead of an Israeli monologue might have come to naught if Walter Cronkite had not taken a hand in the proceedings. Cronkite and his staff at CBS news sensed a big story in the making when they read the wire agency excerpts from Sadat's speech on November 9, a Wednesday, and moved quickly to bring it off and put it on the tube. By the following Monday morning—it took five days to complete the complicated arrangements—Cronkite had taped an interview with President Sadat—who is never shy about appearing on American television—in which he assured the amiable anchorman that he meant every word of his Assembly speech.

"I'm just waiting for the proper invitation," Sadat said between nervous puffs on his pipe. Asked by Cronkite how this might be arranged in view of the lack of diplomatic relations between Egypt and Israel, Sadat replied, "Why not through our mutual friends, the Americans?"

Within hours, the CBS Bureau in Tel Aviv arranged a similar interview with Begin. The Prime Minister had not believed that the diplomatic seeds which he and Dayan had planted only a few weeks before in Bucharest and elsewhere would sprout so soon; he was going ahead with plans to fly to London on November 20. However, Begin assured Cronkite that he and his fellow countrymen would welcome President Sadat's visit. In fact, he said, he planned to send a formal letter of invitation the next day through the United States ambassadors in Tel Aviv and Cairo. He would gladly postpone his projected visit to London, and Sadat could come "any time, any day."

Like the rest of the outside world, Washington was taken by surprise by Sadat's move. Not until the Cronkite interview did the Administration fully understand what had been happening under its very nose.

Later, both Sadat and Begin obligingly credited Carter with responsibility for having brought them together, and this was interpreted by some White House officials as an endorsement of President Carter's diplomacy; actually, that diplomacy, by its inconsistencies, had persuaded Sadat that unless he took some dramatic action outside the framework that had been established by Carter, there was no prospect for meaningful negotiations anywhere.

Sadat's most obvious motive was to overcome the procedural obstacles that had been piling up on the road to Geneva and thus avoid a stalemate in the preparations for that conference. He evidently saw the preparatory diplomatic talks dragging on endlessly, eventually compelling him to resort again to war, something he wished to avoid in view of its high cost to Egypt and its uncertain outcome. The establishment of direct contact with Begin was thus designed to reduce secondary issues to insignificance and lead all parties via the shortest possible route to negotiation on the major substantive matters.

For the same purpose, Sadat sought to remove the "psychological barrier" between Israelis and Arabs which, in his opinion, constituted "seventy percent of the problem." He expected the "shock effect" of his proposed visit to Jerusalem to generate a new atmosphere of greater mutual trust which would facilitate, he hoped, effective communication between the parties. In his opinion, mutual suspicion had reached a danger point, where it not only hindered progress toward a settlement, but also presented a growing threat of escalation towards war.

Sadat was also motivated by a desire to recapture the initiative in Middle East diplomacy and prevent the Superpowers from regulating it at their pace and at their pleasure. To that end, he not only denounced the role played by the Soviet Union since 1967 in various statements to the media, but also indicated his dissatisfaction with the way the United States had handled its diplomatic efforts in the weeks preceding his historic beau geste.

Sadat's reservations concerning the United States' role centered on the

American-Soviet declaration—which was not coordinated with Egypt (or with Israel, for that matter)—and the American tendency to include the recalcitrant and radical Syrians among the "moderates" in the Arab-Israeli conflict. Sadat was also agitated by the concessions made by the United States to Israel within the framework of the American-Israeli Working Paper. Accordingly, one of Sadat's main motives was his determination to bring Middle East diplomacy back where, from his point of view, it belonged—to the region of conflict itself.

Finally, inherent in Sadat's political initiative was his desire to create optimal conditions for an alternative course, should his diplomatic initiative fail to produce results. He evidently calculated that should his style of diplomacy reach a stalemate after all, this would expose Israeli "intransigeance" and allow the Arabs to drive a wedge between Israel and the United States. Such conditions would automatically be conducive to greater American pressure on Israel—or another Arab military campaign against the Jewish state.

The CBS presentation of the evening of November 14—as it was replayed by satellite relay on Israeli television in Jerusalem the next day—opened with pictures of Sadat and Begin on a split screen behind Cronkite. The anchorman, looking more the elder statesman than either of the principals, elicited pledges from both men to come together without "preconditions," thereby eliminating a longtime major roadblock to Arab-Israeli negotiations. A polished diplomat could not have done it more expertly.

Israeli friends with whom I watched the telecast could hardly believe what they saw and heard. Before their very eyes, the leaders of two countries still at war were arranging to meet to discuss peace through the good offices of an enterprising American journalist. Sadat quite probably would have journeyed to Jerusalem without Cronkite's assistance, but it certainly helped to expedite matters considerably, while providing the Great Middle East Peace Drama of the last six weeks of 1977 with a theatrical prologue as neatly packaged as an episode in *Hawaii Five-O* and infinitely more absorbing.

TV network executives quickly discovered that the quiet, unspectacular, intangible wonder called Peace had even greater audience appeal than the noisy, highly visible, tangible phenomenon called War. Correspondents, mainly of the TV genre who have largely taken over journalism since World War II, began converging on Jerusalem from everywhere, mostly from the United States.

There was an infinite amount of detail, however, that the cameras did not—indeed, could not—catch. The electronic cyclops can record the

Who-What-When-Where details of an unfolding story, but rarely the Why
of it. The subtle nuances of events occurring off-camera, such as, for
instance, the content, tone and method of Sadat's reply to Begin's cordial,
formal invitation of November 15 transmitted by Ambassador Lewis to his
opposite number in Cairo, Ambassador Herman Eilts, could not be
recorded.

Begin's letter inviting Sadat to visit Jerusalem was a model of courtesy.
It was addressed to "His Excellency, Mr. Anwar el-Sadat, President of
the Arab Republic of Egypt, Cairo," and said, in part:

> Your Excellency's readiness to undertake such a visit as expressed to
> the People's Council of Egypt has been noted here with deep and
> positive interest, as has been your statement that you would wish to
> address the members of our Parliament, the Knesset, and to meet
> with me . . . May I assure you, Mr. President, that the Parliament,
> the Government and the people of Israel will receive you with
> respect and cordiality.
>
> (signed)   Yours sincerely,
MENAHEM BEGIN

The record shows no comparably courteous personal reply to Premier
Begin from Sadat. Instead, what came from Cairo was an official Egyptian
statement, a polemical document utterly devoid of *politesse* and obviously
addressed to Sadat's Arab constituencies in Egypt and the rest of the
Middle East. A country less eager for peace than Israel might easily have
rejected it, for it said, in part:

> President Anwar el-Sadat has agreed to visit Jerusalem, and his
> Excellency will perform the Eid al Adha prayers in Al Aksa
> Mosque.[3] The President's visit will start Saturday night, November
> 19 *in response to a letter from President Carter that was accompanied
> by an invitation from the Israeli Government.*
>
> The President had intended to perform prayers in Sinai after it
> was liberated in the victorious October War . . . but the call for
> peace based on justice has made the President go this year to Al
> Aksa Mosque for prayers . . . When the President of the Arab
> Republic of Egypt answers the call for peace, it is in the name of
> legal and just Arab rights . . .
>
> President Sadat, who is convinced of the righteousness of the
> Arab cause, accepts the invitation to visit Jerusalem in the name of
> the national responsibility he carries . . . He is also convinced that

putting the facts straight, as he intends to do during his address to the Knesset on Sunday, will have a stronger impact than any other lengthy and tortuous methods.

The trip, since it comes after the October War of 1973, in which the Arabs regained their pride, is therefore not governed by the spirit of defeat and should not be misinterpreted since it aims at a global settlement of the Arab cause . . .

The historic responsibilities of Arab leaders today require them to work for peace in the region so long as it is based on justice, and aims to liberate Arab territories occupied by Israel after the 1967 war and the restoration of Palestinian rights . . .

Menahem Begin swallowed hard when he read the Egyptian answer to his invitation, but to his everlasting credit, he did not reject it as an unseemly prelude to negotiations. A temperamental Rabin, or even a Golda Meir, might have. Begin understood why Sadat found it necessary to couch his response in tendentiously nationalistic prose. The Egyptian, Begin knew, was risking his life as well as his political future in making his overture to the Jewish state.

To old Middle East watchers, it was obvious from the start that there would be no real dialogue between the two men. There would be a meeting of two men but not necessarily of two minds. The prospects were for an intercourse in different idioms. Nevertheless, Sadat's arrival in Israel was awaited with unimaginable enthusiasm. It could not have been greater if Mohammed himself had promised to come on his winged horse instead of a namesake: Mohammed Anwar el-Sadat.

Meanwhile, Sadat's announcement of November 9 sent a shock wave through the Arab world, the likes of which the members of the Arab League had not known since the establishment of Israel. For most Arabs outside of Egypt, it marked a breaking of taboos, a shattering of precedents and conventions.

While stunned disbelief and vehement mistrust were the initial reaction in many Arab quarters, the depth of the inter-Arab rift would only become apparent at the close of Sadat's visit to Damascus on November 17, when Syrian President Haafez el-Asad and his visitor from Cairo publicly acknowledged their differences. Sadat's Arab opponents then set to work to assemble an anti-Sadat coalition and for this purpose scheduled a radical mini-Summit at Tripoli in early December. Another small group of Arab states—Morocco, Tunisia and Sudan—began voicing support for Sadat's initiative, but the majority of Arab League members remained relatively silent—fence-sitting while awaiting developments. A struggle began between Egypt and Syria for the allegiance of this "silent majority" whose most important member, by far, was Saudi Arabia.

I was in Jerusalem before, during and after Sadat's visit to the miraculous city with the miraculous name. There was almost as much excitement in the capital and throughout the country before the arrival of the handsome, magnetic Egyptian as there was during his actual presence in Israel.

Incredible though it may seem, definite word that President Sadat was arriving on the evening of November 19 at 20:00 hours—the date fell on a Saturday and the hour was arranged so as not to conflict with the Jewish Sabbath—did not reach Jerusalem until the early afternoon of Wednesday, November 16.

The police had only about fifty-six hours in which to make the elaborate preparations necessary to guarantee the visitor's safety. More than six thousand police and ten thousand troops were quietly mobilized. A score or so of known West Bank "troublemakers" were "neutralized," i.e., rounded up and placed under temporary arrest. All were Arabs, and most were Communists. The Army speedily sealed the frontiers, the Air Force was placed on partial alert and the Navy strengthened its coastal patrols.

There was some suspicion in Israeli military circles that Sadat's announcement of his readiness to visit Jerusalem might be the harbinger of an attack, Pearl Harbor style. In fact, in the interim before Sadat arrived, General Mordechai Gur, the burly Israeli Chief of Staff, disclosed in an interview with a leading Tel Aviv daily, *Yediot Aharonot,*[4] that "authoritative intelligence reports" in his possession suggested Egypt was really scheming to make war, not peace, and had partially mobilized, the implication being that Sadat was bluffing when he said he wanted to come to Jerusalem to talk peace. (Later, when the two men met, Sadat would say, "See? I wasn't bluffing. Here I am," and Gur would reply, "I'm glad you've come Mr. President, but I wasn't bluffing either.")

Journalistically speaking, "waiting for Sadat" became almost as good a story as his actual visit.

At Ben-Gurion International Airport the long red carpet reserved for state receptions was taken out of storage for cleaning, although at the time there was still some doubt that the Egyptian President would come. Jerusalem's veteran flagmaker, Yitzhak Berman, who had stitched up thousands of American flags for Richard Nixon's 1974 visit, was privately betting "yes, he'll come," and set his workers to manufacturing Egyptian flags of all sizes, even before he had received an order from the Foreign

Ministry. "If Sadat comes and the Ministry orders them, fine and good," he philosophized. "If not, nothing lost. The flags will be snapped up by collectors."

Taking a leaf out of the Nixonian book of Sino-American "ping-pong diplomacy," the Israeli Football Association sent a telegram to the Minister of Education, Zevulum Hammer, asking him to invite the Egyptian national team for a game with a squad composed of Israel's soccer stars.

The irrepressible Abie Nathan, who flew three times to Egypt in unsanctioned and abortive efforts to persuade Cairo and Jerusalem to start talking peace—and in January sailed a "peace ship" through the Suez Canal—requested the honor of conveying Sadat to Israel on his propaganda vessel.

Meanwhile, the protocol experts in the Israeli Foreign Office were struggling with questions they had never faced before. Would it be proper to play the Egyptian national anthem for the arriving President of an enemy country? Should a 21-gun salute be fired in his honor? Would Sadat be willing to address the Knesset when he discovered that he would be standing before the Parliament's only decoration: a portrait of Theodor Herzl, the founder of Zionism, and Israel's official seal?

Yitzhak Graziani, the rotund conductor of the Israeli Defense Forces' band, had a big problem of his own. He was certain his musicians would be required to play the Egyptian national anthem, but it was not in their repertoire, and they had no sheet music. The United States Embassy in Tel Aviv had promised to obtain it for him, but by November 16 it had not yet arrived. Nothing daunted, the maestro recorded the anthem—or what he assumed was the anthem—off a Radio Cairo broadcast, transcribed the melody, had it arranged for the various instruments, and kept his fingers crossed. When the American Embassy finally came through with the official version, his transcription was correct, "right down to the last note." "Now," he said, "let's pray *Hatikva* will be played some day in Cairo."

In less than two days, the Government Press Office, in cooperation with the Ministry of Communications, set up an ultramodern international communications center in the splendid Jerusalem Theatre. Journalists could obtain instant contact with their newsrooms the world over, including Egypt. More than two hundred fifty telephones were installed, literally overnight, enabling direct dialing to the United States and most world capitals. Jerusalemites who had waited months to have telephones installed in their homes quipped, "See how easy it is to cut through bureaucratic red tape when necessary?" They credited Begin with the new efficiency.

By the time Sadat arrived, Jerusalem's hotels were jammed, not only with the several Egyptian delegations that accompanied the President, but with Egyptian journalists and security officers, and with the largest gathering of foreign correspondents ever assembled since World War II. The biggest contingent came from the United States, 580, followed by France with 326 and Japan with 74. Newsmen also came from Iran, Yugoslavia, Bulgaria, Iceland, Morocco and a dozen other countries. They loaded the telephones and telexes with round-the-clock traffic, proving once again, if proof were needed, that Peace is as big a story as War.

Peace news sent prices up on the Tel Aviv Stock Exchange, set Jerusalemites to dancing and jamming traffic in Zion Square, and generated a wave of euphoria throughout Israel such as had not been felt since the state was established. Operation *Yom Sha'ar,* as the welcoming preparations were named, was a smashing success. *Sha'ar* is a Hebrew word meaning "gate." It is also an acronym for *Shalit A ravi Rishon*—"First Arab Ruler" (to come to Israel). Entering into the prevailing spirit, the menu in the Knesset restaurant was captioned *Yom Sha'ar.* The Parliament's chefs decorated the tuna fish salad with tomato strips spelling out *Shalom* (peace) in Hebrew and the Turkish salad with slivers of green peppers forming its equivalent, *Sala'am,* in Arabic.

Early Friday morning, thirty-six hours before Sadat's scheduled arrival, it was decided that the President and his entourage should be housed at Jerusalem's posh King David Hotel. It had sheltered Nixon during his 1974 visit and, of course, Kissinger on his several trips to the capital during his frenetic post-Yom Kippur War "shuttling." All guests, except members of a Congressional delegation from Washington that happened to be in town at the time, were turned out and found accommodations elsewhere.

The "K-D," as longtime clients know it, is not Jerusalem's most modern hotel, but it has by far one of the best grill rooms in town, an excellent bar, an accommodating and courteous staff and easily the most enchanting location. Situated on a promontory overlooking the Kidron Valley, its eastern facade faces the western walls of the Old City. Visible from its terrace and those rooms facing the Old City are the Jaffa Gate, the Tower of David and two edifices most sacred to Islam only after Mecca and Medina: the Mosque of Omar with its golden dome and the ancient silver-domed Mosque of el Aksa from which tradition has it Mohammed ascended into heaven on his winged horse, *Buraq.*

Perhaps the "K-D's" greatest claim to fame, however, is as the hotel which during pre-state days served as headquarters for the Administrative Staff of the British Mandatory Government and which, in 1946, some of Begin's Irgunists blew up.

As the ejected (and dejected) guests left that Friday morning, the carilloneer in the tall, phaliclike YMCA tower across the road from the K-D was practicing changes on an old tune entitled, *Getting to Know You*, in honor of the expected guest.

One who did not share in the general jubilation, according to an item in the *Jerusalem Post*, the local English-language daily, was former Premier Golda Meir, who was quoted as saying: "What's all the messianic euphoria? When Araleh (meaning General Aharon Yariv, then chief of Israeli military intelligence) went to Kilometer 101 (for the disengagement talks after the Yom Kippur War) people were also talking as though the Egyptian general coming to talk to him were the Messiah. I said then: 'I've got one Messiah, and when he comes he's not going to stop at Kilometer 101 or otherwise qualify his coming.' "

Obviously, Mrs. Meir had read Sadat's "reply" to Begin's formal invitation and interpreted it less tolerantly than had Menahem Begin.

It would be superfluous to describe in detail the red-carpet welcome with which the "angel of peace" was received on the evening of November 19. It was a great media event. Both actors in the drama were talking not only to their own people but to the world at large. It was no accident that when Sadat's Boeing 707, gleaming white in the floodlights at Ben-Gurion Airport, came to a full stop on the tarmac, among the first figures in the President's entourage to descend the El-Al Airlines' ramp were the statesmanlike Walter Cronkite of CBS, the teacherish John Chancellor of NBC, and the ubiquitous Barbara Walters of ABC.

Some images stay in the mind and are worth recalling because they bespoke peace in a region that has known very little of it, not merely during the last three decades, but for hundreds, indeed, thousands of years. The sight and sound of the Israeli band, for instance, playing the Egyptian national anthem; the meticulously tailored Sadat standing at attention to the plaintive strains of *Hatikva;* the flags of Egypt and Israel stirring solemnly side by side in the light *khamsin* blowing in from the desert; Sadat, the onetime soldier, and Begin, the former guerilla chieftain, reviewing the seventy-two Israeli soldiers, sailors and airmen that constituted the guest's honor guard—some of its officers undoubtedly had fought the Egyptians on land, sea or in the skies over Sinai.

Memorable also was the hushed and moving tableau following the formalities on arrival: Sadat walking along the receiving line with Menahem Begin to greet old enemies—former Prime Ministers Rabin and Golda Meir (for whom Sadat had a specially warm greeting), then Dayan and Ariel Sharon, Israel's "Patton," who had pushed Israeli armor deep into Egypt in the Yom Kippur War, turning the tide of battle against the

Egyptians and, perhaps, saving Israel. (Sadat to Sharon: "I wanted to catch you there." Sharon to Sadat: "I'm glad to meet you here instead.") Finally, General Gur.

Sadat could not have failed to feel the spontaneity of the cheers and applause of the thousands of Israelis gathered on the upper terrace of the airport's administration building, or the warmth of the greeting that swelled from the hundreds of well-screened guests who filled the specially constructed grandstand. The Israelis were buoyant with a sense of release from fear—and guilt. That Egypt, the proud yet tired giant of the Nile—the old adversary who had grievously injured them and whom they had hurt in return—should now come to welcome them into the Middle Eastern community to which they desperately desired to belong, touched the Israelis to the depths of their being. There was a genuine outpouring of gratitude and affection from a people who had come to believe, not without reason, that they would never see in their midst an Arab leader on a mission of peace.

There were none of the usual speeches at the airport, and at 8:27, exactly thirty minutes after Sadat's arrival, the President entered Israel's only bulletproof and armored limousine—one Kissinger had last used—with Israel's grizzled President Ephraim Katzir, who was almost left behind in the sudden crush of cameramen and Israeli-Egyptian security officers. Premier and Mrs. Begin entered a second car, and the motorcade left the airport for the ninety-minute drive to Jerusalem. The two vehicles, preceded and flanked by a motorcycle escort of heavily armed police, were closely followed by a military ambulance and a mobile cardiac unit—for Sadat, like Begin, also has a history of heart trouble. Along the route from the airport to the capital, police helicopters hovered; security precautions were, to put it mildly, intensive.

When the telecast from the airport ended, Jerusalemites rushed into the streets toward vantage points for a possible glimpse of Sadat on his way to the K-D. In a matter of minutes, a crowd of several thousand gathered at the point where the road from Tel Aviv enters the capital. It was composed of students, old folks, families with small children and many teenagers. The mood was generally jovial, but there were many solemn-faced individuals in the gathering. One, an elderly gentleman who might have been a doctor or a lawyer, said with greater prescience than he probably realized, "I really can't believe anything will come of this; the positions of the two sides are simply too far apart."

Early the next morning, Sadat, fulfilling the promise he had made in his "statement of acceptance" of Israel's invitation, worshipped at el-Aksa. The mosque was crowded with several hundred Moslem holy men who rose in a wave when he entered, applauding and calling his name. He nodded in acknowledgement, and touched heart and forehead in response. Israeli-Egyptian security guards, in stocking feet like everyone else, sat cross-legged on the rich carpets; they rose and nervously scanned the worshippers when they knelt to bow six times toward Mecca. Sadat appeared nervous; he dabbed his forehead frequently with a handkerchief when he stood and listened attentively as an *imam* delivered a decidedly political sermon demanding "justice" for the Palestinians. The 45-minute service ended to shouts of *Allahu akbar* ("God is great") and Sheik Ehkrima Sabri intoned a benediction: "We redeem you with our blood, spirit and faith, Oh Sadat!" The mosque rang with cheers and applause and Sadat's name.

Leaving the mosque, Sadat pointedly avoided visiting the holiest of holies of the Jews, the remnants of the Western Wall of Solomon's Temple, but took care to pay his respects to one of Christianity's holiest shrines, the Church of the Holy Sepulcher, built on what tradition tells us was the site of Christ's crucifixion, burial and resurrection. Sadat did not climb the steep stairs leading to Calvary, but he did stoop low to enter the sepulcher itself to see Christ's tomb.

It gratified the Israelis immensely, however, that Sadat visited the Yad Vashem, the Jewish state's memorial to the victims of the Holocaust. He appeared visibly moved as he walked slowly past its horrifying gallery of wall-size photographs documenting Nazi brutality toward the Jews. His guide was Gideon Hausner, a survivor of a Nazi concentration camp who prosecuted Adolf Eichmann in 1961, and to Hausner's frequent comments on the gravity of the Holocaust's effects on the Jewish people, Sadat nodded solemnly, saying, "I understand," or "I realize that." In the Tent of Remembrance, a stark cavernous room with a blood-chilling array of black plaques, each bearing the name of a Nazi death camp—Auschwitz, Maedanek, Belsen-Buchenwald and a dozen others—Sadat stood for several minutes in silent contemplation of the eternal flame honoring the six million Jewish victims of the Holocaust. Before leaving the Yad Vashem, Sadat wrote in its guest book: "May God guide our steps toward peace. Let us end all suffering for mankind."

Then, the moment of truth. It came when Sadat, the son of Ishmael, stood before the descendants of Isaac in the Knesset and spoke his heart and mind. I saw and heard it all later that day from the crowded press gallery overlooking the austere chamber where the first real test of the peacemaking process that Sadat had started took place. When it was over, many familiar patterns of Middle East politics would need to be reconsidered, recast and rearranged by all concerned, but especially by the Israelis.

NOTES

1. Based on information supplied by two Egyptian correspondents for foreign news agencies—one British, one American—who were present, but requested anonymity.

2. From the unofficial translation provided to *The New York Times* of November 18, 1977, by the *Associated Press*.

3. Prayers marking the end of the Moslem *Qurban Bairam* holiday, or Feast of Sacrifice, that celebrates the end of the *Hadj*, the holy pilgrimage to Mecca.

4. For his "indiscretion," the General was "severely reprimanded" by his boss, Defense Minister Ezer Weizman.

Chapter 4

Encounter in the Knesset

Appropriately enough, the setting for the next episode in the autumn psychodrama was the theatrelike chamber where the Israeli parliament sits. Impressively modern and functional in design, its colors are the natural, tawny tones of leather, native woods and stone. The seats for the Knesset's 120 members are arranged in rows, five deep, that form a sort of horseshoe with the open end facing the Speaker's rostrum and a backdrop whose sculptured panels strongly suggest the Western Wall of the Temple. The wall's starkness is relieved by an unframed portrait of Theodor Herzl done in subdued grays, like a steel engraving, but more evocative of the Founder's wraith than his person, and placed at stage left behind the lectern from which speakers address the assembly. Seating for distinguished visitors, diplomats and the families and friends of politicians is provided in balconies above the three sides of the horseshoe, and the press is accommodated in a steep gallery, sealed off by inch-thick plate glass, but overlooking the entire hall from the side opposite the stage.

Sadat, the acknowledged star of the show, was scheduled to speak at 4 P.M., but the balconies and the gallery were filled nearly to overflowing by three o'clock when the members of the Knesset started drifting in singly and in groups. Among the early arrivals was Shimon Peres, leader of the Labor opposition, who took his seat and busied himself with last-minute changes in the speech he would make later after Sadat and Begin had spoken. Dayan's entrance at 3:30 caused a stir; he came up to the diplomats' balcony just under the press gallery to seat his wife, then went down and took his place in one of the four chairs at the top of the

Knesset's inner horseshoe. He was soon joined there by Begin, Deputy Prime Minister Yigal Yadin, leader of the newly formed DMC [1] and Finance Minister Ehrlich—four bald pates in a row, the first traversed by the black ribbon of the world's most famous eye patch.

The media were present in force. At floor level behind the lateral balconies rose batteries of TV cameras and forests of tripods holding still cameras with long lenses, like so many guns. The speeches would be in Hebrew and Arabic, with simultaneous translations in English and several other languages.

At stage right, near the entrance, stood three Israeli Army trumpeteers, their long instruments at their sides, in the attitude known as parade rest.

By 3:45, nearly all the MKs were in their seats, exchanging greetings and gossiping. Normally, one could easily differentiate the Laborite members from their Likud and other opponents by the open-collared and often coatless informality of their attire. But not today; all were properly dressed, wearing neckties and jackets.

The arrival *en masse* of fifty or sixty Arab dignitaries, some in flowing robes, for whom seats had been reserved in the lateral balconies was warmly applauded, a break with tradition. Applause by visitors is forbidden in the Knesset.

As the hour of Sadat's appearance approached, the atmosphere in the chamber became charged with great expectations. The place almost literally quivered with excitement: a modern Pharaoh had come from Egypt. What message did he bring of peace or war? Everyone present— Israelis and foreigners alike—believed Sadat's mere presence in Jerusalem was deeply significant, meaning recognition at last of Israel's existence as a sovereign state. A succession of Israeli Prime Ministers and their Laborite governments had schooled the Arabs, and the world at large, into believing that recognition was the main ingredient of peace.

Sitting in the press gallery, waiting for Sadat, I recalled an interview with Ben-Gurion in the summer of 1970 in the booklined study of his home in Tel Aviv in which the former Premier told me that if the Arabs simply "recognized Israel—admitted that it was a sovereign Jewish state with a permanent place in the Middle East—they could have all their land back, except Jerusalem, of course. But they'll never do that. Never . . ." Yet, here it was: *de facto* recognition of Israel's existence. Did Sadat's presence in the city also mean acknowledgement of Jerusalem as the capital of the Jewish state? Well, not quite, it developed.

Everyone was in place now, and at precisely four o'clock, the trumpeteers snapped to attention, raised their instruments in unison and sounded a fanfare. Sadat entered, escorted by the short, stocky Speaker of the Knesset, Yitzhak Shamir, and President Katzir. The Parliament's traditional reserve broke again, this time with thunderous applause and a standing ovation from everyone present, including the diplomats. At that moment, it seemed as though the whole world was applauding.

Laurence Olivier at his best could not have made a more impressive entrance than did Sadat in a blue-gray suit that bespoke Saville Row, powder-blue shirt and polka-dotted necktie. He stood there for a few moments, acknowledged the greeting with a dignified bow, then sat at Shamir's right, as Katzir took his place at the Speaker's left. Shamir silenced the house with a single smart rap of his gavel, rose, intoned a brief prayer, and called upon Sadat to speak.

I observed carefully the reactions of the parliamentarians below. The MKs were attentive when Sadat said, "We used to reject you, true. We refused to meet you anywhere, true. At the 1973 Geneva Peace Conference our delegates did not exchange a single direct word with you, true. Yet today we agree to live with you in peace and justice. Israel has become an accomplished fact, recognized by the whole world and the superpowers. We welcome you to live among us in peace and security."

But about twenty minutes into his speech, when Sadat started enumerating the Arabs' "prerequisites for peace"—total withdrawal from all territories occupied by the Israelis in the 1967 war, including Jerusalem, and a homeland for the Palestinians on the West Bank and in Gaza—the MKs began twiddling pencils, fidgeting in their seats and exchanging quick, worried glances.

"My God," muttered the wife of a high-ranking Israeli diplomat seated directly before me. "He wants everything back. Even Jerusalem!"

Sadat read the Israelis a homily on peace, and it was plain that he was addressing himself less to those present than to the world at large, hoping thereby to sway it to his point of view. Peace, he told his global audience, cannot be worth its name unless based "on justice and not on the occupation of the land of others," adding, "it would not be right for you to demand for yourselves what you deny to others." "You must give up once and for all dreams of conquest, and give up the belief that force is the best method for dealing with the Arabs," he said. "You should clearly understand the lesson of confrontation between you and us. Expansion does not pay. To speak frankly, our land does not yield itself to bargaining, it is not even open to argument. To us, the nation's soil is equal to the holy valley where God Almighty spoke to Moses . . . . We cannot accept any attempt to take away one inch of it, nor can we accept the principle of debating or bargaining over it . . ."

Sadat spoke in the manner of a man who had come to reconquer, with the mere gift of his presence, lands lost in wars which the victors had not sought. No one in the chamber doubted his sincerity, and all admired the skill of his presentation, but it was evident to everyone with sufficient historicity in Middle East politics to understand him, that what Sadat wanted was a political settlement which would remove the threat of war and enable Egypt to concentrate on its own problems. He indicated he did not desire a separate or partial agreement, but rather one that would be accepted by all parties to the conflict, including, most particularly, the Palestinians. Their cause, he said, was "the crux of the entire problem." "Nobody in the world could accept today slogans propagated here in Israel, ignoring the existence of a Palestinian people and questioning even their whereabouts," he said. "Because the Palestinian people and their legitimate rights are no longer denied today by anybody; that is nobody who has the ability of judgment, can deny or ignore it . . .

"Even the United States of America, your first ally, which is absolutely committed to safeguard Israel's security and existence and which offered and still offers Israel every moral, material and military support—I say, even the United States has opted to face up to reality and admit that the Palestinian people are entitled to legitimate rights and that the Palestine problem is the cause and essence of the conflict and that so long as it continues to be unresolved, the conflict will continue to aggravate, reaching new dimensions.

"In all sincerity I tell you that there can be no peace without the Palestinians. It is a grave error of unpredictable consequences to overlook or brush aside this cause.

"I shall not indulge in past events such as the Balfour Declaration of sixty years ago. You are well acquainted with the relevant text. If you have found the moral and legal justification to set up a national home on a land that did not all belong to you, it is incumbent upon you to show understanding of the insistence of the people of Palestine for establishment once again of a state on their land. When some extremists ask the Palestinians to give up this sublime objective, this in fact means asking them to renounce their identity and every hope for the future . . .

"You have to face reality bravely, as I have done. There can never be any solution to a problem by evading it or turning a deaf ear to it. Peace cannot last if attempts are made to impose fantasy concepts on which the world has turned its back and announced its unanimous call for the respect of rights and facts."

President Sadat evidently had drawn a great deal of sustenance from President Carter's oft-repeated references to a "homeland" for the Palestinians and to their "legitimate rights." Sadat translated them into "self-determination" and the creation on the West Bank and in the Gaza Strip of an independent Palestinian state. They enabled him to pose a tremendous challenge to Israel, phrased in demands for optimal territorial concessions to which Begin could not respond positively without placing at hazard his country's security and risking his own political life.

From time to time, the freely perspiring Sadat delicately mopped his glistening brow. Fifty-six minutes after he had started, Sadat finished and sat down to generous, but not enthusiastic applause. Most of it, in fact, came from the galleries where the Egyptian and diplomatic delegations were seated. This time there was no standing ovation. The Israelis had heard very little to comfort them. They could only be grateful that Sadat had not once mentioned the PLO.

Begin started speaking at 5 P.M. His voice was strong, vibrant, and he spoke with the ease and style of the great orator, almost entirely extemporaneously with only rare glances at a sheaf of notes, gesturing eloquently with delicate, expressive hands. Sadat followed Begin's address attentively through earphones in simultaneous English translation. The expressions on his mobile face ranged from puzzlement to something close to bewilderment, for he too heard little that he had wanted to hear, though he nodded appreciatively at Begin's praise for his "courage" in making the trip to Israel.

On the whole, Begin's speech was one he might have made—and has—at fund-raising dinners sponsored by Israel Bonds or the United Jewish Appeal in the United States. Like Sadat, he repeatedly drafted the Almighty into his endeavors and invested his cause with holiness, but unlike Sadat, he limited himself to generalities. Mindful, perhaps, of the old cliché that to ignore history is to repeat its mistakes, Begin began by reciting a bit of it for the benefit of the global audience he knew was watching and listening as it had watched and listened to Sadat.

The Prime Minister recalled that when Israel declared its independence, the newly born nation offered peace to all its Arab neighbors and that the offer was rejected. Israel, he said, was attacked on three fronts, "a few against the many, the weak against the strong" in the Arabs' common effort "to destroy the last hope of the Jewish nation in the century of its destruction and redemption."

"No," said Begin, responding to a point Sadat had made, "we do not believe in might, and we never based our relationship with the Arab nation on strength. We believe only in right (and) our hope to this very day has always been for peace . . . . Israel is (still) looking for peace—with Egypt, with Jordan, with Syria, with Lebanon. We want negotiations for a peace treaty (establishing) normal relations between us as they exist between all nations, even after many wars. History teaches us that wars are preventable and that peace is inevitable."

Begin felt obliged to enlighten Sadat—and his worldwide audience—about the nature of the ties that bind the Jewish people to the Land of Israel. In his speech, Sadat had referred to the Balfour Declaration as the instrument in which the Jews had found "the moral and legal justification to set up a national home on a land that did not all belong" to them.

"No, Mr. President," said Begin. "We did not take strange land, we returned to our homeland. The link between our nation and this land is eternal. It began in the dim days of history. It has never been cut. In this land we created our culture, here our prophets prophesied . . . here the kings of Judah and Israel ruled. Here we became a nation. And when we were exiled from our land because of the force that was applied against us, and when we were thrust far from our land, we never forgot this land, even for one day. We prayed for her. We longed for her."

Begin concluded with a plea that despite the known differences in the starting positions of Israel and Egypt, the two countries would enter into active negotiations for an overall settlement in the interests of peace and prosperity for the entire Middle East. His speech left many Israelis feeling somewhat let down; among Begin's critics the consensus was that he should have given Sadat "something more to take home with him" than a reiteration of Israel's desire for peace and a lecture on Jewish history.

Shimon Peres, who followed Begin to the speaker's lectern, spoke briefly but to the point. He urged the Arabs and the Israelis to try to "see things in a new light" and called on both sides to enter into negotiations in a spirit of compromise.

Next day, November 21, before Sadat returned to Cairo and a hero's welcome, only two major events remained on the visitor's crowded schedule.

The first was a meeting with members of the Knesset's various political factions including, of course, representatives of the Labor Alignment. Among them, although she no longer held a seat in the Knesset, was Golda Meir, present at Sadat's request. From her, the Egyptian leader obtained a clearer view of the kind of peace the Israelis envisioned than from anyone else, including Prime Minister Begin.

The ever-present cameras caught all of the byplay—"Grandmother Meir" presenting "Grandfather Sadat" with a tiny golden necklace and earrings for his newborn granddaughter and receiving in return, inveterate smoker that she is, a silver cigarette box inscribed with the President's signature in Arabic—but missed much of the dialogue between the former Prime Minister and the Egyptian leader.

"The old lady," as Sadat had often called her—and they joked about that in their informal tête-à-tête—was at her simple but eloquent best as she reminded the visitor that Israel had never desired "additional territory." Israel, she said, was prepared to live within the territory prescribed by the United Nations Partition Resolution of 1947, but she diplomatically refrained from recalling how this became impossible when the Arabs attacked in 1948.

In the present historical context—ten years after the 1967 war—Mrs.

Meir said, Israel was prepared to make "territorial compromises on all its borders," but "only on one condition: borders that will give us security, that will save us from danger, and from having somebody else come to defend us, God forbid."

On the crucial issue of the Palestinians, Mrs. Meir was far more forthcoming than Begin had been in his Knesset speech.

"We never said," Mrs. Meir continued, "that Palestinians should remain as they are, in camps, in misery, dependent on others. We don't want to be dependent on others, and we don't want them dependent on others. If it had been within our power, there would never have been a problem of this kind. We realize there are Palestinians. We believe there is a solution . . . good for them and good for us.

"There is a connection, therefore, between our unreadiness for another state between us and Jordan—a Palestinian state, small, probably unviable, and which may feel obliged to expand—and our desire for security. If we should agree to such a state, there would be only twelve miles between its western border and the sea. You cannot expect us to feel secure with borders of that kind . . .

"In our peace treaties with Jordan there must be a solution for the Palestinians so that those camps (of theirs) are wiped out, and become a thing of the past. But not at the expense of the security of Israel. If there were no solution, it would be a terrible problem for us. But there is a solution to this problem . . .

"We didn't agree with everything you said last night, but you called for peace, and I believe in your sincere desire for peace. Then let us go on. The process that you started with such courage must continue in face-to-face negotiations between you and us, so that even an old lady like me will live to see the day when there shall be peace between our peoples . . . . I want to live to see that day, the day of peace between you and us, peace between us and all our neighbors."

Sadat was to have spent only an hour with Mrs. Meir and the others—Rabin, Peres, Abba Eban—but he stayed twice as long and was an hour late for the second event on his busy schedule, the joint press conference with Premier Begin at the Jerusalem Theatre. It had been scheduled for twelve o'clock noon, but it did not get under way until shortly after 1 P.M.

The theatre, built to seat eight hundred, was crowded with more than one thousand correspondents. TV cameramen and still photographers filled the aisles and clambered up on every available vantage point. It was mainly another "photo opportunity" sort of thing, and Sadat, a practiced performer—he had long since discovered the importance of television in the conduct of foreign policy—managed to steal the show without overtly upstaging Premier Begin, although the latter displayed a strong sense of political theatre of his own.

The two leaders sat side by side at center stage at a table draped in blue felt, each flanked by an aide. The backdrop behind them combined in broad vertical bands the colors of the flags of the two countries—Israel's blue and white and Egypt's red, white and black—but that was as close as they came to merging their approach to peace.

The reporters had expected a joint communique from the principals but what they got instead was an "Agreed Statement" which ostensibly summed up the results of the visit. It was read aloud in English by Premier Begin, "with the permission of President Sadat," who busied himself with his pipe. Begin spoke in tired, opaque tones that contrasted sharply with the vigorous clarity of his voice when he had addressed the Knesset the night before. Plainly, Sadat and Begin had been unable to concur on the language of a joint formal communique and the "Agreed Statement" was drafted by lesser Israeli and Egyptian officials. Given its rather flowery language, however, Begin's hand was clearly visible:

> In response to the sincere and courageous move by President Sadat, and believing in the need to continue the dialogue along the lines proposed by both sides during their exchanges and the presentation of their positions in their historic meeting in Jerusalem, and in order to enhance the prospect of a fruitful consummation of this significant visit, the Government of Israel, expressing the will of the people of Israel, proposes that this hopeful step be further pursued through dialogue between the two countries concerned, thereby paving the way toward successful negotiations leading to the signing of peace treaties in Geneva with all the neighboring Arab states.

The "Agreed Statement" was an expression of pious hopes rather than an agreement on any substantive issues, or even on a set of principles for the conduct of negotiations. How hard and how long the road to peace would be became dramatically evident in the course of Sadat's replies to questions from the correspondents.

In reply to a question about why he had not reciprocated Israeli hospitality by inviting Begin to Cairo, Sadat said he had discussed the matter with the Prime Minister, and they had mutually agreed to postpone such a visit "for the time being."

Without being prompted, Sadat then stressed what he believed to be the main result of his visit, namely agreement that there should be "no more war after October," meaning, of course, the October War of 1973. But when pressed by another journalist on the same subject, Sadat seemed to modify his "no-war" pledge, refusing to say whether his statement canceled out his previously oft-repeated threat to resort to war should Egypt fail to achieve the peace it seeks by diplomatic means.

Sadat also emphasized that he had agreed with Begin on "the principle of full security," a security achieved by "agreed means" not by "expansion or occupation," adding, somewhat sternly, "Our land is sacred."

Begin felt called upon at that point to explain that "security" to Israel meant "national security" which the Jewish state had been obliged to defend repeatedly. "This," he said, "is going to be our attitude during our negotiations." He closed his brief remarks on the subject by echoing Sadat's words: "*Our* land, too, is sacred."

In his closing remarks, Sadat admitted that Israel's security was an "urgent problem," but he said he considered a "Palestinian state also very important." He hoped, however, that despite differences on the issue it could be settled at Geneva along with all others.

"We are in a crucial moment," he said. "Let us hope, all of us, that we can keep the momentum in Geneva, and may God guide the steps of Premier Begin and the Knesset because there is a great need for hard and drastic decisions. I took my share (of them) in my decision to come here, and I shall be looking forward to those decisions from Premier Begin and the Knesset."

Now it was up to Israel to respond, and the response would need to be in the hard currency of substance. The coin of procedural haggling had been removed from circulation by Sadat's precedent-shattering journey to Jerusalem.

Begin had become, in effect, Sadat's partner in the peacemaking process. But could Begin make peace on the terms Sadat had demanded? Nothing in the Prime Minister's background suggested that he could—or that he would.

If you had programmed a computer with the story of the life and times of Menahem Begin in November 1977, then asked the machine to assess his capacity to make peace between his country and its Arab neighbors, the electronic monster would have coughed a few times with evident embarrassment and sputtered: NEGATIVE. And no matter how many repairmen you summoned, or how viciously you accused the mechanical brain of political prejudice, you would always have received the same reply.

Not because Menahem Begin did not desire peace—he is by nature a striver and an achiever, and nothing would make him happier than to succeed where six Laborite predecessors had failed—but because nothing in his intellectual and political landscape indicated that he was willing to make peace unless the geographic terms of a settlement with the Arabs were congruent with his mental map of *Eretz Yisrael,* "the Land of Israel." It encompasses the entire territory of the Palestine that once was Canaan and became, after World War I, the Palestine of the Mandate granted to Great Britain by the old League of Nations. Begin was and still is willing to forego the part of Palestine east of the Jordan River that became first Transjordania, then the present Kingdom of Jordan. But he was and continues adamant that all of Palestine between the Jordan and the Mediterranean is and shall remain Jewish "by natural and eternal right."

Begin's "mental map" includes, therefore, the West Bank, where about one million Palestinian Arabs live in hopes of someday becoming citizens of a state of their own, a minimal condition for peace which many Israeli "doves" would more or less willingly accept, but which their Prime Minister regards as one that would, if realized, create a "mortal danger" to his country's security.

The roots of Begin's territorialist approach to peacemaking with the Arabs are to be found in his past. His story is strange but typical of his time.

NOTES

1. Democratic Movement for Change, a reformist party composed mainly of ex-Laborites which won 15 seats in the national elections of '77 and joined the Likud government.

Book Two:

Poland 1913–1940

Chapter 5

The Forging of a Rebel

Menahem Begin reported for duty in this world on August 16, 1913, in Brest-Litovsk, a fortress city with a stormy, pendular history and a large Jewish population. Situated on the right bank of the western branch of the River Bug, it lay in the path of the warring armies of the Russian and German Empires at the heart of the region known as the Pale of Settlement within which some five million Jews somehow managed to preserve their way of life despite poverty, persecution and periodic pogroms. Known as Brisk when it was Lithuanian, Brest-Litovsk was Polish when Ze'ev Dov and Hassia Begin welcomed their second son and third child. Rachel was aged six at the time, and Herzl, four going on five.

Menahem's birthday fell on the Sabbath of *Tishah B'Ab*, meaning the "Ninth of Ab," a day for remembering and, therefore, for mourning the destruction of the Temple in Jerusalem, first by the Babylonians in 586 B.C., then by the Romans in A.D. 70. Among the mourners at the synagogue of Brisk's Jewish community that morning was its paid secretary, Ze'ev Dov Begin, who supplemented his meager official salary by jobbing in lumber, one of the principal products of the city's hinterland.

Tishah B'Ab has all the characteristics of *shivah*, the Jewish mourning period for the dead; prohibited during the week of *Tishah Ba'Ab* are bathing, eating, drinking, laughter, conversation, even the exchange of greetings. Ze'ev Dov's joy at having become a father for the third time was therefore tempered by the solemnity of this particular day, another of so many others in Judaism's troubled history that commemorate calamities or narrow deliverances from calamities.

In the synagogue, a black cloth had replaced the decorative parochet over the Ark, and the only light came from the *Ner Tamid,* the Eternal Lamp, which cast a gloomy flicker over the congregation. The recitation, in a subdued minor, was from the Biblical "Book of Lamentations" whose stirring dirges, implausibly attributed to the Prophet Jeremiah, must have been composed by eyewitnesses of the Destruction of the First Temple.

It is customary on *Tishah Ba'Ab* for those Jews who follow tradition to repeat the Prophet Jeremiah's plea for the hastening of Israel's restoration and the rebuilding of Zion in the days of the Messiah. But although he was an Orthodox Jew, Ze'ev Dov believed the Messiah already had come and that his name was Theodor Herzl for whom he had named his first son. Ze'ev Dov was an ardent Zionist and raised his children to see in Zionism the only alternative to life as pariahs in an increasingly hostile Eastern Europe.

Walking slowly back to his modest house in Brisk's Jewish quarter, wearing his one good black suit and top hat—his badge of office—Ze'ev Dov Begin pondered the mournful message of *Tishah Ba'Ab.* Times were hard for the Jews of Brisk, and Ze'ev Dov, being a man who knew several languages and read a great deal in addition to the Old Testament—the daily press in Yiddish and Polish, and the newspapers that frequently came his way from Berlin and Moscow—saw a great war brewing. War only meant even more difficult days ahead for his co-religionists. The Jewish people needed someone to assuage their sorrows. So it was that he named his newborn son Menahem, meaning, "one who consoles."

Menahem's widowed older sister, Mrs. Rachel Halperin, relates that theirs was a closely knit and loving family, bound together by mutual affection and respect, a love of books and pride in their Jewishness. At seventy, Mrs. Halperin is a taut, lively woman with blue-gray eyes like her brother's and graying brown hair caught up in a bun atop her smooth oval face. She lives alone in a spotless three-room apartment in a middle-class section of Tel Aviv, where she gives her visitor breakfast—eggs, toast, fruit and excellent coffee—and talks freely, though in halting French interspersed with German, English and Yiddish, about her beloved Menahem's childhood. When at loss for words to convey her meaning, the voluble lady lapses into Hebrew and a mutual friend, Harry Zinder, translates.

Her visitor's chance remark about a "family resemblance" releases a flash of humor. "Oh no!" she exclaims. "That's not a compliment. My brother is not a handsome man. I'm a lot better looking than he." She is very proud, however, of the photograph of her sibling inscribed in Hebrew, "To my very own sister, With love, Menahem." The picture is displayed on the top shelf of an étagère under photos of a handsome mustachioed papa Ze'ev Dov in his prime and an equally striking likeness of mama Hassia. Oddly, there is no picture of Herzl, "a really beautiful child," Mrs. Halperin recalls, "and smart, even smarter than Menahem."

Menahem, however, was hardly a backward child. He learned to do what he does best—talk—earlier than most children, possibly because when he was not yet even a year old his father would take him up in his arms and point to various objects, repeating their names over and over again. Very soon, the child was pronouncing them clearly enough to be understood, and it wasn't long before he could carry on a conversation.

In 1915, a year after the outbreak of what our fathers and grandfathers called the Great War, the Begins and thousands of other Jewish families fled from Brisk before the advancing Russians. Ze'ev Dov took his brood to Kobriń, in Germany, where he eked out a meager living writing in literary German whatever documents his neighbors needed to establish themselves in their new environment. One of the letters he was called upon to write, Mrs. Halperin recalls with evident relish, was addressed to Kaiser Wilhelm II himself. It was a request for Imperial intervention in some forgotten matter on behalf of the Jewish community of Kobrin.

Anti-Semitism was virtually unknown in the Germany of those days. In fact, the Germans saved many Jews from Russian pogroms and Polish persecution. Ze'ev Dov was something of a Germanophile, an admirer of German culture, and until the rise of Adolf Hitler, a regular subscriber to the *Berliner Tageblatt*. When Menahem was three years old and the family—father, mother and the two older children—were at work in the fields around Kobrin, the small boy was cared for by a kindly old German soldier who acted as babysitter and tutor. With his Yiddish, Menahem learned German.

The Begins returned to Brest-Litovsk, or Brisk as they called it then (and as most East European Jews of that generation still do), early in 1918 after the Russians, now under Bolshevik rule following the Revolution of 1917, made their separate peace with Germany and Austria. By the Treaty of Brest-Litovsk, Russia lost the Ukraine, its Polish and Baltic territories, and Finland—amounting, in all, to a loss of one-third of its population. The Treaty, finally ratified on March 15, 1918 by the Congress of Soviets, would be annulled eight months later by the Armistice of November 11, which marked the Allied defeat of Germany, but Brest-Litovsk was still under German rule when the Begins resumed housekeeping in the fortress town's Jewish quarter.

On the family's return to Brisk, Ze'ev Dov tried to revive the lumber business which he had inherited from his father, but it was hard going. The Begins, Rachel remembers, were "almost always hungry, but whatever there was in the way of food was shared without grumbling."

Ze'ev Dov's only steady income was the small sum he received monthly
from the Jewish community whereof he was not only the secretary but the
acknowledged and highly respected leader. His prestige within it rose
when he persuaded the German military authorities to rebuild the
synagogue and the city's only Jewish hospital, both of which had been
severely damaged during the war.

The grimness of life in the Pale was relieved from time to time by
Jewish festivals. One such was the feast of the *Lag B'Omer,* which occurs
in the early spring on the thirty-third day between Passover and
Pentecost. On the first *Lag B'Omer* after the family's return to Brisk,
Begin père organized an outing in the city's park for the children of his
community. There was a parade with music, followed by singing and
dancing, and a speech by Ze'ev Dov.

"Papa," says Rachel, "was a marvelous orator, and Menahem, who was
five then and would soon be six, listened wide-eyed to every word. I think
that was when Menahem decided that he, too, would be a great speaker
someday.

"He enjoyed himself so much that day. He marched in the parade, and
sang and danced with the other children. Most of all, though, he liked the
bonfires that were lighted at nightfall."

Five years later at the annual *Lag B'Omer* celebration the main speaker
was—Menahem Begin. In knee pants, white shirt with neatly knotted tie
and wearing a yarmulkha, ten-year-old Menahem stood erect on a sturdy
wooden picnic table, hands clasped behind his back, and solemnly
addressed—in Yiddish—an audience of several hundred children and
their parents.

"He held them spellbound," says Rachel.

It is axiomatic that children learn by example, but Menahem learned
more than the art of oratory from his father who was, from all accounts,
not only an ardent Zionist and a Biblical scholar, but a man of exemplary
moral and physical courage. He was called upon to demonstrate it on
several occasions during the difficult period following the Great War and
Poland's reconstitution as an independent republic under its liberator and
national hero, Jozef Pilsudski.

During the early days of the Polish Republic, the Jews of Brisk were
subjected to renewed harassments and humiliations. Inflation was rampant in the city, and black markets flourished in clothing, food, fuel,
medicines—everything. The blame fell on those classical scapegoats of
history's calamities: the Jews.

The situation in Brisk was so critical that Pilsudski himself came to
investigate. The leaders of the Jewish community were summoned to his

presence, and Pilsudski sternly implied that the city's Jews were engaged in "hoarding" and "profiteering." He demanded that they join with the municipal authorities in "fighting the black market" by "exposing the speculators" among them. To everyone's astonishment, Ze'ev Dov Begin boldly denied that Brisk's Jews were guilty of the indicated crimes, and vehemently rejected Pilsudski's proposal that they inform on their own people.

"That is not our task," he said. "We are not detectives, nor are we informers. The Jewish community has no secret police. The authorities, however, do have a secret police. Let them do the job."

Pilsudski flew into a rage—the great man had a low flash point—but soon cooled down. Evidently deeply impressed by Begin's courage and the honorable stand he had taken, he dismissed his visitors with a lecture against patronizing the black market. Shortly afterwards, however, a new wave of anti-Semitism swept the city, inspired mainly by the rough Polish troops quartered in the town. Jews were spat at and stoned.

One day, when Menahem was ten or eleven years old, he was out walking with his father and a rabbi friend. Two Polish soldiers started harassing them, pushing them off the sidewalk, and hurling insults. One, a sergeant, drew a knife and reached for the rabbi's beard. Ze'ev Dov raised his heavy walking stick and brought it down hard on the offender's forearm, a capital offense.

Begin's father and the rabbi were arrested and taken to the city's fortress across the Bug. There they were roughly handled and sentenced to be drowned in the river, but the commanding general, mindful of the important role Polish Jews had played in their country's struggle for independence under Pilsudski, reversed the sentence.

"My father returned home badly beaten," Begin recalls, "but he was in good spirits, for he was convinced he had done what was right, though it might have cost him his life. We were all very proud of our father's behavior—an example for all of the inhabitants of the Jewish community. Incidentally, he subsequently received a letter of apology from the military authorities."

Raised in a bookish environment, Menahem's education started early, almost before he could walk. His mother Hassia read him Bible stories while he was still a toddler, and although Yiddish remained the family language, Menahem's father saw to it that Menahem learned Hebrew. When he was seven years old, the boy was enrolled in Brisk's Mizrachi (Orthodox) elementary school, where the teaching was in Hebrew, and at age thirteen, after his Bar Mitzvah, the "boy-turned-man" matriculated at the Polish Gymnasium, or high school. He had no time for sports; his boyhood and youth were devoted to books—the Bible, Herzl's *Judenstaat;* Leon Pinsker's *Autoemancipation,* which called on Jews everywhere not to wait for others to grant them freedom, and *Rome and Jerusalem,* wherein its author, Moses Hess, developed the thesis that Judaism could only flourish if and when the Jews rebuilt their ancient homeland in Palestine. All appealed strongly to a maturing Menahem who saw even in youth the futility of passive assimilation in the overwhelmingly Judophobe context of the mid-1920s. By the time he had reached his middle teens, Menahem Begin was already a militant Zionist. He enrolled in *Betar,* the nationalist youth organization associated with the Zionist Revisionist Movement founded by Vladimir Jabotinsky, ultimately Begin's idol and mentor.

Earlier, Menahem had joined a leftist Zionist youth organization, the radical *Hashomer Hatzair* (The Young Watchmen) but resigned when his father informed him that the organization's leadership and many of its members were Bolsheviks. "We must fight for our own freedom as Jews," said papa Begin, "before we can fight for the freedom of others."

It seems relevant and useful at this point to explain that Zionism was no longer merely an expression of a homeless people's longing for its ancient homeland, but considerably more. The Zionist movement had developed into a revolutionary process which, while of a piece with the whole history and tradition of the Jewish people, was also inextricably a part of the nation-making phenomenon of the middle decades of the nineteenth century that witnessed the making of modern Italy in the time of the *Risorgimento.* This, incidentally, strongly influenced the early pre-Herzl Zionist ideologue, Moses Hess and, subsequently, Vladimir Jabotinsky.

Nonconformity, however, is a primary characteristic of the Jewish people, and this trait soon manifested itself in the development of a multiplicity of parties and sub-parties in the Zionist movement. Zionism's followers held widely divergent views on religious, social, economic and political problems. Every Zionist, it seemed, wanted the National Home promised in the Balfour Declaration of 1917 and authorized under the League of Nations Mandate over Palestine granted to Great Britain, but he wanted a National Home in his own image.

All Zionists were united on such matters as the revival of Hebrew as a national language, maximum immigration, the establishment of agriculture as the basis of the Jewish economy in the state-to-be *and the inclusion of Transjordan in the eventual area of Jewish settlement.* Most Zionists also favored cooperation with the existing Arab population in Palestine, with neither people dominating the other, regardless of their relative numbers.

Beyond these fundamentals, however, opinions varied widely—as they do to this day—on such far-reaching issues as the social and economic shape of the ultimate Israel and the political course to be taken in any given set of circumstances, particularly as they related to territorial matters. Differences of this sort eventuated in Vladimir Jabotinsky's

Revisionism. Within its ranks, at an early age—he was only sixteen at the time—Menahem Begin found the particular expression of Zionism that most appealed to him, a Zionism best described, perhaps, as conservative maximalism. To understand Jabotinsky is to understand Menahem Begin, politically his lineal descendant.

Jabotinsky, like Ben-Gurion, belonged to the grand old generation, bred in the Diaspora, that produced Chaim Weizmann, Levi Eshkol and Golda Meir, i.e., the acknowledged founders of the modern Jewish state. Weizmann, who later became Israel's first President, was politically a conservative. Ben-Gurion and the others were Socialists, but Jabotinsky was not. All, however, were ardent Zionists, faithful followers of Theodor Herzl.

Herzl was a nineteenth-century Austrian journalist who personally regarded assimilation as most desirable, but impossible to realize in view of the anti-Semitism then rampant throughout most of Europe, particularly in Poland and Russia, where it often took the violent form of bloody pogroms. Although essentially a dreamer, Herzl was also a political realist. He realized that the Jewish people could attain nationhood only if the Great Powers of the time could be persuaded to bestow upon them the necessary territory. This, Herzl saw, required political action on a grand scale. In his *Judenstaat,* he advocated the creation of a Jewish state, and in 1897 he organized the Zionist Congress at Basel, Switzerland, which drafted a program stating that Zionism would strive "to create for the Jewish people a home in Palestine secured by public law." During the next seven years, Herzl tried to obtain a charter for Palestine from the Sultan in Constantinople and to enlist the help of Kaiser Wilhelm, the Russian Czar and others in his efforts, but in vain. He died of cardiac arrest in 1904 at the age of forty-four.

Herzl's political Zionism inspired the creation of a democratically organized worldwide movement. It developed an active propaganda through orators and pamphlets, created its own newspapers in many languages and gave impetus to a Jewish "Renaissance" in arts and letters. The development of the modern Hebrew language took place during the decade immediately following Herzl's death.

The movement received additional momentum from the failure of the Russian revolution of 1905 and the wave of pogroms and repressions that followed, causing growing numbers of Jewish youth to emigrate to Palestine as pioneer settlers.

With the Great War, the leadership of political Zionism became centered in Russian Jews living in England. Weizmann was one of them, and he was instrumental in obtaining from Great Britain the Balfour

Declaration which promised British support for the creation in Palestine of a Jewish national homeland. When the Declaration was incorporated in Britain's League of Nations Mandate in 1922, Zionist hopes soared. Mighty Albion had reversed the Diaspora by a stroke of the pen. Or so it seemed at the time.

In the early 1920s a movement developed within the World Zionist Organization in opposition to Weizmann's now well-established leadership and the policies of accommodation to British interests which he pursued. It was headed by Vladimir (Ze'ev) Jabotinsky, a brilliant, Russian-born journalist whom the British took to calling Jug-O-Whisky, possibly because they couldn't pronounce his name, but also, perhaps, because he was short, stocky and full of fire.

Jabotinsky was a foreign correspondent for newspapers published in Odessa, his native city, first as resident journalist in Bern, then Rome. There he studied law and Italian history, with particular attention to the Risorgimento, which produced such giants as Cavour, Garibaldi and Mazzini, the makers of modern Italy. To a degree, the Risorgimento— meaning Renaissance or Rebirth—became Jabotinsky's inspiration for his own brand of Zionism, which essentially entailed achieving Jewish nationhood by the use of force if political means failed.

Jabotinsky began expounding his activist brand of Zionism in 1903, both in his writings and in his oratory, of which he was an acknowledged master. During the next decade, he continued working as a journalist, crystallizing his views, which tended increasingly to be uncompromising, in contrast to those of Weizmann and his inner circle.

During World War I, Jabotinsky became persuaded that the Ottoman Empire, then the ruling power in Palestine, an area that historically had never had an identity of its own, would fall and that in the resultant vacuum the Jews could colonize the territory. With the aid of a like-minded Zionist, Joseph Trumpeldor, Jabotinsky petitioned the British Government to permit the formation of Jewish refugees from Turkey into military units. He was motivated by the assumption that if the Jews helped Britain militarily against Turkey, England would perceive the Jews as a useful ally, hence be more inclined to help them realize their Zionist dream. He succeeded in organizing companies of Jewish mule drivers— the Zion Mule Corps that distinguished itself in the debacle at Gallipoli— to act as ammunition carriers and engineers. Later in the war, when the British Government allowed the formation of three regular Jewish battalions, which helped General Allenby liberate Jerusalem from the Turks in 1917, Jabotinsky enlisted and became a lieutenant.

In 1920 Jabotinsky saw the need for a Jewish military force to police Palestine under British auspices, both for the protection of the growing Jewish community there and to convince the British that the Jews could become a valuable ally in an area strategically important to the British Empire. He organized and led a Jewish self-defense movement, later known as the *Haganah,* against Arab predators in Palestine. The British didn't like this; by then, they were Palestine's rulers and had every intention, despite the promises made to the Jews in the Balfour Declaration, of holding onto the country to defend the eastern approaches to the Suez Canal and the southern accesses to the oil fields of Iraq and Saudi Arabia.

Jabotinsky was arrested and sentenced to fifteen years at hard labor, but this provoked such an outcry that he was soon reprieved. Within the Zionist movement, however, his militancy caused him to go his own way. The source of widespread Jewish suffering, Jabotinsky believed, was not merely anti-Semitism, but the Diaspora—the Great Dispersion—itself. "Liquidate the Diaspora," he urged audiences in Eastern Europe in the 1920s and early 1930s, "or the Diaspora will liquidate you."

Perspicacious in matters political, Jabotinsky foresaw earlier than most that the rising tide of Nazism threatened to engulf and destroy European Jewry and he proposed mass evacuation of Europe's Jews to Palestine. The establishmentarian Zionists had been talking about intensifying emigration to the Holy Land in order to create there a Jewish majority. For this, Jabotinsky said, the departure from Europe of a million Jews would suffice, adding: "But one million will no longer solve the Jewish problem. Today much larger masses urgently require emigration."

Earlier, Jabotinsky had founded Betar, a movement designed to prepare young people physically and psychologically for emigration to Palestine. The name was taken from the fortress where Bar Kochba made his last heroic stand in the revolt of the Jews against Roman rule in Palestine in the Second Century A.D. Jabotinsky told the Jewish boys in the ghettos of Eastern Europe that they were the lineal descendants of kings and prophets, the heirs of great judges and warriors. Betar instructors taught self-discipline, good manners, physical cleanliness and neatness, tact, quiet speech, loyalty, courage, self-esteem and self-denial.

The *Betarim* wore uniforms, marched in parades and were trained in the use of weapons. In this respect, they were not unlike similar formations then popular in Italy and Germany. Jewish intellectuals raised eyebrows and muttered words like "Fascist" and "Nazi." Militarism ran counter to widespread acceptance of Jewish powerlessness as an ethical heritage. Jabotinsky argued that history obliged them to radically change their perspective. "If you don't know how to shoot," he said, "you have no hope. But if you know how to shoot, you have some hope."

Eastern European nations with large Jewish minorities looked favorably upon Jabotinsky's "Evacuation Plan" as a means of jettisoning Jews in substantial numbers. Poland was an outstanding example, and in Warsaw

Jabotinsky succeeded in obtaining the use of military training camps and arms for his Betarim.

The crucial issue that placed Jabotinsky irrevocably in opposition to the mainstream of the Zionist movement, however, was territorial. The growing need in the mid-1930s for Palestine to absorb millions of European Jews instead of mere tens or even hundreds of thousands caused Jabotinsky to cling to the original definition of the British Mandate as including Transjordan, the area east of the Jordan River. In the British White Paper of 1922, Transjordan, while remaining part of the Mandate, was arbitrarily excluded from the provisions regarding the eventual Jewish National Homeland.

In Jabotinsky's view, Transjordan remained part of historical Palestine. In 1925 the territorial concept became a central plank of Jabotinsky's Revisionist Party platform, and later, after failing repeatedly to win elections for the presidency of the World Zionist Organization, he created—in 1935—the New Zionist Organization. Its membership was open to all Zionists who would commit themselves to the creation of a Jewish state "on both sides of the Jordan" wherein there would be "social justice without class war within Palestine Jewry."

Not surprisingly, Jabotinsky vigorously opposed the partition of Palestine west of the Jordan into Jewish and Arab states, with a British zone, as proposed by the Peel Commission of 1937, a proposal which the mainstream Zionists were prepared to accept. To his way of thinking, the Jews had achieved international recognition of their claim to Palestine in the Balfour Declaration which was incorporated in the League of Nations Mandate and endorsed by the Great Powers, including the United states. In the long run, Jabotinsky argued, to give up part of the claim for the apparent immediate advantage of being able to proclaim an independent Israel risked losing it all. "Let no Christian hand touch our right," he said, "but first of all let no Hebrew hand do so . . . . Our right is eternal and to the whole land, and it cannot be conceded."

There was a great deal more to Jabotinsky than is indicated above. Unlike the followers of Ben-Gurion, for instance, Jabotinsky did not believe in combining Zionism with Socialist programs. He considered Socialism an encroachment upon basic human freedoms. Moreover, Jabotinsky, unlike Weizmann and Ben-Gurion, saw no possibility of obtaining Arab agreement to the creation of a Jewish state. Nor did he believe the Arabs could be "bribed" by prospects of economic development. The Arabs, he warned, would never sell the future of their land "as long as they have the slightest hope to get rid of us one way or another."

For Jabotinsky, the most powerful weapon the Jews owned, apart from military force, was morality. "This is by no means a weak weapon," he said. On the contrary, it is a very strong one. But the nature of this weapon is that it cannot be used in secret." He believed the "conscience of the world" was a political force which the Jews could successfully exploit, but it was a force that had to be mobilized worldwide and over the head of the British Government whenever necessary.

One who did not agree with Jabotinsky on this particular point and dared to challenge him publicly—at the Third Betar World Congress held in Warsaw in the early autumn of 1938, shortly after the sellout of democratic Czechoslovakia to the Nazis by Britain and France at Munich—was Menahem Begin. He had grown up in the ranks of Betar and was himself by then an acknowledged "great orator" and leader in the Revisionist movement.

What follows is the story of his rise within Betar as told by various older Revisionists, among them the talented musicologist, Zvi Propess,¹ who in 1930 was Betar Commissioner for the whole of Poland. Propess heard Menahem Begin speak at one of the organization's rallies in Brisk. "He was magnificent," says Propess, "I knew that before us that day stood a young man endowed with great talents."

By his own account, young Begin was "fascinated by the total Zionism of Betar." All those elements, which from reading and listening to others he had accepted as gospel, "found expression in Betar," he says, "and I had no doubt whatsoever that this was the movement in which I would want to serve the Jewish people all my life."

Begin rose rapidly in the Betar movement, which he entered while still a student in the Polish Gymnasium and where he organized a "defense squad" against the school's anti-Semites. When attacked, Begin and his Betarim would fight back, often going home beaten and bloody, but satisfied that they had given at least as much punishment as they had absorbed. The bullying of Jews in Brisk's Polish high school gradually diminished, then ceased altogether.

By the time he finished his studies at the Gymnasium in 1930, Begin was Betar Commander for the Brisk District and had decided to become a lawyer—"for social reasons," he wrote at the time, "so that I might be able to defend the poor and the oppressed." Early the following year, before his eighteenth birthday, he enrolled in the Law School of the University of Warsaw, where his sister Rachel was studying history and his brother Herzl was majoring in mathematics. For the Jews of the Pale, no sacrifice was too great that their children might have university educations, and it was one of Ze'ev Dov's proudest achievements that not only his sons but also his daughter received higher education.

In Warsaw, where he arrived with very few personal effects but with a Bible and a boxful or two of books, Menahem reported at once to the offices of the Betar High Commission, where he met his commander, Aharon Zvi Propess. It seemed only logical to the latter that Begin, despite his youth and his unprepossessing appearance—"he was very thin, very pale," Propess told me—should become one of the Commission's officers.

"Although obviously not very strong, physically," says Propess, "Begin was disciplined, well-liked by his comrades and, I must say, clearly very ambitious. The moment I met him, I decided to co-opt him. He became one of the Commission's nine top officers, and we entrusted him with what we called the Organization Portfolio."

In the Polish capital, Begin lived at the Jewish students' hostel and supported himself by tutoring high school students in his best subject: Latin. As Betar's chief organizer, Begin traveled extensively throughout Poland, making passionate Zionist speeches in Hebrew, Yiddish and Polish, creating new cells in the country's main cities and towns and increasing membership. In less than four years, Begin had more than tripled the number of cells to seven hundred and quadrupled the organization's enrollment to seventy thousand.

Begin was one of the main speakers at the Betar World Conference in Crakow in 1935, the year he was graduated in law from Warsaw University. As Propess tells it, Begin was already looked upon as the movement's most promising future leader. At one point during the conference, with Jabotinsky on the platform, Begin took the floor. No one seems to remember what he said, but Propess, who was there, recalls that when the speaker had finished, the Revisionist leader leaped to his feet and led the applause. "It lasted several minutes," says Propess, "and a murmuring could be heard among those present: 'The heir!' "

Begin's success as an organizer led Jabotinsky to send him to Czechoslovakia, where the movement had to be built up from scratch. The young Commissioner, however, had only limited resources at his disposal and barely managed food and lodging, often not even the latter.

"I know that for months on end Begin made do with only one meal a day," Propess relates, "and I received reports—not from him but from other Betarim—that he was seen in Prague sleeping on a bench in one of the city's public parks. Begin never thought about himself and never complained. As far as he was concerned, the main thing was to carry out his mission. That's the operative word with Begin—a sense of 'mission.' "

On his return to Warsaw, Begin was exhausted and came down with pneumonia. "My wife and I," Propess remembers, "persuaded him to take a rest and found him a place in a boarding house in Otwock, a suburb. That was on a Wednesday or Thursday. When we went to visit him on the Sabbath, Begin was gone. He had gone off somewhere—to make a speech."

The tide of events was now running strongly against the Jews not only in Europe but in Palestine itself. In 1936, sporadic Arab terrorism became full-scale guerrilla warfare against the Jewish community and the Mandatory Government. The Arab attacks were organized by the sinister Haj Amin el-Husseini,[2] the Mufti of Jerusalem, who would soon become Hitler's aide and counselor in execution of the latter's "Final Solution" of the "Jewish problem." Arab attacks in cities, towns, and villages and on remote settlements increased in frequency and intensity. The Jews suffered arson, the deforestation of their land, and destruction of homes, wells, pipelines and other valuable property, but thanks to two underground forces—the *Haganah* and the *Irgun Zvai Leumi*—actual Jewish casualties in dead and wounded were not heavy.

The Haganah, as previously indicated, was the underground military organization originally created by Jabotinsky in the early 1920s "to defend Jewish life, property and honor." It soon became closely linked with the *Histadrut* (the Labor Federation) and operated under the jurisdiction and orders of the Jewish Agency for Palestine, the *yishuv's* representative body, recognized as such by the British Mandatory authorities. The Jewish Agency represented, in other words, the establishmentarian Zionism of Weizmann, Ben-Gurion, et. al., which opposed aggressive military operations against the Arabs. During the mid-1930s and most of the 1940s the Haganah acted primarily as a defensive force, arguing that retaliation against Arab guerrilla bases would foreclose eventual agreement with the Arabs and result in injury to innocent people.

The Irgun Zvai Leumi, or National Military Organization, on the other hand, represented the Revisionist Zionist Movement. Founded in 1931 by a group of Haganah commanders who disagreed with Haganah's character as a purely defensive organization, the IZL proposed offensive military action against the increasing Arab attacks on the *yishuv,* and joined forces with Betar. It received the support of Palestine's nonlaborite center and right wing political parties.

Following a split in 1937, when about half its members returned to the Haganah, IZL was reorganized and became ideologically linked with Jabotinsky's Revisionist Zionist movement. Rejecting the *havlagah* ("restraint") policy of the Haganah, the Irgun began making sharp armed attacks on Arab bases and vehicles which the Jewish Agency publicly condemned. The Irgun argued that its attacks were aimed at deterring further Arab assaults on Jewish life and property; its aim was to take the war to the Arabs, which it did, and force the British to leave Palestine and declare the country's independence. Its ranks swelled with every act of Arab terrorism.

Alarmed at the rising crescendo of violence, the British government appointed the Peel Commission to study the situation in Palestine and recommend a solution. If Whitehall had hoped for a whitewash of British administration of the Mandate, it was bitterly disappointed. The Commission noted with pleasure the sharpness of "the contrast between this intensely democratic and highly organized modern (Jewish) community and the old-fashioned Arab world around it," and conceded that nowhere in the world was the spirit of nationalism "more intense than among the Jews of Palestine." Accordingly, the Commission recommended partition of the country into separate Jewish and Arab states.

Weizmann's Zionists realized that acceptance would mean further whittling down of the original Balfour boundaries, but they saw partition as the only immediate means of opening Palestine's doors to co-religionists fleeing in increasing numbers from the spreading Nazi terror in Europe. For the refugees, Palestine was now the only hope—nobody else wanted them, not even the United States. Reluctantly, the establishmentarian Zionists accepted the Peel proposal. The Arabs, assuming—as always—an "all-or-nothing" attitude, rejected partition outright and stepped up terrorist activities. For three years the country echoed to the sounds of rifle and machine gun fire, and exploding grenades and mines.

Under Husseini's leadership, the Arabs stopped bickering among themselves and achieved a measure of unity. They established a permanent executive organ known as the Arab High Committee, with Husseini as chairman. The committee demanded a cessation of Jewish immigration and a prohibition of land transfers from Arabs to Jews. A general strike developed into a rebellion against British authority. The British countered by removing Husseini from the Committee's chairmanship and declaring the organization illegal in Palestine. In October 1937, Husseini, the Yassir Arafat of his time, fled to Beirut, where he reconstituted the committee under his domination and continued its operations.

The rebellion Husseini fomented forced the British to make substantial concessions to Arab demands, among them severe restrictions on Jewish immigration at a crucial moment in the history of European Jewry. The gates of Palestine were closing, and both the Haganah and the Irgun intensified their efforts to bring in immigrants "illegally" because the British had taken to withholding immigration certificates.

As Nazi-inspired racism advanced through eastern and central Europe, the Haganah and the Irgun organized clandestine ways to bring in refugees in spite of regulations. A traffic in human beings sprang up in the Mediterranean. Secret organizations cooperated with profiteers who owned ships flying Greek or Turkish flags. Together they worked out a racket that provided fabulous profits for a few shipowners in Athens and Istanbul, but salvation for thousands. Refugees from the Nazi-Fascist areas filtered down to Greek or Turkish ports. There they were loaded like cattle onto waiting vessels, paying as much as four hundred dollars per head for passage in the dark, stinking holds of foul, unseaworthy tubs for a trip normally costing sixty dollars in first-class cabins with bath. The ships sailed as near as they dared to the Palestinian coast at points where small boats from shore met them to take off their passengers. At first, the British authorities, aware that these people—frightened, sick and penniless—had nowhere else to go, closed an eye. But the Arabs screamed disapproval, and the British banned the traffic, making it a criminal offense to transport or aid the "illegal" refugees.

A coast-guard patrol was organized, but the shipowners were making too much money to be easily discouraged. They obtained other, even less seaworthy vessels and loaded these to the gunwhales with passengers. On dark nights, they would beach the ships. There was nothing for the coast guard to do but rescue the refugees as the vessels began breaking up. Men, women and children—often babies born on board without medical aid—landed in Palestine with no passports or papers of identification of any kind. Most of the time they had no money, no clothes. Sometimes they swam ashore and many drowned in the effort.

But the influx from Europe, and from Germany in particular, provided the Jewish homeland with much-needed managers, engineers, physicians, chemists, research scientists, and experts of all kinds not only to help increase productivity, but to improve the quality of goods and enable Palestine to compete in the world's agricultural and industrial markets. More important, perhaps, eminent scholars arrived, to staff the Hebrew University in Jerusalem and the homeland's expanding educational system. With them came economists and men trained in government service to help create the framework of self-government, even while Palestine remained a Mandate under British rule.

Husseini and his extremist clique saw what was happening. If the Jews and the nation they were building were to be destroyed, it would have to be done soon. To that end, the Mufti entered into a secret alliance with the Nazis: he promised Hitler Arab support in the Middle East in the event of war with England in exchange for German money and weapons.

In the face of mounting Arab violence and British obstruction of Zionist objectives, the Irgun adopted a philosophy of armed power against both the Arabs and the British. It chose as its symbol a hand holding a rifle over the map of the original Palestine of the Mandate, which had included Transjordan, with the motto *Rak Kakh* ("Only Thus"). Jabotinsky and his followers reaffirmed the three principal objectives of Revisionist Zionism:

(1) creation of a Jewish state within the historical boundaries of *Eretz Yisrael,* (2) the evacuation to Palestine of the threatened Jews of the Diaspora, and (3) revival of the Jewish fighting spirit for actual warfare against the British overlords of Palestine.

It was a revolutionary program for the making of a Jewish nation. Unfortunately the Zionist revolution had appeared late on the international scene and had not developed a Cavour or a Mazzini, much less a Garibaldi, although Jabotinsky possessed some of the qualities of the first two; like Cavour he was far-sighted and like Mazzini a fiery ideologue. Worse yet, as Walter Laqueur has said, "there were no longer empty spaces on the world map." Palestine, though underdeveloped, was by no means "empty." Moreover, Britain held it and had no intention of yielding it to either its Jewish or Arab inhabitants.

Meanwhile, according to Propess and others who were closely associated with the Revisionist leader at the time, Jabotinsky did not believe that a major European war was imminent as a result of Hitler's triumph at Munich. Begin, on the other hand, was convinced that no time should be lost in creating an army of Jews in Europe and transporting it to Palestine to liberate the Holy Land from the British. He had read *Mein Kampf* and did not trust Hitler's assertion that he would have no further territorial demands after having obtained "repatriation" of Czechoslovakia's Sudeten Germans with the acquisition of Bohemia at Munich. In retrospect, Begin was right and Jabotinsky was wrong.

The Munich Conference, it will be recalled, was attended by Britain's Neville Chamberlain, France's Edouard Daladier and Italy's Benito Mussolini at the "invitation" of Adolf Hitler. The Soviet Union, which had a mutual defense alliance with Czechoslovakia, was excluded. So was Czechoslovakia itself. The meeting began shortly after noon on September 29, 1938, and lasted through the night into the early hours of the next day, by which time "agreement" had been reached. Chamberlain and Daladier accepted Hitler's terms, then put enormous pressure on the Czech government to yield—to sign its own death warrant.

France, urged by England into a pacific course that it was only too willing to follow, repudiated its treaty obligation to defend Czechoslovakia, ignored the Russians, who had affirmed their willingness to help protect the Czechs if France also acted, and dismantled its whole defensive system in the Little Entente, leaving the Balkans at the mercy of the Rome-Berlin axis.

It was agreed at Munich that Germany should annex outright adjoining Bohemia with its German majority. But Bohemia, in addition to Germans, contained the mountainous approaches to Czechoslovakia and the major Czech fortifications. The loss of Bohemia left Czechoslovakia virtually defenseless militarily—as defenseless as Israel would be in the 1970s if it allowed the creation on the West Bank of an independent Arab state dominated by the PLO.

After solemn guarantees by all concerned that the territorial and political integrity of what remained of Czechoslovakia would be respected, the conference disbanded. Chamberlain, Daladier, even Mussolini were received at home with cheers and deep sighs of relief. Chamberlain happily, if naively, reported to the British people that he had brought them "peace in our time." In the House of Commons, Winston Churchill disagreed, saying that all that the Prime Minister had gained was that "the German dictator, instead of snatching the victuals from the table, has been content to have them served to him course by course . . . We are in the presence of a disaster of the first magnitude, which has befallen Great Britain and France."

In the weeks following the Munich crisis the dismemberment of Czechoslovakia, freest and most democratic regime in Middle Europe, was completed. The country was brought under total German hegemony, with race laws, the Gestapo, wholesale arrests of dissidents, and a tightly controlled press. "This," wrote *The New York Times*, "is the twilight of liberty in Central Europe."

The annihilation of Czechoslovakia placed in Germany's power all of the subjugated country's natural and industrial resources. Bohemia-Moravia gave Germany 18,000 square miles of additional territory, a population of about seven million, large armament plants, and the gold and foreign exchange reserves of the Czech National Bank. Slovakia added another 15,000 square miles and a population of about two and a half million.

The expansion of the Third Reich by the annexation of territory inhabited by a non-Germanic people created a novel and preposterous situation. Until then, Hitler had appealed to the Wilsonian principle of self-determination—the principle that would be invoked in 1977-78 on behalf of the Palestinian Arabs residing in Judea and Samaria—in defense of his claim to adjacent lands inhabited by Germans, and though his methods were brutal and overbearing, it was held in many quarters that he had a plausible "case." If he learned nothing else at the time, Begin learned that invocation of the principle of "self-determination" could have disastrous consequences for the nation against which the principle was applied.

Menahem Begin, as indicated earlier, was one of the principal speakers at the Third World Congress of Betar, held in Warsaw, shortly after the

Munich Conference. In recent years, he had become the spokesman of a
"young guard" bloc whose members had grown impatient with Jabotinsky's inclination to temporize with what, in their view, had become a
desperate situation for Jewry in Palestine.

"Until now," said Begin, "the Zionist movement's answer (to Arab and
British opposition to Zionist objectives in Palestine) had consisted of
political activity, settlement, mass immigration, moral pressure, making
common cause with the British and maintaining faith in the League of
Nations and the conscience of the world. Now, all is changed: the
conscience of the world has ceased to react, and the League of Nations has
lost its value. Our British partner leads us to the gallows [3] and imprisons
the finest of our nation.

"Our good friends the British offer us five percent of *Eretz Yisrael* [4] and
give primary consideration to the Arabs in appeasement of their nationalist ambitions. If we continue on this course, the realization of Zionism will
be deferred. We want to fight—to conquer or perish. After political
Zionism, after practical Zionism, we must now enter the age of military
Zionism. We must amass strength that will not be dependent upon the
mercies of others. If such a force is created, the world too will come to our
assistance."

Warming to his subject, Begin went further. He called for armed revolt
against the British in Palestine, for "rebellion in the Irish style." He had
in mind, of course, the formation in the Holy Land of a Jewish force
similar to the Irish Republican Army which had fought British rule in
Ireland. The activity of the IRA between 1919 and 1921—guerrilla tactics,
ambushes, raids and sabotage—forced the British to negotiate a political
settlement providing for the creation of the Irish Free State.

In reply, Jabotinsky called for restraint and moderation, and attacked
his disciple in words dripping sarcasm.

"There is all manner of creaking," he said. "There is the kind that
merely grates and the kind that is of some use, such as the grating of the
wheels of a carriage in movement. But there is also a kind that is
superfluous, such as a door creaking on its hinges. Menahem Begin's
words are like the creaking of a door. What kind of 'Irish-style' rebellion
would we be capable of waging in Eretz Yisrael? The Irish live on their
own soil. But we? Are we living in our own land?"

Propess, who attended the Warsaw Congress with a musician's ear and
a conductor's memory, remembers the nature and intensity of the debate
that ensued. Begin, he recalls, had the support of a number of Irgunists
who had just arrived from Palestine with reports of increasing evidence of
British reluctance to fulfill the pledges of the Balfour Declaration and of
indications of growing Arab resistance to Zionist objectives. Among the
Irgunists were Arieh Ben-Eliezer, Uri Zvi Greenberg, Avraham Stern—

who would soon break away from the Irgun to form the extremist Freedom Fighters for Israel (FFI) later known as "The Stern Gang"—and several others who ultimately would help Begin lead the Irgun in the Jews' pre-state struggle for independence. All spoke in support of Begin's position.

At one point, the debate centered on an amendment to the fourth article of the seven-point Betar oath of allegiance which Jabotinsky had drafted prior to the Second Betar World Congress of 1935, but which had not yet been approved in plenary session. The article in question stated, "I will train my arm for the defense of my people but I will not raise my arm except in self-defense." The aim of this formulation had been to restrain Betar members from striking fellow Jewish adversaries unless they were attacked first. Begin proposed that the vow be amended to read, "I will train my arm for the defense of my people *and for the conquest of my homeland."* (Italics added.)

A spirited debate broke out between the master and his pupil; Jabotinsky, the humanist and liberal, agreed in principle to the amendment but took issue with the tone of despair in Begin's remarks about his lack of faith in "the conscience of the world."

"I understand the pain," he said, "but to let it lead you into despair is dangerous, a slamming of the door which is neither beneficial nor necessary. The Jewish people are not living in a world of robbers. It is, after all, a world of law and justice, and conscience still holds sway in it."

At this, an impatient Begin leaped to his feet and interrupted. "After Munich," he cried, "who can have faith in the conscience of the world?"

David Yutan—now a member of the executive of the Municipality of Tel Aviv—who was present, says that Jabotinsky was visibly shaken by Begin's interruption. His brilliant disciple was publicly attacking him and questioning what with Jabotinsky had become an article of faith: confidence in the "collective humanity of mankind," which he called "the conscience of the civilized world."

"Sir," said Jabotinsky, sternly addressing himself directly to Begin, "if you, sir, have stopped believing in the conscience of the world, you'd best go to the Vistula"—and here he pointed in the direction of the river that flows past Warsaw—"and drown yourself in it. Your alternative would be to take up Communism!"

Although Jabotinsky was incensed, he understood the spirit that motivated the youngster whom he had trained and led as commander of both Betar and the Irgun. He accepted the decision of the Congress on Begin's amendment which meant, in effect, a merging of Betar and the Irgun Zvai Leumi. It was decided, among other things, that an IZL representative would direct a department for military education within Betar.

In April 1939, after Hitler had swallowed all of Czechoslovakia, Jabotinsky finally realized that the ground was burning under the feet of European Jewry. He ordered his organization to hasten the creation of a Jewish army in Poland and the departure of as many Jews as possible for Palestine. Propess was sent on a fund-raising mission to the United States, but enroute stopped in Haifa, where he was arrested by the British and deported to East Africa. Begin replaced Propess as Betar High Commissioner for Poland.

Then came the May 1939, British White Paper renouncing the Balfour Declaration and the Mandate on which British authority rested. The document carried the imprimatur of Neville Chamberlain and constituted an act of appeasement of the forces of evil that rivaled, and in some ways even surpassed in its iniquitous consequences, Hitler's triumph at Munich of the previous autumn.

The White Paper proposed that Jewish immigration to Palestine be limited to fifteen thousand a year for five years, then cease completely. The Jewish population of Palestine was to be frozen at one-third the total, and within ten years the country was to become an independent state wherein the Jews would have permanent minority status. This as hundreds of thousands of Jews were already being herded into concentration camps preparatory to extermination in accordance with the formula of the Final Solution.

Soon after the White Paper was proclaimed, Menahem Begin led a Betar protest demonstration outside the gates of the British Embassy in Warsaw. He was arrested and quickly released, but not before the police had shaved his head. It would not be his last experience with the *polizei*.

NOTES

1. Now in his late seventies, Propess is Director of the Israel Choir Competition and the Israel Harp Contest, annual events which he manages from his offices in Tel Aviv.

2. Haj Amin el-Husseini was the first to employ the techniques of anti-Semitism to political purpose in the Middle East and, in a very real sense, invented genocide before Hitler. Between 1939-1945, Husseini spent most of his time in Berlin and was often in Hitler's company. If the mindless doctrine of extermination of Jews subsequently preached by Arab leaders can be traced to a single source, that source is unquestionably Husseini. He was responsible for the severe outbreaks of Arab violence in 1920 and 1929, and again in the mid-1930s. Born in 1896 or thereabouts, he died in

Beirut, July 4, 1974, one of many unpunished War Criminals of World War II.

3. This was a reference to the hanging by the British of a young Irgunist, Shlomo Ben-Yosef, following his abortive attack on an Arab bus in Galilee.

4. The portion of Palestine allotted to the Jews by the Peel Commission in 1937.

Chapter 6

Time Runs Out

After Jabotinsky appointed him Betar Commissioner for Poland in the spring of 1939, Menahem Begin traveled extensively about the country, organizing Irgun cells within the youth movement's local chapters, making speeches wherever he went. Touring the branches, he exhorted members to participate more actively in Betar's programs and did his utmost to woo Jews away from communism which was making some headway as an antidote to Nazism.

Lacking funds for hotel accommodations and restaurants, Begin slept and took his meals in the homes of provincial Betar functionaries and Revisionist Party leaders. In the home of one of the latter, Zvi Arnold, in the town of Drohobycz, he met his host's twin daughters. They were nineteen years old, had just completed their studies at the Gymnasium, and, like their father, were deeply involved in the movement. Both were active members of Betar.

The girls were a lively pair, small, sturdy, athletic and almost as alike physically as the proverbial two peas in a pod, but one took Begin's fancy. Remembering that moment, Begin says, "I looked at one of them and said to myself, 'That one is going to be my wife,' although I was much older. I was an old man of twenty-six!" His choice was Aliza, whom he would thereafter call Ala.

After a brief courtship, Menahem and Aliza were married in his parents' home in Brisk on May 29, 1939. They both appeared before the rabbi in brown Betar uniforms and the wedding was easily the social event of the year for the city's large Jewish community. It was attended by

Jabotinsky and several hundred Betarim from all over Poland. The couple went to Warsaw to live in Begin's rented room, but not for long. The shadow of Hitler's swastika already loomed large on the horizon.

Begin's frantic comings and goings between Warsaw and a score or more of Poland's major cities and towns had a two-fold purpose: first, to raise a Jewish Legion within the Polish army, ostensibly to help in the country's defense when the Germans attacked, but actually for eventual action against the British in Palestine; second, to encourage Poland's three million Jews to leave the country with all possible haste by whatever means available.

According to David Yutan, then an officer in the Betar High Commission, Jabotinsky had obtained the Polish government's approval for both projects. Jabotinsky was constantly looking for alliances, and as the British connection deteriorated, Polish assistance was solicited and secured at both the civilian and military levels.

Polish endorsement of Jabotinsky's plans—whose execution he entrusted to Begin and Yutan while he himself went to the United States on a fund-raising and propaganda mission—was not surprising. The Poles saw in Zionism, especially in Revisionist Zionism, a solution to their "Jewish problem." The Jews constituted upwards of ten per cent of Poland's population. They were prominent in the country's economic life, in some areas even dominant, and were under constant attack by Polish anti-Semites. The authorities in Warsaw perceived in Zionism a way of ridding themselves of their "surplus Jews."

Another of Begin's collaborators of those days, Eytan Livni—later a member of the Irgun's general staff in Palestine—recalls signs on Warsaw's walls reading: "Jews! Go to Palestine!" In short, endemically anti-Semitic, Poland preferred helping the Jews to emigrate instead of ostracizing them from the Polish society.

As Jabotinsky's official delegate to the Polish Foreign Office, Yutan, in addition to his other duties, was in charge of obtaining passports and emigration certificates for Polish Jews. During the first nine months of 1939—before the Nazis attacked Poland—approximately one million Jews, Yutan recalls, applied for the necessary documents.

Meanwhile, plans were going forward for training and arming one hundred thousand young men for the Jewish Legion and for transporting them to Palestine in a fleet of chartered ships. The Poles organized a training school for Irgun battalion commanders at a remote village named Zielonka and the military phase of the operation was actually proceeding so well, Yutan recalls, that a date was set for its launching. Jewry's "army of liberation" was to have sailed during Passover in the early spring of 1940!

The collaboration between the Revisionists and the Polish government angered the British, but Whitehall's ire was mild compared to the bitter reaction of the preponderantly Laborite Zionist establishment. The Jewish Agency's representatives in Poland went to great lengths to help "illegal" immigrants if they were Laborites, but allegedly withheld the required certificates from Revisionist Zionists.

The split between Jabotinsky and the Weizmann-Ben-Gurion faction was undoubtedly one of Zionism's major tragedies, for it complicated and delayed the process of saving Jewish lives while there was still time. Jabotinsky remained an uncompromising nineteenth-century-style democrat, but in the general fear of Fascism during the late 1930s, his Betar movement gave rise to suspicion and downright hatred. His wooing of the right wing Polish government was vigorously denounced by Ben-Gurion who went so far as to refer to Jabotinsky as "Vladimir Hitler." [1] Jabotinsky's insistence that Zionism's objective should be a single-minded effort to achieve a Jewish state was misinterpreted as "deification of the state." Even Rabbi Stephen Wise, head of the American Jewish Congress, who previously had shown considerable sympathy for Jabotinsky's movement, was influenced by the prevailing opinion and asserted: "For the Revisionists as for the Fascists the state is everything and the individual nothing." [2]

In seeking the support of the Polish government for his "evacuation" scheme, Jabotinsky was seen by the Labor Zionists and their allies as pandering to the worst anti-Semitic tendencies of the Eastern European states. Sholom Asch, the Hebrew writer, said at the time, "One had to have a heart of stone, to be devoid of any feeling for human sufferings, to be so brazen as to come to Poland with such proposals at such a terrible time . . . . Heaven help a people with such leaders!" Unlike Ben-Gurion and other critics, however, Sholem Asch later acknowledged Jabotinsky had been prophetically right and subsequently publicly expressed "deep regret" that he had opposed Jabotinsky's evacuation plan.

The hostility of the Labor Zionists to many of Jabotinsky's ideas is difficult to understand. History has proved him right in many areas that in his day provoked great controversy and weakened the dynamics of the Zionist revolution. The charge of Fascism, a standard weapon in the hands of the left in those days, was unfair. Actually, Jabotinsky hated the very idea of totalitarianism, whether of the Communist or Fascist variety. He preferred, he said, "old-fashioned parliamentarianism however clumsy or inefficient it might be" to any *Polizeistaat*, and he believed that ninety-nine percent of his party comrades, among them his pupil Menahem Begin, shared his views.

According to one authority, Jabotinsky had an almost physical sense of the approaching doom of European Jewry long before other Zionist leaders and gave it dramatic expression at the Founding Conference of the New Zionist (Revisionist) Organization in September 1935, only days after Adolf Hitler had proclaimed his infamous Nuremberg Laws depriving the Jews of Germany of citizenship, and confining them to the status of "subjects." In a memorable speech, Jabotinsky declared, "We apparently are living on the threshold of the last portal to hell, on the eve of the final holocaust in the global ghetto." Prophetic words indeed.

Although slow to realize that Hitler meant war after Munich, Jabotinsky's doubts were swept away by the Fuehrer's subsequent demands for the return to Germany of Danzig, landlocked Poland's outlet to the Baltic, and the territory known as the Polish Corridor, which separated East Prussia from the main body of the German Reich. There was no doubt then in Jabotinsky's mind that Poland was next on Hitler's schedule of European conquest. At a public meeting in Warsaw in May 1939, Jabotinsky made one final appeal to Jewry to abandon Europe, a task he left Begin to carry out.

Through the spring and early summer of 1939—while Hitler occupied the Lithuanian port of Memel, agitated for the return of Danzig and the Corridor, and massed some two hundred fifty thousand troops in Czechoslovakia with armor and air power—Begin shuttled by railway between Warsaw and Sniatyn, a town on the Romanian border, escorting Betar members on their way to Palestine via Black Sea ports. How many Polish Jews were saved in this fashion, no one seems to know exactly. Yutan, Livni and other Irgunists put the figure at "about thirty thousand," but agree it would have been considerably higher if there had been unity in the Zionist movement instead of hostility between the Jewish Agency and the Revisionists.

The relationship between the Revisionists and the Labor Zionists of the Jewish Agency had become embittered to a degree difficult to imagine in the 1970s. Labor saw Jabotinsky's Revisionism not merely as a threat to the fundamental values and institutions of an eventual Israel, but to the physical existence of the *yishuv,* the Jewish community in Palestine itself. For the Labor Zionists it was an obvious principle that any Zionist policy had to be built on the premise that the practical colonizing achievements in Palestine—the development of agriculture and industry, the revival of Hebrew, the establishment of settlements etcetera—took precedence over all other considerations. Jabotinsky, on the other hand, explicitly asserted that he was prepared to risk even the *yishuv*'s accomplishments for what he conceived to be the dominant goal: the global salvation of European

Jewry, which was the policy Begin pursued.³

Early in August 1939, Begin accompanied a trainload of about one thousand Betarim along the railway escape route to the Romanian border and found the frontier closed. Begin remained there for nearly three weeks trying to arrange Romanian permission for the convoy to proceed. In the end, he was obliged to return to the Polish capital with the disappointed and now despairing would-be emigrants.⁴

To make Begin's task even more difficult, opposition to his efforts to evacuate Poland's Jewish population arose from within the country's Jewish leadership. In an outburst of Polish patriotism, one of the community's leaders, Yitzhak Gruenbaum, known for his statement that Poland had "two million superfluous Jews," did not agree that even these, at least, should evacuate. Like many others, Gruenbaum believed Poland was militarily strong and could successfully defend itself if Hitler attacked. It was a view shared by many Polish Jews who argued that in any event Poland would not be alone if war came; the country would have the (already promised) support of mighty Britain and of France, whose army was still regarded by the experts as being "the best in Europe."

Meanwhile, time was running out—for Poland and for its three million Jews. Poland itself was caught in the Nazi vise, much as Austria and Czechoslovakia had been earlier. And Poland's Jews were trapped by the British White Paper, dissension in the Zionist ranks and the imminence of war.

In Moscow, in the early morning hours of August 24, Hitler's Foreign Minister, Joachim von Ribbentrop and his Soviet counterpart, Vyacheslav Molotov, signed the historic German-Soviet Pact. There were two documents. One, for public consumption, merely stated that the two powers had agreed not to make war on each other for a period of ten years and each promised to give no help to the enemies of the other in the event of attack by third parties. The second document, kept secret at the time, provided that in any future territorial rearrangements, Russia and Germany would divide Poland and the Baltic states between them.

The German-Soviet Pact stupefied the world. Communism and Nazism, supposedly ideological opposites, had come to terms. It was a humiliating rebuff to the West in general, and to Britain and France in particular. It was also a startling indication of the cynicism of Nazis and Communists alike, and a dramatic demonstration of the ruthless realities of power politics.

At about this time Hitler received bad news from two directions. From London came word that the British government had formalized into an actual mutual assistance pact the assurances of support in case of attack that Chamberlain already had given the Poles verbally. And from Mussolini came a coded telegram saying Italy would be unable to give Germany military aid if the Western powers attacked in the defense of Poland. The two items depressed Hitler and the invasion of Poland, originally fixed for August 26, was postponed.

As Hitler hesitated, Europe teetered on the brink of catastrophe. It had been a warm summer and the crops were ripening in the fields. It was difficult to realize how close to war the Continent really was. Except for air raid drills in London and Berlin, and quiet mobilization in Poland, there were few signs of imminent conflict anywhere. People still traveled freely enough, and everywhere people were saying what they earnestly hoped would be true: "There will be no war. You'll see. There will be another Munich."

People often believe what they want to believe, even though it be contrary to reality. This human weakness may explain why a policy of appeasement was followed toward the Nazis by statesmen who ought to have known better, but who dreaded the prospect of war. It may also explain why Hitler, up to the eleventh hour, believed Britain and France would back down and abandon Poland to its fate. But they didn't and on September 1, 1939, the first Nazi bombs fell on Warsaw.

David Yutan recalls that he accompanied Begin to Polish Army headquarters and proposed that special units of Betar members be constituted to help resist the German attack. "The Polish officers listened politely," says Yutan, "took notes on our proposal and promised to pass it on to their superiors. Yet with each passing day it became clearer that the fate of Poland was sealed. Soon, there was no one to talk to at headquarters—the officers were too busy or away at the front."

On September 5, Aliza and Menahem Begin were witnesses at the wedding of a Betar leader, Natan Yellin-Mor,[5] and his fiancee, Frieda, who had somehow managed to come to Warsaw from her parents' home in Bialystok. The ceremony, a reasonable interlude in an unreasonable world, took place in the home of Warsaw's last Chief Rabbi, Shlomo David Kahana.

By now, the railways and roads were heavy with military traffic. Nevertheless, Begin continued to organize and escort Betar groups that left the capital for Sniatyn, where the frontier had been temporarily reopened to allow Jews to escape. Toward the end of September, upon returning from what Begin knew would be the last of his trips to the Romanian border, Uri Zvi Greenberg, the "poet laureate" of the Betar movement, was amazed to find Menahem in his office at the organization's headquarters.

"Why are you still here?" Greenberg asked. "We've got passports for you and Aliza for Palestine. Take them and go!"

Begin replied that he would "think about it," but decided later not to leave. "Flight," he said, "is the road of despair." He occupied himself with plans to transfer Betar headquarters to Lublin, but soon gave up the idea as impractical. Poland was disintegrating before the German onslaught, a spectacular, perfectly executed example of lightning war by tanks and planes that gave our dictionaries a new word: *blitzkrieg*.

Begin and his wife finally left Warsaw when the Germans were about to lay siege to the capital, and headed south for the Romanian border. They set out by rail with the Yellin-Mors but were obliged to leave the train and continue their journey through the German lines by wagon and on foot. At Lvov, Begin was arrested by the Russians, but was quickly released, and allowed to proceed with the others to Vilna, which the advancing Soviets had already handed over to Lithuania, but had not yet physically occupied it.

While Vilna still remained "Lithuanian" under "Soviet supervision," the city became briefly what it had been for a century and a half, a center of eastern European Jewish cultural life. Between 1799 and 1938, Vilna became renowned for the rabbinical studies that produced texts of the Mishna, the Jerusalem Talmud and other works that are still standard. By the turn of the twentieth century, it had also become the focal point of the Socialist-oriented Zionist movement in Russia.

Into Vilna after the fall of Warsaw flowed hundreds of Jewish refugees from all over Poland, among them Betarim who sought out Begin for assistance in escaping to Palestine. With the help of another Betar official, Dr. Israel Sheib—later known in the Irgun as "Eldad"—Begin did what he could for his followers, finding them shelter in Vilna proper and its environs, and helping many on their way to the Holy Land.

The Begins rented an apartment in the Polish quarter of the city with Dr. Sheib and his wife, Batya. Twice he was offered immigration certificates to Palestine by leaders of the Jewish community in Vilna, but Begin refused to go. "Let others save themselves while there's still time," he said. "I'll wait. I have work to do here."

One day in the summer of 1940, Begin was invited to speak at the city's University—renowned in recent years as a hotbed of anti-Semitism—in a ceremony memorializing Theodor Herzl and celebrating, at the same time, the fifteenth anniversary of the founding of the Hebrew University in Jerusalem. Never before had anyone lectured in Hebrew on the Vilna campus. "It was," says Dr. Sheib, "an exciting and exhilirating occasion."

In the midst of the ceremony, a note was brought to the dais stating that Soviet tanks were at the city's gates. When the news was read to the audience, there was pandemonium in the packed auditorium. Many called for immediate adjournment, but Begin took the floor, and calmed the crowd. "Let us indeed adjourn," he said, "but let us do it with dignity. Let us sing our national anthem." Three thousand Jewish students made the walls ring to the plangent sounds of *Hatikva* while Soviet tanks rolled into the city.

Later that summer, on August 4, a Betar member entered the restaurant in Vilna where Jewish refugees congregated, with sad news for Revisionists: he had heard on the radio that Ze'ev Jabotinsky had died in the United States.[6] At considerable personal risk, traveling under the very noses of NKVD agents, Begin made his way to Kovno. There, in the town's main synagogue, before a large gathering of mourners, Menahem Begin delivered a eulogy for his departed mentor.

The western half of Poland was now under German occupation, including Brest-Litovsk, where Begin's father, Ze'ev Dov, was struggling to hold together his family and what remained of the Jewish community. When the Nazis entered the city, their first move was to arrest five hundred Jews who were then herded into the town's central market place and ordered to stand facing a wall. Among those arrested was Menahem's older brother, Herzl, then thirty years old. There was a command: "Fire!" But the volley was merely intended to frighten. It was fired in the air, over the heads of the terrified crowd.

Ze'ev Dov, meanwhile, was at Nazi headquarters waving under the Commandant's nose the old World War I German document certifying his position as official representative of the Jewish community of Brisk. Addressing the *Herr Komandant* as though they were equals, Ze'ev Dov Begin declared the Germans had no right to arrest those people in the market place and demanded their immediate release.

The German officer was astonished. He examined the document that Ze'ev Dov handed him and remarked that it might well have been issued by his grandfather. He reassured his caller, however, that he had no intention of shooting any Jews, not for the time being, anyway. What he wanted from the community was money, watches, clothing and food for five hundred men.

Ze'ev Dov understood at once what was afoot. At Bereza Kartuska, near Brisk, there was a Polish concentration camp for Germans suspected of having collaborated with the Nazis prior to the invasion. The Wehrmacht had liberated the prisoners, and they now had to be clothed and equipped for repatriation before Brisk was given over to the Russians in accordance with the secret clauses of the German-Soviet pact.

But the Jews of Brisk were not spared for long. They were not much better off under their new masters than they had been under the

Germans. For when the Russians occupied eastern Poland and the Baltic countries, they arrested many Jewish communal leaders, whom they regarded as anti-Communist, and either shot them outright or exiled them to Siberia for "re-education" in labor camps.

Among those arrested were a pair of newlyweds, Rachel Begin and Yehoshua Halperin, an attorney. Rachel recalls that as she and her husband were being taken away in a Russian lorry, her father ran after the truck, caught up with it and handed her a miniature Book of Psalms containing a special prayer for travelers. To this day, whenever Menahem leaves Ben-Gurion Airport for a foreign destination, Rachel is there to give him her blessing and to hand him a similar tiny volume with the prayer. Menahem has come to believe, says Rachel, that if she is not present at his departure, "something untoward will happen." [7]

During the Russian occupation, Brisk's Jewish community ceased to exist as a corporate entity. All political parties went underground, while Jewish service organizations—schools, hospitals, students' hostels, orphanages, libraries—were taken over and operated by the government. Yet, worse was to come.

In the summer of 1941, when Hitler launched "Operation Barbarossa" against his erstwhile Russian "ally," fortified Brisk was among the first key cities to fall, although only after a fierce resistance. The surviving members of the Begin family—Ze'ev Dov, his wife Hassia and their son Herzl—were among the early victims of the "Final Solution." The entire Jewish community of several thousand was killed by one means or another. Many, among them Ze'ev Dov, were weighted with sacks filled with rocks and drowned in the River Bug. It is said that as he was being led to the river's banks with his co-religionists, Ze'ev Dov led them in a "confessional" prayer and that even as the weights were being tied about his neck he sang *Hatikva*. The lives of Hassia and Herzl were extinguished at Auschwitz.

Later, when Stalin's Russia became an ally of the Western Powers, Rachel and her husband were released and moved to Uzbekistan, where Rachel earned a precarious living for herself and her lawyer husband teaching Russian. In 1944, the couple were allowed to proceed to Palestine. They settled in Tel Aviv where, in 1966, Halperin died after a long illness.

During the spring and summer of 1940—after the collapse of Poland and the fall of France—Lithuania, which had been theoretically "liberated" by the Red Army, remained under Soviet political and military domination as did the adjoining Baltic states, Latvia and Estonia. In Vilna, the NKVD, the Russian secret police, started a purge of all Zionists among the thousands of Jewish refugees who had congregated in the ancient Lithuanian capital and its environs.

The Begins and the Sheibs had found refuge in the home of a friendly family of Polish Catholics in a small village near the big city. But there was no hiding from the NKVD; its Lithuanian agents kept the house under round-the-clock surveillance.

One day—September 1, 1940—a messenger arrived from the municipality with an official-looking document "inviting" Menahem Begin to present himself immediately at a certain office at the Vilna Town Hall to discuss an "application" which he was supposed to have deposited with the authorities. Having filed no "application" of any kind with the municipality, Begin sensed an NKVD trap and ignored the summons.

Several days later, while he and Dr. Sheib were absorbed in their daily game of chess, a black sedan drew up outside the house and discharged three husky men. Moments later came the sharp "knock on the door" all Jewish refugees everywhere had come to dread. When the lady of the house admitted the callers, the biggest and burliest of the trio wanted to know why Begin had not responded to the municipality's "invitation."

As Dr. Sheib relates the incident, Begin put on a great show of innocence, replying that since he had not submitted an "application" of any sort at the municipality or anywhere else, he had assumed there had been a mistake, hence had seen no reason to respond. When the men insisted he accompany them to Vilna anyhow, Begin firmly refused and demanded to see their credentials. The boss cop produced a card identifying him as an agent of the "Lithuanian Intelligence Service," and Begin knew the men had come to arrest him. The police had no warrant, but they made it clear that unless Begin came willingly, he would be taken by force.

"Menahem was most polite to his 'guests'," Dr. Sheib recalls. "He asked them to come in and make themselves comfortable while he dressed. He even invited them to have tea, which they declined. Then Menahem polished his shoes, put on his best suit, carefully knotted his necktie and asked permission to take along some books. 'No need,' one of the men said. 'You'll be back before long.' But Begin refused to go without at least his Bible, which he took down from its accustomed place and thrust under his arm together with another book he had been reading—Maurois' biography of Disraeli.

"At the door, Begin stopped, turned and said, 'After you, gentlemen. This is my house, and I would not dream of allowing my guests to leave after me.' He embraced me and my wife Batya, who burst into tears. But young Aliza—she was only twenty at the time—retained her composure.

She was allowed to accompany her husband to the car parked outside, and there they said their goodbyes.

"Before they parted, Menahem told Aliza to tell me that he conceded the chess game because I was ahead when we were interrupted. We did not see Menahem again for two years. We next met in *Eretz Yisrael* . . ."

On his way to the car, Begin caught a glimpse of his friend, David Yutan, who was also wanted by the NKVD and for weeks had expected arrest. The two men exchanged glances that bespoke more than words could have expressed.

The Soviet authorities, more specifically the NKVD, accused Begin of "serving the interests of British imperialism" and declared him "a dangerous element in society." There was no trial, of course, and Begin subsequently was sentenced to eight years "service" in a "correctional labor camp," a Muscovite euphemism for the horrors of a Siberian gulag.

For several months, until January 1941, Begin was confined in the gloomy old Lukishki Prison, in the heart of Vilna proper, and from there was transferred to the Pechora concentration camp in northern Russia. Then, in the harsh winter of that terrible year, he was sent by ship to yet another Arctic gulag with many other prisoners—mostly "politicals" like himself, but many of them hardened criminals—to serve out what remained of his sentence building a railway line across the northern steppes.

Menahem Begin did not, however, serve out his time. History had ordained for him a different destiny from the one decreed by the NKVD.

NOTES

1. Erich and Rael Jean Isaac, *Middle East Review*, Vol. X, No. 1, Fall, 1977.

2. Ibid.

3. The hostility dated back to an incident that occurred in 1933 when the Revisionists were accused of responsibility for the murder of a Zionist labor leader, Chaim Arlosoroff. A broad anti-Revisionist coalition was formed at the time including centrist General Zionists as well as Socialists which asserted: "We declare that the moral responsibility for this brutal assassination (on a beach in Tel Aviv) falls upon the entire Revisionist movement . . . . Let our motto be: Expel the Revisionist gangs from Jewish life." Evidence subsequently emerged in the 1950s and again in the 1970s that Arabs, not Jews, had been responsible for Arlosoroff's murder, but the breach never healed.

4. Aharon Dolav, "White Nights and Tempestuous Days in the Life of Menahem Begin," *Ma'ariv,* Tel Aviv, June 10, 1977.

5. Yellin-Mor was Betar High Commission officer in charge of the illegal emigration of Betar members and Revisionists, but soon resigned to become editor of the Yiddish daily *Die Tat* (Action), Irgun organ in Poland that provided detailed accounts of events in Palestine.

6. Jabotinsky died August 3, 1940, in Hunter, New York, of a heart attack. He was in the United States visiting newly formed Betar chapters, raising funds and promoting Revisionist ideas. In his will, he specified he wished to be buried eventually in Israel, which he felt certain would achieve national independence during or immediately after World War II. Ben-Gurion refused to listen to repeated pleas that Jabotinsky's body be brought to Israel. For all his greatness, "B.-G." had his blind spots, and Jabotinsky was certainly one of them. It was due to the intercession of Teddy Kollek, when "B.-G." was out of the government and Levi Eshkol was Prime Minister, that Jabotinsky's remains were brought to Israel and laid to rest on Mount Herzl, the Jewish state's "Arlington."

7. In an interview with the author, to whom Mrs. Halperin later graciously presented one of the prayer books.

8. Interview with the author.

Book Three:

Soviet Russia 1941-1942

Chapter 7

Through Hell to Freedom: Part One

From his home, Menahem Begin was taken first to the squat, gloomy building in mid-city Vilna that once had housed the District Court of Poland but was now the headquarters of the NKVD, Lavrenti Beria's instrument for organizing terror, espionage and forced labor in the Soviet Union on behalf of his master, Josef Stalin, whom he served as Commissar for Internal Affairs. Beria's minions were experts in the art of "interrogation" and in the application of the draconic Section 58 of the Soviet Criminal Code. This particular piece of legislation was sufficiently broad and vague to provide a semblance of legal rationale for proscribing and punishing any form of behavior, real or imagined, considered inimical to the interests of the State. Merely being a Zionist was crime enough, and it was under Section 58 that Begin was charged, although he did not know this when he was arrested.

However, Begin was aware that when he entered the NKVD's offices he had stepped into "a new world full of unknown horrors." [1] He had reason to believe he would never again see his wife and friends, never reach the *Eretz Israel* of his longings, for he knew that few survived the kind of "justice" meted out by the NKVD under Soviet law. Yet, he faced the uncertainties of the future calmly, almost serenely, determined to survive, come what might.

His ordeal in the toils of the NKVD, Lukishki Prison and the Siberian labor camp at Pechora would span approximately twelve months—the longest year in his life—and it started with an interrogation, Cheka-OGPU style, with questions that were really accusations. It lasted sixty hours—longer than Begin believed a man could endure—without water, without food and without sleep. But Begin endured, for Begin is a stubborn man.

The interrogation took place in an ordinary room, before an ordinary desk behind which sat Begin's burly interrogator, who tried at first to disguise the proceedings as merely a "conversation." "Answer a few questions truthfully," he said, "and you can go right home to your wife." Had Begin engaged in politics? Yes. What kind? Zionist; he had headed the Betar organization in Poland. Then, sharply, "What were your activities in Vilna against the Soviet authorities?" Begin calmly denied any such activities. The interrogator stiffened. "You're lying," he said.

After some time, seeing he was getting nowhere, the man abandoned his tough style and switched to the familiar *ti* form in Russian used between bosom friends or by masters to servants. Begin politely reminded his inquisitor that by law "representatives of the Soviet authorities must behave courteously to citizens." "So," he said, "I would ask you not to address me as *'ti.'* Furthermore, I am not telling you lies." The NKVD man apologized. "I didn't mean to insult you," he said. "It's obvious you are an educated man. But don't be so proud."

Several hours later, Begin was told he was hurting his chances of being released by withholding the truth and was left alone with paper and ink, and orders to "Write—write everything" concerning his life and activities. "But you had better write the truth," Begin was advised. "You still have a chance of returning to your wife. Think carefully, and write the truth."

Begin understood Russian, having picked it up by hearing it spoken, but he had not yet learned to write it. He asked whether he should compose his *curriculum vitae* in Polish or Yiddish. The reply surprised him, but only mildly, for it merely confirmed what he had suspected all along.

"It's all the same," the man said. "We translate from many languages here, but from my own point of view it would be better if you wrote in Yiddish, because I am a Jew, too."

"Really?" Begin blurted, feigning amazement.

"Yes, I am a Jew, and as a Jew you can trust me. You write the truth!"

When the interrogator left, an armed Russian soldier entered and planted himself before the door. Thereafter, Begin was never alone again, not until some time later, when he was sentenced to seven days in solitary confinement in Lukishki Prison.

His inquisitor returned after several hours, glanced at what Begin had written without reading it, tossed it to one side and asked his prisoner whether he was now ready "to tell the truth." Begin said he had written the truth and had nothing further to add.

"We have ways," the man said, "of compelling you to tell the truth."

Begin interrupted a flow of threats to ask for something to drink. He had been arrested around mid-day, and it was now well after dark. He was hungry and, above all, thirsty. The interrogator left, promising to "organize" tea for him. Begin resumed reading Maurois' life of the First Lord of Beaconsfield in English, a language he had studied at the University and could read with ease.

The tea never came. When the door opened again it was to admit a new guard, bigger and more brutish than the one he replaced. The replacement, a sergeant, found Begin absorbed in the portion of Maurois' biography dealing with Disraeli's youth and took away the book. "From now on, no more reading here." Begin protested, stating he had been given permission to read by the interrogator. The sergeant said the interrogator had no authority here and that he, a soldier of the Soviet Union, was in charge.

The sergeant then ordered Begin to take the chair in which he had been sitting facing the desk and put it in a far corner of the room, facing the wall. He sat in that position, knees touching the masonry, for almost sixty hours, eyes focused on one point. He held onto his sanity by mentally reliving his boyhood in a Gentile Polish school, his first meeting with Jabotinsky, his missions on behalf of Betar, his first experience in jail for having demonstrated against the White Paper outside the British Embassy in Warsaw, his journeys to the Romanian border with Betarim on their way to Palestine, his pride in his Jewishness. They could separate Begin from his wife, his books, his freedom, but not from his thoughts, and these, he would write later, were not only about the past but also about the future. He saw himself reaching *Eretz Israel* . . .

Begin dozed off from time to time, but the guard would waken him in a low voice. "No sleeping, now. No reading and no sleeping."

From time to time, the interrogator returned to ask whether Begin was ready "to tell the truth." To these routine questions, the prisoner gave routine replies and repeatedly asked for the tea he had been promised. The man feigned surprise that it had not been brought, gave reassurances that it would soon be forthcoming and disappeared. Begin ate a bit of bread he had brought with him, but it wasn't hunger that tormented him; it was thirst and lack of sleep. Depriving a man of sleep, Begin realized, was a special means of NKVD pressure, possibly the worst ever conceived by inquisitorial science.

Finally, two days and twelve hours after his arrest, Begin was crowded into an automobile with several other prisoners and taken to Lukishki Prison. In a cell shared by two others, Begin collapsed onto a straw-ticked mattress and fell into a deep sleep.

Vilna's central prison, built more than a century earlier by the Czars, had survived many revolutions by Polish and Lithuanian nationalists. Several Slavic languages, to which Begin added Hebrew, were engraved on the thick, concrete walls of the "human cage" that Begin found himself sharing with a former major in the Polish reserve and a corporal in the Polish regular army. Each had a straw-filled mattress, a rickety stool, a shelf for personal belongings and a small bowl in which their "food" was served. A rough wooden table was common property. So was the pail that functioned as a toilet.

The Polish officer was serving time for having belonged to some secret organization or other. He was middle-aged, highly educated and well-mannered. Obsessively orderly about everything, he would sulk if utensils were not properly laid out at meals, then cleaned and replaced exactly where they belonged.

The noncom was a tailor by trade and had no clear idea about why he had been arrested and jailed. Poorly educated, he was eager to make up in prison what he had missed in school, and Begin obliged by giving him lessons in European and Polish history. The "courses" were conducted without books or writing materials which, of course, were forbidden.

Both cellmates were hopeful that Germany would attack and defeat Russia. A German victory, they believed, would mean freedom from Lukishki. Begin disagreed, explaining that in the event of a Russo-German war, Poland would disappear as a nation and more millions of Jews were likely to fall into Hitler's hands.

"Yes," he said, "I also want to get out of here, but when I think of them, I tell myself that if I have to be released at such a price, I would rather remain in Lukishki, if that would prevent Jews from falling into the hands of the Gestapo."

The officer and the corporal sneered. "That's the way it is with Jews," they said. "They always stick together."

"Gentlemen," Begin replied. "What you call Jewish solidarity—I wish it really existed."

A shadow fell between Begin and his cellmates, not to be lifted completely for some time.

The days lengthened into weeks, and Begin learned what it meant to be not merely hungry but starving. The NKVD menu was not remarkable either for its variety or its abundance. It consisted, invariably, of watery soup, a sort of thin gruel, and stale bread, all in minute quantities. Begin's cellmates avidly licked their bowls, gathered bread crumbs into little balls and gazed at them like so many "precious pearls" before gulping them down. They counted the grains of the daily half-teaspoonful of sugar which they were given to sweeten the dubious brown liquid called coffee that came with "breakfast."

Nevertheless, one Yom Kippur, Menahem Begin fasted. His warder called him a "half-wit" for observing the ritual of the Day of Atonement, but Begin found solace in identifying himself "with all that is good in man's life."

Immediately after Yom Kippur, the interrogations resumed.

Late one night, Begin was awakened by his warden, marched down the long corridor of his cell block and into another wing of the prison where he was led into a small, warm, well-lighted room. A uniformed captain, armed with a revolver, entered and sat opposite the prisoner at a desk. The officer said he had read what Begin had written and had found it "worthless." Begin had better start "telling the truth," he said, and started asking questions. How long had Begin been a Zionist?

"Since childhood," said Begin. "From the age of ten to thirteen, I was in the *Hashomer Hatzair,* and from the age of fifteen onwards I was in the Betar."

"I see you began your criminal activities early," the captain said.

"Why criminal?" Begin replied. "I think my activities were right and proper."

Begin was told he was "worse than a murderer" because all his activities were "anti-Soviet and anti-revolutionary." Why had he joined Betar? Because of Jabotinsky, said Begin. The interrogator bridled: "Jabotinsky is the leader of Jewish Fascism." Begin denied this and launched into an explanation.

"Jabotinsky," he said, "was anti-Fascist. He was my teacher. I am a prisoner and I know I must answer questions, but I will defend the honor of my teacher as long as I am able to do so. Wouldn't you, citizen-judge, do the same if someone were to offend the memory of Lenin?"

The interrogator was incensed by the comparison, but calmed down after another tirade against Jabotinsky the "Fascist." He asked where Jabotinsky was now. "He is dead," said Begin. Did Begin know him well?

Yes, he knew Jabotinsky well. Yes, he had met him several times. What did they talk about? Various things—the education of Hebrew youth, organizational problems, the situation in Palestine, the iniquities of British policy, immigration.

But by joining Betar, the interrogator pointed out, the young *did not join the Communist Party*. The inquisitor stressed this in the manner of a man scoring a most significant point in what was less an interrogation than a debate between Communism and Zionism, "an argument," Begin would write later, "at times stormy, between two worlds brought together in a small room, the nocturnal workroom of an officer of the OGPU, a State security officer of the Soviet Union."

At two o'clock in the morning, after four hours of questions, answers and argument, the interrogator wrote out what Begin had said. Begin found it incomplete and asked that certain items be added. No need, he was told. He could say whatever else he wished at "the trial."

"So, there will be a trial?" Begin asked, but with mixed feelings. He was surprised and delighted, but also anxious.

"Of course there will be a trial," said the officer, red-faced with indignation. "You are in the Soviet Union, where every man is given the right to defend himself even if he is a criminal. Now—sign!"

Begin signed what the interrogator had written but requested that an interpreter be present at future meetings. He feared his Russian wasn't up to another encounter with an officer of the Soviet Union. The interrogator promised to provide one for their next "conversation."

Back in his cell, Begin went to sleep but was awakened at daybreak by the shrill whistle that started every monotonous day of life in Lukishki. Life? Living death . . .

Next day, the questioning was resumed in the presence of an interpreter. Begin could now express himself more clearly in Yiddish. His inquisitor wanted to know exactly what the Betar movement was all about. Calmly, patiently, Begin explained.

"Our program," he said, "is very simple. The Jewish people have no country of their own, and we (of Betar) want to give them back their Homeland. We want to turn *Eretz Yisrael* into a Jewish state and settle in it millions of Jews who have no future whatsoever in the countries of the Diaspora."

Begin asked the interpreter to translate exactly his phrase about converting *"Eretz Yisrael* into a Jewish state." This was a very important definition, Begin said, "because the British wrote in the Balfour Declaration: 'the establishment in Palestine of a National Home for the Jewish people'—and they have taken advantage of the many interpretations of this sentence in order to get out of their commitment . . . . That is fraud on their part."

Begin soon wished he had never asked for an interpreter; his interpreter turned out to be another anti-Zionist Jew. Instead of translating, the interpreter proceeded, in Yiddish, to attack Zionism, denouncing it as a "farce," a movement designed to divert Jewish youth from the revolution and declaring that the idea of a Jewish state was a chimera, for Britain had no intention of creating such a state.

Begin hotly defended Zionism as no "farce" but possibly "the most serious national liberation movement history has ever known," a movement that was not "created" but that "arose" out of persecution and an ages-old longing to return to Judaism's historical Homeland. He insisted that the Jewish state would arise, although he realized, he said, that he might not ever see it. The interrogator assured him on that point. "No," he said, "you won't ever see it."

As before, the interrogation lasted many hours, again ending at daybreak. This time, however, no minutes were recorded, and on his way back to his cell, Begin felt as though he had been attending a conference and was now returning to his hotel room. Elated at how well he had defended Zionism, he practically ran back to his quarters. On his way, he asked a puzzled duty officer whether any messages had come for Menahem Begin during his absence.

Begin got no sleep. The reveille whistle sounded only minutes after the iron door of his cell closed behind him.

There was no "interpreter" at the next interrogation that evening. Now the officer accused Begin and his Zionists of wanting "to deprive the Arab farmers of their land." Begin explained there was room enough in geographic Palestine—the Palestine of the original British Mandate—for its Arab population *and* for millions of Jews. The officer then charged Zionists with being "agents of British imperialism." To this, Begin replied with a question of his own.

"If we Zionists are British agents," he asked, "why don't the British let us into Palestine . . . . Why did they say in their latest White Paper (1939) that, in a few years' time, they will not let one more Jew enter Palestine? If we were indeed serving British interests, the logical thing would be for Britain to help us, not hinder us . . . . The fact of the matter is that before the war we had to break through the British blockade to bring people to the shores of Palestine, as Garibaldi did in his time in Italy."

The interrogator objected to Begin's comparison with Garibaldi, "a true fighter for freedom." It was the first time that Begin had ever heard Garibaldi praised by a Communist. He was astonished to learn that the quintessentially democratic Garibaldi was considered a hero in the Soviet Union.

The interrogation continued, night after night, often without a break. Begin realized the "conversations" were really interrogations and that he was condemned *a priori* to disappear. But he never hesitated to argue points of law with his captors, or to call them to order whenever they used abusive language. When an interrogator cursed him, Begin reminded him that swearing was forbidden by law in the Soviet Union, and the astounded inquisitor desisted. On another occasion, Begin demanded to know how the Russians could hold him responsible for alleged crimes committed not in the Soviet Union but in Poland *before* the Red Army had occupied it. The interrogator smiled. Did Begin know under what section he was accused? Begin did not.

"You are charged," the official said, "under Section 58 of the Criminal Law of the Soviet Socialist Russian Republic . . ."

"But how can you apply it to what I did in Poland?" Begin asked.

"Ach!" snorted the inquisitor. "You are a strange fellow, Menahem Begin. Section 58 applies to everyone in the world. Do you hear? *In the whole world*. It is only a question of when (the criminal) will get to us, or we to him."

At yet another session, Begin was told that a visitor was joining the interrogation. For several terrified hours, Begin feared his wife had been arrested and had been summoned to a confrontation, a common tactic of Soviet police methods. But the visitor turned out to be Dr. Jacob Shechter, one of the leaders of the Revisionist Party in Cracow. The police simply wanted to know who had authorized the exit visas for Palestine that both Begin and Shechter held. Each replied he had authorized his own and nothing came of the crude attempt to have the two men hurl accusations at each other.

At what proved to be the final interrogation, Begin was asked to sign a statement declaring: "I confess that I am guilty of having been the chairman of the Betar organization in Poland, of being responsible for the work of Betar and of calling upon the Jewish Youth to join the ranks of Betar."

Begin refused to sign. Throughout an entire night he fought to persuade his inquisitor to substitute the word "confess" with the word "admit" and to strike out "guilty." In the end, the exhausted interrogator made the changes Begin demanded. The prisoner signed the revised statement and was returned to his cell.

The interrogations were over at last. In *White Nights* Begin was careful to underscore the fact that he was never physically maltreated, never tortured or beaten. The NKVD's weapons were thirst, hunger, isolation, and, above all, sleeplessness. Deprived of sleep long enough, a man will sign anything, and many did, signing away their lives with admissions of guilt for crimes they probably had not committed.

Although the interrogations bordered on cruelty, they had kept Begin busy mentally, a lawyer matching wits with his lawyer-interrogators, arguing political philosophy, history, even the finer points of Soviet jurisprudence. When they ceased, Begin knew he faced an uncertain future and became somewhat depressed. He seriously considered drafting a bill of divorcement that would have enabled his young wife to remarry— she was only twenty at the time, eight years his junior—in the event the NKVD really meant for him to "disappear."

Begin discussed the matter with his cellmates, both bachelors. "If my own future is doubtful," Begin said, "why should I destroy the future of my wife who would be hoping for my return—in vain?" The major agreed Begin should draft a divorce, but only to relieve his mind. "I am sure," the older man said, "your wife will not accept your 'gift' and that someday the two of you will laugh together about this 'divorce.' " Begin decided to draw up a paper granting Aliza a divorce if he had not returned to her within five years. However, unable to obtain pen and ink from his warders, the document was never actually drafted.

One day was indistinguishable from another in Lukishki Prison, but Begin and his cellmates knew the New Year 1941 was approaching and decided to "celebrate" its arrival. On the last day of 1940 they were given the same aqueous coffee and stale bread in the morning, the same thin soup at midday, the same watery gruel in the evening. By the exercise of considerable willpower, each saved half his morning "coffee" to drink a toast at midnight.

A few days later, a warder ordered Begin to gather up his belongings; he was being moved. Where? Begin wasn't told. All he heard was the shouts of the prison guards, *"Davai! Paskareya!—Hurry! Hurry up!"* He made a bundle of his clothing, his precious toothbrush, bowl, mug and spoon, embraced his cellmates and left. He never saw them again.

Begin spent the next two months in a communal cell. Built to accommodate sixteen inmates, it held nearly sixty. With few exceptions, all were "political" prisoners, and among them the newcomer found three Jews. Two—Mordecai Bernstein and a Dr. Lifshitz—were high-ranking members of a Socialist anti-Zionist Jewish organization known as The Bund. The third was a common thief. With Bernstein, Begin struck up a friendship and held long conversations in Hebrew, disagreeing about everything, especially Zionism.

Between them, Begin and Bernstein organized lecture courses in history, languages, political science and other subjects, but one of the most interesting was a "course" given by an uneducated beekeeper about—bees! A favorite pastime was chess, played with chessmen moulded from hoarded bits of bread.

One afternoon, Begin was amusing a group of fellow inmates with Yiddish jokes. One story was about a nitwit. A Jewish warder overheard him, mistakenly assumed Begin was referring to him personally and reported the "insult" to the prison superintendent. Begin was arbitrarily sentenced to seven days solitary confinement, where he learned there was a worse place than an ordinary prison cell. In his dark, windowless cage, the heat was stifling by day, the cold unbearable by night. He had no blanket and no "pail," and he slept on a fouled cement floor, his head pillowed on a bony arm, fighting off the rats when they became too "friendly."

"Man's imagination," he would write later, "did not invent degrees in Paradise. It did create them in Hell. Happiness is indivisible, suffering is graded. When I returned . . . to my cell, I was the happiest prisoner in the world."

Shortly after Begin's sojourn in solitary, he and his cellmates went on a hunger strike. For weeks their diet had consisted entirely of *kasha,* a gritty gruel served twice daily. Although already verging on starvation, the mere sight of the *kasha* sickened the prisoners. Refusing it, they subsisted entirely on the morning "coffee" and bread. When it seemed they could hold out no longer, they were given a soup made of rotting cabbage leaves. The men considered this a great victory. Thereafter it was cabbage soup twice a week and five times weekly—*kasha.*

On March 31, 1941, the prison "telegraph"—messages tapped out in Morse code on the water pipes—carried important news: the sentences which the prisoners were to serve. The "telegraphers" in a distant wing were asked by their "correspondents" in Begin's cell: "When did the trials take place?" Back came the reply: "No trials—just sentences," which ranged from five to eight years for each prisoner. The information turned out to be painfully accurate.

Next day, April 1, Begin and his companions were marched down a long corridor to a table behind which sat two men. Each in turn stated his name and was handed a slip of paper to sign. It said: "The special Advisory Commission to the People's Commissariat for Internal Affairs finds that Menahem Begin is an element dangerous to society, and orders that he be imprisoned in a Correctional Labor Camp for a period of eight years." April Fool's day prank? Not at all. Begin read his slip and signed as ordered.

Soviet "justice" had done its work. There was no appeal from the sentence, just as there had been no trial, no judge, no witnesses, no attorney, no defense. Eight years at hard labor in Siberia. More than ever Begin wished he had somehow managed to send his beloved Aliza a "bill of divorcement," for surely he would not survive eight years in the frozen north. His week in solitary had weakened him considerably, and on prison fare he had not regained his strength.

The prisoners knew they were going to a cold place somewhere when each was allowed to receive parcels of warm clothing from friends and relatives. Begin's parcel contained a handkerchief embroidered with the Latin letters O-L-A. He was puzzled. Why not ALA, his wife's nickname? Bernstein solved the mystery. He explained the letters as a Hebrew feminine contraction of "Aliyah," meaning "going to settle in Palestine." Whether the shrewd Bernstein knew what he was talking about, was merely trying to assuage Begin's anxiety, or simply guessing, was not clear. It happened, however, that he was right. Aliza was in fact on her way to Palestine, friends having persuaded her she could be of more help to her husband there than waiting in Vilna. It was, Begin would recall, his "best day in prison."

During the next few days, some prisoners were moved out to Begin's cell, others took their place. Among the new arrivals was an old friend of Begin's from Betar days, Meir Sheshkin. Together, they "celebrated" Passover, the most beloved of all Jewish holy days.

In its most meaningful sense, Passover represents a cherished traditional value—a love of freedom. In the religious literature of the Jews, the festival is referred to pridefully as "the Season of Our Freedom."

The memory of the Bondage in Egypt, although it occurred some thirty-two centuries ago, has continued to rankle in the macerated consciousness of the Jewish people. In reality, the Jew has never considered—except for the Golden Age of his people's greatness in the Land of Israel—that the bondage ever ended. This idea is touchingly projected in the Aramaic prayer at the Seder—the home-service that opens the celebration of Passover—which states the theme of the holy day like the opening chorus in a Greek tragedy. The head of the household, robed in his white *kittel* and skullcap and acting the role of celebrant-priest, gravely raises his tray with the ceremonial matzoh, shows it to the assembled company and intones in the minor key of well-remembered sorrow: "Behold! This is as the bread of affliction that our fathers ate in the land of Egypt . . . Now we are here—may we be next year in the land of Israel! Now we are slaves—may we be free men in the year to come!"

For Begin and Sheshkin and the few Jews remaining in their cell, the "bread of affliction" was the stale crust saved from "breakfast" and the ceremonial wine was NKVD "coffee." But very real indeed were the "bondage" and the "affliction," and quite probably no men anywhere at that particular moment uttered more prayerfully the words . . . "may we next year be in Jerusalem!"

It was spring outside now, and the crowded communal cell was stiflingly hot. Sometime in May, the prisoners were told they would be leaving soon and would be allowed a farewell visit by *one* relative. Begin submitted Aliza's name. Always long, the days of waiting for the promised visit became interminable. But at last Begin's turn to be called came. The visitor had arrived.

A long room, crowded, noisy and smelly. Prisoners on one side, visitors on the other, behind a stout wire grille. Begin's visitor was not Aliza, of course, but someone who resembled her, was of approximately the same age, and who, at great personal risk, was impersonating her. She was Paula Daiches, whom Begin knew in Vilna as a member of Betar. They spoke rapidly in Polish.

"Everything is all right," Paula assured him quickly. "Aunt Ala is with Uncle Shimshon." Begin understood. "Uncle Shimshon" was Dr. Shimshon Yunichtman, head of Betar *in Palestine*. "I've already had a letter from her," Paula said, adding that his *brothers,* were in good health. Begin had only one brother, Herzl, and correctly translated the plural of brother to mean his colleagues in Betar. So, they too were safe.

"I've also brought you regards," said Paula, "from Aunt *Iggeret-besabon,*" Hebrew meaning "note in soap." They tried to continue in Hebrew, but were cut short by an eavesdropping guard who ordered them to speak only Russian or Polish. Begin told Paula to write "Aunt Ala" that he was proud of her, that he was "strong and healthy," and not to worry. He would be back . . .

Paula had brought a parcel. The warder who inspected it found food, personal linens and a bar of soap. He confiscated the food, causing Paula to burst into tears, but allowed Begin to keep the linen—several collar-attached shirts, fur-lined gloves, underwear and handkerchiefs—and handed him the soap in two pieces. The warder had cut it into halves, but had not found what he was looking for.

Paula and Begin said their goodbyes. They would never meet again.

In prison, soap is a precious commodity, so it was with the care of a surgeon that a cellmate "operated" on Begin's two pieces in search of the hidden note. For a scalpel, the prisoner used the sharpened edge of a spoon, making three cuts, layer by layer. He found the tightly rolled message in an outer layer, the warder having missed it by cutting the soap in half. The note merely confirmed what Paula had told Begin, adding only that friends in Palestine and in America were working for his release with "good prospects" that they would succeed. Begin's spirits rose considerably.

One day early in June, Lukishki's prisoners, numbering about two thousand, were herded into the prison's central courtyard. There they were counted, divided into groups, searched, made to strip and—searched again. Begin would remember the scene as resembling a "slave market," which, of course, was what it was. Beria's NKVD was recruiting slaves for his labor camps.

On command, the prisoners put on their clothes, and gathered up their belongings. In groups of fifteen, they were packed into prison vans. They knew they were headed for Siberia, but Begin recalls that a Jew in his vehicle whispered: "The journey has begun—to *Eretz Yisrael.*" He was right, but the route lay through a hell named Pechora.

NOTES

1. Menahem Begin, *White Nights,* Steimatzsky, Ltd., Jerusalem, 1977. *White Nights* was written seventeen years after his arrest by the NKVD. It is the story, in infinite detail, of his incarceration in Lukishki prison, his experiences in the Pechora "correctional camp" and his ultimate release in the summer of 1941. Nature must have endowed Begin with a phenomenal memory, for in *White Nights,* he reproduces entire conversations with NKVD interrogators and warders as well as fellow prisoners. Since the cruel conditions of his long confinement make it highly unlikely that he was able to keep any sort of a diary, Begin must have reconstructed his story entirely from memory. First published in 1957, and reissued twenty years later when Begin became Prime Minister, *White Nights* is a remarkable tale written in the author's discursive style. It is well worth reading today, not only as the personal history of a particularly harrowing period in his life, but as evidence of the excessive cruelty of Stalinism at its worst.

2. Paula Daiches remained in Vilna and died fighting in the Jewish underground when the Germans came in that summer, 1941.

Chapter 8

Through Hell To Freedom: Part Two

A train composed of wooden boxcars awaited the prisoners at a remote freight yard siding in the vicinity of Vilna's railroad station. It was guarded by uniformed NKVD troops—Lavrenti Beria's equivalent of Hitler's SS—with bayonets in their rifles and snarling police dogs on long leashes.

The cars were of the kind normally used to transport "forty men *or* eight horses." Into each wagon the guards loaded seventy prisoners. Inside, the men found double tiers of bunks made of rough planking, a small barred window at either end for "ventilation" and a communal toilet—a central hole in the flooring, large enough for its intended function, but too small for escape.

As each of the mobile prisons was fully loaded, its sliding doors were slammed home and bolted from the outside, but even after the loading was completed the train did not move. It remained in the yard for hours.

The congestion was unbearable and the heat soon became almost intolerable. The prisoners gasped for air and banged on the wooden walls begging the guards to open the doors, but there was no response. What they could not cure, the men endured and eventually found relief in the sleep of exhaustion.

When the prisoners awakened, the train was moving, headed for Siberia. They traveled for many days and nights, exactly how many Menahem Begin later could not recall, but he would remember vividly the terrible thirst, the hunger, the stench, the nausea induced by the crazy swaying of the overloaded cars and the sickening sounds that accompanied it.

The train stopped every morning and evening to enable the guards who traveled in the caboose to make body counts. The counters touched each man, and if the count did not tally, it was repeated over and over again until it did.

At the morning stops, the prisoners were given their allotment of food for the day: black bread, salted dried fish and cloudy water from a communal drinking pail. In the circumstances, the water was never enough and the prisoners cried out for more. Once, during a halt in a swamp, they were given the slimy green stuff from wayside puddles alive with frogs and slithery creatures.

In the course of their journey, Begin became aware of trains moving in the opposite direction loaded with troops and military equipment. Begin could see them through slits and knotholes in his car's walls. What was happening? The guards at the various stops either did not know or were under orders not to impart any information.

The men now craved news almost as much as they craved clean water. Eventually, they learned via "prison telegraph" the reason for the southward movement of soldiers and weapons: Hitler's Germany had attacked its "friend" Stalin's Russia.

Begin's car, in which he was the only Jew, was filled with Poles and Lithuanians in approximately equal numbers. When word came some days later that Vilna had fallen, the Lithuanians rejoiced at the setback to their ancient enemies, the Poles. The latter mourned, for they knew now their country was lost, perhaps forever. Begin himself, was merely grateful that Aliza and his friends had escaped.

Day telescoped into night and into day in one interminable nightmare of thirst, hunger and retching. Soon there were no more nights, for they had penetrated deep into northern Russia where the nights are indistinguishable from the days, hence the title *White Nights* of Begin's subsequent memoir.

The train finally reached its destination, and the men were ordered out of their mobile prisons. They found themselves standing in an open field surrounded by swampland and low-lying scrub vegetation. They were in the Taiga, the northern tundra, in the vicinity of Koshva, a concentration camp operated by the NKVD. It was not exactly a health resort.

During a short rest in the field, Begin met three Jewish friends, Sheshkin, Kroll and Shechter. Then a whistle sounded. The men were formed up into fours in marching order, told they were going to a transit camp, and warned to keep strictly in line. One step to the right or left would be taken as an attempt to escape, and the guards were entitled to shoot without warning.

It was a long way to the camp, over a narrow muddy route, sometimes across bridges merely the width of a wooden plank, and it was not always possible to stay in line. Marchers obliged to break ranks, had to shout back to the guards for permission to "diverge to the right . . . or left."

From time to time Begin looked behind him down row on row of "candidates for re-education," thousands of them bent under their bundles, moving on legs rendered unsteady by weakness and disuse, a pitiful parade of doctors, engineers, lawyers, professors, laborers, judges, army officers and common thieves, flanked on both sides by soldiers with bayoneted rifles and growling dogs. At a brief rest stop, a sadistic NKVD guard gratuitously informed Begin that none of them would ever "get out of here."

The prisoners slogged through the mud for hours before they reached the barbed wire fence that enclosed the camp, a huge area of barrackslike hutments with watchtowers at the corners. Inside the gates, the prisoners were divided into groups of one hundred. Sheshkin and Kroll were included in Begin's lot, but Shechter was sent elsewhere.

After stripping, each man had a bucketful of tepid water thrown over him for a shower. Then, all were given a thick hot soup, the first decent food they had had in many weeks, and that night they slept in the tiered bunks of the camp's many long wooden "dormitories."

Next morning, the prisoners were summoned to the central office in small groups to be registered. Begin was told he would be released on September 20, 1948, eight years from the day he was arrested, not from the date of sentencing.

"What were you convicted of?" he was asked.

"I don't know exactly," Begin replied. "The Judge-Interrogator told me that I was being charged under Section 58." The man behind the desk fidgeted. "What did they say when they sentenced you?" he asked.

"They said: *'sozialno-opasni element'*—element dangerous to society," Begin replied.

On an index card, the man wrote the letters "S.O.E.," and as he handed it to Begin for his signature, he whispered: "Never say Section 58. Say what was in the sentence—S.O.E."

It was sound advice. Section 58 covered a multitude of crimes far worse than the one with which Begin had been charged, including treason and sabotage, which were punishable by death or its equivalent—permanent exile to a Siberian labor camp.

A few days later, the prisoners again marched for many hours, this time to the bank of the Pechora river where they were loaded on barges and ferried to Pechor-Lag, the Pechora labor camp.

At the camp, Begin, Sheshkin and Kroll went for their first medical examination. A member of the office staff, a thieving veteran prisoner, took their temperatures, and asked the three if they had "shirts with collars" to barter for a favor. For nine shirts, three from each, the man would certify them for transfer to the camp hospital for "further examination." There, he hinted, they would sleep in proper beds and receive decent food.

Begin's friends actually did have slight fevers, but he didn't. Nevertheless, not wishing to be separated from them, he contributed his "three shirts with collars" to make up the total the blackmailer had demanded. At the hospital, Begin developed a temperature, and remained for nearly a fortnight. "But in that time," he wrote later, "I learned more about the Soviet Union than it is possible to learn in years from . . . books."

The "hospital" turned out to be a wooden hut half buried in the ground as protection against the severe weather in an area where the winters are nine months long and where most of the time the thermometer hovers at 75 degrees below zero. The bathhouse, which the patients used—going and coming in their underwear and wrapped in a thin blanket— was located nearly half a mile away. "You'll get used to it," Begin was told, "and if you don't you die."

Begin's first night was neither white with the northern lights nor black with the shuttered hospital hut's darkness, but red with the blood of innumerable bedbug bites. The veterans, accustomed to the vermin, slept soundly. He didn't. He lay awake all night, listening to the others' snores, and killing bugs—when he could find them.

During his hospitalization, a fellow prisoner in an adjoining bed asked Begin, "Are you not the head of Betar in Poland?" Begin wondered how the man had recognized him. "By the name on your knapsack," the man replied, and identified himself as Marmelstein, a fellow-member of Betar.

Tears welled in Marmelstein's eyes as he recounted the horrors of life in a Soviet labor camp. He warned Begin not to try to escape, for in the tundra, in summer time, he would encounter a species of flies whose bite was infinitely worse than that of mosquitoes. Escapees never returned; they died from hunger, thirst and exposure, or were captured. One who came back voluntarily looked more beast than man, barely recognizable as human after being nearly eaten alive by the flies.

Marmelstein also cautioned Begin against an apparently incurable disease they called *tsinga*, which many contracted. It caused a man's body to break out all over in pus-filled sores and his teeth to loosen in their sockets and drop out. Prisoners ailing with *tsinga* were given an ineffective ointment as treatment, but were not hospitalized or excused from work. Finally, there was *panos*, an intestinal disorder that produced almost constant diarrhea. It exempted the prisoners from work only when blood appeared in their stools.

During his stay in Pechor-Lag, Begin met scores of men in the last stages of *tsinga* and *panos*. There were also many so-called *chleno-rubi*, prisoners who purposely crippled themselves to escape work; they would chop off fingers with an axe merely for a chance to be hospitalized and get some sleep, a few days' relief from work in the bitter cold of the Arctic winters. But it was a losing game. Each self-inflicted wound added a month to the prisoner's term "for sabotaging State property!"

While still a "patient" in the Pechor-Lag "hospital" Begin's education in the inner workings of the Soviet political system was furthered by a fellow inmate named Garin. He was an anti-Zionist Jew who, until his arrest some years back, had been an associate editor of *Pravda*. He told his life story to Begin who related it in his *White Nights*. Briefly, Garin's account went somewhat as follows:

A Bolshevik at the age of seventeen, he fought in the Red Army of the Revolution, rose quickly in party ranks to General Secretary in the Ukraine and was rewarded for his loyalty with an assistant editorship on the staff of the prestigious Moscow daily. His wife was also highly regarded in the party and held an important position in one of the ministries. The Garins lived happily in the Soviet paradise until 1937 when, for no ascertainable reason, Mrs. Garin was arrested. Knowing herself to be innocent of any wrong-doing, she wrote a letter to Stalin. Amazingly, he received it and, even more surprisingly, he ordered her release and immediate reinstatement.

A few months later, however, she was re-arrested. It was the time of the "treason trials" of 1936-1938, when Stalin was purging the party of Trotskyites. Garin was also arrested, and charged with Trotskyism, a crime tantamount to treason. He had written numerous articles in *Pravda* attacking Trotsky and his "theory of permanent revolution," but at his "trial" his essays were used as evidence that he was merely "camouflaging" his Trotskyite activities.

"I tell you," Begin quoted Garin as saying, "that in 1937, they went stark crazy. The center of gravity in the leadership shifted from the party to the NKVD."

Garin's interrogation, during which he attempted suicide several times, lasted four years. Often severely beaten by his interrogators, Garin developed a heart condition, but this did not prevent him from being sentenced to eight years at hard labor and he wound up in Pechor-Lag.

Released from the "hospital," Begin joined his fellow prisoners in the work gangs, a motley of Slavic nationalities—Russians, Poles, Lithuanians, Latvians, Estonians and Romanians from Bessarabia with a sprinkling of Jews. The prisoners were divided "vertically" into two groups: the politicals and the criminals—in NKVD language, the SOEs were the element dangerous to society and the SVE *(sotzialno vredni element)*, the "element harmful to society," the criminals, known in camp argot as Urki. The politicals were at the mercy of the criminals, who were given all managerial posts and derived satisfaction from humiliating their social and intellectual betters.

Early one morning, Begin was marched with the others to a hillock overlooking the Pechora river where the Camp Superintendent made a patriotic speech. "Remember," he declared, "that you are working for the Soviet mother-country . . . You are far from the front, and you must be grateful to those who are defending you from the German cannibals," adding that it was their "duty" to help the home front. "Today a spade," he concluded, "tomorrow you may be wielding a rifle!" There were loud "Hurrahs!" but only from the *Urki*.

Behind the speaker, a band was assembled, brass instruments gleaming in the feeble sunlight. It struck up a rousing marching tune to which the prisoners quick-marched down the slope to the river bank where a barge loaded with steel railroad sleepers had docked. The prisoners' job was to unload the barge of the steel ties that were to be used to construct a segment of the Kotlas-Varkuta railway. The minimum quota for each prisoner was two sleepers per trip up the muddy slope from the barge to waiting trucks.

The sleepers were carried across the shoulders. After a few hours, the upper part of Begin's rather bony back was scraped raw, and he padded it with rags provided by older fellow prisoners during the break for their midday meal: a bowlful of soup made from the heads and tails of river fish. In the afternoon, the men worked without music. The band left at noon and never returned. Fourteen hours after reveille, the prisoners were marched back to camp. They had actually worked twelve hours; the remaining two hours were spent marching to and from their labors, eating their "lunch," smoking coarse tobacco rolled in newsprint and being counted. Supper that night was more fish soup, the taste of which made Begin and his fellow prisoners from Lukishki "homesick for the gruel that once revolted us." While he slept, an *Urki* stole most of Begin's belongings.

Day after day the men hauled iron and steel from the barge, first the sleepers, which were deck cargo, then the rails from the barge's hold. The rail-hauling was the hardest work of all, and was done collectively, by gangs of twelve men, six on each side, who dragged the rails up the slippery slope to the trucks with steel cables. The *Urki* overseers cursed when the men slid and fell. One became particularly abusive to Garin. Day in, day out the man who had been an assistant editor of *Pravda* heard himself called a dirty *zhid*, the Russian equivalent of such English pejoratives as "yid" and "kike." Garin said nothing. He was running a fever and was almost too weak to stand.

There was no doctor in the camp, only a *lek-pom*, an orderly who took temperatures, dealt out aspirin for headaches and could distinguish serious *panos* (with blood) and simple *panos*, without it. *Lek-poms* were themselves prisoners who lived in fear of having their sentences lengthened for showing mercy, thereby laying themselves open to charges of sabotage or treason. They were understandably disinclined to allow sick prisoners time off from work for a slight fever.

After a sleepless, fevered night, Begin and Garin went together to their *lek-pom* to have their temperatures checked. Garin's thermometer registered a mere 100; he was sent back to work. Begin was found to have a 103-degree fever and was allowed three days' rest. "For three days," he would recall, "I lay on my lice-infested bunk, burning . . ." On the fourth day, pronounced fit for duty, he rejoined his group on the muddy river bank, wondering how long a human being could endure such treatment and go on living.

Poor medical care, however, was less a problem for the prisoners than constant, gnawing hunger, which defied comparison with what they had experienced in Lukishki. There, they sat in cells, hungry, but sheltered from the elements and physically more or less inactive. In Pechor-Lag they worked fourteen to sixteen hours daily in the open, in fair weather or foul, attacked by swarms of flies and mosquitoes while performing back-breaking labor. The men became, in Begin's words, "animals walking on two legs . . ."

To squeeze out of the prisoners the last possible erg of human energy, the NKVD invented a quota system to determine the *katiol*, the daily food ration, including bread. Prisoners delivering less than 30 percent of their work quota, received only 200 grams of bread and a bowl of soup once daily; those meeting 60 percent of their quota got 400 grams of bread and soup twice a day; fulfillment of from 60 to 80 percent meant 500 grams of bread, a better soup with cereal, dried potatoes and an occasional biscuit. Workers who exceeded their quotas were served a "banquet": up to 900 grams of bread and good rich soups, a ration Begin never tasted, although apparently he did manage to qualify for at least 400 grams of bread. He must have, or he would not have survived the rigors of Pechor-Lag. A will to survive alone could not have ensured his survival.

The prisoners' daily performances were registered on tally sheets to determine the amount of food they would receive. The "norms" set by the NKVD were utterly unrealistic, and to avoid starving to death, the prisoners resorted to *blat,* meaning bribery, to have their percentages raised. In return for higher percentages, the guards accepted whatever the prisoners had to offer: money, articles of clothing, spare tobacco, anything. There is no evidence in *White Nights*, however, that Begin resorted to *blat.*

*   *   *

Then came rumors of a forthcoming *etap*, the camp word for transfer to another place, but it had evil connotations. Marmelstein had instructed him about *etap*. His friend, Begin recalled, had warned him that the transfers were made by long overland marches in unreliable trucks, on foot or in ships, and that often more men died enroute than reached their destination, especially in winter in freezing winds with thermometer readings of 100 degrees below zero. However, days passed and no *etap*.

One morning, the sentry who escorted Begin's group to work turned to him and asked: "Are you a Pollak?" Begin answered that he was "a Jew, but a Polish citizen." The soldier shrugged off the rebuke, and volunteered important information: "All the Pollaks are being set free." At this, Begin went "weak in the knees" and wanted to know the source of the sentry's information. The soldier assured him it was true; he had heard the news on the camp's radio at headquarters in a broadcast from Moscow which, the man reminded him, always reported only the truth.

The news spread with electric speed throughout the camp but the Poles, fearing a trap, refrained from asking the Camp Commandant for confirmation. They went on hauling iron as before, until one day they were summoned to a meeting at which a Russian government official confirmed that the Soviet Union and the Polish Government in Exile had signed an agreement freeing all Poles held in Russian prisons and/or labor camps.

At the meeting, the Poles were told that final instructions had not yet been received, and that until further orders the prisoners were to continue working as before. In fact, they were exhorted to work even harder now that Poland and the Soviet Union were allies against "the German cannibals." Meanwhile, rumors of an impending *etap* continued to circulate, and fears grew among the Poles that instead of being amnestied they would be sent farther north and to certain death in the approaching winter.

Begin was talked into acting as the Poles' spokesman to ascertain whether the rumors about a transfer were correct. The Camp Commandant assured him that the reports were true, because there was no longer enough work for the men at Pechor-Lag. *Etap* was unavoidable. He promised, however, that he would release all Poles the moment he received official word to do so. His friend Kroll was sure Begin had seriously hurt his chances of being released by having agreed to represent the Polish contingent.

Finally, after weeks of tension, Pechor-Lag's living dead were given cursory medical examinations, counted over and over again and marched down to the river bank to a ship. But the vessel was not ready for boarding. The men lay on the damp ground for three days and two nights, subsisting on reduced rations of bread and water. After all, they weren't working! On the third night, they were brought back to empty huts, and they slept in bunks that by contrast to the hard ground seemed like comfortable beds. But during the night, all of Begin's belongings were stolen. He had tied them in a bundle to his wrist; when he awakened, he found only a bit of string dangling from it. An *Urki* had left Begin with only the clothes he stood in.

At daybreak the next day, the prisoners, numbering about eight hundred, mostly *Urki*, were escorted aboard the vessel. Compared to the ship's hold, Begin wrote, "the solitary confinement cell at Lukishki was a (health) resort." The men were crowded into three tiers of bunks built along the dank walls of the hull. Below deck, it was impossible to sit, stand or move. The men could only lie quietly in eternal darkness.

The ship sailed northwards for three weeks. Drinking only river water, nearly all the prisoners suffered from severe *panos* and spent most of the time lining up on the main deck to use the two available "heads." The hold itself became a communal dungeon in which the *Urki* terrorized the "politicals." Begin saw his fur-lined gloves being gambled away by one *Urki*, but prudently said nothing.

One of the *Urki*'s other victims was Garin, who was certain the criminals meant to kill him. They had stolen all his money, but they wouldn't believe him when he told them he had no more. He kept close to Begin day and night, trembling with fear, and at one point asked Begin, in Yiddish, to sing for him a song he remembered from childhood, the "Lashuv song," as he called it, "the song the Zionists sang in Odessa about Eretz Israel."

Begin understood that Garin meant the *Hatikva* and sang it for him, the other six or seven Jews in the ship's foul hold joining in: "Lashuv Le 'eretz avot Israel . . . To return to the land of our fathers . . ."

On arrival at its destination upriver, the vessel lay at anchor for several days. Then, one day, a sentry shouted down into the hold: "Be—gin!" The *Urki* who stood alongside the hatchway took up the shout: "Be—gin!"

"Here I am," Begin shouted back.

"Name and father's name?"

Begin responded as ordered.

"Correct," the sentry said, and called other names alphabetically.

"All those whose names I have called, collect your belongings. An order has come to release the Poles. You are going free."

Begin said goodbye to Garin and dashed for the hatchway. He had no belongings. An *Urki*, quite probably the one who had stolen them, tried to stop him, shouting, "He's a *zhid*, not a Pollak."

On deck there were a few other Jews and some Poles, not many. All were transferred by boat to a concentration camp where they were released.

Begin wandered through Russia for several months. He traversed the vast area between the Barends Sea to the shores of the Caspian, passing through large cities, small towns and out-of-the-way villages. He slept in railway stations, in public parks and in people's backyards. In his wanderings, he covered hundreds of miles standing on the steps of railway coaches, clinging to the door handles or to some other Polish wanderer who, like himself, had no money for train tickets.

Begin was looking for a recruiting station for the Polish Army which he had been told was being formed on Russian soil in accordance with the Sikorski-Stalin agreement. He was also looking for his sister Rachel and her husband, both of whom had been deported before he himself was arrested in Vilna.

Pure chance led Begin to his sister and brother-in-law. Dozing late one night in a squalid railway station with a number of other penniless wanderers waiting for a free ride on a train, he overheard a woman mention the name Halperin. Instantly awake, he questioned her. Was this Halperin she was talking about a lawyer? Yes, he was. From Warsaw, perhaps? Yes. And was the name of the lawyer's wife Rachel? It was.

With the stranger's help, Begin found his sister in a Tartar shack in the small Uzbekian town of Dzhizak, between Tashkent and Samarkand. He settled in with Rachel and her husband for some time, regaining his strength, and trying in vain to obtain a Soviet exit visa for Palestine. Discouraged, he thought he would try his luck in Margilan, the second oldest city in the Fergana Valley, where a Polish Army division was stationed. There, he believed, he might meet helpful friends. And he did.

In Margilan, Begin found his friend Sheskin. He had joined the Polish Army, was serving in the Supply Corps at Divisional Headquarters and apparently had established a cordial rapport with highly placed members of the General Staff. But Sheskin couldn't help Begin obtain a Soviet exit visa, and between them decided to consult a mutual friend, Dr. Yohanan Bader, about what to do. Begin had received word from his sister that an "unknown person" was looking for him, which he interpreted to mean the police were looking for him. Zionists were not popular in the Soviet Union, and Begin was now anxious to quit Russia by whatever means possible.

Dr. Bader, himself a Betar leader and leading Revisionist, lived hundreds of miles away in Mari, the capital of Turkomen, but made the long journey to Margilan to talk with Begin, when he received word from Sheskin that his advice was needed. Dr. Bader told Begin it had become impossible for Jews to obtain exit permits for Palestine and advised him to make every effort to join the Polish Army which was destined for service in the endangered Middle East.

Begin did as Dr. Bader suggested and presented himself to the Divisional Draft Board. The examining physician turned him down: bad heart, weak lungs, poor vision. "The doctor," said Begin later, "almost succeeded in frightening me."

In view of the disturbing news he had received from his sister, Begin decided to try again by applying directly, in a personal letter to the Chief of Staff stating that if the army didn't accept him he might be re-arrested. Sheskin saw to it that the letter actually reached the Chief of Staff, who subsequently summoned Begin and ordered him to report to the Draft Board. Begin told him he had already done so and had been turned down. "Never mind," the officer said. "This time, there will be a letter from me. Go again."

The promised letter arrived at the Draft Board and the examining doctor, the same one who had flunked him before, declared Begin fit for military service. A few days later, Menahem Begin was inducted as a private in the Free Polish Army of General Wladyslaw Anders. He was undoubtedly the most unsoldierly looking soldier in the entire outfit, thin to the point of scrawniness and wearing thick eyeglasses. A few weeks later, the army left Russia for the Middle East.

NOTES

1. The amnesty was the result of a pact negotiated with Stalin by General Wladyslaw Sikorski, Prime Minister of the Polish government in Exile. The accord was signed in 1941, shortly after the German invasion of the Soviet Union. Among other things, it provided for the formation of a Polish Allied Army. Stalin broke off Soviet-Polish diplomatic relations in 1943, following Sikorski's request that the International Red Cross be permitted to investigate the murder at Katyn of thousands of Polish officers previously in Russian hands. The same year, on July 4, Sikorski was killed in an air crash over Gibraltar.

Book Four:

Palestine 1942–1948

Chapter 9

The Irgun Finds a Commander

Enroute to Palestine, the vanguard of General Anders' army of 80,000 Polish refugees and deportees, riding rickety lorries supplied by the Russians and the British, traversed Persia and Iraq and entered Transjordan. On arrival there, Menahem Begin was elated. To him, as to all Zionists who shared Jabotinsky's vision of the future Jewish state, the barren land he was crossing was an integral part of the Eretz Israel of his dreams—dreams that had helped sustain him during his long ordeal of imprisonment and the Soviet Union's labor camps. He saw the country's "broad, neglected, unpopulated fields" and realized why the Romans had called that part of ancient Palestine *Palestina Salutaris*. In their time it had been the granary of the Roman Empire, the source of much of its corn and wheat.

"And here was Transjordan," he would write years later,[1] "Our heritage. . . . Now, despite neglect, bursting forth from underneath the stones covering the infinite fields, there is grass, green, tall and pleasant. The region is almost entirely empty. Here and there, in the wide expanse, you see a Bedouin hovel, or a camel. Only as you approach the Jordan itself do you see a few people and fields of welcome corn. The eastern bank of the Jordan—Eretz Israel. The military convoy stopped. We rested. I . . . waded a little way into the grass, and drank in the odor of the fields of my Homeland."

There at Mafrak, in Transjordan, where Anders' army of Free Poles made camp before pushing on into Palestine—or what remained of it after the British had arbitrarily truncated it by creating Transjordan in 1922—

141

Begin received distressing news. From a Jewish soldier serving in the area with His Britannic Majesty's forces, Begin learned that the commander of the Irgun Zvai Leumi, the almost legendary David Raziel, had been killed the year before in Iraq while helping the British suppress an Arab pro-Nazi rebellion led by Rashid Ali el-Khilani. The IZL, he was told, was in total disarray and held together only by the faith of a few remaining followers.

The news depressed Begin. He had met Raziel in Poland several times when the Irgun's leader had visited the Polish training camp for battalion commanders at Zielonka and had been greatly impressed. Broad-shouldered, of medium height, soft-spoken but a stern disciplinarian and meticulous planner, Raziel was every inch the military man. Had he lived, he might well have become the Garibaldi of the Zionist revolution. Unlike other Irgun chiefs, Raziel had never been a member of Betar but shared their belief that a Jewish state ultimately could be achieved only by force. Deeply religious, Raziel had majored in Talmudic studies at the Hebrew University in Jerusalem, written a training manual with Avraham Stern— another militant who was impatient with the cautious military policies of previous Irgun commanders—and Begin had looked forward to serving under him if it could be arranged. Now Raziel was gone.

Nevertheless, it was a happy Begin who arrived in Palestine early in May 1942, emaciated, travel-weary, and an almost comical figure in the ill-fitting khaki of a private in the army of the Polish government in exile. His arrival was eagerly awaited in Jerusalem by Aliza, with whom he was soon joyously reunited, and by a host of friends, among them Ya'acov Meridor, Raziel's successor as commander of the IZL and David Yutan, Dr. Sheib, Eliahu Lankin, Yehuram (Eytan) Livni and others who had managed with luck and by roundabout routes to make their way safely to the Promised Land.

Upon arrival, Begin was assigned to the staff of the Polish Town Major in Jerusalem, where he and Aliza set up housekeeping in her one room apartment on the ground floor of No. 25 Alfassi Street. Among those with whom he made contact as soon as he could was Meridor, who gave Begin a discouraging account of the IZL's situation: fewer than six hundred activists remained in the organization; its stores of arms and explosives were gone—lost, stolen by the Arabs or confiscated by the British—and there was no money, no radio, no communications equipment of any kind, and worse yet, no printing press—after dynamite the Irgun's best weapon. In short, the years since September 1939 had virtually wrecked the IZL, and it now had to be rebuilt from the ground up.

The main damage came after publication of the British White Paper in the spring of 1939. The Irgun reacted violently, attacking British military and government installations and causing considerable damage and bloodshed. During this period, the Irgun bore the brunt of British retaliation. Hundreds of its members were imprisoned, among them practically the entire IZL leadership, including Raziel and several others, leaving only Meridor to carry on. And Meridor, Begin could see, did not relish the awesome task of reorganization that had become imperative if the Irgun was to resume its mission: the expulsion of the British from Palestine.

Meridor had more bad news. The truce that was declared when the war erupted, he explained, led to yet another split in the organization. In 1940, those who wanted to continue fighting the British, war or no war, formed a new underground group, the *Lohamei Herut Israel*, or "Fighters for the Freedom of Israel," known to the Jewish community as LEHI and to the British as the "Stern Gang," for it was led at the time by the able Avraham Stern. Stern, a handsome intellectual, probably was the most extreme of the anti-British leaders of the time, the one who most sincerely believed, until Begin came along, that only through military action would the Jews of Palestine succeed in creating an independent state.

If Begin needed evidence of British indifference to the fate of European Jewry to fortify his convictions, there was plenty of it. Throughout the war the White Paper of 1939 remained in being, and the British went to great lengths to enforce it. Thousands of Jewish refugees who had managed to reach Romanian and Turkish ports and found ships to transport them to Palestine were denied permission to land when their vessels reached their destination. In case after case the British behaved abominably.

In the early winter of 1940, two tramp steamers, the *Pacific* and the *Milos*, carrying between them about 1,800 refugees, were intercepted by British patrol vessels in Mediterranean waters and convoyed into Haifa harbor. The passengers had no sooner set foot on the soil of the Promised Land, kneeling and kissing the ground, when they were led into internment camps, held for several days behind barbed wire, then herded aboard a British freighter, the *S.S. Patria*, for deportation to the island of Mauritius in the Indian Ocean, on orders from Sir Harold MacMichael, High Commissioner for Palestine.

The Jewish Agency protested vehemently to Sir Harold that most of the passengers were *halutzim*, agricultural workers who had trained nearly all their lives for settlement in the Holy Land. If war had not broken out, they would not be in the country. But MacMichael was adamant; not only would the refugees not be permitted to remain, but as punishment they would never be allowed to enter Palestine, not even *after* the war. As a warning to those who might be nourishing hopes of fleeing Europe, he added: "Similar action will be taken in the case of any further parties who may succeed in reaching Palestine with a view to illegal entry."

Forced aboard the *Patria*, the refugees, in one final act of desperation, blew up their ship as it was preparing to sail. The explosion shook all Haifa. More than two hundred and fifty men, women and children drowned as the vessel sank. Despite the catastrophe, MacMichael informed the Jewish Agency that the deportation order still remained in force. The survivors would be exiled to Mauritius as soon as another ship was available. He was overruled by London when Weizmann personally appealed to MacMichael's superiors in Whitehall, and the survivors were allowed to remain in what the High Commissioner announced as "an exceptional act of mercy." But the survivors were counted and their precise total was deducted from the next allotment of immigration certificates.

On the heels of the *Patria* tragedy came yet another. About one thousand seven hundred refugees from Poland, Austria and Czechoslovakia arrived aboard a typhoid-infested old tub named the *Atlantic*. The passengers were quarantined at the Haifa detention camp, then ordered deported. The refugees fought to remain in Palestine; in the end, soldiers dragged men and women by their arms and legs, even by their hair, and drove them aboard ship with batons.

Shortly afterwards, still another refugee-laden vessel, the *Salvatore*, unable to land its passengers because they did not possess valid British visas for Palestine, sank mysteriously in the Sea of Marmora. The death toll was two hundred and thirty-one men, women and children.

But perhaps the most tragic of many such episodes involved the *Struma*, a 180-ton Romanian vessel which normally carried about one hundred passengers on coastal runs in the Black Sea. On December 16, 1941, the *Struma* boarded 769 Jewish refugees at Costanza, and though none of her passengers had British permits, sailed for Haifa. Critically overloaded and endangered by sprung plates in her hull and defective engines, the ship broke down off Istanbul. The Turkish authorities would not allow the passengers to disembark unless they obtained British certificates for Palestine. The British refused.

The *Struma* lay at anchor off Istanbul for two and a half months. Finally, on February 24, despite protests by the captain that his ship was not seaworthy, the Turks towed the *Struma* out to sea. Before the vessel faded from view the people on shore read the large banner made by the passengers. It said: SAVE US!

Six miles from shore the *Struma* sank. Whether it struck a mine, simply capsized, or was torpedoed by German or Italian submarines lurking in those waters, was never determined. Two passengers survived by swimming to shore; 70 children, 269 women and 428 men drowned. Ironically, immediately after the *Struma*'s enforced departure from Istanbul, local British officials received a cable authorizing them to issue Palestine certificates *for the seventy children.*

The world was shocked by the incident, but the British remained unmoved. In the House of Commons, Harold Macmillan, then Undersecretary for the Colonies, said, blandly, "It is not in our power to give guarantees nor to take measures of a nature that may compromise the present policy regarding illegal immigration." His superior, Lord Cranborne, taking into account the outraged reaction of some Englishmen to the tragedy, declared, "Under the present unhappy situation in the world, it is to a certain extent inevitable that we should be hardened to such horrors."

The fate of the refugee ships aroused widespread indignation in Palestine's Jewish community, but after Raziel's death, the Irgun had virtually disintegrated. Only the FFI, or Stern group, remained active. After the sinking of the *Struma*, placards appeared everywhere—in Tel Aviv, Jerusalem, Haifa, Hebron and Safad—bearing a photograph of the High Commissioner and reading, in Hebrew and English:

WANTED FOR MURDER!

Sir Harold MacMichael, known as the High Commissioner for Palestine, *Wanted for Murder* by drowning of 800 refugees aboard the *S.S. Struma.*

But by then, Avraham Stern, alias Yair, was already dead. On the morning of February 12, 1942, as he hid in a cupboard in the fourth-floor apartment of a follower in Tel Aviv, British police found him, shot him several times, wrapped his body in a blanket and rolled it down four flights of stairs to the street. The official records would say, "Shot while attempting to escape."

Resistance had virtually ceased since late 1940 when the British finally accepted Jewish volunteers in His Majesty's Forces, though only in units performing the dreariest and most onerous tasks—hauling supplies, or prodding the western desert of Egypt for German mines as sappers. By the time Begin arrived in Palestine, virtually every able-bodied man and woman in the Jewish population of approximately four hundred and eighty-five thousand had enlisted in Britain's service. There was no comparable outpouring of volunteers among the Arab inhabitants of Palestine, who numbered approximately one million and represented a potential of seventy-five thousand to one hundred thousand recruits. In four years they produced only 8,745 volunteers for Britain's so-called Pioneer Battalions.

Generally speaking, the prevailing mood of the Jewish community in Palestine in the late spring of 1942 was one of acceptance of its existing position under the restrictions imposed by the White Paper while waiting for better times. Like the Haganah, the Irgun had decided it would be sheer madness to oppose Hitler's most effective democratic enemy and ceased operations against the British in Palestine. Jabotinsky himself, on September 5, 1939, had announced the NZO's full support for the British war effort and hundreds of Irgunists joined the thousands of Palestinian Jews who volunteered for service in Britain's armed forces. Raziel himself had endorsed Jabotinsky's call to arms against the common enemy in a letter written from his cell in the British jail, from which he was released for his ill-fated mission to Iraq.

Begin's experiences before reaching Palestine had moulded a rebel, a nonconformist. He had suffered privation, imprisonment and ill-treatment from the Russians during the earlier part of his long journey, when Russia was still allied to Nazi Germany, and he was embittered by the Hitlerian Holocaust that had taken his father, mother and brother. In Palestine, Begin saw Britain as the perfidious Albion that would never keep its promise of nationhood to the Jews, hence had to be driven from the territory by force as soon as opportunity offered. A man of concentrated will, he was not easily distracted from his target, which was British rule in the Palestine that, in his view, had been pledged to the Jews in the Balfour Declaration.

A lawyer by profession and a Biblical scholar and Latinist, Begin had little military training and no experience at all in the dark art of underground conspiracy. But an enviable reputation as an orator, patriot and organizer had preceded him, and in the autumn of 1942—after Britain's Eighth Army had defeated the Nazi-Fascist Afrika Korps at El Alamein—the Revisionist leaders in Palestine offered Begin the office of Betar Commissioner for Eretz Israel. He accepted, but did not hold the position very long. Informers saw to it that the British learned of Begin's appointment, and they, in turn, notified the Polish authorities, whereupon Begin resigned, realizing he had made a mistake: he could not serve Betar while still in uniform. Repeatedly urged to desert, Begin steadfastly refused, contending that he had sworn loyalty to the Polish Army and would under no circumstances violate his oath of allegiance to the flag he served.

The great Battle of El Alamein, which began on October 23, turned the tide of war in Africa against the forces of the Rome-Berlin axis and, in fact, as the defeated Marshall Rommel would write later, "probably represented the turning point in the whole vast struggle." Within less than a year, the entire southern littoral of the Mediterranean was cleared of enemy troops, and the war hopscotched from North Africa to Sicily, thence to Italy.

With an ultimate Allied victory no longer in doubt, Palestine's Revisionist leaders secretly planned to terminate the armistice with the

British, and to that end offered Begin the post of IZL commander. Efforts were made to obtain his release from the Polish Army, which was due to be transported to the Italian front, but the negotiations dragged on for weeks into the spring of 1943. They were finally brought to a successful conclusion by Mark Kahan, who had recently arrived with another contingent of Free Poles from the Soviet Union.

In the U.S.S.R., Kahan, a Revisionist functionary from Warsaw, had tried to set up Jewish units within the framework of General Anders' army, ostensibly to counteract the excessive anti-Semitism prevalent among its Polish troops, but in reality to enable thousands of Jews headed for Palestine to obtain military training in anticipation of future developments in the Jewish homeland. Kahan was not very successful, but he developed excellent relations within the Polish General Staff. He found it no simple task, however, to secure Begin's release.

Kahan's efforts were helped by the arrival in Palestine of Arieh Ben-Eliezer, an IZL veteran active in a recently created organization known as the League for the Nation's Liberation, established by Hillel Kook and Shmuel Merlin in the United States. Ben-Eliezer came to Jerusalem as an emissary of a League affiliate, the Committee to Save the Jews of Europe. His mission was to enlist the help of the Polish General Staff in liberating more than a quarter of a million Polish Jews still incarcerated in Soviet prisons and labor camps.

For this purpose, Ben-Eliezer required the approval of the Anders headquarters staff in Jerusalem for the release of five Jewish soldiers from the Polish Army in Palestine for propaganda work in the United States. Kahan arranged for Ben-Eliezer to meet with General Okulicki, Chief of Staff of the Polish Army in the Middle East. Ben-Eliezer gave the General five names, including that of Menahem Begin as leader of the proposed delegation. The General said he would think about it.

Some time later, Okulicki was posted to London, seat of several governments in exile at the time, including Free Poland's. At a farewell party in his honor, the General informed Kahan that the last document he had signed upon terminating his assignment in Palestine was for the release of the five Jewish soldiers.

The delegation did not go to the United States, but Begin was at last released from the Polish Army. At the time, the late autumn of 1943, a Jewish state, even an Irgun rebellion against British authority, seemed a distant goal to everyone except Menahem Begin: he had not only a vision of the future, but iron-willed determination and a plan.

At a hastily summoned meeting of IZL leaders, he was unanimously appointed Commander of the Irgun and charged with the task of setting up a general staff. Meridor only too gladly transferred command to him in a special order of the day, and was appointed Begin's deputy.

At thirty, a new chapter opened in the life of Menahem Begin. He had been arrested, charged, sentenced and exiled by the Russians as an "agent of British Imperialism." Ironically, those selfsame British would henceforth hunt him as a common criminal with a price on his head for trying to smash their rule in Palestine.

"In this new chapter," Begin would write later, "fate played another of its tricks on me. Conspiratorial work was to me quite unknown before I plunged perforce into its depths. I knew nothing of underground activities, beyond what I had read in an occasional book. I had never dreamt I would fight underground. In all things I always preferred the open to the secret, and yet . . ."

Into the underground he plunged to lead a revolution that would do infinitely more to create the modern state of Israel than its official Zionist leadership would admit for more than a generation. Had he possessed the physique, military talents and experience of David Raziel, Menahem Begin might have become the Garibaldi of the Zionist revolution, fighting in the field against a foreign oppressor, emerging eventually—as did the immortal Giuseppe in the middle decades of the nineteenth century—a heroic figure admired, even revered by lovers of freedom everywhere. But this was another century, and a world emerging from the greatest, costliest, bloodiest war mankind had ever known saw Menahem Begin not as a patriot fighting for the liberation of his country, but as a "terrorist," a felon guilty of crimes against constituted authority, and as a "terrorist" he would enter his country's history books, thanks mainly to his enemy and arch-rival David Ben-Gurion. He was, however, considerably more.

NOTES

1. Menahem Begin, *The Revolt*, Steimatzky's Agency, Limited, Jerusalem, 1951, translated by Samuel (Shmuel) Katz. English version edited by Ivan M. Greenberg.
2. *The Revolt*, Ibid.

Chapter 10

The Revolt:
Part One

The new commander of the Irgun Zvai Leumi was a thoughtful, meticulous, indefatigable planner. In a matter of days, Menahem Begin evolved a highly imaginative plan for reorganizing the IZL and blasting the British out of Palestine to make way for a Jewish state.

Begin's scheme called for a series of violent underground operations that would compel vigorous British retaliation. By forcing the authorities to adopt repressive countermeasures, Begin reasoned, Great Britain would alienate her anti-colonialist allies, Russia and the United States, arouse the antagonism of the Jewish community both in Palestine and abroad, and weaken support for the Mandatory Government back home.

Begin's logic was clear. The English people, proud of their reputation as defenders of human rights, would deeply resent the mass arrests, interrogations, confinements, even executions that were bound to result from the kind of underground warfare the Irgun would wage. In the end, Begin figured, the British in Palestine would be compelled to behave like Nazis to quell the rebellion, or withdraw, and he was certain that they would rather retreat than sully their image as champions of democracy. For once, Begin believed, history was on the side of the Jews.

It was understood, however, that while Britain continued fighting the Nazis, operations against the British would be confined to nonmilitary objectives. Furthermore, before any bombs were exploded in occupied buildings, the occupants were to be given sufficient warning to enable them to evacuate the endangered premises; there was to be no needless bloodshed.

Although it had its "soldiers," the Irgun as Begin reorganized it was essentially a *political* organization. As soon as he became its commander, one of his first moves was to sever the IZL's connection with the Revisionist Party. This made the Irgun solely responsible for its actions, minimized intramural friction and gave Begin maximum control over policy as well as operations. Its declared purpose was to destroy the British government's prestige in Palestine "deliberately, tirelessly, unceasingly," in accordance with Begin's theory that by undermining the authority of the British, the Irgun would oblige them to depart before their power structure collapsed and buried them in iniquity.

Begin did not see his planned offensive as "terrorism" as it would soon be labeled by the British and also by the Irgun's political opponents in the Jewish Agency, but as terrorism's direct opposite, a necessary element in the struggle of the Jewish people against oppression and subjugations.

"Our purpose," he wrote later, "was precisely the reverse of 'terrorism.' The whole essence of our struggle was the determination to free our people of its chief affliction—fear. How could we continue to live in a hostile world in which the Jew was attacked (simply) because he was a Jew—how could we go on living without arms, without a Homeland, without elementary means of defense? We of the Irgun Zvai Leumi arose, therefore, to rebel and fight, not in order to instill fear. . . . Historically we were not 'terrorists.' We were, strictly speaking, antiterrorists. . . . In building our organization, . . . we created no group of assassins to lurk in wait for important victims." [1]

The organizational structure devised by Begin was simple enough. At its head stood a high command advised by a general staff organized in departments appropriate to underground requirements. The body of the Irgun was divided into sections suited to the peculiar needs of an underground operation of the magnitude Begin proposed. The overall administrative "machine," as he called it, was always very small. There were never more than a few dozen members—often fewer than twenty, seldom more than thirty or forty—on full-time service. All the rest of the hundreds, and subsequently thousands, of Irgunists carried on with their ordinary daily work although they remained at the disposal of the IZL whenever needed. "It was in truth," Begin said, "a People's Army . . ."

The high command controlled all of the Irgun's activities, both military and political. Decisions were usually unanimous among the members of the high command though they were rarely if ever put to a formal vote. Begin's voice invariably carried the arguments; his views, even when opposed by others, inevitably prevailed. He approached each major operation like a lawyer arguing a case, seeing the pros and cons, and winning over opponents by the sheer power of his logic and his amazing grasp of the strategic consequences of what were often purely military actions. Very soon, Begin's influence permeated the entire Irgun. His ideas and ideals were reflected in and reinforced by his writings in *Herut*, the underground's news sheet which made its appearance shortly after his advent as *Adoni Hamefaked*.

When Begin doffed his uniform he also shed his identity and became Ben Zeev, an ordinary-looking Polish Jew in neat but unstylish civilian clothes, wearing tortoise-shell glasses and felt hat and carrying under one arm a battered brief case. He moved to Tel Aviv and "pitched his tent," as he put it, in the rather gloomy, nondescript Savoy Hotel in a side street off the Allenby Road, a thoroughfare named for the British general who had liberated Jerusalem from the Turks in 1917.

In the Savoy he met frequently with Arieh Ben-Eliezer, the newcomer from the United States, who quickly became his close friend and adviser. At times the two would also meet at the home of Menahem's sister Rachel, whose cooking both appreciated. Frequently they walked the ill-lighted streets at night, talking as they went, two friends out for an evening's constitutional, taking no special precautions beyond making certain they were not saying anything important when they encountered occasional passersby. At the time the "underground" was still very much above ground.

There were frequent consultations with members of Begin's general staff, among them Meridor, of course, Eliahu Lankin and Shlomo Levi. All contributed in drafting the Irgun's Order of Battle which established four administrative divisions: (1) AR—Army of the Revolution; (2) SU—Shock Units; (3) AF—Assault Force, and (4) RPF—Revolutionary Propaganda Force. The AR existed only in theory, however, and the SU was never actually created, its work being assigned to an already existing Irgun unit variously known as the "Red Section" or the "Black Squad."

In the early stages of the revolt, the most important work was done by the RPF. Its assignment was to explain to the public the reasons for Irgun's military operations and to prepare them psychologically for the IZL's attacks. It acquired an underground radio station and, eventually, an underground press. For a while, printer's ink was practically the only weapon the Irgun possessed, and the RPF often operated independently of military operations, using "leaflets instead of bullets."

Dynamite, however, would soon come into play. By the end of 1943 the appalling extent of the tragedy that had overtaken the Jewish people in Nazi-occupied Europe was becoming known to Ben-Eliezer and others in close touch with the situation. The Irgun almost literally vibrated with a new sense of urgency, and it permeated the proclamation calling for open revolt throughout Palestine which Begin actually had drafted early in 1943, while he was still a private in the Polish Army, but was not published until after he had become IZL's commander.

The proclamation was a masterful indictment of the British regime which, Begin wrote, had "shamefully betrayed the Jewish people" by having failed to open Palestine's gates to Jewish immigration, thereby sealing the fate of Jews caught in the Nazi Holocaust. There was no longer any moral basis for the British presence in Eretz Israel, Begin declared, nor for the existence of an armistice between the *yishuv* and a British administration which "hands our brothers over to Hitler."

"Our people," the declaration stated, "is at war with this regime—war to the end. This war will demand many and heavy sacrifices, but we enter on it in the consciousness that we are being faithful to the children of our people who have been and are being slaughtered. It is for their sake that we fight, and to their dying testimony that we remain loyal. This, then, is our demand: Immediate transfer of power in Eretz Israel to a Provisional Hebrew Government. We shall fight, every Jew in the Homeland will fight. The God of Israel, the Lord of Hosts, will aid us. There will be no retreat. Freedom—or death."

The proclamation was reminiscent in tone and content to the words of one of Begin's heroes, Giuseppe Garibaldi, when the latter summoned his famous One Thousand to battle against Italy's foreign oppressors with the cry of *Roma o Morte*—Rome or Death—in 1859. Doubts arose within the Irgun's high command, however, about whether the manifesto should be published or not. Some argued that it might be wiser simply to start military operations without actually proclaiming the revolt. It was finally published early in 1944, while Hitler still held most of Europe, upon Begin's insistence that, since the coming struggle in Palestine undoubtedly would be a long and difficult one, the public should be informed in advance of the nature of the rebellion and its objectives.

In the underground, the proclamation—clandestinely printed, of course, and pasted on the walls of all the major cities and towns by youngsters, some mere boys and girls—came to be known as the *palabra*, Spanish for "word;" the printer who turned it out on a flatbed press was a Sephardic Jew. Begin admits what when he first heard his declaration of war called the *palabra*, he didn't know what the word meant. There were mixed reactions among members of the Jewish community. The commander himself overheard one worker say, "Begin is a public speaker, and now that he's gone underground and can't make speeches he's started writing them on the walls." Most people refused to take the proclamation seriously, expressing doubts that its appearance would be followed by action. They were soon proved wrong.

When the call to arms came, the Irgun was as ready as it could be under the circumstances. It had about six hundred fully trained activists, and although Begin had broken relations with the Revisionist movement, the

Irgun could count on considerable support from National Zionist Organization (NZO) sympathizers. However, volunteers were needed, and for the newcomers, a secret "training school" was created. After careful screening to weed out undesirables, the new recruits were gathered in small groups and instructed in Irgunist ideology, the rigid rules of underground warfare, the use and maintenance of weapons and guerilla tactics. The courses were in the form of seminars, lasted about four months and were conducted, usually at night, in "safe" houses.

New volunteers also attended weekend sessions outdoors in isolated training camps where, out of sight and sound behind wind-sculptured sand dunes along the seacoast, they learned to fire their weapons and participated in tactical exercises with live ammunition. The most intensive training of all, however, was in the delicate business of making and planting explosives. It was a one-year course, and only the most skillful were graduated. The Irgunists knew from long experience the perils of entrusting the handling of high explosives to untrained people.

On the whole, historians have never fully appreciated the enormity of the task that Begin undertook when he proclaimed the Irgun's revolt. At the time, his six hundred men—of whom, incidentally, he could arm barely one hundred—represented a minute minority within the Jewish community which was overwhelmingly committed to the "official Zionism" of the Jewish Agency headed by Ben-Gurion, and from which Begin could expect only suspicion and enmity or worse.

It was not a situation that Begin relished. He had tried to arrange an alliance with Lohamei Herut Israel (LEHI) in the fall of 1943 that would have included some of the more militant members of the Haganah and formed at least the semblance of a truly national resistance movement. LEHI, whose operations chief at the time was Yitzhak Shamir,[2] the present Speaker of the Knesset—and as tough an underground fighter as ever planted a bomb in an enemy's cellar—was willing to join the Irgun, which he trusted completely, but wanted no part of the Haganah, which he mistrusted totally. Ergo, no common front, although eventually LEHI and the Irgun came to a tacit understanding that was tantamount to a "mutual assistance pact" for specific operations.

Shamir was delighted when, on the night of February 12, 1944, Irgunist incendiary bombs exploded simultaneously in the offices of the Department of Immigration in Jerusalem, Tel Aviv and Haifa. A fortnight later, more bombs went off in the offices of the Income Tax Collectors in the same three cities. It was obvious, now, that the Irgun meant business. If further proof were needed, on March 23 there were simultaneous attacks by Irgun commandos on several offices of the British Criminal Investigation Department (CID). Both sides suffered casualties and the revolt was on in earnest.

For only the third time in its long imperial history, Great Britain had a rebellion on its hands. First those pesky Americans back in 1776, then the always troublesome Irish in 1919 and now the Jews, "the fossil remnants of the Syriac Society." [3] Their consternation when the revolt erupted was evident throughout the Mandated Territory. First, bombs in empty government offices, then dead policemen and shootouts in midtown Haifa and Jerusalem. The British overlords of Palestine reacted precisely as Begin had anticipated. The repressive measures began.

The British imposed a curfew on Jerusalem, Haifa and Jaffa, reinvoked the death sentence for possessing arms and explosives which had been enacted during "the troubles" in 1936 but had been allowed to lapse, and officially denounced the Irgunists as "political gangsters" against whom the Security Forces would adopt "a firm policy of suppression." After the successful attacks on the various headquarters of the CID, Begin and Ben-Eliezer agreed that it no longer mattered if they themselves were captured and killed. They were certain that after those operations, "the continuance of the revolt was assured."

One of the positive results of these early operations was the sobering effect they had on the Arab population. The Arabs could see for themselves the destruction the Irgun had wrought and reacted with mingled wonderment, admiration—and fear. It dawned on them that they could no longer count on help from the authorities. "There are no more police," some were heard to say as they viewed what remained of the General Headquarters of CID in Jerusalem in the area between Barclay's Bank and the Post Office.

A decidedly negative consequence of the bombings, however, was the reaction of the official Zionist establishment. Its newspapers denounced the Irgunists as "nihilists," "maniacs," "charlatans," "fascists," "murderers" and "bandits." Even the Revisionist *Hamashkif* openly declared its opposition to the Irgun, heaping contempt on its "pretensions." It called for support of official Zionism's "partnership" with Great Britain, and faith in the efficacy of political negotiation as the route to a Jewish state and cooperated with the British to the extent of publishing photographs of "wanted terrorists" supplied by the CID. In the remoter rural areas where Irgun literature did not penetrate, the opposition propaganda proved effective. Many accepted the idea that the Irgun—and LEHI—were "stabbing Zionism in the back."

The unfavorable propaganda temporarily hurt the Irgun more financially than politically. At the outset, the revolt was strictly a low budget operation with expenses running at between $4,000 and $5,000 a month, but a large sum for those days. Much of the money was raised locally in the form of contributions from sympathizers, but these fell off sharply when the press attacks appeared, and the Irgun was obliged to resort to other means to finance its rebellion. Eytan Livni,[4] who was chief of operations until his arrest in April 1946, recalls that on one occasion an Irgunist team of two young men and a girl "lifted" diamonds worth the equivalent of $200,000 from a British post office. An equal sum was taken later during a raid on a heavily guarded train carrying the monthly payroll of the British-owned Palestine Railroad.

Such thefts, euphemistically called "confiscations," were frowned upon by Begin, but even he had to admit, in the end, that it was the only way the increasing expenses of the steadily burgeoning revolution could be met. Funds were needed for weapons, explosives, radio equipment, ammunition, medical supplies, car rentals and bribes. It took money, too, to maintain the several "safe" houses where Irgunist chiefs met, absconded or conducted training seminars. Finally, there were the personal expenses of the high command, whose members could not continue working at their jobs or professions after the police started their hunt for the members of the underground. After the war in Europe ended in 1945, some financial assistance came from abroad, mostly South Africa and the United States. But until then, the Irgun had to depend on what money it could steal from the British or wheedle from supporters in Palestine itself.

Far more disturbing to Begin was the open antagonism of David Ben-Gurion, who denounced the revolt as a betrayal of Zionist goals by narrow-minded men with dubious motives. The Jewish Agency's leader saw in the rebellion a challenge to his authority that imperilled his Biltmore Program, named for the New York hotel where, early in 1944, Ben-Gurion declared that after World War II the Jews aspired to create in Palestine not merely a "national homeland" but an independent Jewish state. At that juncture, Ben-Gurion's definition of Zionism's objectives was considered "novel," even "radical," for only a few years before he had tried to persuade the Peel Commission that what the Jews needed and demanded was merely a "national homeland." In other words, Ben-Gurion seemed ready at long last to settle for a Jewish state in *western* Palestine, far less than Herzl, or Jabotinsky or Menahem Begin deemed adequate for Jewry's territorial needs.

"We were delighted at his change," Begin would write later, "and bore no grudge against Mr. Ben-Gurion. It was Jabotinsky himself who always taught us to resist 'black memories.' He used to say: 'Any man may make a mistake or say foolish things. . . . . Forget what must be forgotten and give him your hand.' "

Early attempts by Ben-Gurion—through emissaries—to persuade the Irgun to abandon its revolution came to naught, and in the summer of 1944 a meeting was arranged between him and Begin. The latter was keen to meet the great man who had suddenly demonstrated a new militancy against Palestine's rulers by actually calling for the creation of a Jewish state. Begin was ready to join forces and follow Ben-Gurion, if he was prepared to lead an all-out struggle for the establishment of Jewish sovereignty over all of what remained of Palestine. Common fears and common purposes, to paraphrase Aristotle, bring even enemies together.

The meeting between the two leaders never took place, which is a pity, for Ben-Gurion probably missed an opportunity to become the Cavour of the Zionist revolution. A union of the *yishuv*'s forces, ably led by one mind toward a common goal—the creation of a Jewish state in the *whole* of western Palestine—might well have spared much Jewish and Arab blood. The resultant Israel would have been a state with the "defensible borders" it now seeks to achieve. What the Jews got, instead, after the UN Partition Resolution of 1947 and the War of Independence was the vulnerable gerrymandered state that fell far short of the magnanimous though admittedly ambiguous promise of the Balfour Declaration. Worse still, the Israel of 1948 was a poor reward indeed for the price the Jews had paid in human life and treasure during World War II out of which sprang independence for the Arabs in a score of nations covering some four million five hundred thousand miles of territory formerly held by the victorious empires of modern history's bloodiest struggle. But I digress.

To the scheduled meeting, Ben-Gurion sent two personal representatives, Moshe Sneh, one of the several gray eminences in his entourage, who later on became a Communist, and Eliahu Golomb, commander of the Haganah. Sneh, a squarely built man with inscrutable eyes, bluntly advised Begin that the responsibility for the fate of the Jewish community in Palestine rested in the Jewish Agency and the Haganah, not the Irgun. The revolt, Sneh said, was jeopardizing a "good" British "partition scheme" which the Jewish leadership was seriously considering.

Begin responded that there was no such thing as a "good" or "bad" partition and reiterated his belief that the Homeland could not be cut up like a joint of beef by its British trustees. British promises to reward the Jews with a state of their own after the war were not to be trusted, Begin declared, adding that the only way to create a Jewish state was to continue fighting for it. "A people can have only one army and only one policy," Sneh retorted, to which Begin replied that "the only policy for an oppressed people under foreign rule is to struggle for liberation."

Before the meeting ended, Sneh demanded that the Irgun submit its plans to the Jewish Agency or the Haganah. Begin refused. "If you fight," he said, "not only shall we fight with you, but we shall follow you. Until that time comes, however, we cannot submit to you our operational plans. Our struggle requires absolute secrecy in planning and execution . . ."

Begin did not know at the time that Ben-Gurion and the Haganah already were making plans to liquidate the Irgun.

*　　*　　*

The British, however, were even more anxious than Ben-Gurion to destroy the Irgun and intensified their hunt for "terrorists." Begin, of course, was at the top of their "wanted" list, but apparently they had no clear idea of where he might be hiding or even what he really looked like, for they were seeking a "hump-backed, hawk-nosed former law student at Warsaw University with thick horn-rimmed eyeglasses and bad teeth, aged about thirty-eight." Actually, during the first few months of the rebellion, Begin was still living openly as Ben Zeev in the Savoy Hotel, virtually under the noses of the CID.

Mrs. Begin was in Jerusalem where, in 1943, she had given birth to her first child, Benny, and Begin was now anxious to bring mother and son to Tel Aviv, but was undecided whether to stay where he was or move. A narrow escape from capture in the Savoy Hotel decided the matter in favor of moving to safer quarters. With his wife and infant son, Begin settled in Mahne Yehuda, on the outskirts of the Yemenite Quarter of Petah Tikva, not far from Tel Aviv. Shortly afterwards, the Begins took a small house in the Hassidof Quarter, another tiny suburb of Petah Tikva where everyone knew everyone else. There Menahem Begin became Israel Halperin, and lived in what he called "open underground." Only one neighbor ever penetrated the Halperin pseudonym, but he never betrayed Begin's real identity.

The house in the Hassidof Quarter remained the Irgun's headquarters for nearly a year. In the small kitchen, by lamplight or candlelight, the members of the high command held meetings, discussed policy and planned operations. They often helped to make up a *minyan* for prayers in the suburb's modest little synagogue.

Early in September 1944, the British decided Petah Tikva was a devil's nest of terrorists and swept through the entire town right up to the edge of the Hassidof Quarter, but did not enter it. They arrested many inhabitants of Petah Tikva, and from the front windows of their house the Begins watched the prisoners being hauled away in army lorries.

The Irgun grew in numbers and strength during the Hasidoff Quarter period. Many who had left the organization in the late 1930s returned, and many others volunteered. There was, however, a shortage of weapons. According to Livni, the only weapons the Irgun possessed when the revolt started were "almost entirely of the kind that could easily be hidden under a man's jacket or carried in a girl's handbag" —automatic pistols and grenades. The IZL's heaviest weapons at the time were three German Schmeiser submachine guns.

Later, Livni relates, the Irgun acquired hundreds of British Bren guns, bought illegally from soldiers or stolen or captured in raids on military depots. Subsequently, the Irgun manufactured its own grenades, mortars and land mines, including an especially ingenious one that operated on the pressure principle and could not be safely disarmed. Militarily, however, the Irgun was never a powerful force. At its peak strength—about three thousand activists in 1947—the Irgun had weapons for fewer than one thousand.

But the Irgun had no shortage of courage and plenty of dynamite. During Begin's residence in the Hasidoff Quarter, the high command planned and executed a number of daring operations. Activists blew up the CID's central headquarters in Jerusalem, blasted a number of police stations in the Tel Aviv-Jaffa area and successfully raided several Tegart fortresses, the name given to the strongly built, dun-colored police posts erected by the British Mandatory Administration in key spots throughout the country in the late 1930s on the recommendation of Sir Charles Tegart (who had been brought in as an adviser on security). The raids reaped a rich harvest in weapons but cost the Irgun several dead and many wounded.

The casualties inspired Begin to write a pamphlet entitled "We Believe" —one of many he turned out during his underground days— proclaiming the Irgun's "unshakeable belief" that the blood spilled by its members would "nourish the tree of freedom in our country and the tree of life for our people."

But the blood-letting had barely begun.

NOTES

1. *The Revolt*, Ibid.

2. Yitzhak Shamir, in an interview with the author.

3. Arnold J. Toynbee, *A Study of History* (London: Oxford University Press, 1947).

4. In an interview with the author.

Chapter 11

The Revolt:
Part Two

Palestine soon became a battlefield. Few days passed without bloodshed in the streets of Jerusalem and Tel Aviv, Haifa and Jaffa and a dozen other communities. Here an Irgunist bomb, there a LEHI grenade, everywhere the British retaliating.

Realizing they had a full-blown rebellion on their hands, the British replaced High Commissioner MacMichael—after several LEHI attempts on his life—with a prestigious military man, Field Marshal Lord Gort, hero of the battle of Malta. MacMichael's transfer to Malaya was fortuitous for him. The Irgun and the LEHI had jointly planned to kidnap him and demand in return cancellation of the White Paper to allow the remnants of European Jewry to enter Palestine.

The underground's fury was in response to the dreadful news reaching Palestine from abroad. Every day came word of Jews being gassed to death and burned, machine-gunned in rows alongside mass graves they themselves had been forced to dig at gunpoint, or being destroyed by other no less barbarous means: starvation, the ghetto system, slave labor, deportations under inhuman conditions. New arrivals, eyewitnesses to such horrors, testified to what they had seen and what had been dismissed in some Allied circles as mere "wartime atrocity stories" were proving only too hideously true. The policy of total destruction of the Jews which had been repeatedly proclaimed by Hitler was actually being carried out.

It was common knowledge in Palestine that hundreds of thousands of Jews had been shot by the *Einsatzgruppen*, mobile "killing units" which followed the Nazi armies for just that purpose. Their scale of murder was so massive that it could not be hidden by the most elaborate German security precautions. Detailed reports of their operations had reached Washington and London, but for all their awareness of the enormity of Nazi barbarism, neither the United States nor Great Britain could be stirred from their apathy about the plight of the Jews. For reasons unexplained to this day no Allied bombers could be spared from strictly military operations for the demolition of Hitler's gas chambers and crematoria.

On May 17, 1944, the fifth anniversary of the White Paper, three truckloads of armed Irgunists, using for the first time their homemade mortar—later famous as the *Davidkah* or "Little David"—stormed and captured the Government Broadcasting Station at Ramallah. The plan was to silence its official "Palestinian" program and broadcast an appeal to the world at large to help save Europe's Jews and liberate Palestine from the British. But the scheme misfired: there was no *studio* at Ramallah—it was in Jerusalem, and heavily guarded.

The British responded with lightning raids and police sweeps wherever they thought the rebels might be hiding. They even invaded remote agricultural settlements, using Indian troops for the purpose. Innocent farmers were herded into wire cages for body searches and were beaten when they resisted; their wives hurled pots and pans at the soldiers and fought furiously rather than submit to arrest; hundreds were thrown in jail without charge or trial.[1]

With the approach of Yom Kippur, the Irgun warned the British not to disturb the Jews who would be praying at the Western Wall—it was still called the "Wailing Wall" in those days—during services on the Day of Atonement. The warnings were repeated daily for ten days, and the British, persuaded that the Irgun planned to attack them at the Wall, deployed a strong force in the area. But the Irgun had no intention of taking on the British army in what would have been a bloody shootout while Jews were praying at the Wall. The IZL's warnings were a tactical ruse, and it worked. In the early morning hours of the day after Yom Kippur, the Irgun simultaneously attacked the Tegart fortresses at Haifa, Beit-Dajan, Kalkiliah and Katara with total surprise, and came away with much-needed stocks of weapons and ammunition.

In the darkness before dawn on October 21, the British retaliated. Surrounding the detention center at Latrun with troops to prevent any attempt at a mass rescue, they dragged 251 Irgunist and LEHI prisoners from their beds, manacled them and flew them in Royal Air Force transports to an East African concentration camp in Eritrea. Among those deported were some of the Irgun's best officers and men. Their loss was a severe blow to the revolt and caused Begin to wonder whether he and the high command "had the right to impose, even indirectly, so much suffering and so much sorrow on so many comrades and their relatives."

At this juncture, the Jewish Agency renewed its pressure on the Irgun to cease all operations. Golomb, the Haganah's commander, had visited London and received "assurances" from British Labor Party leaders that after the war—and an anticipated Laborite victory over the Conservatives in the upcoming national elections—they would offer their "good friends" the Labor Zionists in Palestine a "fair deal." They warned, however, that continued "terrorism" would make a favorable settlement "impossible."

On October 25, the inner council of the Jewish Agency, at a secret meeting called by Ben-Gurion, decided to declare all-out war on the IZL, but before going into action made another attempt to persuade Begin to give up the fight. Golomb and Sneh met again with Begin and Lankin, this time at a café on the corner of one of Tel Aviv's busiest streets, Allenby Road.

Golomb and Sneh, speaking in the name of the Jewish Agency, again demanded immediate cessation of all Irgun activities. They said Begin had totally misread British intentions and tried to persuade him that after the war ended in Europe, British policy would change substantially in favor of Zionist objectives in Palestine. Begin, responding, reiterated his mistrust of British policy and repeated the Irgun's willingness to join forces with the Haganah against the Mandatory Government. The discussion continued until well after midnight but accomplished nothing. Begin and Lankin flatly refused to accede to the Haganah's *diktat*, and Golomb countered by threatening to liquidate the Irgun. His parting words to Begin were: "We shall step in and finish you."

Begin returned to his home in the Hassidof Quarter that night with a heavy heart. He knew Golomb to be a man of immense authority within the Jewish Agency, a soldier not given to idle threats. Convinced Golomb meant business, Begin feared the worst—civil war—something he was determined to avert at any cost short of disbanding the Irgun. The mere thought of Jew killing Jew filled him with dread.

In the circumstances, the Irgun and LEHI—which meanwhile had secretly promised Golomb to suspend operations against the British—resumed negotiations for joint action designed to oblige the authorities to release their deported comrades and issued an ultimatum demanding their return. Night after night, Irgunists and members of LEHI drew up battle plans "not so much to avenge the exiles," said Begin later, "as to prove to the authorities that their attempt to strike fear into the hearts of Jewish youth and frighten them away from our ranks was abysmally wrong."

But on November 6, 1944, something momentous happened that caused the Irgun and LEHI leaders to abandon their plans. That evening, while Begin waited with Yaacov Meridor for Yitzhak Shamir and Friedman-Yellin of the LEHI to work out final details for a major joint offensive against their common enemy, Yaacov casually turned on a radio. A news flash from Cairo announced that the Right Honorable Walter Edward Guinness, first Baron Moyne, Resident British Minister in the Middle East, had been assassinated by two young Jews belonging to a splinter group of LEHI, which was also known as the Fighters for the Freedom of Israel, or Stern Gang.

The youthful assassins, Eliahu Bet-Zouri and Eliahu Hakin, had acted on orders from Shamir, the FFI's tough, bushy-browed operations chief, in accordance with long-standing plans apparently made before the parent organization's pledge to the Haganah to suspend anti-British activities. Whether Shamir was unable to abort the Cairo plot due to communications problems or simply felt the LEHI's promise to Golomb applied only to anti-British operations in Palestine remains a moot question. In any event, he had given the Irgun no hint of the Cairo mission, which greatly distressed Begin. Despite this, the two organizations remained on friendly terms. It would be the Irgun, however, not LEHI or the FFI, that would shoulder the consequences.

The murder of Lord Moyne, a close personal friend of Prime Minister Winston Churchill, raised a storm of anger and indignation in England. In London, "Parliament met in a cold fury. Churchill could not trust himself to speak at length, and it was Foreign Minister Anthony Eden who gave the details of the shooting to the House of Commons. King George and Queen Elizabeth telegraphed condolences to the bereaved family . . ."[2]

Chaim Weizmann, the godhead of official Zionism, who happened to be in London at the time—in fact, he had lunched with Churchill on November 4, two days before the assassination—issued a statement saying that the shock of Moyne's murder had been "far more severe and numbing than that of the death of my own son," RAF flight lieutenant Michael Weizmann, reported "missing in action" over Germany. That the revered world leader of Zionism could bring himself to use such grief-laden words perhaps more than anything else jolted the Jews of Palestine into a realization of the enormity of what had happened.

In Jerusalem, the Jewish Agency hastened to express officially its horror "at this revolting crime," and the Hebrew press reached for the strongest words in its dictionaries to denounce "the abominable deed." The influential *Haaretz* lamented, "Since Zionism began, no more grievous blow has been struck at our cause." The country's Jewish community was psychologically conditioned by the press to believe rumors that the British planned a general massacre to avenge the death of their Minister of State. As Begin later described it, "An atmosphere of fear and terror developed in the country which, it must be remembered, was still largely isolated from the world at large by wartime conditions. In such an atmosphere it was easy to condemn those who, it was alleged, were 'trying to bring down catastrophe on the nation.' " [3]

Riding the wave of popular resentment and fear generated by Moyne's murder, Ben-Gurion made a speech to the Histadrut outlining his plan for liquidating the underground. Its members, when found, were to be fired from their jobs, and there was to be no sentimental hesitancy about handing them over to the British. Furthermore, Ben-Gurion emphasized, the Jewish Agency and its security forces—the Haganah and the Palmach—were to cooperate fully with the authorities in pursuit of "common interests."

In fairness to Ben-Gurion it must be said, however, that he sincerely believed he was acting in Zionism's best interests. He had received word from Weizmann, after the latter's luncheon with Churchill, that the Prime Minister had accepted as viable a proposal to allow one million five hundred thousand Jews into Palestine during the decade following cessation of hostilities in Europe and had agreed to permit from one hundred thousand to one hundred and fifty thousand orphans to enter immediately. It was Weizmann's impression, apparently, that the White Paper was a dead letter and that the War Cabinet had agreed on a "good partition," meaning, presumably, a fair division of Palestine between Arab and Jewish claimants to the territory.

Clearly, from the point of view of the Jewish Agency, Moyne's assassination had imperiled whatever arrangements Weizmann had made with Churchill and such "assurances" as Golomb had received from the Labor Party. Seen in that light, the killing in Cairo had been a fateful blunder. Indications of a change of heart on the part of the prestigious occupant of No. 10 Downing Street came in his speech in the House of Commons on November 17.

"If our dreams for Zionism should be dissolved in the smoke of the revolvers of assassins," Churchill said, "and if our efforts for its future should provoke a new wave of banditry worthy of the Nazi Germans, many persons like myself will have to reconsider the position that we have maintained so firmly for such a long time. In order to hold out a possibility for future peace, these harmful activities must cease and those responsible for them must be radically destroyed and eliminated."

Three days later, on November 20, Ben-Gurion announced his plan for crushing the underground. The Haganah and the Palmach went to work. The brunt of their attack, when it came, was borne almost entirely by the Irgun, the LEHI having exculpated itself by its agreement with the Haganah's Golomb. Specially formed and trained units hunted down Irgunists everywhere. At the same time, the British military authorities and police were handed lists of Irgun members known to the Haganah.

Meridor was betrayed to the police and so was Lankin. Both were deported to Eritrea.

Shlomo Levi, the youngest member of Begin's staff, was arrested on his way from Tel Aviv to take over Lankin's post as Jerusalem's regional commander. In short order, the only one left of the Irgun's top leadership was Begin himself, Ben-Eliezer having been arrested earlier, in the spring, by the Haganah. Expulsions of young Irgunists from high schools, dismissals from jobs—with resultant hardship to dependents—kidnapping, beatings, even torture became the sole occupation of the Jewish Agency's action-starved security forces, and the police fattened their files, said Begin, with material "worth its weight in gold: names, addresses, descriptions, types of duty, rank . . ."

Although when the hunt started the situation verged perilously close to civil war, it never developed into a fratricidal struggle. This was because Begin strictly forbade retaliation. The Irgun, he reminded his followers, was not "fighting for power, but to liberate Palestine." Sooner or later, he said, the Jewish Agency and its security forces would realize the immutability of British policy and would join with the Irgun in a united effort against the Mandatory power. It was imperative, Begin declared, that the Irgun not retaliate—but "suffer and wait."

And, as always, the Irgun obeyed. Although its ranks were seriously depleted and operations were virtually suspended, not a single act of retaliation against either the Haganah or the somewhat rowdier Palmach were carried out by the Irgun during the entire six-month period of what the hunters called "The Season."

From the standpoint of the Jewish Agency, "The Season" was a disaster. When it was over, the Irgun was stronger than ever physically and politically. New men came and joined Begin's high command, among them Bezalel Amitzur, Amihai Paglin, Haim Landau, Samuel (Shmuel) Katz, and others whom the world would know only by code names. More important, the Irgun acquired stature in the eyes of the public. By doggedly pursuing its policy of restraint toward its tormenters, the Irgun gained the sympathy of many who before had abhorred its politics and suspected its motives. Even critics who continued to question the revolt's objectives could no longer impugn the Irgun's loyalty to Zionism and the Jewish community. As matters turned out, the Jewish Agency not only had failed to destroy the Irgun, but had unwittingly invested the organization and its revolt with a legitimacy it had not previously enjoyed.

By the spring of 1945, when "The Season" ended, Menahem Begin had not only survived the first of the many crises that would mark his leadership, but had won a major moral victory over his future arch-rival and implacable enemy: David Ben-Gurion.

*   *   *

During the early days of the intensive British hunt for Irgunists, their most important quarry remained unmolested in his lair in the Hasidoff Quarter. Some of the search parties came too close for comfort, however, and the Begins moved to a small, detached house in Rehov Joshua Bin-Nun, a side street in North Tel Aviv, then an area of open fields and citrus groves. Their new home was near the Yarkon River—still a pleasant stream in those days, not the foul ditch it has since become—with a garden in front and orange trees in the rear. But the place had its disadvantages; it was situated roughly midway between the municipal abattoir and the city's dog pound. Begin recalls "an almost incessant cacophony of dogs howling for freedom and doomed animals crying for their lives. And smells . . ."

In the Joshua Bin-Nun house "Israel Halperin" grew a bushy beard and became "Israel Sassover." He dressed in a longish black coat, like an Orthodox Jew, and sufficiently resembled a Rabbi to be mistaken for one. He was soon a regular participant at prayers in the local synagogue just down the road from his home and the *schule* became an important part of Begin's life during one of the most difficult periods of the Irgun's struggle.

While the Begins were living in Rehov Joshua Bin-Nun, they had their second child, a daughter, whom they named Hassia after Menahem's dead mother. The baby was registered illegally by Begin's friend, Israel Epstein, as his own daughter; Begin obviously could not record her birth under his own name, and the "Sassover" identity was, of course, not registered. Providentially, the addition of Hassia to the Begin menage helped Menahem maintain his incognito. The British never knew that Begin had more than one child and consequently in all their searches they looked for a man with a wife and one small boy.

For the "full-timers"—Begin and the high command plus a few others—life in the underground was no bed of roses, however romantic it might have seemed to some in retrospect. They moved about only by night, using circuitous routes through back streets. Begin himself often did not see daylight for months at a time. When he had to meet anyone he was fetched in a car after dark and brought back the same night, or else he spent the following day at the residence where the meeting had taken place, returning home only after nightfall. Begin had not yet given up smoking; he and everyone else lived mostly on cigarettes and coffee. Nevertheless, despite its hardships, underground existence seemed to agree with the Commander; he was ill only once during the years of the revolt, suffering for a while from a severe loss of appetite, which his doctor attributed to lack of fresh air and sunshine while residing at the Joshua Bin-Nun address. Once he was obliged to hide in a closet without food or water for four days with the police encamped in his garden. When he emerged, seriously dehydrated, he had the presence of mind not to drink; he merely soaked his head in a bucket of water.

Living in the shadows was harder on Aliza, whom everyone including Begin called "Ala." Mrs. Begin hardly ever left their home. She couldn't go visiting or be visited by friends and spent most of her time doing housework and caring for the children. Her only companions from the "outside" were the members of the IZL high command who came to confer with her husband, and the wives of those who were married. Her marketing was done by an "Uncle Meir," a trusted longtime friend and one of the oldest members of the IZL. Aliza's only recreation was sitting on the secluded back porch and knitting. A friend who knew her well at the time described Aliza as "small, thin and stooped from long, endless days and nights of knitting and reading to tide over the interminable solitude of life in the underground." [4] Like her husband, Aliza was nearsighted and wore glasses.

Throughout the years of the revolt, Aliza Begin demonstrated quiet courage of the steady kind, without heroics. It manifested itself in an amazing cheerfulness in all circumstances, including childbirth, when unlike most women she was obliged to forego the bedside sympathy of an attentive husband and the pampering of relatives and friends. Each time no loving husband brought her flowers and gifts, no friends helped to while away the days. She lay alone in a "safe" hospital, unvisited, unknown, and she returned home each time to tackle the additional burden smilingly and cheerfully. Aliza's greatest burden, of course, was constant worry over her husband's safety and the success of the revolt.

Aliza could have no domestic help, so Menahem helped her with the household chores. Fellow Irgunists who came to plan daring new deeds often found their chief washing dishes or the baby's diapers, sweeping out the kitchen or mopping the floors. However, he insisted he liked housework, saying it provided much-needed exercise and relaxation. He frequently washed, dressed and fed the children while discussing matters of high policy with one or more members of the high command.

One of the matters periodically debated by Begin and his advisers while they were still being hunted during "The Season" was how to transform their revolution into a unified national effort. As the war in Europe drew to a close in the early spring of 1945, Begin believed the time had come to intensify and continue the Irgun's struggle in a new and broader context.

On May 15, a week after the German collapse, Begin circulated among two hundred and fifty leaders of the Jewish community a memorandum soliciting their individual and collective support for the immediate proclamation of a Provisional National Government and the creation of a Supreme National Council. What Begin proposed, in short, was that the

Jews of Palestine declare their independence under a government of their own.

Begin envisaged "the establishment of a free, democratic regime, with equality of rights for all inhabitants," organized to provide "social insurance, agrarian reform and public ownership" of essential services. Begin also suggested the creation of a general staff "to direct the military uprising," and the formation of a legislative council "to set up independent courts and to draft a constitution for the Hebrew Republic."

The plan Begin outlined was essentially what was fulfilled three years later, in May 1948, but in May 1945, it was unanimously rejected by the representative cross-section of leading politicians, economists, scientists, lawyers and others to whom he submitted it. The official Jewish leadership awaited a Labor Party victory in the impending national elections in Great Britain and fulfillment of its promised "fair deal" to its "socialist brothers" in Palestine. Said Ben-Gurion, confidently, "The British workers will understand our aims."

Quite apart from the "assurances" the British Laborites had given Golomb, the Labor Party had vigorously opposed the 1939 White Paper, and its spokesmen had proclaimed day and night their unalterable attachment to the Balfour Declaration. Moreover, at its 1945 pre-election Blackpool Conference the Party had announced a Zionist program that was more ambitious than the official Zionist blueprint. At Blackpool, the Labor Party actually demanded the establishment of a Jewish state in Palestine, even if some Arabs had to be moved out to make room for the Jews.

It was not surprising, therefore, that Ben-Gurion and his Laborite *Mapainiks* jumped for joy when Clement Atlee and Ernest Bevin, "the workingman's friend," replaced Churchill and Eden. *Davar*, the official organ of the Histadrut, wrote: "The victory of the Labor Party, which raised the banner of undiluted Zionism during the election campaign, is a clear victory for the demands of Zionism . . ." There was even some dancing in the streets of Tel Aviv when the returns were announced over the radio.

Disillusionment came almost with the speed of light. No sooner had the Labor Government assumed office in July than it went back on the word and the spirit of the Party's promises, old and new. The leaders of the Jewish Agency, bitterly disappointed, realized they could no longer collaborate with the British and ordered its security forces to stop hounding the Irgun: no more betrayals, no more kidnappings, no more handing over of prisoners to the authorities.

Begin's prognosis that the British Laborites would deal no more generously with Zionism than the Conservatives was fulfilled to the letter. One of the Laborites' election-campaign promises had been to scrap the

White Paper. Once in power, however, Bevin, as Foreign Minister, did an about face. Arguing that the Arab countries would rise against Britain if the government changed its policy, the White Paper remained the law of the land in Palestine. Consequently, the tens of thousands of Jews who had somehow survived gas chambers, firing squads, typhus and starvation, and who after the war pleaded to be allowed to go to Palestine, had to be told to wait; the Jewish homeland was still closed to them.

Meanwhile, the end of the war in Europe had disclosed the full extent of the horrors to which European Jews had been submitted. At the various death camps located in areas liberated by British and American troops, correspondents could see the cattle cars in which men, women and children were hauled to the camps; the wooden huts where Jews awaited their turn for the privilege of dying in the gas cells; the furnaces where the bodies were later disposed of; and the offices where the gruesome tallies of the names and numbers of those exterminated were meticulously kept with Teutonic efficiency. Even the amounts of gold taken from the victims' teeth were neatly registered. At Auschwitz, where 2,300,000 were put to death, reporters found warehouses full of clothing, shorn hair and valuables taken from Jews when they arrived for Hitler's "Final Solution."

It soon became abundantly evident that in the conduct of Middle East affairs, Bevin, apparently unmoved by the tragedy that had befallen European Jewry, would follow religiously his Tory predecessors' policy of propping up the area's Arab potentates and feudalistic regimes in hopes of building a *cordon sanitaire* against the new-old bugaboo of Mediterranean history—Russian power—and ensuring continuation of Britain's then dominant position in the Middle East's oil region. Bevin's traditionalist approach demonstrated an almost complete lack of comprehension of the changes wrought by World War II in the Arabs' attitudes toward Britain, for it assumed, on the one hand, that the Arabs would fight on Britain's side in another world war, and, on the other, that Arab Moslems and Russian atheists had nothing in common, an assumption which Egypt, Syria and Iraq, among others, would demolish from the mid-1950s onward. Bevin blindly wooed Arab help in upholding "democratic civilization" in the Middle East, although the only friends democracy had in the area were the Jews, who had fought a war for it whereas the overwhelming majority of the Arabs had not.

Public opinion in Britain and the United States, aroused by correspondents' descriptions of the death camps, demanded justice for the Jews, but "Ernie" Bevin, the former Baptist lay preacher, ignored the popular outcry at home and abroad, crushed opposition within his own party and did everything he could to prevent Jews from reaching Palestine. He started by countering an urgent appeal from President Harry Truman for immediate admission of one hundred thousand refugees to Palestine with a proposal that an Anglo-American committee of inquiry be created "to study the matter," an obvious delaying tactic, and poured additional troops into the area that was to have been the Jewish National Homeland. Eventually, the British garrison in Palestine numbered between eighty-five thousand and one hundred thousand well-armed men.

Persuaded at last that Great Britain had no intention of allowing Zionist hopes of nationhood to be realized in any substantial portion of Palestine, the Jewish Agency's leaders fulfilled another of Begin's prophecies: they decided to resist Bevin's policy with violence and turned to the dissidents of the underground—the Irgun and LEHI—for help. The initiative was Ben-Gurion's, but the negotiations for the establishment of a common resistance front were conducted on his behalf by Israel Galili and Moshe Sneh, with Begin representing the IZL and Nathan Friedman acting for LEHI.

Sneh and Galili, who had succeeded Golomb following the latter's death from a heart attack, proposed that the Irgun's members should join the ranks of the Haganah, which would have meant the end of the IZL as an independent organization. Having only minimal confidence in the Haganah's staying powers, Begin refused to disband the Irgun. In order to achieve the unity he himself had long advocated, however, he agreed to accept the Haganah's leadership in the coming struggle for national independence. LEHI followed suit.[5]

From the ensuing three-cornered negotiations emerged what was called *Tenuat Hameri*, or Resistance Movement, under Haganah command. The Irgun and the LEHI leadership agreed thenceforth to carry out only operations approved by the Haganah which, oddly, were to be limited only to attacks on the British whenever they tried to prevent the arrival of "illegal" immigrants. The limitation irked Begin but his great objective had been achieved: the Jews as a people were at war with the oppressor. The Irgun and LEHI could, however, carry out "confiscations" of weapons and money on their own.

By the early autumn of 1945, the Resistance Movement was fully organized and it swung into action. Three British patrol boats used for hunting immigrant ships off the coast were sunk by the Irgun, two in the harbor at Haifa and the third at Jaffa. Railway lines were cut by the Haganah at 186 points, and traffic was suspended from the Syrian border to Gaza, from Haifa to Samakh and from Lydda to Jerusalem. The Irgun attacked the Lydda station, causing serious damage and casualties among British troops. That same month, LEHI damaged the oil refineries at Haifa.

The struggle for national independence now entered a new and seemingly decisive phase. The operations of *Tenuat Hameri* were massive.

Radar stations and installations of the Mobile Police were attacked by the Haganah. LEHI heavily damaged railway workshops and an aerodrome. The Irgun destroyed and/or severely damaged a number of key railroad stations and police headquarters and raided airfields at Lydda, Kfar Sirkin and Kastine, blowing up several four-engined Halifax bombers.

Begin was in his element. He would look back on the period of *Tenuat Hameri* as one of "the happiest times in my life," although working with the Jewish Agency presented problems. There was a tendency on the part of the Agency's political leadership to test British reactions after each operation, to "slow down" in the hope that maybe with every blow the enemy had "had enough" and would be reasonable about allowing the free flow of immigration. Instead, Bevin's response to every attack was to send more troops. In December 1945, the Sixth Airborne Division of about twenty thousand men was moved into Palestine to reinforce the eighty-five thousand troops already there.

In addition to their regular forces, the British could call upon thousands of uniformed police, some units from Transjordan's well-trained Arab Legion and unknown numbers of secret police in plain clothes. At sea, to seal the coast against the "illegal" immigration, Britain had several destroyers, two cruisers, and a number of patrol vessels.

By early 1946, the Mandated Territory was literally an armed camp. Tegart fortresses and tented British army camps studded the countryside. Troops manned heavy roadblocks at strategic intersections. Bunkered observation posts guarded the approaches to major urban centers. Motorized patrols circulated constantly in the cities.

Government buildings everywhere were protected by sandbag breast-works, rolls of barbed wire and spiked cheval-defrise. Sentries challenged visitors at every entrance. In most cities, the British wired and sandbagged themselves into ghettolike areas for protection against almost constant attacks by the underground groups of *Tenuat Hameri* acting singly or in concert. The largest of these compounds was in Jerusalem, and it soon became known as "Bevingrad." British and American correspondents who had covered World War II felt completely at home. What they saw were preparations for all out war, and the censorship which they encountered was fully as rigid as that they had known while following the Allied armies in North Africa, Italy, France and Germany.

As J. Bowyer Bell pointed out in his excellent *Terror Out of Zion,*[6] "There were curfews, confiscations, searches in the streets, sweeps through the countryside, collective fines, detentions, and arrests for cause. Once the vast interrogation apparatus had filtered out the few hard cases, they were often exiled to camps in East Africa. The newspapers in the Mandate were censored and travel was restricted. The mails were monitored, as was all overseas cable traffic. The Mandate became a garrison state under internal siege, and the garrison, despite its size, equipment and determination, proved ineffectual and self-defeating."

Thus, when the Anglo-American Committee arrived early in 1946 to conduct yet another inquiry in the long succession of inquiries into the "Palestine Problem," it found a country sandbagged, ribbed with barbed wire, and taut with tension. The Committee had met with Bevin in London beforehand, and the Foreign Minister had promised that if the group's conclusions were unanimous, he would honor their recommendations.

The Committee's final report recommended immediate removal of the White Paper restrictions on immigration and proposed abolition of the Land Laws of 1940 which prohibited Jews from buying land in four-fifths of western Palestine. It reaffirmed President Truman's recommendation for immediate admission of one hundred thousand refugees who were too sick or too poor to qualify for admission anywhere else, including, alas, the United States. Lastly, it called for the dissolution of all "private armies," claiming their existence endangered "world peace."

Pending a reply from London, the Haganah proposed suspension of all armed action so as not to impede the anticipated admission of the one hundred thousand refugees. Begin and the Irgun agreed, but with strong reservations; they did not believe Bevin would allow any Jews to enter Palestine or that there had been any perceptible change in overall British policy. In the meantime, the movement of Jewish refugees from eastern Europe into the American zone in Germany gathered momentum. More than ninety thousand arrived in the area during the spring and summer, and by the end of 1946, the displaced persons' camps were packed to overflowing with about two hundred and fifty thousand Jews. American military and Jewish philanthropic resources were strained to the utmost.

As Begin had foreseen, Bevin rejected the Anglo-American Committee's proposals. Moreover, the Foreign Secretary made it clear that he intended to postpone indefinitely fulfillment of Britain's promise to Zionism and to use Palestine—a country created almost entirely by Jewish money, ingenuity and hard work—as a base for British troops no longer welcome in Egypt, Syria and Iraq. The realization that London's policy had in fact remained unchanged, and the explosion of refugees from eastern Europe, aroused the resistance movement to new and greater militancy. Its leaders decided that additional pressure would have to be exerted on the British, and on May 12, 1946, the underground's secret radio broadcast a warning which said, in part:

> . . . Britain obviously intends to concentrate her military bases in Palestine . . . We warn His Majesty's Government that if it does not fulfill its responsibilities under the Mandate—above all with regard

to immigration—the Jewish resistance movement will make every effort to hinder the transfer of British bases to Palestine and to prevent their establishment in this country . . .

The Irgun had been active even before the warning, blowing up bridges, sabotaging railway workshops at Haifa and raiding the Sarafand Armory, Britain's biggest military camp in Palestine, making off with a large store of arms and ammunition later confiscated by the Haganah. Then, on the night of June 17, Haganah units launched their most daring attack thus far. They blew up ten of the eleven bridges connecting Palestine with surrounding countries, thereby effectively isolating the Mandate from overland communications with its neighbors.

In the morning of June 29, a Saturday—a day that thereafter would be known as "Black Sabbath"—the British counterattacked. Lieutenant General Sir Evelyn Hugh Barker, Britain's G.O.C. in Palestine, sent into action some ten thousand troops. They fanned out over the country, imposed curfews everywhere, and led nearly three thousand Jews away to detention centers at Latrun and Rafa, in Sinai. The building of the Jewish Agency in Jerusalem was occupied. A number of prominent Zionist leaders were arrested, but most of the main ones, including Ben-Gurion— who was in Paris—were out of the country at the time. Detained, also, were nearly half of the members of the Haganah.

Begin and his Irgunists fared much better. The authorities did not know where to start looking for them. They were everywhere—and nowhere.

The sweep lasted for two weeks and was nationwide. Tel Aviv was combed block by block, its houses and buildings searched from basements to rooftops. Hospitals were not immune; casts were chipped off some patients to make certain their wearers were bonafide patients. Nevertheless, the British were unsuccessful in finding any high-ranking underground commanders. Nor were arms caches of any importance discovered by General Barker's men.

But the days of a united Resistance Movement were numbered. *Tenuat Hameri* was beginning to feel internal stresses and strains. The massive arrests and detentions of "Black Sabbath" had begun to erode the Jewish Agency's will to resist. Its leaders feared that continued assaults on military bases risked even more paralyzing British countermeasures, and the Haganah was ordered to stop fighting and concentrate on facilitating illegal immigration. Sneh flew to Paris to try to persuade Ben-Gurion to continue armed resistance jointly with the Irgun and LEHI, but returned with a firm "No," much to the relief of Galili and others in the movement who had started having second thoughts about taking on the British Empire after Black Sabbath. Sitting in Paris, Ben-Gurion must have known that the Irgun and LEHI would go on fighting, leaving him and the

Agency free to negotiate in the international arena with "clean hands."
Ben-Gurion was nothing if not a political pragmatist.

In the summer of 1946, less than a month after Black Sabbath, the Irgun
made its most violent single attack on the British. Begin was determined
to carry out a spectacular operation that would simultaneously deal the
British a heavy blow and dramatize Jewish resistance beyond the frontiers
of Palestine or Great Britain itself. He succeeded.

NOTES

1. Gerold Frank, *The Deed* (New York: Simon and Schuster, 1963).

2. *The Deed*, op. cit.

3. *The Revolt*, op. cit.

4. Doris Katz, *The Lady Was a Terrorist* (New York: Shiloni Publishers, 1953).

5. One of Begin's conditions for joining the Resistance Movement
under its command was the release of his friend Ben-Eliezer, who had
been captured by the Haganah and held for several months. He was freed,
and smuggled out to Italy on a tanker with another Irgun officer to
organize the IZL in the Diaspora.

6. J. Bowyer Bell, *Terror Out of Zion*, Irgun Zvai Leumi, LEHI, and
the Palestine Underground, 1929–1949 (New York: St. Martin's Press,
1977).

Chapter 12

The Revolt:
Part Three

On July 1, two days after General Barker's massive Black Sabbath sweep, the Irgun received a message from the Haganah command to proceed "as soon as possible" with "Operation Chick," the code name for an attack on the King David Hotel. Begin had submitted plans for Chick" to the resistance movement back in the spring. They were approved in principle, but were deemed "too provocative" at the time, and action was deferred. Now, suddenly, there was a green light.

The reason for the urgency was obvious. When Barker's men raided the headquarters of the Jewish Agency, they carted off with their prisoners a truckload of documents containing proof of Haganah's involvement in *Tenuat Hameri*. The material was now in the possession of the British Secretariat which was housed in the southwest wing of the King David. Begin was only too willing to oblige; it was precisely the spectacular kind of attack he had been thinking about for some time, but it could not be carried out immediately. Curfews were still in effect, and the roadblocks were still in place. Moreover, security around the King David had been tightened considerably since spring.

The hotel had become the hub of the activities of the British Administration under Sir John Shaw. A new High Commissioner, Lieutenant General Sir Alan G. Cunningham, an old "Kenya hand" who had liberated Abyssinia from Mussolini's Blackshirts in 1941, had replaced the aged and ailing Lord Gort in 1945. British Military Police and the staff of the Special Investigations Branch occupied an adjoining building in the rear of the hotel, and the entire area, including a car park, was enclosed in heavy barbed wire barricades above which stretched anti-grenade screens. All entrances were guarded by armed sentries behind waist-high sandbag revetments, and the enclave as a whole was additionally protected by an elaborate alarm system which linked the Secretariat, the hotel and the police to a central control located in town on Mamillah Road. At the first sign of trouble a siren would sound and bring a small army to the endangered "mini-Bevingrad."

Except for the southwest wing, however, the rest of the King David—roughly three quarters of it—continued functioning as a fashionable hotel, the best in Jerusalem. It was a center of British social life for civilians, diplomats and the military. The "K-D," as everyone called it, was *the* place for rather boozy luncheons, afternoon teas, cocktail parties and formal dinners, often with dancing. The hotel's bar was always well patronized, as was its grill room, The Régence, complete with Arab waiters in tarbushes and flowing gallabeahs, and turbaned Sudanese busboys. In those twilight days of Empire, the King David was to Jerusalem what Shepherd's was to Cairo, and Raffles to Singapore.

The man in charge of "Chick" was Amihai Paglin, the Irgun's young—he was twenty-three—and resourceful chief of operations. Known in the underground as Gideon,' he was a careful planner and spent weeks gathering data on how best to penetrate the hotel's rather formidable defenses. Information provided by agents disguised as repairmen, delivery boys and lobby loiterers, as well as patrons who regularly frequented the grill room, led Gideon to conclude that success would depend on precise timing and proper placement of a heavy charge of dynamite. The operation had to be timed to avoid civilian casualties, and the required quantities of explosives had to be located where they would bring down only the wing housing the Secretariat.

Gideon's information indicated that the Régence was usually empty during the mornings and early afternoons. Moreover, its kitchens were located, like the grill room itself, in the basement almost directly under the Government wing. Gideon also noted that the hotel used substantial amounts of milk delivered in large cylindrical metal cans. Clearly, the way through the Secretariat's defenses lay via the kitchens, and the most practicable means for delivering the explosives was to substitute them for the milk in those huge cans.

By mid-July, when the curfews were lifted and the roadblocks removed, "Chick" was ready to go. The plan for its execution, as it evolved in meetings between Begin and other leaders of the resistance movement—Moshe Sneh acting for the Haganah and Yellin-Mor for LEHI—called for the attack to take place at about 11 A.M. to coincide with a simultaneous LEHI operation against the David Brothers Building where other Government offices were located. But no date could be set. The LEHI people were having difficulty completing their preparations.

After several postponements, the Irgun decided to go ahead alone on July 22. Last-minute consultations delayed the operation for an hour. It actually got under way at high noon. The date, incidentally, fell on a Monday, a day when the mental and physical reactions of the British were most apt to be at lowest ebb after a bibulous weekend.

At noon, there was a small explosion at some distance from the south end of the hotel's spacious grounds. Seconds later, there was another explosion in the side road leading to the French Consulate. These were "cracker-bombs," noisy but harmless, set off to keep pedestrians away. Meanwhile, a "dairy truck" turned into the hotel drive in the rear and clattered down to the basement entrance to the grill room and the kitchens. There, the fourteen members of the Assault Force got out. Most of them, including Gideon, were dressed in Arab robes, and all were armed with revolvers and Sten guns. They quickly unloaded seven milk cans, each filled with approximately seventy pounds of TNT mixed with gelignite and equipped with timing devices.

The Assault Force then divided into two groups, one for the actual breakthrough, and the other to cover the first. Led by Gideon, the first group carried the milk-can bombs into the basement by way of the grill room, overwhelmed fifteen waiters and members of the kitchen staff and locked them up in a side storeroom. Two British soldiers who happened by, became suspicious and drew their pistols. Both men were shot in an exchange of fire which wounded two Irgunists. Outside, the cover unit engaged British M.P.s who had started firing in the general direction of the kitchen.

During the gunfight outside, Gideon and his men muscled the milk-can bombs into position in the basement, clearly labeled each of them "Mines—Do Not Touch" and set the timers to detonate in exactly thirty minutes. Gideon then freed the Arab workers in the storeroom and ordered them to run for their lives. They obeyed with alacrity, the Irgun "Arabs" mingling with them as they poured out of the hotel's rear entrance.

Gideon and his men piled into their waiting truck under cover of a smoke bomb that exploded at 12:08 on the sidewalk outside the King David and got away. At 12:10 the Irgun's telephonist, a woman, rang the hotel and shouted to the operator: "The hotel has been mined—Evacuate the entire building!" She then telephoned the *Palestine Post*, stating that time bombs had been placed in the King David Hotel and that the people there had been warned to evacuate the building. A third telephone call alerted the French Consulate, situated about one hundred and fifty yards from the hotel, to open its windows as there would soon be a major explosion.

At 12:15, Inspector J.C. Taylor at the control center in Mamillah Road received word of "a disturbance of some sort" at the King David, and the siren started screaming. But by then, Gideon's bombs were in place, and he and his force were gone. Believing, apparently, that with their departure the danger had passed, Inspector Taylor called off the general alert.

The telephone operator at the hotel reported to one of the assistant managers that she had received an anonymous call from a woman who had told her the King David was about to blow up and to evacuate the building. But the guests were not alerted, nor were the members of the Secretariat staff upstairs. At 12:30, the hotel lobby was filled, civilians and men in uniform were in the bar, sipping pre-luncheon cocktails; the lounges were crowded. After the flurry in the basement and the shootout in the street, all seemed suddenly to have turned back to normal—it was just another hot, somnolent Jerusalem noontime in July.

Gideon's well-placed charges exploded at precisely 12:37 P.M. and shook the entire city. The southwest wing of the King David Hotel bulged outward for an instant, them crumbled. The results were greater than expected. A Haganah expert, Yitzhak Sadeh, had doubted whether more than two or three floors would be affected; all six collapsed in a heap of stone and mortar, sheared girders and crumpled concrete. It took days to dig through the rubble for some of the bodies. When the grisly work was completed on August 4, the toll was ninety-one dead and forty-five injured. Among the casualties were a few high-ranking British officers, many civilian employees of the Secretariat, several aliens, a number of Arabs and fifteen Jews.[2]

The fact that many innocent people had been killed and wounded deeply disturbed Begin. His satisfaction "at the success of the great operation," he admitted later, "was bitterly marred by the heavy casualties it had caused." He said he went through "days of pain and nights of sorrow for the blood that need not have been shed."[3] The reactions of the Hebrew press, Ben-Gurion and the Haganah gave him further cause for "pain and sorrow." From these sources came an unexpected flood of denunciations.

The morning after the bombing, *Kol Israel*, the Haganah-controlled radio, broadcast a highly significant statement. "The Hebrew Resistance Movement," it said, "denounces the heavy toll of lives caused in the dissidents' operation at the King David Hotel." The Haganah thus disclaimed an attack that had been jointly planned, and that had been executed at its request. Begin was dumbfounded. He demanded an explanation from Israel Galili, but received in return an order that the Irgun take sole responsibility for the bombing in the interest of future good relations. The Irgun loyally complied.

Meanwhile, the outcry in the press rose to unprecedented levels of stridency. *Al Hamishmar*, a leftwing organ, headlined "Treason and Murder" an article calling for "a campaign of extermination" against the Irgun. *Haaretz* inveighed against "redemption proclaimed by a leper" and called the King David incident, "A frightful blow to all the hopes of the Jewish people." However, the unkindest cut of all came from Ben-Gurion himself who, in an interview in Paris, told a reporter on July 24 that "The Irgun is the enemy of the Jewish people—it has always opposed me."

Clearly Ben-Gurion and the Haganah were washing their hands of the King David business in hopes of reestablishing good relations with the Mandatory Government and with Whitehall. Moreover, they were anxious to obtain the release of hundreds of followers being held by the British. Of the nearly four hundred detained at Latrun, the more than two hundred and sixty held at the Rafa camp in Sinai and the upwards of three hundred exiled to Eritrea, most were Haganah men. Ben-Gurion now furiously anathematized the Irgun and urged Palestine Jewry to turn in Irgunists wherever they were discovered.

The British were unimpressed by Ben-Gurion's disclaimers, and forty-eight hours after the King David blast they issued a White Paper detailing the Haganah's involvement in the Resistance Movement. Among the documents they had captured in their Black Sabbath sweep of the Jewish Agency headquarters, they had found a report by Moshe Sharett (later Shertok), a member of the Agency's Inner Council, praising the Haganah for having destroyed the ten bridges linking Palestine to the surrounding countries and explaining the action's political significance. It was not the only incriminating document that the British had carried away to the King David.

The punitive measures that followed the explosion were directed not against any single underground group but against the entire Jewish community. Jerusalem and Tel Aviv were placed under strict curfew. In both cities, a reinforced division of British troops—about twenty thousand men—conducted search operations as before, but this time with orders from General Barker to shoot curfew violators on the spot. Angrily branding all Jews guilty of complicity in terrorist crimes, Barker put the nation's Jewish homes and shops out of bounds to his officers and men. In addition, he issued a secret order forbidding Anglo-Jewish fraternization in language that was patently anti-Semitic. It said, in part:

> I am determined that they should be punished and made aware of our feelings of contempt and disgust at their behavior. I understand that these measures will create difficulties for the troops, but I am certain (that) if my reasons are explained to them, they will understand their duty and will punish the Jews in the manner this race dislikes most: by hitting them in the pocket . . .

The order was not "secret" for long. A few days after it was circulated among General Barker's officers, it was pasted up on the walls by the Irgun's couriers, and its author was branded a self-confessed anti-Semite.

On the night of July 23, just before the curfew descended on Tel Aviv, Begin left a routine meeting with Yellin-Mor and Shamir, and walked back to his house in Rehov Joshua Bin-Nun, accompanied by his close friend and new adviser, Haim Landau. Early the following morning when British troops came looking for "Rabbi Sassover," they were told that he had gone to Jerusalem. Alerted in time, Begin was hidden in a secret cupboard that Yaacov Meridor had built for him months earlier for just such an emergency. Aliza did not dare open the cupboard to give him food or water, a platoon of British soldiers having chosen to camp out in the garden of the house, under the windows of Begin's groundfloor apartment. She could not take the risk of the children's reactions or of a Tommy walking in—as happened from time to time—to ask for a drink of water or a box of matches.[4] If the troops wondered why the radio was turned up nearly all the time, they made no point of it. Actually, that was how Begin was keeping track of time and the progress of the house-to-house search. He remained in his cramped quarters for four days and four nights—reliving his experiences in solitary confinement in Lukishki Prison—without food or water, in the heat of midsummer. When the Tommies left, he emerged starved and half dead of thirst.

The bombs that blasted the King David Hotel also tore apart *Tenuat Hameri*. Late the following month, the Haganah withdrew from the resistance movement, and the Irgun and LEHI went their separate ways, keeping in touch to avoid duplication of effort, but operating unilaterally. Behind the Haganah's withdrawal, Begin saw the Machiavellian hand of Ben-Gurion at work, but there was little he could do about it except to continue fighting in accordance with his unshakeable belief that by relentless action against them the British would be persuaded to give up and go home.

In September, after a brief pause, the Irgun resumed operations. Three bridges were destroyed, railway lines carrying military traffic were sabotaged at various points and road mines made the highways perilous for army vehicles, especially at night when the hair-thin wires that tripped these particular devices were invisible. So it went throughout the autumn, a season of almost continuous attacks that resulted in a number of British dead and wounded, and sorely tried British nerves. At one point, a gang of soldiers, acting on their own, took revenge. They descended upon several cafés on one of Tel Aviv's busier streets and beat up whatever Jews came their way. About thirty victims were more or less seriously injured.

Then, in December came the floggings. Two teenaged Irgunists were

arrested, tried by a Military Court, found guilty of violating the
Mandatory Government's emergency regulations against carrying arms
and sentenced to fifteen years' imprisonment. In addition, each of the
boys was to receive eighteen lashes. Begin was furious over the "degrad-
ing addendum" to an already severe sentence, which he interpreted as a
"very serious matter with far-reaching moral and political implications."
In 1920, in Brisk, at the age of seven, he had seen Jewish citizens whipped
by Polish troops after the Russian retreat for alleged sympathy with the
Bolsheviks, and he remembered that one of the Jews had died from the
flogging. In Persia, on his way to Palestine from Russia, he had seen
British officers regularly "emphasize" their orders to the "natives" with
their swagger sticks. The thought of Britons flogging Jews in their
homeland was more than Begin could bear.

It was decided at a hastily summoned meeting of the Irgun's high
command to warn the military authorities that for every Jew they flogged
a British *officer* would be similarly dealt with. Begin wrote the warning in
English himself, having added to his knowledge of the language by
listening daily to the broadcasts from London of the B.B.C. It was not
exactly a literary masterpiece, but it made its point clearly enough, and
for obvious psychological reasons—rankers are not always overly fond of
their superiors—the warning was addressed specifically to British officers.
Its message was clear: "If you whip us we shall whip you." The warning
was posted on the walls of Tel Aviv, Jerusalem and Haifa, and across one
of them a British private scrawled in large letters: "Please don't forget my
sergeant-major!"

On December 27, a Friday, young Ben Kimche, one of the two
condemned Irgunists, was taken from his cell in the Jerusalem jail and
given eighteen strokes with a cane as prescribed by the Military Court. A
second warning posted late Saturday evening after sundown reminded the
authorities that "Zion is not Exile. Jews are not Zulus. You will not whip
Jews in their Homeland." Two days later, a British major and three
noncommissioned officers were nabbed by Irgunists in and around Tel
Aviv. Each was given eighteen strokes with a cane and released to tell
about it.

The other boy, a chap named Katz, was still under sentence. The Irgun
issued a third warning stating that if the military dared again to "abuse the
bodies and the human and national honor of Jewish youths," the Irgun
would not reply with the whip, but "with fire." Katz was not beaten; he
was amnestied along with a gaggle of Arabs. No Jew ever again was
flogged by the British in Palestine.

Begin's handling of the flogging episode was no mere application of

Biblical "eye for an eye" retribution; it reflected his fierce devotion to the sanctity of his fellow Jews as human beings. Whatever happened to them, happened to him personally. A humiliated, maltreated or otherwise tyrannized Jew was a humiliated, maltreated, tyrannized Menahem Begin who, during his Siberian exile, had evolved a philosophy about dealing with tyranny. The gist of it was that while not *"every* end" justified *"all* means," the odious principle that "the end justifies the means," so dear to dictators, was in fact applicable in fighting tyranny.[5]

Begin saw the British in Palestine not merely as a "foreign government" but as a tyrannical regime to be got rid of by whatever means the accepted laws of warfare allowed short of assassination, which remained the province of the FFI. British personnel were not, except in a few specific instances, the target of Irgun attack. This was not, as one member of the high command[6] has said, "a manifestation of superior virtue or half-heartedness, but the rational tactic of an underground movement facing a power infinitely greater in both manpower and firepower." Indeed, during the four fierce years of Irgun activity the number of casualties inflicted on the British forces was amazingly small, a little over two hundred out of an army that numbered between eighty thousand and one hundred thousand troops. This included casualties inflicted by LEHI and the FFI, which recognized no restrictions, and by the Haganah in the seven months of its own participation in joint operations.

From the outset, the Irgun's mission—the "end" it sought to achieve—was the liberation of Palestine from its British overlords. The "means" the Irgun employed were destruction of British military and governmental installations, harassment of their communications and humiliation of their personnel by revealing them to their fellow-countrymen back home—and to the world at large—as incapable of governing a people determined to achieve national independence. As the year 1946 ended, evidence mounted that the Irgun was succeeding in swaying public opinion in London and elsewhere, especially in the United States. There various committees and individuals, among them author Ben Hecht, were collecting substantial amounts of funds and organizing supportive meetings and demonstrations on behalf of the Irgun and its objectives.

Psychologically, the flogging of the British major and three noncoms had a greater impact than the King David blast. The incident literally resounded round the world, and British prestige suffered a damaging blow. From his seat in the benches of the opposition, Winston Churchill, always deeply concerned about his country's prestige, accused the government of not knowing "how to behave like men." "You whip a Jewish terrorist," he cried, "and the terrorists catch a British major and three noncommissioned officers and whip them the next day. You then cancel the whipping of another terrorist. Do you know what this means?"

Whether His Majesty's Government knew what it meant or not, the rest of the world did.

Begin received congratulatory telegrams from proud Diaspora Jews, Irishmen, Americans, Canadians and Frenchmen. A French newspaper published a howler of a cartoon showing a British soldier holding his steel helmet over his exposed backside. The caption explained that after their men had been flogged, the British military authorities had decided helmets should be worn not on the head but to protect the other area. France, Begin said later, "rumbled with laughter . . . ridicule can be more destructive than high explosive bombs."

After caning, the British tried hanging. The consequences proved infinitely more corrosive of British authority in Palestine than the whippings. Whitehall seemed to have learned nothing from the use of the gallows against rebels in Ireland. There the rope had merely created martyrs, not respect for law and order. So it was in Palestine.

In the spring of 1946, the Irgun had invaded the Tegart fortress at Ramat-Gan, near Tel Aviv. In the ensuing battle three Irgunists were killed and a fourth, Dov Gruner, was captured. Tried by the usual three-man Military Court, he was sentenced "to be hanged by the neck until dead." Three other Irgunists—Yehiel Drezner, Mordechai Alkochi and Eliezer Kashani, captured on their way to attack installations at Lydda Airport—were also under sentence of death by hanging, having wounded a British soldier when they attempted to run through a roadblock on the road leading to the airport.

Begin and the high command did not believe the British would actually execute men who should be regarded as prisoners of war and stepped up operations. Irgunists struck at military headquarters in Tel Aviv's Citrus House, at the Importers Building where police were billeted and at the Jaffa police headquarters. An attack on the army's East Surrey camp on the shores of Haifa Bay resulted in the death of a British officer, and there were five casualties in another raid on the camp at Kiryat Haim.

The rising crescendo of violence brought more troops, more barbed wire, more roadblocks, more sandbagged guard posts and new plans for tightening British security in the Mandate. In mid-January, High Commissioner Cunningham, newly returned from a London conference with his superior, Chief of the General Staff Montgomery, announced the imminent arrival in Palestine of yet another crack division. Simultaneously, stringent restrictions were imposed on British security forces to reduce their vulnerability to attack from the Irgun and LEHI. Existing "Bevingrads" in Jerusalem and Haifa were greatly enlarged, and additional ones were created. Cafés and movie houses were placed out of bounds, and the wives and children of British government personnel, military and civilian, were moved into the expanded "security zones" preparatory to sending them back to England. Jewish residents in the areas taken over by the British for their extended Anglo-Saxon "ghettos" were forced to leave their homes. The Crown's troops were instructed never to walk alone but in groups of no less than four. In the name of security, the British turned Palestine into a prison and locked themselves into it.[7] They could leave it only in convoys of cars escorted by Bren-gun carriers.

On January 24, a Friday, Gruner's death sentence was confirmed. The Irgun learned of the decision late the next day, and Begin summoned his high command. A plan was quickly devised and swiftly executed. As many British officers as possible—four or five—were to be kidnapped and held until Gruner's death sentence was successfully appealed. But even plain noncommissioned British soldiers were hard to come by under the new regulations; they walked in fours as ordered and were always well-armed. After twenty-four hours, the Irgunists were still empty-handed.

On Monday, January 27, however, they netted two "big fish" in Tel Aviv. One was Major H.A.I. Collins, a British intelligence officer masking as a retired business man, the other was a well-known jurist, Judge Ralph Windham. Major Collins was "taken" at his home, and Judge Windham was "captured" in a hallway outside the courtroom in Rehov Yehuda Halevi where he was trying a case.

The British promptly clamped a curfew on Tel Aviv and parts of Haifa and Jerusalem, and threatened to invoke countrywide statutorial martial law. The Haganah informed the Irgun that Dov Gruner's sentence would not be carried out because it was under appeal, and prevailed on Begin to release the captives. Justice Windham was set free on Tuesday evening, and Major Collins the following day. The authorities accordingly postponed Gruner's execution because, they said, an appeal was pending before the Privy Council.

Begin was no longer directing the Irgun's operations from the old headquarters in the house in Rehov Joshua Bin-Nun. A hotel was being built next door, and the police were zeroing in on the neighborhood. Early in 1947, before the new security measures went into effect, he had been obliged to move again.

A new and spacious apartment was rented for the Begins on Yosef Eliahu Street in a modern residential section of Tel Aviv near the Habimah Theatre. Its selection was entrusted to "Uncle" Meir, who based his choice on its two-fold advantages: it was on the ground floor and had a separate main entrance, so that none of the family needed to use the communal staircase, and it had no fewer than five exits—in case of emergency.

With the new home came a new identity. Quite by chance, a passport was found in a public library, a document formerly the property of a Dr. Yonah Koenigshoffer, a name which suited perfectly, a friend said, because it "sounded Germanic and simply reeked of loyalty and law and order." Begin shaved his beard, keeping only a bushy moustache and discarded the long black coat for gray flannels, a tweedy jacket, proper shirt and necktie. *Rebbe* Israel Sassover became Dr. Koenigshoffer, non-practicing attorney-at-law. To confuse matters further, the doorplate on the new apartment read: "Mr. and Mrs. Oppenheimer." The Polish Jew from Brisk became a proper *Yekke*, a Jew of German origin.

British Intelligence still had no idea what Begin looked like. Rumors were circulated by Irgun agents that plastic surgery had so altered his features that he was no longer recognizable as the emaciated little Polish soldier with the toothbrush moustache who had arrived in Palestine in 1943 and whose photograph was in the CID files. Back in February, 1945, while Yaacov Meridor was still interned in Eritrea—he subsequently escaped to Italy—he had occasion to "confirm" the rumored transformation. An interrogator told Meridor that according to information in the army's possession, Begin had undergone "a plastic operation which makes it difficult to recognize him." He asked, "Is that true?" Meridor took pains to seem confused and shocked, and cried out: "No. It's not true. He wouldn't do such a thing. I would have known about it." Yaacov's reply and manner convinced his interrogator that Begin had entirely changed his features surgically and so informed the CID in Palestine.[8]

Nevertheless, security around Begin was tightened considerably. There were no armed bodyguards or sentries, no dramatics, but extreme care was taken to limit his contacts with the outside world. Rare visitors were carefully screened long before they were brought to the house.

Within the Irgun "family"—the high command—Begin was now called "Ben David" (Son of David), after David Raziel. His lieutenants shortened this to "Bad"—pronounced in Hebrew with a broad "a"—and this was the name generally applied to him, except in his own home where everyone called him "Aba," for "father." Neither "Menahem" nor "Begin" was ever used by his most intimate collaborators, even in the strictest privacy. Closest to him at the time were Samuel Katz, a cultured and literate Revisionist from South Africa, known as Shmuel, and Haim Landau, whose underground name was Avraham. Both were members of the high command.

The new "Aba" puzzled little Benny, who was now four years old, a bright, observant child. With his beard gone, Begin looked ten years younger. On seeing his father for the first time with only a moustache and attired like a normal middle-class citizen, Benny asked his mother whether an uncle had come to visit. Then Begin spoke, and Benny knew it was "Aba."

Benny was something of a "security problem." In his presence, conversations had to be considerably camouflaged lest he let something slip to his playmates at kindergarten. But if Benny was puzzled by the strange goings on at home, he never let on at school. "Perhaps," Begin decided, "he sensed something, instinctively . . ." Nevertheless, it was thought safer not to rely entirely on the boy's discretion, and everything discussed in the house had a code name, while everyone who came to meetings there had a pseudonym with "uncle" or "aunt" attached to it. Katz, for instance, was "Dod Yaacov," and his wife, Doris, who often acted as Begin's chauffeur, was "Dodah Rivka." [9]

It was while residing in Yosef Eliahu Street, where at last he had a study all to himself, that "Ben David" faced the most difficult decisions of the Irgun's rebellion. Four Irgunists were sentenced to death by hanging, and Begin almost hourly lived their fears and anxieties. Their sentences were confirmed by General Barker in mid-February as his last official act before leaving Palestine, and Gruner, Drezner, Alkochi and Kashani knew they were doomed. "In those days," Begin later wrote, "I pondered . . . the heroism of men awaiting death in the cells of the condemned. Which is nobler, I reflected, bravery in battle, or fortitude in a death-cell?"

What to do? How to save these brave men? Gruner, for one, wanted no mercy from the British. During his trial, he had refused to sign a paper that would have commuted his sentence to life imprisonment. Instead, he made a ringingly patriotic statement:

Of course I want to live. Who does not? . . . The right way to my mind, is the way of the people in these days; to stand up for what is ours and be ready for battle even if in some instances it leads to the gallows. For the world knows that a land is redeemed by blood . . . I swear that if I had the choice of starting again I would choose the same road, regardless of the possible consequences to me.

After Barker departed, however, the executions were postponed, and Begin clung to the hope that the men would not be hanged after all.

Meanwhile, the Irgun's rebellion continued. Revolutions, like wars, develop their own inner kinetics. "A revolution," wrote Victor Hugo, "is not cut off square. It has always some necessary undulations before returning to the condition of peace, like a mountain on descending towards the plain." [10] Begin knew he could not "cut off square" the Irgun's revolt against the British, and the high command met regularly at the new address to plan more spectacular operations.

No drama surrounded the sessions of the high command. Its members would slip in one by one, giving only a code ring at the doorbell to announce themselves. Full meetings concentrated on the tactical conduct of the struggle, the detail and timing—and political impact—of major operations. Such meetings, however, were infrequent and irregular. None lasted more than three hours, the maximum Begin would allow for fruitful discussion. Often, the meetings were held sequentially, Begin sounding out each member as he came, to consult on the problem of the hour. If an emergency decision had to be made, one member of the high command would speed around the city for consultation with his scattered colleagues.

In February 1947, the British declared the Mandate "unworkable" and laid the problem of the future of Palestine in the lap of the United Nations.

And that spring, the revolt entered a period of agony for the *yishuv*, the Irgun *and* Great Britain, bled white by World War II.

One member of the Irgun's high command—Shmuel Katz, Begin's expert on propaganda and foreign relations—saw in Britain's United Nations move the beginning of the end of the British presence in Palestine. England's growing economic difficulties at home in the grim winter of 1946–1947 and unrest in the Empire at large—India clamored for independence and verged on civil war, and nationalist movements were making themselves heard in Malaya, Kenya and Egypt—would force her to cut her overseas commitments. Besides, Katz argued, pressure was mounting in London to "bring the boys home" from Palestine. Another six months of a united effort—Irgun fighting side by side with the Haganah and LEHI—and Britain would be obliged to leave, Katz said.

Sobered by bitter experience, Begin was not optimistic. To start with, he had little faith that *Tenuat Hameri*, the Humpty Dumpty of resistance, could be put back together again. Moreover, there were indications Britain actually had no real intention of getting out. In the House of Commons, Colonial Secretary Sir Arthur Creech-Jones corroborated this when he sought to placate Conservative opposition by declaring that England "was not going to the United Nations to surrender the Mandate," and Bevin added, Britain was only asking the UN for advice on how to handle the situation in Palestine. At the War Office, General Montgomery was stressing Palestine's strategic importance as a base from which to defend the eastern approaches to the Suez Canal and to protect the oil fields of the Middle East. If the British meant to pull out, argued Begin, why then were they expanding their "security zones" in Palestine, bringing in more troops and recruiting more policemen? "Join the Palestine Police and See the World," the posters said. (Local wits altered the text to read ". . . and See the '*Next*' World.")

No, Begin decided, the fight was far from over yet. The Irgun stepped up its campaign.

On March 1, a Saturday, Begin ordered more than a dozen major operations. All came after sunset in keeping with Irgun's rule never to attack on the Sabbath. The main assault was directed against Goldschmidt House, the British Officers' Club, in the heart of Jerusalem's "Bevingrad" compound. Sunday morning's newspapers described the Club as a total wreck from satchel bombs tossed in by Irgunists who had crashed the outer defense perimeter in a heavy truck under covering fire from a well-placed machine gun on King George Avenue opposite the Yeshorun Synagogue. Total casualties were listed at more than twenty killed and thirty wounded, including several women.

In London, Lord Beaverbrook's Empire-minded *Sunday Express* headlined the story: GOVERN OR GET OUT. That morning, martial law was proclaimed in Palestine, with a strict curfew on Jewish areas. Anyone was liable to be shot and killed. Automatically, all soldiers now had police powers. The curfew was accompanied by an intensive search in Jerusalem and Tel Aviv. General Sir Gordon MacMillan, Barker's replacement, was determined to "stamp out terrorism," and appropriately code-named the process Operation Elephant in Tel Aviv and Operation Hippo in Jerusalem. But neither Elephant nor Hippo achieved the desired result.

For all its severity, martial law failed in preventing Irgun and LEHI from continuing their attacks. Although the country's telephone system had virtually ceased operating and traffic on the roads was limited to military and government vehicles traveling under armed escort, the underground seemed to have little difficulty with communications, and its assault forces somehow managed to arrive at their pre-determined targets, many of them within the well-protected "security zones." The Irgun and LEHI hit here, there, everywhere. There was constant sniping; fires erupted suddenly in unexpected places; road mines exploded under army jeeps and personnel carriers; grenades burst among groups of soldiers patrolling the streets.

In mid-March, martial law was lifted, and Operations Elephant and Hippo were scrubbed. In the House of Commons, Churchill was not alone in demanding to know how much longer the "squalid warfare" would be allowed to continue.

Early in April, Britain sent an urgent message to Trygve Lie, the Secretary General of the United Nations, asking him to summon a special session of the General Assembly to examine the Palestine problem. At the same time, however, Britain's representative at the United Nations, then housed, ironically, at Lake Success, made it clear that London reserved the right to reject any United Nations decision. Then, to demonstrate to the world body that Britain was still in "firm and resolute authority" in Palestine, and not, as many supposed, too weak to administer the Mandate, Whitehall authorized the execution of the four men held in jail in Jerusalem.

The impending fate of Dov Gruner, Drezner, Alkochi and Kashani had weighed heavily on Begin and the high command. Dov had been severely wounded in the jaw when he was captured months before in the Irgun's raid on the army camp at Ramat Gan. He had undergone several operations and known much pain. Begin had wanted to send a specialist to him, but the young man refused, protesting it was too great an expense for "the family"—the Irgun—to bear. Long before Dov's first appeal went to the Privy Council, Gideon, the Irgun's chief of operations and the IZL's military genius, had devised a daring plan to "spring" Dov Gruner and the others from the Jerusalem jail. But it required a British armored car captured intact at precisely the right time and place in order to arrive— manned by Irgunists disguised as soldiers—at the prison during the afternoon exercise period in the jail's courtyard. Once there, the condemned men would rush to the vehicle which would then shoot its way out. The plan was found impractical and was discarded. In the meantime, two more captured underground fighters, Moshe Barzani of the LEHI and Meir Feinstein of the Irgun, were also sentenced to death.

On March 31, two weeks after martial law was raised, the LEHI's activists exploded bombs inside the huge refinery at Haifa. The resultant flames burned for days. The harbor-side city was under a pall of greasy black clouds of smoke from the burning oil tanks. They were still burning on April 14, when the four condemned Irgunists were taken from their cells in Jerusalem and transferred, under heavy guard, to the fortress prison at Acre.

On April 16, another strict curfew was imposed, and on that day, in the gray half light before dawn, the narrow corridor outside the cells of the condemned men in Acre filled with troops. Gruner, refusing to stand on command, was rudely yanked to his feet. There was no last meal, no final request, no rabbi, no warning.[11] Dov and the others began singing *Hatikvah*.

> As long as within the heart
> A Jewish soul yearns,
> And forward towards the east,
> An eye turns to Zion . . .

Across the yard, another prisoner, Chaim Wasserman, turned in his cot and glanced at his watch. It was just after four o'clock, yet he thought he heard singing. He listened intently and could make out the words of what is undoubtedly the most solemn anthem in the world.

> . . . Our hope is not yet lost,
> Our hope of two thousand years
> To be a free people in our land
> The land of Zion and Jerusalem

Then he knew. He started shouting to the others in his cell block. "They're hanging Dov Gruner!" [12] The other prisoners—about ninety LEHI and Irgun men—stood up and began singing too. Dov Gruner, Drezner, Alkochi and Kashani did not die alone.

Next morning, Thursday, April 17, the British announced that the four men had been executed by hanging. The curfew, they said, would remain in force until further notice. The execution of Barzani and Feinstein was set for April 21.

Begin immediately issued orders to kidnap British soldiers to be hanged in retaliation. Over its underground radio, the Irgun broadcast a communique warning the British what the executions would mean. Drafted by Begin, it said, in part:

> . . . We will no longer be bound by the normal rules of warfare. In future every combatant unit of Irgun will be accompanied by a war court of the Jewish underground movement. Every enemy subject . . . taken prisoner will immediately be brought before the court, irrespective of whether he is a member of the army or the civilian administration. Both are criminal organizations. He will be tried for entering illegally into Palestine, for illegal possession of arms and their use against civilians, for murder, oppression and exploitation; there will be no appeal against the decision of the people's court. Those condemned will be hanged or shot. [13]

Day after day Irgun patrols searched the streets and back roads for unwary British soldiers but none was to be found. HMG's troops were abroad only in force and heavily armed or rode in armored personnel carriers. Most of the British garrison was confined to barracks or remained beyond reach within the barbed wire perimeters of their

"Bevingrads." Meanwhile, Barazani and Feinstein, who had lost an arm in the raid that had resulted in his capture, saw no possibility of escape. They realized, also, that a break-in operation from the outside involved greater risks than their respective operations could afford. Knowing themselves to be doomed, they could at least deprive the British of the privilege of executing them, and, perhaps, take their executioners with them. They smuggled out a request for grenades.

This too proved impossible from the outside, but Irgun comrades in a nearby cell—men who had not been condemned to death—manufactured a single grenade from smuggled materials and somehow managed to pass it on in a scooped out Jaffa orange. In the third night watch, after they had received the spiritual solace of prayers with a Rabbi, the two condemned men clasped each other in brotherly embrace in their common cell, placed the grenade between them chest high, released the pin, and pressed yet closer to each other . . .

Barazani and Feinstein died at approximately 11:40 on the night of April 21. News of their death only stimulated the Irgun to greater efforts to find hostages. Failing, both the Irgun and LEHI intensified their struggle against the British.

Meanwhile, on April 28, in faraway Lake Success, the General Assembly met in special session and created UNSCOP—the United Nations Special Committee on Palestine. Composed of representatives from eleven countries, none a major power, UNSCOP was to travel to Europe and the Middle East and hear the testimony of the interested parties—Britain, the Jews and the Arabs—and produce a proposal for consideration by the world body.

The Irgun and LEHI were not impressed. As far as they were concerned, the British would stay in Palestine no matter what any committee might suggest to the contrary. In their view, a Jewish state would not emerge from the revolution as a result of another inquiry. Both Begin and his counterpart in the LEHI command planned new and heavier blows against the common enemy.

NOTES

1. Gideon, Amihai Paglin, died February 25, 1978, of injuries sustained in an automobile accident January 30 that killed his wife. He was 55 years old. The couple left a son and a daughter.

2. Why the King David was not evacuated was never satisfactorily

explained. One witness, who was in the hotel at the time, told the Haganah that when he and others tried to leave after the first warning explosions outside, their way was barred by British troops with rifles. Begin later claimed, based on information from Galili, that when the alarm reached an unidentified high British official, that gentleman exclaimed, "We don't take orders from the Jews here, we give them." It seems possible, even probable, that Monday morning hangovers in high places accounted for the failure of the British to react promptly to the repeated warnings. In any event, there was no official investigation.

3. *The Revolt*, op. cit.

4. Samuel Katz, *Days of Fire* (London: W.H. Allen, 1968).

5. Begin, *White Nights*, op. cit.

6. Samuel Katz, *Days of Fire*, op. cit.

7. Bell, *Terror Out of Zion*, op.cit.

8. Ya'acov Meridor, *Long Is the Road to Freedom* (South Africa: Newzo Press and Publishing Company, 1955). (Translated from Hebrew)

9. Doris Katz, *The Lady was a Terrorist*, op.cit.

10. Victor Hugo, *Les Miséarables*.

11. Bell, *Terror Out of Zion*, op.cit.

12. Jan Gitlin, *Conquest of Acre Prison* (Tel Aviv: Hadar, 1962).

13. Begin, *The Revolt*, op.cit.

August, 1948. As chief of the Irgun Zvei Leumi, Begin addresses a crowd of Jerusalemites in Zion Square. *Wide World Photos*

November, 1948. Begin with his wife, Aliza, and children Leah, Hassia, and Benjamin Zeev. *Wide World Photos*

March, 1957. The Begins enjoy a game of chess. *Wide World Photos*

May, 1950. Menahem Begin speaks at a party rally in Tel Aviv.
Wide World Photos

1967. Menahem Begin, member of the Knesset. *Wide World Photos*

August, 1959. Begin calls for "no violence" in Haifa. *Wide World Photos*

November, 1977. Egyptian President Sadat whispers into Premier Begin's ear during a state dinner at the King David Hotel in Jerusalem.

Wide World Photos

December, 1977. President Sadat and Prime Minister Begin during peace talks in Ismailia, Egypt. *Wide World Photos*

November, 1977. Prime Minister Begin and President Sadat shake hands after the press conference in Jerusalem. *Wide World Photos*

March, 1978. President Carter and Prime Minister Begin walk toward the White House for a day of talks on the Mideast situation. *Wide World Photos*

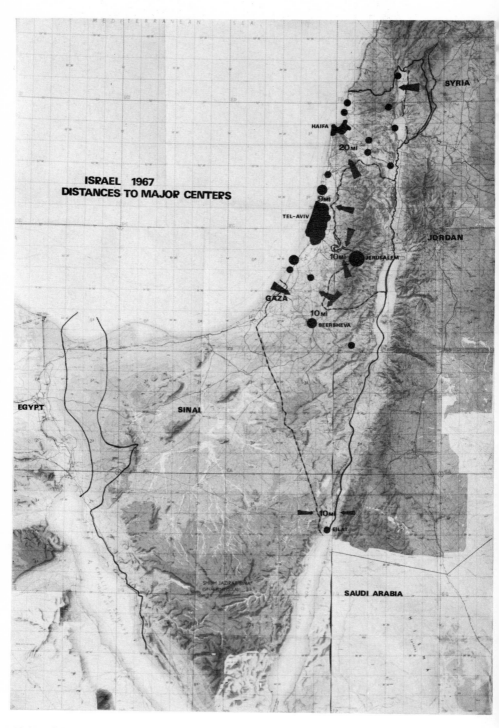

1967. Distances to major centers in Israel.

Chapter 13

The Revolt:
Part Four

What spurred the underground to more strenuous endeavors in the burgeoning spring of 1947 was the knowledge of British brutality to the condemned men while they were held in the Jerusalem jail. Stories, that until then had been just so much hearsay, were documented by a long message written by Drezner and smuggled out before he and the others were transferred to the fortress prison at Acre. Correspondents, especially those who had covered British units during World War II and recalled their gallantry in battle and their—on the whole—decent treatment of POWs, found the reports unbelievable. Confirmation of British cruelty comparable to that of the Nazis in occupied Europe came as a shock to them—and to Englishmen back home who increasingly doubted the wisdom of continuing in Palestine what was rapidly becoming a losing campaign of repression.

Reporters covering "the troubles" in Palestine demanded proof, and the Irgun was only too happy to provide it. Begin had received a complete account of what Drezner, Alkoshi and Kashani had endured from the time of their capture, with a fourth comrade during "Operation Wilhelma"—when they ran into a British roadblock in their attempted attack on Lydda Airport several months before—until shortly before their execution. The prisoners' report was written in tiny Hebrew characters on sheets of toilet tissue which had then been tightly wadded and spirited out by well-paid Arab warders. Smoothed and pieced together, the slips told a horrendous story. It is reproduced below in full that the reader may better understand, perhaps, what motivated some of the more desperate operations undertaken by Begin and the Irgun during the final year of the underground's revolt:

Before Wilhelma, I decided to stop the car and jump into the orange-grove. But the driver lost control of the car and it ran into a barbed-wire barrier set up on the road by the Army. The barrier was dragged along by the car and it was only the second barrier we hit that stopped us. At that moment a Bren-gun opened fire on us from behind, and then the car was surrounded by "anemones" with their revolvers aimed at us. We had no choice but to leave the car with our hands up. Eliezer got a bullet in his back and Mordechai (the driver) in the shoulder. The bullet went right through and came out. As we came out I got a blow in the back and rolled into the ditch. As I lay I heard a revolver-shot and I saw a soldier pointing his revolver at Mordechai. He fired, missed Mordechai and killed his brother-Britisher. He at once hit Mordechai over the head with his revolver and threw him on to me in the ditch. We both got to our feet while, with their revolvers trained on us, they kicked us. We heard more shots. I thought they would finish us all off. When they finally took us into an armoured car we found two others. Eliezer was not there. After that we did not see him. The others had also not seen what had happened to him. He had had some difficulty in getting out of the car and they were under the impression that the soldiers had shot him in the car.

Then began the chapter of beatings which ended only the next day at seventeen hours—about twenty hours consecutively.

Amid blows, we were taken into a small armoured car, each of us guarded by a soldier. The guards at once emptied our pockets, ordering us to keep our hands up. They took everything: our watches, about fifty pounds in cash, purses and notebooks, pens and pencils, even a handkerchief and a comb. When they had done with this, they all began to hit us. They aimed particularly at our faces and stomachs. When we doubled up from blows to the stomach they would hit us in the face to straighten us up again. I remember how my nose ran blood like water from a tap and the soldiers called out happily: "I have broken his nose."

This journey ended in a camp I do not know. They shoved us out and took us to an open field. They stood us in a row, about ten soldiers formed a line in front of us and loaded their rifles. I must mention that we all stood the test, and nobody lowered his head. At that moment an officer came running up and reprimanded the soldiers, who had apparently really meant to finish us off. We were led to a room. They kept us there about half an hour. All the time—

from the time we were caught—we had our hands up. After half an hour, when our hands had turned to stone, they put us into a big truck and laid us on the floor. They saw a ring on Mordechai's finger and tried to take it off. When it would not come off they pulled his finger with all their might until they thought it was broken, and then gave up. We came to an anemones' camp and there an officer ordered us to be taken into one of the huts. It was a kitchen which had not been used for some time, about fifteen by forty-five feet. There they undressed us. They took everything off . . . but as we were manacled to each other the clothes remained hanging on our hands. To get them off they pulled with all their strength and injured our hands. What they did not manage to tear off this way they cut off with a razor blade. We were left as naked as on the day we were born.

They began an organized attack for which they had apparently got an officer's permission or orders. They hit each of us in turn and then all together. Four or five soldiers took part in this. When they got tired, they were relieved by others. They hit us with their fists in the head and the feet, and they kicked us in all parts of the body not even omitting the testicles. Among the beaters were two policemen who had apparently been sent to guard us. One of them moved around with a big baton which he brought down on our backs, or legs or stomachs. One of these blows broke Eliezer's hand and caused a sprain in Haim Golor's back. One blow I got on my neck almost made me faint. This went on until late at night. An officer came in then and ordered them to stop hitting us, to wash us and give us blankets for sleeping. They poured water over our heads and each of us had to wash the other. The wash did not help much as our wounds were bleeding and we immediately became dirty again. The four of us, wet and naked and shivering with cold, lay down in one blanket and covered ourselves with two other blankets. (That was all they gave us). But no sooner had we dozed off than the guard came, kicked us awake and pulled off the blankets. We had such visits about every fifteen minutes.

Towards morning they ordered us to get up and "wash" again. The blanket we had lain on was soaked in blood and had changed its colour. After we had washed they gave us clothes so that we should dress. Three of us were not given our shoes. So, covered in our rags, we were made to run all the way to the "hospital-room." On the way every soldier we met hit at us with his fists or his rifle-butt, and our guards did not spare us either. We ran with our hands above our heads. In the dispensary they kept us for about three-quarters of an hour with our hands up until the doctor came.

A doctor, a short elderly man, looked at our wounds and asked the soldiers if they wanted to go on "playing" with us. The soldiers replied in the affirmative. "All right then," said the doctor, "I'll bandage their wounds afterwards." (They did not realize that I understood English).

They made us run back the same way to the place we had come from. They again undressed us and took us outside, and there poured slop-water over us. Then soldiers standing around were invited to volunteer to hit us, and there was no lack of volunteers. They then took us inside again and ordered us to wash the floor and scratch our blood off the walls. Only then I saw what that kitchen looked like. There were pieces of dried blood on the walls and we had to scratch them off with our nails. They beat us as we did it. Suddenly the policeman pulled us away and ordered us to kneel and kiss the ground. When we refused we were beaten with a cudgel. But we did not do as he asked. They put another pair of handcuffs on me—apparently they had noticed that I was encouraging my comrades in their rebelliousness. When they handcuffed me I did not want to do anything, and they again hit me. Finally they took off the extra handcuffs.

At about nine o'clock they washed us again . . . and gave each of us a pair of trousers. The same doctor came again and had plasters put on two of us. After that a police officer came, accompanied by the Jewish officer Karlik and several detectives. They hardly questioned us, asked only our names and addresses. All day the police came and went and meantime the soldiers did not stop "playing" with us. Towards evening only Karlik remained in the next-door room and they took us out to get us to sign the charge-sheet. While Karlik was sitting in the next room a giant corporal came in and ordered us to do all kinds of humiliating things. When we refused he beat us mercilessly. I told the boys not to keep quiet this time so that our cries should reach Karlik. I had told him clearly that he was the only Jew we had met and that he must do everything to get us out of there otherwise they would beat us to death. He promised . . .[1]

Irgunists went looking for the camp mentioned in the report and for the perpetrators—the paratroopers who wore crimson berets and were therefore called "anemones" in the underground—but in vain. The CID man in question was shadowed persistently, but it was found impossible to lay hands on him. He always traveled in an armored car and after a while was transferred out of the country. An Irgun "court" sentenced him to death in absentia.

Meanwhile, the search for hostages continued. Irgun units patrolled country roads and the streets of cities and towns, but the military literally were not to be found. They left their camps only in convoys escorted by tanks. "We could, of course, have attacked them too," Begin said, "but in those angry days that was not the retaliation we aimed at. It was our duty to pay the hangman in precisely his own coin. And we did not succeed. The army dug in more deeply in their hiding-places . . . (and) the big debt remained unpaid." [2] But not for long.

In the early afternoon of May 4, 1947, a Sunday, one of Paglin's most daring operations was set into motion. Its objective was to break into the ancient citadel at Acre that served the British as a prison. It was where Gruner, Drezner, Alkoshi and Kashani had been hanged, and where sixty-one other Irgunists, among them Eytan Livni, as well as about thirty other underground fighters, were serving long sentences. In 1799, the fortress had withstood Napoleon's siege and had never been successfully forced, not even when the city itself surrendered to the Egyptian viceroy Ibrahim Pasha in 1832. Until British officers could be found for hanging, what better revenge than to release imprisoned comrades?

A detailed story of how Gideon Paglin, working from the outside, and Eytan Livni, his predecessor as the Irgun's chief of operations, planning from within, managed the simultaneous break-in and break-out which Begin later likened to "storming another Bastille," would require at least a long separate chapter. [3] As the Irgun's commander subsequently related it in his wordy memoirs, it was another glorious episode in his country's struggle for independence. Actually, it proved more important for its consequences than its accomplishments. None can dispute its daring, but insufficient allowance was made for the risks attending the getaway. The result was death and grievous injury to many of the Irgunist and LEHI prisoners involved. Here, briefly, is what happened.

Inside the prison, impregnable from its normal northern approaches, Livni discovered a vulnerable spot, a room where kerosene was stored for the jail's cookstoves and heaters. The room was on the south side and reachable from neighboring rooftops. Livni reported this to Begin in a smuggled note, and the Irgun's commander assigned Gideon to reconnoiter. For two weeks, Gideon and an aide—disguised at times as Arabs, at others as English businessmen—surveyed an approach to the high window of the kerosene room and an escape through the narrow, winding, always crowded alleys that served Arab Acre proper as streets.

With the aid of a map of Acre provided by an Irgun agent employed in Haifa's Department of Public Works, Gideon developed a somewhat complicated route for entering the city's maze of alleys and lanes with a small truck and getting out again. He also plotted a way over an outer wall and onto the rooftop of an Arab house that could serve as a platform from which to reach the barred windows of the kerosene room.

From the inside, Eytan assured Gideon that with some help from the outside, the prisoners could make their way to the designated room. Eytan said he needed explosives to blast two stout iron gates along the passageway leading from the prisoners' cells to the kerosene room, and civilian clothing for the men who would be escaping. The explosives were smuggled into the prison in jars of jam and marmalade, and the detonators came in the false bottom of a large tin of olive oil. Prisoners serving time for minor offenses received special treatment, which included permission to wear civilian clothes on the Sabbath; they were persuaded to ask for additional clothing. Obliging friends and relatives complied, and soon all was ready at Livni's end. The clothing and the explosives were hidden in an escape tunnel which LEHI men had started earlier, but which was abandoned at Livni's insistence after he had established contact with Gideon and knew that a "break-in" was "in the works." [4]

Obviously, however, not all the Irgunist and other prisoners could be liberated. It was left to Begin to decide who should escape and who should remain behind. It was a difficult decision to make, but Begin was pragmatic about it. The Irgun and its underground allies needed men experienced in handling weapons and in performing the kind of often complex sabotage operations the struggle against the British required. Besides, only a limited amount of transport would be available. The final figure decided upon after much discussion was "no more than forty-one," the maximum number that could be accommodated in the planned convoy and safely hidden in pre-determined places. The figure worked out to thirty seasoned Irgunists and eleven veterans of LEHI. Begin stubbornly refused to increase the total.

The selection of the escapees was left to Livni and the two LEHI commanders, Matti Shmulevitz and a man named Zettler. However, they did not immediately make their choices, or communicate details of the impending break-out outside their circle, with one exception, Michael Ashbel, a demolitions expert and composer of the underground's popular ballad, "On the Barricades." He would make the charges needed to blast the two gates between the cells and the kerosene room.

The attack on the "impregnable" fortress-prison would be made by a force composed of thirty-four handpicked men uniformed as members of the British Royal Engineers. They would travel in convoy, in three vehicles—two three-quarter-ton trucks and one three-tonner—all properly painted a greenish color and correctly marked. The convoy would be led by a "Captain" and two privates in a regular army jeep.

As operational commander, Begin picked Shimshon (Dov Cohen), who had served with the British in Africa and Europe and was promoted to staff sergeant and decorated for bravery beyond the call of duty. He had a fine, clipped, British accent and manner, and possessed the daring and knowledge of military operations which the Acre assignment required. With him in the jeep traveled "privates" Kabtzan and Shmulik.

In addition, an Irgun squad of "Arabs" would move separately to an area overlooking the encampment of a British unit outside Acre's defense perimeter. The Irgun "Arabs" were to provide diversionary fire during the actual attack and covering fire for the withdrawal with two-inch mortars and automatic weapons.

The convoy was to start from the Irgun's hilltop settlement at Shumi, in Samaria, about forty miles from Acre, and wind its way slowly down into the Valley of the Crocodile until it reached the main north-south coastal highway. Then it would head north with official-looking Movement Orders specifying the convoy's destination as Beirut. The vehicles were to reach their designated objective at Acre before 4 o'clock in the afternoon, in full daylight, so that the operation, set for 4:15, would be completed before curfew time at nightfall when there would be too many British roadblocks and careful inspection of all suspicious-looking vehicles.

On reaching the main highway, the convoy sped northward carrying cases of mines, high explosives and weapons, mostly Bren-guns. Officers and men moving in the opposite direction, bona-fide Britishers headed for Tel Aviv and Jerusalem, smartly saluted the three pips on Shimson's shoulder tabs, and Shimshon returned the salutes. Passing troops waved in comradely fashion.

As Shimshon's convoy approached the outskirts of Acre, small groups of Irgunists dropped off here and there to set up roadblocks against the possibility that the British might bring up reenforcements when the "balloon went up" at the prison. Just before the convoy entered Acre proper, the Irgun "Arabs" started lobbing small-calibre mortar shells on the nearby army camp, at once a diversionary and preventive action.

Minutes later, the first of the convoy's two small trucks, driven by Solomon, second in command, managed to maneuver its way through a heavy traffic of donkeys, handcarts and Arab pedestrians to the south side of the citadel out of sight of the few guards on the fort's watch towers. From the vehicle jumped a "telephone repair crew" with a ladder which was placed against the wall of the Arab house abutting the prison wall. Up went Yehuda Afirion with boxes of "telephone equipment"—high-explosives and detonating devices to blast through three feet of stone. Solomon handed up a second, slightly longer ladder, with which to reach the windows of the kerosene room. Heavily burdened, Afirion scaled the second ladder, placed the explosives and set the detonators. Then he and Solomon came down and returned to their truck parked at the end of the alley. It was 4:15.

Inside, Livni waited. The signal for the break-out operations to start was the expected explosion. Every minute seemed an eternity. Each of the men slated to depart had donned civilian clothes, shaved—except Livni, who kept his red beard—and listened intently for the blast that would mean freedom or death. Those who by now knew they weren't leaving also waited, but to carry out assigned tasks. Some armed with weighted socks were to fight off Arab warders and Arab prisoners who might try to escape with the others.

The explosion came at 4:22. The citadel shuddered much as it must have during Napoleon's bombardment, but only momentarily. Solomon and Afirion looked up, saw that the breach they had made was small, and wondered whether it would serve its purpose. The fort's 450-odd Arab prisoners, many of whom were listed in prison records as "criminally insane," began screaming. The Arab warders seemed stunned, not knowing what was happening or what to do. The British guards on the towers started shooting down in the direction of the alley and into the courtyard which had suddenly turned into a mass of hysterical Arabs running this way and that through clouds of dust.

Inside, Livni and his men went into action the instant the external charge exploded. Menahem Malatzky and Michael Ashbel blasted the first iron gate, then the second, and opened the passageway to the kerosene room. A group of Irgunists, led by Dov Efrat, soaked rags and discarded prison clothing in olive oil, lighted them and created a wall of flame and thick black smoke behind their escaping comrades and against an onrush of Arab prisoners who had broken out of their cells. It worked.

Breaching the wall, however, was only half the task. The exit of the escapees and their route to the waiting vehicles had to be secured. A party of Irgunists subjected the watch towers to a steady fire with Bren-guns and rifles. Every one of the chosen prisoners got through the breach—plus more than two hundred Arabs who saw a chance at freedom, took it, and vanished into the old city's labyrinth of souks and alleys.

The bewildered fortress staff, on reduced Sunday strength, reacted slowly to the emergency but managed to call for reinforcements. A police station dispatched an armed patrol. A military party rushed toward the scene from an army camp inside the Acre defense perimeter. Haifa, thirteen miles away, sent a truckload of troops. According to an official British account published later, however, none of the units reached the prison area in time to cut off entirely the prisoners' escape. The police were stopped by one of the minefields laid by Shimshon's men. The troops were halted by another Irgun roadblock. The speeding truck from Haifa hit an Irgun mine and was wrecked enroute. In the camp outside Acre the Irgun's mini-mortars (mere two-inchers) caused so much confusion that no effective action was taken. The "security ring" which the Irgunists had constructed within the army's prison defenses had done its job.

From then on, however, everything seemed to go wrong. When Shimshon took off on his mission, he airily promised to "bring back Eytan and all the other boys hale and hearty." [6] Eytan and most of the Irgun and LEHI prisoners were in fact brought safely back to an underground base. But Shimshon himself and several others never returned.

Once down in the alley, most of the escapees hurried through swarms of Arab peddlers, strollers and shoppers toward the Continental Gate, the main entrance to the old city, where the three-tonner waited. The others piled into the small truck parked at the end of the lane in the shadow of the prison's south wall. Loaded, the vehicle took off, then stalled. Restarted by vigorous pushing through the excited crowd, the driver suddenly found himself confronted by a mob between him and the gate where other Arabs were attempting to close the heavy wooden doors, but a noisy grenade dispersed them. The truck clattered through the gate and joined the other vehicle parked just outside. The two trucks then moved off in convoy following a pre-determined roundabout route that would take them onto the Haifa-Beirut road at a point beyond British road-blocks. As the second vehicle moved off, however, a burst from a policeman's Bren gun hit the rear end. Haim Appelbaum, a LEHI man, was mortally wounded. He was the only casualty in the first two vehicles.

But the third lorry—the second of the two small trucks—ran into serious trouble. What happened to it and to its occupants was subsequently related in a letter to Livni from Matti Shmulewitz, one of the survivors. A party of British soldiers had gone bathing that fine Sunday afternoon on a beach just south of Acre. When the Tommies heard the explosion and the sounds of battle coming from the direction of the prison, they hurriedly donned their uniforms, grabbed their stacked weapons, ran up to the main road and set a roadblock *inside* the mined impediments laid by the Irgunists. Matti's letter said, in part:

> As you know we ran into a road-block and into crossfire. . . . Several seconds previously our driver had seen Shimshon running towards us on the road and signalling us . . . not to go on to the road. By the time the driver had grasped the meaning of the signals he had reached the bend. He swerved round the road-block at speed and in trying to straighten out he brought the truck off the road and ran into a cactus fence. The engine stalled. The machine-gun fire was heavy but we heard clearly Shimshon's call "After me!" Mike (Ashbel) was wounded while still in the truck and others were wounded while they were jumping out at the back. For a few seconds we ran around looking for a way out of the zone of fire, but wherever we turned we faced machine-gun barrels. When we were all wounded and had begun to run along the ditch by the side of the

road we suddenly saw Shimson running towards an army vehicle standing in the road. We ran after him and jumped on to it. There were two unarmed soldiers in it and a driver. Shimshon forced the driver to start and the more lightly-wounded among us jumped on to the soldiers and held them down. There were now only nine of us left. Haim Brenner had been killed in the ditch by a bullet in the neck. Mendel had been wounded in the back and could run no further. Nitcha too had remained wounded in the ditch and Yitshak Kuzinevsky remained with him to bind his wounds and did not succeed in reaching the vehicle.

It seemed that we were saved. We got out of the range of fire and began to take stock of the wounded. We could hold the soldiers no longer as we had no arms and most of us were wounded.

We passed Shimshon's jeep and there he ordered the driver to stop. When he learnt there was a driver among us (Shemesh) we turned the soldiers out and transferred the Bren-gun and ammunition from the jeep. Meanwhile the troops were approaching us again and we again came under fire. Shemesh took the wheel—and discovered that the engine would not fire. He started to repair it, when suddenly a truck appeared coming towards us. We jumped out and ran towards it. Shimshon fired a round in the air, and the truck stopped. With Shimshon were Shemesh and Amnon. I dragged Barukh Shmukler and Shimon (Shimon Amrami). They were both wounded in the legs and other parts of the body. Barukh's right elbow was terribly shattered and as we ran under the rain of bullets, he said to me: "To hell with it. I shall get used to writing with my left hand. They'll definitely take off my right."

The Arabs in the truck jumped out, and (among) them was a soldier with a rifle. The driver began to argue with Shimshon as he stood with the Bren by the door, with Shemesh at his side. Shimshon fired and the driver fell out of the truck, (shot) in the head. At that moment the catastrophe occurred which sealed our fate. Shemesh, as he saw the driver falling out, too hastily jumped into the driver's seat and in his haste got in front of the barrel of the Bren before Shimshon had had time to stop his fire. Shemesh fell dead on the spot. We were left without a driver. Amnon took the wheel and tried to turn the truck round, but he could not. He was wounded in the ribs and the elbow. Shimshon ran back to the jeep, took up a position behind it and held up the advancing soldiers. There he fell. I had never met him before but from the moment I saw him in action he aroused my admiration. . . .

Nissim Kazas flung himself empty-handed on to the soldier who aimed his rifle at him, threw him to the ground and knocked him out with the butt. . . . We dispersed in the field on the other side of the road. Mike, Barukh and Shimon did not run far. The three of them lay down together, all seriously wounded, particularly in the hands and legs. Shimon was wounded in the shoulder. Moshe Salamon, Joseph Dahar and I got farther than the others. We reached a cornfield and there lay down to survey the ground. In front of us was corn and we saw soldiers running about. . . . The road on the other side of the cornfield was steadily filling up with soldiers and police. The cornfield was small and the only way out of it was through an open field beside the road; but there we should have been discovered at once. We decided to lie where we were till dusk.

After about fifteen minutes soldiers came into the field and found us. They fired at us after we had surrendered and only by a miracle did we come out alive. Joseph was wounded again. We were saved by the intervention of a police officer who (ordered) the soldiers not to kill us. Shimon, Mike and Barukh did not have this good fortune, and as they lay wounded on the ground each of them had three shots fired at his stomach. Barukh miraculously was not hit.

They took us to a truck. The wounded were dragged along the ground and were thrown into it as one throws chattels. We lay in a single heap, the wounded and the dead together. Only Moshe Salamon, who was unhurt, and I, wounded only in the hand, were able to help the others. . . .

After managing to pull the dead . . . off the wounded I spent most of the journey talking to Shimon. He knew he was dying. I tried to deny it and to cheer him up. Mike (Ashbel), who also knew his end was near, lay and joked. It was hard to believe that this man was going to die. From time to time he would sigh, but then added at once: "It will still be good. Don't worry." An Egged (tourist) bus, full of Jews, stood on the road as we pulled up to take on another wounded man, Amnon. Mike, lying on the bench, saw their faces as they looked at the frightful spectacle, and called out to them: "Jews, see, we are dying for your sakes."

On the way to the hospital they took us to the Acre Police Station. There they threw the wounded on to the pavement. To my shouting, my appeals, and my demands that a doctor should be brought, there was one reply: "Shut up!"

The first to die was Shimon. I was with him all the time. He was conscious to the last. I cannot tell you what went on inside me as I saw my good friend dying. His chief anxiety was the sorrow his death would bring to his parents and his friends. . . . His last words were "Matti, avenge, a-v-e-n-g-e."

Levi died in horrible pain. He was wounded in the lungs and was suffocating. . . .

Mike joked up to the last moment. The same old Mike. I held his hand, felt him growing cold and yet could not believe he was dying. He continued to comfort me to the end. "Don't worry, it will still be good. We'll pay 'em yet."

Nichto lay quietly. As he lay on his back I saw the blood oozing from the hole in his back. I turned him over on his side and told him not to move. He was wounded in the leg too and it was hard for him to lie on his side. After a few minutes he said in a submissive voice: "Matti, may I turn over. It's hard lying this way". . . . the doctor came at long last . . .

It is certain that most of the boys who died of wounds could have been saved had they been given medical aid. As it was, they were left to bleed for *six hours*. . . .

What Begin called "the greatest jail-break in history" made headlines in the world press and focused attention more sharply than ever on the Jews' struggle in Palestine. Operation Acre was undeniably a dramatic episode. An underground Jewish force had attacked an apparently impregnable British stronghold in the heart of an Arab city, blasting its way in and shooting its way out. But Begin and Paglin counted the cost: five of the attackers captured and four killed; of the would-be escapees, five killed, seven wounded, and several recaptured. Next day, Homer Bigart wrote in *The New York Herald-Tribune*, "the heart of the Irgun Commander is very bitter at the heavy casualties." The reporter, Begin said, was quite right.

Begin could derive some comfort, however, from the report on the Acre attack published on June 4 by High Commissioner Cunningham in which he admitted that "no mere numbers of troops or police can guarantee security against attack on many thousands of buildings, bridges . . . postoffices, hundreds of miles of roads, railways and oil pipelines." Complete defense of all such installations against "organized attacks which are liable to be carried out anywhere and at any time of the day or night for years on end," Cunningham said, "is not a practical proposition. It must be borne in mind that the dissidents are trained in underground tactics. . . ."

Cunningham's message was clear: It was impossible for the British government to impose order in Palestine by force. yet it was the only method London seemed to know, and on June 16 three of the five Irgunists captured by the British during the fighting outside Acre— Avshalom Haviv, Meir Nakar and Yaacov Weiss—were sentenced to be hanged.

At the trial, Weiss, a Hungarian Jew who had saved hundreds of co-religionists from the Nazis during World War II and had fought in the underground in Budapest, testified to the barbarous treatment accorded the wounded at Acre. He warned the authorities that retaliation would follow. "And though we shall not compete with you in maltreatment of wounded men and sadism," he declared, "you will be repaid . . . in full."

His comrade, Meir Nakar, delivered a scathing denunciation of the Mandatory Government. "British rule in Eretz Israel," he said, "is bankrupt . . . A government whose officials have to sit in barbed-wire ghettos—is that a government? A government which spends half its budget on police purposes and yet remains helpless in face of the anger of the people in revolt—is that a government?"

Avshalom Haviv equated what was happening in Palestine to what had happened a generation earlier in Ireland. "When the sons of Ireland rose up against you," he said, "you tried to drown the rising in rivers of blood. You set up gallows, you murdered in the streets, you exiled, you ran amok and stupidly believed that by dint of persecution you would break the spirit of resistance which is God's gift to every man worthy of the name. You were wrong. Free Ireland rose in spite of you. If you were wise, you British tyrants, you would hurry out of our country . . . now."

The three British officer judges listened stonily, put on their hats and pronounced the fateful words:

"You will be hanged by the neck until dead."

The condemned men stood up and sang *Hatikvah*.

Earlier, on May 15, the General Assembly of the United Nations had passed a resolution calling upon all parties in the Palestine dispute to refrain from violence *or the threat of violence*. (Italics mine–F.G.) At the time, the Irgun and LEHI formally notified the United Nations that they would respect the appeal of the world body provided the British did likewise. The verdict of the Military Court of June 16 coincided with the arrival in Jerusalem of the United Nations Special Committee on Palestine. The Committee actually was holding its first meeting when the sentence was passed. On behalf of the Irgun, Begin addressed a memorandum to the Committee reminding its members of the United Nations resolution of the previous month, pointing out that death sentences were "acts of hostility and violence." Begin asked that the Committee intervene on behalf of the doomed men.

The Committee took up Begin's appeal and cabled Secretary General Trygve Lie its concern that the execution of the death sentences might seriously interfere with UNSCOP's work. Relayed back from the United Nations to Sir Henry Gurney, Secretary to the Palestine government, the petition was rudely rejected. Obviously, while Britain welcomed an UNSCOP inquiry into the situation in the Mandate, it would countenance no interference in the administration of British justice in the territory.

Realizing that UNSCOP could not save the condemned men, the Irgun intensified its hunt for hostages. After several unsuccessful attempts to kidnap high-ranking British officers in Jerusalem and Herzliah, on July 12, an Irgunist patrol captured two unarmed noncoms in Netanya. They were Sergeants Mervyn Paice and Cliff Martin. The captives were hidden in a soundproof underground bunker in the basement of a factory in Netanya for cutting and polishing diamonds. They were told what would happen to them if the three Irgun men were hanged and left in the airless chamber with water, a week's supply of food, a bucket for a latrine, and two cylinders of oxygen.

Netanya and surrounding settlements were placed under martial law by the British and an intensive house-to-house search was instituted. Five thousand troops descended on the area. They seized and questioned nearly fifteen hundred inhabitants in and around Netanya, but the captives were not found, not even during two thorough searches of the diamond factory itself.

Then, on the evening of July 17 came news that swept the drama of the missing sergeants from the front pages. Royal Navy destroyers patrolling off Haifa sighted and intercepted a weird-looking, high-decked single-stacker making for port. The ship was the *Exodus*, a four-thousand-ton, wooden-hulled vessel built in the mid-1920s for the Chesapeake Bay excursion trade. Aboard her were more than forty-five hundred men, women and children whom the *Exodus*, after sailing across the Atlantic, had taken aboard at Sète, near Marseilles, in southern France.

The saga of the *Exodus* is too well known to warrant repetition in detail here. The ship docked at Haifa, the refugees were debarked, herded into stockades, sprayed with DDT, and after barely touching Palestinian soil, were reembarked on three prison ships whose decks were caged in with wire. The reloading completed, the vessels steamed out to sea and presumably headed for Cyprus, the usual destination of intercepted "illegals." The passengers were taken, instead, back to Sète, and ordered to debark. They refused. Then, an ultimatum arrived for the refugees from London: Disembark in France within forty-eight hours or be taken to the British-occupied zone of Germany. Eighteen days later the refugees were in Hamburg and once more behind barbed wire in a land they had hoped never to see again.

The departure of the three British prison ships— "floating Ausch-witzes," a French priest called them—was a signal for renewed under-ground violence. Even the Haganah, quiescent since the arrival of the United Nations Special Committee on Palestine, resumed operations. There were bloody attacks in Haifa, Jerusalem and Hadar Hacarmel.

Mine explosions, ambushes, night raids and sniping resulted in thirteen British killed and nearly eighty wounded. In Haifa harbor, the Haganah, using limpet mines, sank the British lighter *Empire Lifeguard*. In Tel Aviv there was a general strike; in Netanya the curfew continued and the search for the missing sergeants went on and on, and was finally suspended.

The British were more determined than ever to prove to the United Nations Committee and to the world at large that they were still masters in their own house. On the evening of July 28, Yaacov Weiss, Meir Nakar and Avshalom Haviv were advised by their jailers that they would be hanged in the morning. The three men responded by standing up in their cell and singing *Hatikvah*. Jewish fellow prisoners heard them and joined in the macabre concert. No British lives were lost in the escape operation at Acre. Yet, the three were to be hanged. Major Charlton, the prison superintendent, was astonished, and refused to carry out the sentence; he was discharged and sent back to England. His replacement was Captain Clough, the superintendent of the Nablus prison, who had supervised the hanging of Dov Gruner and his comrades.

Gideon Paglin was relaxing at a movie on the evening of July 28 when an aide brought him word that the three Irgunists were to be hanged the following morning. He slipped out of the theatre and hurried to Begin's house where a meeting of the high command was being held. Gideon took Begin aside and proposed that the captive sergeants be hanged immediately. There was no time to be lost; the British intended putting the entire country under curfew by 11 o'clock on the morning of hanging day. The execution of the hostages had to be carried out, therefore, before the roadblocks went up and intensive searches of vehicles began. The deed could be done in the factory basement, Gideon explained, and the bodies moved elsewhere.

Begin hesitated; he was reluctant to allow Paglin to go into an area heavily patrolled by the British, but finally consented. Policy, not revenge, however, motivated Begin's decision. The Irgun was politically committed. In an article in the underground Irgun press, Shmuel Katz had written: "We recognize no one-sided laws of war. If the British are determined that their way out of the country should be lined by an avenue of gallows and of weeping fathers, mothers, wives and sweethearts, we shall see to it that in this there is no racial discrimination. The gallows will be all of one color. Their price will be paid in full."

At Acre prison, the three Irgunists were hanged between four and five A.M. on the morning of July 29 as scheduled. All three died singing

Hatikvah and Michael Ashbel's stirring "On the Barricades." Avshalom Haviv's voice was silenced by the hangman's noose at 4:03; Meir Nakar's at 4:28 and Yaacov Weiss' at 5:02. From each, the last words their friends heard were "Avenge us!" The Irgun did not fail them.

Early the same morning, Paglin sped his small car, a dilapidated-looking Morris Minor, toward Netanya. There he picked up three other members of the execution "team," and threaded his way through British security traffic to the diamond factory. They were not challenged on the way; the curfew was not yet in effect. There was still time, several hours, in fact. Nevertheless, a sense of urgency seized Gideon and his men. Even as they lifted the sandbagged hatch of the underground bunker where their captives had lived for seventeen days on the oxygen and food Paglin had provided, the Irgunists could hear army vehicles rushing by outside, moving into place ahead of curfew time.

The first sergeant was dragged out, groggy from confinement in a limited space with barely enough oxygen to sustain life. He was whiskered, red-eyed and more dead than alive. Taken into a raftered room, he was hooded, bound hand and foot and unsteadily propped up on a stool under a noose dangling from a beam. At a signal from Paglin, the stool was kicked out from under him. The grim business was repeated with the second sergeant and another noose.

Twenty minutes later the two bodies were taken down, placed in the rear of a jeep, covered with a tarpaulin and driven several miles over back roads to a eucalyptus grove near a settlement on the outskirts of Netanya. There the ropes were tossed over the limbs of adjoining trees, the bodies were lifted free of the ground and left dangling. In the vicinity of the bodies, the departing Irgunists planted a mine.

The executions were announced by the Irgun over its secret radio and in its Wall newspapers. However, the British were unable to find the victims until the Irgun, worried that Jewish settlement guards who were aiding the search might set off the mine and themselves be injured or killed, telephoned the police the location of the eucalyptus grove. Aware the area might be booby-trapped, the British cut down the bodies with long pruning hooks, but then exploded the mine when they dragged one of the bodies across it from a safe distance.

The messy business shocked the world. Loudest in the ensuing denunciations was the Jewish Agency, which condemned the deed as "a vile murder by a gang of criminals." In Geneva, where he was attending sessions of the ongoing UNSCOP investigation, Moshe Shertok declared, "It is mortifying to think that some Jews should have become so depraved by the horrible iniquities in Europe as to be capable of such vileness." [7]

Anti-Semitic violence erupted in London, Liverpool, Manchester and Glasgow. Here and there Jewish shops were broken into and looted; Jewish synagogues were smeared with lurid slogans; some Jewish cemeteries were desecrated. In the House of Commons, Creech-Jones expressed the view of most Englishmen when he said, "In the long history of Palestine there has scarcely been a more dastardly act than the cold-blooded and calculated murder of these innocent young men after holding them hostage for more than a fortnight."

With one exception, the British press uniformly condemned the Irgun's deed and called for reprisals; the theme was set by the *Daily Telegraph* which urged the British security forces to "Take the gloves off." The lone exception was the liberal *Manchester Guardian* whose chief editorial writer clearly saw the handwriting on the wall and headed a leader: "Time to Go." Obviously, the time for the evacuation of Palestine had arrived. But the British were not yet prepared to accept the inevitable, and the blood-letting in the Mandate continued. Britain in general, but Bevin in particular, seemed engaged in a baffling contest of wills with Palestine's Jews.

The British were ready to evacuate Egypt, India, even Greece—where Britain had shifted the economic, political and military burden of preventing a Communist takeover to the United States which accepted it in March 1947 with the Truman Doctrine—but not Palestine. The upkeep of their armed forces in the Mandate was a colossal economic drain, as well as the cause of a grave manpower shortage at home. In all other sectors, even at the risk of imperial insecurity, the British were reducing their military commitments. Yet they hung on by their nails to the sliver of Mediterranean real estate called Palestine, maintaining there upwards of one hundred thousand armed men to protect mysterious interests no one could fathom.

Like India and Egypt, Palestine had become an expensive nuisance, yet the War Office was spending on it millions of pounds sterling contributed by hard-pressed postwar British taxpayers. The crux of the problem was the adverse balance of payments. Britain had forfeited most of its overseas investments and the bulk of its maritime trade revenues during World War II without devising substitutes. Under the circumstances, the experts advocated as a sole panacea the reduction of military commitments which would save Britain many tens of millions of pounds and tens of thousands of essential workers. Drastic cutbacks of army establishments were being carried out in India, Egypt, Greece, even Germany, but not in Palestine. On the contrary, the government was recruiting more policemen and troops for service in the Mandate.

Bevin, who had rejected a traditional *pro*-Zionist policy on the ground that it would require another division in Palestine for enforcement of his government's policies, was now compelled to send more than another division to impose an *anti*-Zionist policy. It was evident that he regarded the Zionist struggle as a plot against himself personally, and at one point went so far as to threaten to resign—and bring down the Labor Government—if his Palestine policy were altered.

Despite Bevin's personal attitude, however, a consensus was forming in Britain and within the Labor Party itself that the only hope of peace in Palestine rested with the United Nations. During the late summer and autumn of 1947, the center of world interest shifted gradually away from Palestine toward Geneva and Lake Success. The underground's struggle in the Israel-to-be, however, was far from ended. Indeed, it entered a new, more intensive phase describable only as all-out war, first against the British, then against Arab aggression.

NOTES

1. Begin, *Ibid*.
2. Begin, *Ibid*.
3. A fine account appears in J. Bowyer Bell's *Terror Out of Zion*, op.cit.
4. Livni, interview with the author.
5. Bell, op.cit.
6. Begin, op.cit.
7. *Palestine Post*, August 4, 1947.

Chapter 14

And So to War

In the late summer of 1947, the United Nations Special Committee on Palestine completed its study of the crisis in the Holy Land, and on August 31 submitted to the General Assembly at Lake Success a report in which seven of the eleven members—Canada, Czechoslovakia, Guatemala, the Netherlands, Peru, Sweden and Uruguay—recommended partition. The three members against it were India, Iran and Yugoslavia, which favored a federated, binational Arab-Jewish state. The eleventh member, Australia, abstained.

The Committee called for the creation of independent Jewish and Arab states in the territory west of the Jordan River, the internationalization of Jerusalem under a United Nations Trusteeship and economic union of the three areas. Basically, the proposals differed little from those previously put forward over the years by half a dozen other committees and commissions charged with the task of reconciling the conflicting interests of Arab and Jewish claimants to the same area.

What the Committee had sought, no doubt, was an alternative to blood and fire in the Holy Land. What they produced, however, was another truncation of Palestine, the second since Britain's arbitrary creation of Transjordan in 1921. Although Transjordan remained under British Mandate, it was subsequently exempted from those clauses in the Mandate that provided for the development therein of a Jewish national home in accordance with the Balfour Declaration of 1917. The creation of Transjordan reduced the territory pledged to the Jews for their future state from forty-five thousand square miles—an area approximately equal to the size of Pennsylvania—to the 10,000 square miles lying between the Jordan River and the Mediterranean Sea, an area about the size of Maryland.

Transjordan was "manufactured" in Jerusalem in the summer of 1921 at a conference attended by Winston Churchill, then Secretary for War and Near Eastern Affairs in David Lloyd George's government; Sir Herbert Samuel, the newly appointed British High Commissioner for Palestine, and the Emir Abdullah, a Bedouin chieftain from the distant Hejaz, fetched to the meeting by Colonel T. E. Lawrence, indefatigable Arabophile and intriguer. Churchill represented a government that stood in mortal fear of the Russian Revolution, then in full cry, and that was anxious to solidify Britain's position with the Arabs, possessors of enormous oil resources. Samuel, although Jewish, was more eager to serve his government than his fellow Jews. Lawrence was his usual persuasive self, and Abdullah was, from his point of view, a man with a genuine grievance—he had not been sufficiently rewarded for his contribution to the Allied victory over the Turks in World War I. The matter was settled, history records, in thirty minutes: Churchill simply lopped Transjordan from Palestine, and a kingdom of Hashemite Bedouins from faraway Hejaz, with no prior claim whatever on the land of Palestine, was created.

It was this initial amputation of Palestine, incidentally, that led to the major struggle within the Zionist movement between the followers of Weizmann and those of Jabotinsky. It resulted in the latter's defection and the emergence of the New Zionist Organization. Weizmann and his followers were inclined to accept the drastic reduction in the area of the Jewish state-to-be, whereas Jabotinsky's followers—the Revisionists—thought it inexpedient and illegal. In a celebrated witticism, Jabotinsky defined Palestine as "a territory whose chief geographical feature is this: the Jordan River does not delineate its frontiers but flows through its center." His pupil, Menahem Begin, would so define it throughout his career as underground fighter, politician and, within the limits of the possible, as statesman.

In the UNSCOP plan presented to the United Nations in the summer of 1947, the Balfour Declaration's "Pennsylvania" shrank further and even more drastically to an only slightly larger "Connecticut" of less than six thousand square miles. Quite apart from the proposed reduction in territory, however, the plan was full of weaknesses: The boundaries were arbitrary and artificial; the provisions for economic union were unrealistic; Jerusalem was entirely surrounded by Arab territory, physically removed from Jewish Palestine and without its own outlet to the sea. Geographically, the proposed Jewish and Arab states were entwined in an inimical embrace like two fighting pythons each bent on swallowing the other.

Begin and his advisers—Haim Landau and Shmuel Katz—had tried to influence the Committee in the direction of a more favorable territorial solution, but without success.

During its month-long sojourn in Palestine before moving on to Geneva to ponder what they had seen and heard, the Committee's members, individually and in groups, visited factories and *kibbutzim* and interviewed Arab and Jewish leaders. They saw a country at war, the British virtually isolated in their "Bevingrads," the inhabitants restricted to their homes by nightlong curfews, the roads filled, mainly with military traffic, and everywhere Tegart fortresses, sandbag breastworks and barbed wire. Few of the members possessed the historicity—or the inclination—to view the situation for what it was—the struggle of a Jewish people for independence and nationhood in the Promised Land. Most seemed inclined to the idea that what was going on in Palestine was simply a tragic, irrational Jewish-Arab conflict, an inevitable stroke of fate over which the peoples concerned had no control. That, of course, is what it would become, but not what it was in June and July, when the Committee toured the Holy Land and when the British still had the military muscle to impose a Zionist solution in the *whole* of western Palestine had they so desired.

The Zionist point of view was presented to the Committee by Ben-Gurion, Shertok, Abba Eban and other members of the Jewish Agency. They saw in UNSCOP the representatives of a supreme international body, Zionism's court of last resort whose epochal judgment would decide Zionism's political and historical destiny. When, inevitably, the idea of partition was broached to them, they eagerly grasped it as an acceptable solution, for they had been instructed by the Inner Council of the Jewish Agency to work for the creation of a Jewish state "in a suitable area."

There were only two meetings with the Irgun, both very secret, neither of them with the Committee as a whole but with those few members who truly desired to hear "all sides." The first was held in the home of the poet, Yaacov Cohen, on June 26, 1947. It was arranged by a newspaperman, Carter Davidson, chief correspondent in Palestine of the Associated Press, who had made contact with the Irgun's Shmuel Katz, and was overtly sympathetic to Begin's cause. Present were Menahem Begin, Haim Landau and Katz for the Irgun. The Committee was represented by its chairman, Justice Emil Sandström, an elderly Swede, reticent and almost pathologically neutral, Dr. Victor Hoo, Assistant Secretary General of the United Nations, a Chinese, long-time diplomat, aloof, not really interested in the Palestine issue, and Dr. Ralph Bunche, the profoundly intelligent black American, and the driving force that kept

UNSCOP's wheels turning. As chairman of the United Nations' Trustee-ship Council, he had been seconded to UNSCOP as head of its three-man Secretariat.

During the meeting, Begin apparently launched into a passionate denunciation of British behavior in Palestine, citing the barbaric treat-ment of Irgun captives—Gruner and three of his comrades, said Begin, his voice rising, were at that very moment "waiting in the shadow of the gallows." Dr. Hoo and Dr. Bunche were visibly moved by Begin's emotional speech, but Judge Sandström shushed him, fearing he might be heard outside the house. The Judge evidently imagined the place surrounded by British troops. It wouldn't do for an eminent Swedish jurist to be caught interviewing "terrorists." Begin apologized and calmed down.

Sandström asked only one question of any importance. He wanted to know what would happen if the Arabs attacked the Jews after a British evacuation. The prospect of an Arab-Jewish war was the chief argument the British were using against evacuating the country, maintaining they were in Palestine to protect the Jews from the Arabs. Begin pointed out that the Arabs would not attack unless "a certain third party encouraged and aided them." He emphasized, however, that should the Arabs decide to wage war they would be roundly defeated. In modern warfare, Begin reminded the Judge, brains and high morale, not numbers, decided the issue.

In his exposition, Begin stressed Jewry's claim to the *whole* of Palestine (including Transjordan), which prompted Dr. Hoo to ask: "Assuming you get Palestine on both sides of the Jordan as a Jewish state and you bring in several million people, what will you do about the increase in population? The country is small. What is going to happen in three hundred years' time?" Begin turned the question around, stressing the absurdity of any plan that would set up a small Jewish state in only a part of what remained of the country. It was Katz, however, who caused Dr. Hoo to drop the subject. "That is a universal problem," he said. "What do you think is going to happen to China in three hundred years?"

Throughout the meeting, which lasted three and a half hours, Dr. Bunche asked many questions and took copious notes. He elicited from Begin the Irgun's desire for complete evacuation of Palestine by the British, the removal of British rule, the setting up of a provisional government and the creation of a free, independent, democratic Jewish state. Dr. Bunche's questions enabled Begin to stress that the Jews had lost six million people in the Hitlerian Holocaust, that tens of thousands of Jews were languishing in intolerable conditions in British displaced persons' camps in Cyprus and elsewhere, and that British air and naval forces were being used to intercept ships at sea carrying Jews wishing to come to Palestine.

As the meeting drew to a close, the elderly Judge Sandström unbent sufficiently to express his regrets to Begin that other members of the Committee would not hear the Commander's testimony. Dr. Hoo left with, "*Au revoir* in an independent Palestine." Dr. Bunche, however, was the warmest of all. Shaking Begin's hand, he exclaimed, feelingly, "I can understand you. I, too, am a member of a persecuted minority."

When news of the meeting leaked, the British were furious. In Parliament, the government's spokesmen were subjected to scathing criticism. British troops and police had been looking for Menahem Begin for five years without success, despite a posted reward for his capture of 10,000 pounds Sterling (about $50,000 at the time). Yet, the Chairman of UNSCOP had found him with the greatest of ease. Incredible! The British press was scandalized.

A second international incident occurred when Begin met later with the South American members of UNSCOP: Dr. Jorge García-Granados, Guatemala's Ambassador to the United States, a short, stormy man given to quick, original thought, and his friend Professor Enrique Rodríguez Fabregat, of Uruguay, a left wing liberal with a brilliant political past. Both humanitarians and revolutionaries in their own right, Granados and Fabregat proved highly susceptible to Begin's argument for liquidation of the British Mandate and the creation of a Jewish state in the whole of Palestine.

"The Arabs and the British," Begin urged, "have unofficial mouthpieces on the Committee. Our people has none. You two, who do not hide your feelings, should counter the demand that Palestine should be Arab or British, by the demand that Palestine should be Jewish . . ."

García's reply was candid and illuminating. He said he was under the impression that the majority of the Committee were inclined to recommend the liquidation of British rule, but they had to take into account the presence of the Arabs in Palestine. "They feel," he said, "that they cannot be 'one-sided.' Moreover, it would be strange indeed if Rodríguez and I were to demand more than Mr. Shertok. And you know as well as we do that the Jewish Agency is proposing partition."

Begin knew then that the underground's cause was beaten. The Jewish Agency had cut the ground out from under the feet of the Irgun and LEHI. Begin realized that no foreigner, no matter how friendly and well-intentioned, could claim for a nation more than its own official representatives demanded. He was sure, after talking with García and Rodríguez, that UNSCOP would propose partition—and that the Jewish Agency would accept it.

In the bitter debate that followed UNSCOP's presentation to the General Assembly, Rabbi Hillel Silver, as spokesman for Palestine Jewry and the World Zionist Movement, did in fact accept the proferred one-fifth of the "Balfour loaf" as better than none. "If heavy sacrifice is the inescapable condition of a final solution," he said, "if it makes possible the immediate reestablishment of the Jewish state, the ideal for which a people has ceaselessly striven, then the Jewish Agency is prepared to recommend acceptance of the partition solution. This sacrifice would be the Jewish contribution to the solution of a painful problem and would bear witness to the Jewish people's spirit of international cooperation and its desire for peace."

On the other hand, the Arabs opposed the proposal and threatened war to prevent its being carried out, demonstrating an intransigeance that would characterize their attitude thereafter. Egypt's Mahmoud Fawzi declared the partition scheme lay beyond the scope of the United Nations' Charter, which, of course, it did not. Iraq's Dr. Fadhil Jamali said his country would not recognize the validity of the United Nations decision. Syria's Adel Arslan stated his government would "never recognize" the proposed partition. Camille Chamoun, later president of Lebanon, called the plan "unjust and inequitable." The Emir Faisal, of Saudi Arabia, said his government would not consider itself bound by the United Nations decision. Yemen's Prince Seif el Islam Abdullah characterized the proposal as "illegal and unworkable" and flatly announced the Arabs "would not agree to it."

While the diplomats haggled at Lake Success, Begin repeatedly warned of behind-the-scenes maneuverings by the British to "influence" an invasion of Palestine by the surrounding Arab states. On at least one occasion, in 1946, a high-ranking British officer—Brigadier L. N. Clayton, a renowned Arabophile—had participated in the deliberations of the Arab League, constituted in the spring of 1945 mainly in order to fight Zionism. Each of the League members—Egypt, Saudi Arabia, Iraq, Transjordan, Yemen, Syria and Lebanon—wanted as much of Palestine as it could grab, but all were agreed that the Jews should have none of it.

One Arab leader wanted it *all*. He was the ex-Mufti of Jerusalem, Hitler's quondam partner in the "final solution," back in Cairo from exile and intriguing to organize a campaign to "drive the Jews into the sea." For this and other reasons, Begin and his high command had little faith that the proposed partition would—or could—be carried out peacefully. They saw the Jewish Agency's acceptance of the UNSCOP proposals as an absurdity wrapped in illusions.

On October 1, over its underground radio, "The Voice of Fighting Zion," and in its wall posters, the Irgun cautioned the Jewish community that the United Nations had no military force to impose peace and that Britain was well aware of this. A second warning was issued on October 12 that the British intended to continue their naval blockade against

Palestine while they evacuated only those areas bordering on the Arab states so as to enable Arab bands to prepare an armed attack on the future state. A third warning was broadcast on November 16:

The public is harboring three illusions fostered by its leaders. Number one: that the partition of the country, if it is accepted by a two-thirds majority in the United Nations Assembly, will be implemented by peaceful means. Number two: that if a war breaks out in Eretz Israel as the result of an attack engineered by British agents, the United Nations Committee sitting in Jerusalem will soon restore peace. Number three: that if the United Nations representatives fail in their mission as angels of peace, the Security Council will intervene, issue a command, and stop the war with a wave of the hand. . . .

Begin contended that the "peace" for which Ben-Gurion and his colleagues were willing to sacrifice more territory was not only a mirage, a delusion, but a gross illegality. On the day the General Assembly of the United Nations approved the UNSCOP's partition proposal—the fateful afternoon of November 29, 1947—the Irgun again warned the people that war was imminent, and added:

The partition of the Homeland is illegal. It will never be recognized. The signature by institutions and individuals of the partition agreement is invalid. It will not bind the Jewish people. Jerusalem was and will for ever be our capital. Eretz Israel will be restored to the people of Israel. All of it. And forever.

On the same day, Begin issued a special Order of the Day to all soldiers of the Irgun Zvai Leumi predicting war would break out because the British government would do their utmost to see that it did. His message ended on this solemn note:

We who have offered our lives for the day of redemption are not rejoicing. For the Homeland has not been liberated but mutilated. The State for which we have striven from our early youth, the State which will give freedom to the people and assure the future of its sons—that State still remains the goal of our generation!

The UNSCOP proposal for partition of Palestine into Jewish and Arab states was adopted in the General Assembly by a vote of thirty-three to thirteen.[1] The decision was hailed with joy throughout the free world. In Palestine, Jews embraced each other in the streets of Tel Aviv and

Jerusalem, their eyes glistening with happy tears. Thirty years of struggle under the British Mandate, fifteen years of heartache over the plight of Jewry in Hitler's Europe, and two thousand years of longing for a homeland had ended—or so it seemed to most Jewish inhabitants of Palestine. Civilization as represented by a more than two-thirds majority of the members of the United Nations had at long last invested the Jewish people with nationhood—though only in a gerrymandered fragment of the Promised Land. It was, in fact, Zion without Zion.

Nevertheless, along Jerusalem's King George V Avenue, named for the monarch who had ruled Britain in the time of Balfour and the Declaration, Jews waved their blue and white national flag, sang *Hatikvah*, and danced the hora. Independence was theirs at last, and the United Nations had won a great moral victory—Trygve Lie called it its "first rounded, positive achievement."

Significantly, four British Dominions—Australia, Canada, New Zealand and South Africa—voted with the majority in ordering partition, in creating a special United Nations Palestine Commission[2] to take over administration of the country and in requesting Britain to leave the area by February 1, 1948, to make way for the independent Jewish and Arab states. The General Assembly's resolution also called on the British to make available adequate harbor and reception facilities for immediate entry of Jewish immigrants, and appealed to everyone concerned to refrain from any action which might hamper or delay the carrying out of the partition plan.

Bevin, however, announced on December 11, 1947, that the Mandate would not be terminated until May 15 of the following year and that British evacuation of Palestine would not be completed by August 1. Britain, furthermore, refused to participate in any collective effort to enforce the United Nations resolution and denied the newly formed Palestine Commission facilities to enable it to operate effectively.

It seems unbelievable, in retrospect, that a country whose record for conscientious administration as an imperial power surpassed that of any since the Roman Empire could behave in such a manner, but it did. In effect, Britain refused to cooperate in carrying out a United Nations decision that did not conform with her own colonial policy. In Palestine, the result was anarchy, for the Arabs were encouraged to believe that they could proceed to undo the collective will of the United Nations with impunity—indeed, with British connivance or acquiescence. And they did.

The seeds of all future Arab-Israeli conflict were sown during the years 1947–1949, years which saw the triumphant emergence of an independent if territorially mutilated Israel—and the adoption by the Arab states of annihilation as a policy, with war as an instrument thereof. The bloodshed of the wars of 1956, 1967 and 1973, the economic dislocations, the painful refugee problems—Jewish as well as Arab—and the political turmoil of the last thirty years are traceable to Arab refusal in 1947 to accept Resolution 181 of the General Assembly of the United Nations, proposing for Palestine "partition with economic union."

Had the Arabs accepted partition in 1947, an independent Arab Palestine would have been created. Ergo, had they not launched their war of conquest, there would have been no Arab refugee problem. But let us begin at the beginning.

Partition provided for the establishment of a Palestinian Arab state to include western Galilee, the hill country of Samaria and Judea—minus Jerusalem—and the coastal plain from Ashdod to the Egyptian frontier. The Jewish state was to comprise eastern Galilee, the Plain of Esdraelon and most of the coastal region, plus the Negev. Thus each state was split into three sections, linked at three points. The city of Jerusalem was to become a United Nations demilitarized trusteeship of holy places and minorities, with freedom of access and exit to all faiths. Economic union of the two states and Jerusalem envisioned a common currency and joint communications, postal services, seaports and airports, utilities and developmental agencies.

From the Jewish point of view, the plan offered only minimal satisfaction of long-held dreams. Jerusalem, the Zion of their aspirations, lay within an enclave entirely surrounded by Arab territory, without direct access to the sea. Yet, faced with the urgent need of providing a homeland for the remnants of European Jewry, the Zionists accepted partition. It was not a good solution, but it held, however vaguely, the promise of peace.

Partition could not be effected, however, unless both Arabs and Jews wholly accepted the General Assembly's integral resolution. Failure to implement any one of the specific provisions creating the independent Arab and Jewish states, and the Jerusalem enclave, meant failure of the whole. But although the Jews accepted the decision of the United Nations as their contribution to a peaceful solution of the problem, the Palestine Arabs, represented by their Higher Committee, and supported by the armed intervention of the surrounding Arab states, not only refused to accept the resolution, but destroyed it by their attempted conquest of the whole country.

The partition of the territory was to have been a matter between the Palestine Arab community and Palestine Jewry. The Arab states had no claim to even an inch of the land involved, but forty-eight hours after the General Assembly had acted, the Arabs moved to frustrate its decision.

Convinced that the British armed forces were on their side, eight hundred Arabs from Syria invaded Palestine and attacked Jewish settlements in the north. Another force of approximately the same strength crossed from Transjordan and encamped in Samaria, setting up a local "government" at Nablus. Subsequently, Egyptian troops occupied the Gaza area. Britain did nothing to stop the incursions or to expel the invaders.

Occupation of the West Bank area by Transjordanian troops and annexation of the Gaza region by Egyptian soldiers—clear acts of aggression by countries whose sovereignty was not even remotely affected by the United Nations partition proposal—prevented the birth of a Palestine Arab state and the internationalization of Jerusalem. This is a point forgotten or ignored, by the defenders of Arab claims to Palestine. The result of the dual aggression by Transjordan and Egypt was territorial expansion of both those states at the expense of what would have been a Palestine Arab state and an internationalized Jerusalem.

Both aggressions, furthermore, plainly contravened the will of more than two-thirds of the members of the United Nations and, in so doing, dealt a serious blow to the moral authority of an institution born of history's costliest, most destructive, deadliest war. In the demolition of the first important United Nations step toward preservation of the world's hard-won peace, the Axis won through its wartime Arab friends a posthumous political victory. It succeeded in doing in peacetime what it had failed to do in war—breaking the unity of the Allies.

In a very real sense, what followed was a continuation of Hitler's war against the United Nations, Judaism, Christianity and democracy itself, directed by the same Haj Amin el Husseini who, only twenty-four hours before Germany surrendered, in consideration of gold monies paid him to date, had agreed to set up a new Pan-Arab empire to fight against the common enemy. During his association with Hitler, the not-so-grand Mufti had repeatedly suggested "the extermination of European Jewry" as a "comfortable solution to the Palestine problem."

Now he was leading what was in effect not only a war against the Jews but also a war against the United Nations and all it represented. His field commander was the notorious brigand Fawzi Bey el Kaukji, who had served with the Turks against the British in World War I, participated in the 1936–1939 disturbances in Palestine and spent the World War II years in Nazi Germany. Kaukji began actual military operations in January 1948.

To prevent Jews and Arabs from obtaining the means for mutual annihilation, the United States placed an embargo on arms shipments to the Middle East and shamed the British into announcing, but not into enforcing, a similar policy. Britain continued to send weapons to the Arab states "in fulfillment of treaty obligations." London had no treaty obligations to Fawzi el Kaukji, but this difficulty was quickly surmounted: The civil administration, in settling up accounts preparatory to departure, handed over to the Supreme Moslem Council a tidy one million five hundred thousand dollars—a sum that went straight into Haj Amin's war chest.

In the its first report to the Security Council in February 1948, the United Nations Commission on Palestine complained that the administration had declined to establish procedures for transferring its authority to the United Nations' representatives, failed to provide port facilities for Jewish immigration and denied the Commission either the right or the protection to enter Palestine a reasonable time in advance of termination of the Mandate and British evacuation of the country. The report added that "powerful Arab interests, both inside and outside Palestine, are defying the resolution of the General Assembly and are engaged in a deliberate effort to alter by force the settlement envisaged therein." [3]

Arab hostility to partition was not a spontaneous, last-moment, emotional reaction to a United Nations decision, but as Menahem Begin had warned, was deliberately planned and organized. Armed invasion, as part of what Dr. Hussein Khalidi, acting Chairman of the Palestine Arab Higher Committee, later called a "crusade against the Jews," was decided at a secret meeting of the Arab League governments in Sofar, Lebanon, on September 19, more than two months before the General Assembly proposed partition. [4] A training center for a so-called Arab Army of Liberation of five thousand men was established in Damascus. The training was conducted by Syrian officers under the supervision and command of Kaukji.

Actual armed invasion, which began in January, was preceded by systematic Arab attacks in Jerusalem, Jaffa, Haifa, Safad and Ramleh; ambushes along the Tel Aviv-Jerusalem road and the Haifa-Tel Aviv highway; raids against Jewish settlements in Galilee, the Hebron area, the Sharon and the Negev and assaults on the Jewish quarters of the Old City of Jerusalem and the Jaffa outskirts of Tel Aviv. Within a week of the United Nations' decision to partition Palestine, 105 Jews were killed and many times that number were wounded.

Arabs shot down Jews as they rode buses home from work in Jerusalem or Haifa, as they tilled their fields in the settlements near Kfar Etzion, as they walked the streets of Beersheba or drove their battered jalopies along the highway between Tel Aviv and Lydda. The toll in Jewish dead mounted daily: five killed here, nine there, fourteen somewhere else. By mid-December the dead numbered more than two hundred.

Spokesman Khalidi attempted to dignify the Arabs' aggression as "holy war," but by any name, it was armed insurrection against a majority decision of civilized mankind to grant Arabs and Jews equal self-determination in their own land. It succeeded only in killing partition and, with it, self-determination for Palestine's Arabs. Worse, it set into motion events which years later would culminate in defeats for the armies of Egypt in 1956, and for the armies of Egypt, Jordan and Syria in 1967 and 1973.

NOTES

1. Those in favor: Australia, Belgium, Bolivia, Brazil, Byelorussia, Canada, Costa Rica, Czechoslovakia, Denmark, Dominican Republic, Ecuador, France, Guatemala, Haiti, Iceland, Liberia, Luxembourg, Netherlands, New Zealand, Nicaragua, Norway, Panama, Paraguay, Peru, Philippines, Poland, Sweden, Ukraine, South Africa, Uruguay, U.S.S.R., United States, Venezuela. Those against: Afghanistan, Cuba, Egypt, Greece, India, Iran, Iraq, Lebanon, Pakistan, Saudi Arabia, Syria, Turkey, Yemen. Those abstaining: Argentina, Chile, China, Colombia, El Salvador, Ethiopia, Honduras, Mexico, United Kingdom, Yugoslavia. Thailand was absent.

2. Composed of representatives from Bolivia, Czechoslovakia, Denmark, Panama and the Philippines.

3. First Special Report to the Security Council by the United Nations Palestine Commission, A/AC $^{2/9}$, February 16, 1948.

4. B.Y. Boutros-Gali, *The Arab League* (Cairo: University of Cairo, 1954), p. 411.

Chapter 15

War and Politics

Menahem Begin foresaw a head-on clash with the Arabs as a result of the United Nations decision to partition Palestine. He decided the time had come for reunification of the Irgun and the Haganah in a common effort against the Arabs, just as together, however briefly, they had fought the British. Neither organization was militarily strong enough to prevent early successes by the marauding Arab irregulars, and much Jewish blood was spilled while the British stood by, unwilling to risk their lives to keep the Arabs in check, much less defend the Jews. But the mutual suspicions, jealousies and ideological rivalries that for more than a decade had envenomed relations between the Irgun and the Jewish Agency persisted, and negotiations for establishing a united front, initiated in mid-December, dragged on for months.

To Begin's credit, it must be said that he persistently advocated unity while Ben-Gurion stubbornly resisted a merger. Rightly or wrongly, Ben-Gurion had developed an almost pathological mistrust of Begin, in whom he saw a rival for political power after the establishment of a Jewish state. And when Begin, early in December 1947, appealed to the Jewish Agency to join forces while there was yet time and by so doing, "end our defensive posture, take the offensive and attack the Arab marauders' bases," Ben-Gurion at first turned a deaf ear.

Meanwhile, in anticipation of full-scale war with the Arabs, Begin ordered the Irgun's fighters reorganized into regular field units. Irgun military camps were established under canvas in the orange groves around Petah Tikvah and Ramat Gan. From training for partisan sallies, the

Irgun passed to intensive instruction in the techniques of open battle, and by mid-December Irgunist assault forces were hammering at Arab bases in the environs of Haifa, Jaffa, Jerusalem and Tireh. At the time, the Haganah was busy defending scattered Jewish settlements against attacks by Kaukji's irregulars in Samaria, which British troops had evacuated, and fighting off the ex-Mufti's gangs, assembled in Judea under the command of one of his kinsmen, Abdul Kader el Husseini, to whom, incidentally, Yassir Arafat is distantly related.

The Haganah's modest successes against Kaukji and Kader, however, were not indicative of the organization's true military strength. Theoretically, the Haganah could field fifty-four thousand men. But of these, thirty-two thousand were men in their late forties or early fifties, too old for anything but guard duty, and nine thousand, five hundred were inexperienced teenagers too young for field service. Actual fighting men who had military training numbered only about twelve thousand, five hundred, of whom nine thousand constituted the regular Haganah defense force and approximately three thousand comprised Yigal Allon's Palmach, the elite corps that had had intensive commando training back when the British organized the Jewish underground that was to have continued the war against the Axis in the event Rommel overran the Middle East.

Weapons, moreover, were in critically short supply. The Haganah's secret workshops had not yet produced sufficient quantities of small arms, mortars and ammunition to equip adequate field forces, and the flow of weapons from Czechoslovakia and France had not yet begun. The Haganah's total arsenal consisted of some ten thousand, five hundred rifles, most of World War I vintage; three thousand, five hundred submachine guns of various makes; 775 light machine guns and about 160 mediums; 672 one-inch mortars and 84 three-inchers which Haganah officers smilingly referred to as their "heavy artillery." Haganah had no field pieces, no armored vehicles of any kind, and its "air force" consisted of a few Piper Cubs and British trainers assembled from components salvaged from postwar junkheaps and hidden away in secret places in the hills.

A shortage of arms and of money with which to purchase them, also seriously handicapped the Irgun. It did not have weapons enough for all its fighting men or for the volunteers who were now offering themselves by the hundreds. As the ranks of the Irgun swelled, so did its budget, which rose from about fifteen thousand dollars a week to over fifty thousand dollars. However, unlike the Jewish Agency, which had the support of the overwhelming majority of the Jews of the Diaspora— especially in the United States where the "official" Zionists raised millions for arms and munitions—most of the Irgun's funds had to be levied locally.

Some financial help came from Jewish communities in Latin America, South Africa and the United States, where Ben Hecht's Committee for National Liberation had been organizing support for Begin's cause. Most of the Irgun's financial needs, however, were raised in Palestine by aboveground public appeals such as the so-called "Iron Fund." As British security forces increasingly withdrew from Jewish sectors, the "Iron Fund" held rallies in those areas to explain Irgun policy and the urgency of the crisis the country faced.

In the meantime, in mid-December, negotiations had begun between Begin and representatives of the Jewish Agency for joining forces against the Arabs, but the discussions dragged on endlessly. Begin was unable to persuade the Agency's delegates that the British would not open a port on February 1, as the United Nations had proposed. Ben-Gurion counted on the opening of the port to bring in arms and ammunition, hence believed he could dispense with the Irgun's help. He delayed entering into an effective alliance with Begin.

As if to demonstrate their contempt for the Irgun, Haganah men dispersed a nocturnal "Iron Fund" rally in Tel Aviv's Mograbi Square by tossing several hand grenades into the crowd that had assembled around an IZL sound truck. No one was killed, but many were injured, some severely. The incident interrupted further serious discussions about a Haganah-Irgun alliance, but psychologically it worked to the Irgun's advantage. At a second "Iron Fund" rally held in Mograbi Square a few nights later in mid-December the crowds were bigger than ever.

That evening Menahem Begin came out into the open for the first time in years. He walked down the Allenby Road to the meeting in plain sight of everyone, startling a few Irgunists who recognized him but who prudently turned their faces without speaking. Begin had emerged from his underground headquarters to listen to the public's comments about the Haganah's grenade-tossing and what he heard heartened him considerably: The criticism was general and bitter. Evidently, the Haganah had angered the people instead of frightening them.

The chances of reconstituting a united resistance movement to face the new and growing Arab threat were further reduced early in January when the Haganah, in violation of previous commitments, kidnapped Yedidiah Segal, one of the Irgun's best officers in Haifa. Only a fortnight earlier, the Haganah's commander had personally promised there would be no more kidnappings or reprisals of any kind against the Irgun, which promptly retaliated by detaining one of the Haganah's intelligence chiefs. On January 12, an exchange was arranged, and the Haganah man was freed; he returned to his unit in good health. But Yedidiah Segal never came home. His mother went looking for him and was informed by the Haganah that he had been released. His body was found in Tireh, an Arab town, on January 15. Next day, the Haganah published a statement explaining that Yedidiah had "escaped" before being exchanged and "had been killed by Tireh Arabs." Begin was deeply distressed.

"We were again in a dilemma," he recalls. "We did not know the details of Yedidiah's murder. Among my men, the call for revenge was general. Suddenly we found ourselves—all of us of the Irgun—on the edge of an abyss. The Jewish people were fighting for their very existence. And on the horizon—as we knew—was an Arab invasion. Was it fated that at such an hour brothers should turn and kill each other? The bereaved mother came to our aid. She said: 'I do not want the shedding of my son's blood to cause a civil war.' Again we halted at the very edge of disaster, the tragic cycle which nineteen centuries ago had sealed the fate of besieged Jerusalem."

Begin obviously had in mind how Jerusalem's Jews wasted their strength and resources in internal quarrels before Titus laid siege to the city and leveled it in A.D. 70. Within the capital bloody civil wars and subcivil wars rent the defenders, who displayed a common front only when the Romans were visible from the city's ramparts. By then it was too late. It was mainly as a result of the intramural quarrels that preceded the siege, according to Josephus, that the city fell, and one million, one hundred thousand Jews were slaughtered.

Begin forbade reprisals for Yedidiah Segal's death. Instead, he informed the Jewish Agency that the Irgun would not continue negotiations for an alliance with the Haganah until an impartial committee was set up to investigate the tragic affair. This done, the negotiations were resumed, and a secret agreement was signed between the two organizations defining their respective roles much along the lines of the old *Tenuat Hameri*: Irgun defense posts would be subject to the sector commander appointed by the Haganah; Irgun's plans for attacks on the Arabs and/or the British would require prior approval by the Haganah; operations for arms seizures from the British would be planned and carried out jointly; the Irgun would refrain from "confiscating" monies in areas policed by Jews but would be free to collect funds locally.

Ben-Gurion finally realized that a full-blown war with the Arabs was inevitable. At that very moment, in fact, five Arab states—Egypt, Iraq, Syria, Lebanon and Transjordan—were preparing for concerted aggression. Ben-Gurion grudgingly welcomed Begin's cooperation, but extracted from him a pledge that when a Jewish Provisional Government was proclaimed as planned on May 15, 1948, Begin would wholeheartedly support it. Begin unhesitatingly promised to do so, adding that when the government came into being, the Irgun's fighting men would be disbanded and integrated into the future state's defense forces.

*　　*　　*

Early in February, while the negotiations with the Haganah lumbered along, Begin was advised of the arrival off the coast of southern France of the long-awaited *Altalena*, a 4000-ton American LST purchased in the United States with funds raised by Ben Hecht's Hebrew Committee for National Liberation. The vessel bore Jabotinsky's *nom de plume* and was to be used to transport arms and volunteers assembled in France by a team of Irgunists that included Shmuel Katz and two recent fugitives from the Gilgil concentration camp in British Kenya—Yaacov Meridor and Eliahu Lankin, who had reached Paris by way of Rome.

The *Altalena* was in excellent operational condition, had a 14-knot capability and could have carried five thousand men without baggage. It was bought as part of the Irgun's Operation *Palest*, a plan to recruit and equip an International Brigade and ship it to Palestine. Its arrival there was to coincide with the proclamation of the Jewish state on May 15 in order to make certain the survival of the newly created nation. Without its weapons and troops, the state might not last more than a few days, but with them, Begin believed, all of Palestine might be won.

When the *Altalena* dropped anchor off Sète, near Marseilles, however, Katz and the others had not yet succeeded in persuading the French government to release the requested arms and the *Altalena* earned her keep by making commercial runs between Italian, North African and French ports. Meanwhile, Lankin and Meridor recruited and trained nearly one thousand European and North African Jews. It would be many weeks, however, before the *Altalena* would sail for Palestine and become a *cause célèbre* in Israel's early history.

Meanwhile, the Irgun went ahead with its own plans for an offensive against the Arabs. At the end of January, at a meeting of the high command, Begin and Paglin outlined four "strategic objectives": (1) Jerusalem, (2) Jaffa, (3) the Lydda-Ramleh plain, and (4) the Triangle, the largely Arab-populated area lying within Nablus, Jenin and Tulkarm. To this day military control of the Triangle is vital to Israel's security; it lies wholly within Samaria. It would be some time, however, before the Irgun could put its "strategy of conquest," as Begin called it, into operation. The men were not yet fully trained and weapons were still in short supply.

In February, as Begin had predicted, the British refused to open a port which would have enabled the Haganah (and the Irgun) to bring in arms and ammunition as well as immigrants. Furthermore, although they had authorized a Jewish militia, the British forbade its creation while the Union Jack still floated over Palestine. "Law and order," said Bevin in London, "is still an exclusive British responsibility." The British hunted

Irgunists without success but many Haganah members were caught, disarmed and jailed.

Britain's Palestine garrison—an army large enough to have waged successful war against the combined armies of all the Arab countries of the Middle East—made no serious effort to put down the Arabs' insurrection against constituted international authority. Consequently, by the end of February, after three months of almost uninterrupted Jewish-Arab fighting, casualties on both sides totaled upwards of two thousand, five hundred.

Despite the presence in Palestine of British troops in overwhelming numbers, the Arabs managed to occupy hilltops overlooking the main highways and commanding lesser roads leading in and out of Jewish settlements. It became increasingly difficult for the Haganah to supply the scattered *kibbutzim* and villages and to keep communications open between Jerusalem and the coastal cities. By mid-March, Jerusalem and its large Jewish population were in serious danger of being isolated by Kader's forces. The roadway and water conduit from Tel Aviv had been cut, and Jerusalem was on a starvation diet. The city echoed day and night to the sound of mortar and machine gun fire; it literally reeked of uncollected garbage and unflushed sewage.

At this juncture Ben-Gurion did what Begin had urged him to do for some time—he became at last more warrior than politician. With the fate of Jerusalem in the balance, he knew the time had come to fight. But how, and with what? Grimly, he summoned the high command of the Haganah. The commanders painted a gloomy picture. It might be possible, they said, to hold out against local guerrillas, perhaps even defeat them, but if the Arab states actually invaded, the situation could become grave. The scattered settlements were difficult to defend. Someone proposed that it might be wise for the inhabitants of the *kibbutzim* to withdraw behind redoubts along the coastal area, but the idea was quickly dismissed. In any case, the defense of Jerusalem was generally deemed inadvisable; aside from the obvious difficulties of supply, the city was slated to be internationalized. It seemed bootless to expend the Haganah's limited resources in its defense. In the circumstances, Ben-Gurion did what men in his position of maximum responsibility usually do when faced with a military crisis: He appointed a new Haganah commander.

The new man was David Shaltiel, a tall, severe-looking man with steel-rimmed eyeglasses who had been a sergeant in the French Foreign Legion and had spent some time in Dachau as a Zionist prisoner of the Nazis before arriving in Palestine and joining the Haganah. From the standpoint of the Irgun and LEHI, Ben-Gurion could not have made a worse choice: Shaltiel had been heavily involved in hunting down members of the underground during "The Season." Consequently, neither Begin nor

Yellin-Mor trusted Shaltiel, in whom they saw a foil for Ben-Gurion rather than a first-rate military commander. In the end, he proved less able than Ben-Gurion had hoped, but it should be recorded in Shaltiel's defense that he took over command in Jerusalem at a time when the city's situation seemed hopeless, and that while eventually he lost the Old City, he did save West Jerusalem where one hundred thousand Jews lived.

The deterioration of the Zionists' military position in that first terrible winter of 1947–1948 was at least partly attributable to the embargo imposed by the United States on arms shipments to the Middle East. It had the effect of depriving the Jews of weapons while the Arabs were receiving ample supplies of arms from the British, along with a stream of men and military materiel from neighboring countries.

Politically, too, the United States suddenly began shifting ground. When, in February, Britain's formal reply to the United Nations Palestine Commission made it abundantly evident that the committee would not be allowed to function, Washington did not even enter a formal protest. By the end of the month, American participation in the discussions at Lake Success was largely confined to cataloging reasons why it was constitutionally impossible for the Security Council to enforce partition. As a United Nations project, the division of Palestine into Jewish and Arab states seemed headed for the diplomatic graveyard. Paradoxically, it was being pushed in that direction by the United States, previously the boldest, strongest supporter of the partition idea.

News of the extent of Arab opposition to partition—and none-too-subtle pressure from powerful oil interests—had shaken Washington. On March 18, President Truman had promised the ailing Chaim Weizmann full support for Jewish statehood, but two days later the American Ambassador to the United Nations, Warren Austin, proposed shelving partition in favor of a total United Nations trusteeship over an undivided Palestine, something for which the British had been lobbying.

The sudden collapse of American support for Jewish independence sprang from the traditional policy of the State Department that the Arabs had to be appeased in order to ensure continued access to the oil resources of the Middle East for defense purposes—and to safeguard the profits of American oil companies operating in Arab territories. In his memoirs, President Truman subsequently suggested that perhaps some of the Arab experts in the State Department "were also inclined to be anti-Semitic." *Toujours ça change . . .*

American policy probably would not have faltered, however, if at the same time there had not occurred a rapid deterioration of relations between Washington and Moscow. The breach, which had inspired Bevin's belief in the inevitability of American acquiescence in the British solution for Palestine, widened ominously.

The outlines of two solid, hostile blocs had become increasingly evident ever since the Soviet Union, in the summer of 1947, set its face against the Marshall Plan, history's most magnanimous effort for postwar reconstruction of the ruined economies of friends and foes, and Western statesmen occupied themselves with the practical problems of a possible Third World War. Relations between Washington and London, however, grew closer and warmer, and the pressure of British representatives in Washington on their American colleagues to reverse their Palestine policy assumed new and greater significance.

The erosion of American support for the Zionist cause in Palestine was undoubtedly also influenced by the press. By and large, it reported the Zionists' life-and-death struggle for nationhood in Palestine as though what was happening there was just another dispute between Jews and Arabs. Rarely was the conflict related to the United Nations and Arab violations of its historic decision of November 29, 1947; seldom was any distinction made between Arab aggressors and aggressed Jews. The dispatches dealt mainly with Arab victories, and the general view was that the Jews' prospects of surviving were at best only remote. Emphasis was laid on atrocity stories, with particular stress on "atrocities" committed by Jews fighting for survival against great odds.

A case in point was the battle for Deir Yassin in which the Irgun killed some two hundred and fifty Arabs, including many women and children. It was the "atrocity" story par excellence of the fighting in the early spring of 1948. There was no blinking the fact that innocents were slaughtered in that unhappy event, but to be understood, if not condoned, the incident must be seen against the background of a besieged Jerusalem.

The Arab ring around Jerusalem tightened during the last two weeks in March. More than one hundred thousand Jews in the New City and seventeen hundred in the Jewish quarter of the Old City, were surrounded. Food stocks ran low. There was no running water—the Arabs cut if off as often as it was restored. The Arabs controlled the approaches to Jerusalem and had ambushed numerous Jewish convoys, causing heavy loss of life and equipment. As long as they held Kastel, on the heights overlooking the road leading down to Tel Aviv, the Arabs retained full command of the situation. A convoy which had taken supplies from Jerusalem to the besieged Etzion Bloc of Jewish villages south of the city, was ambushed on its return. In an unequal battle—two hundred Jews against three thousand Arabs—which lasted until the British decided to intervene, the Jews lost 40 men, many were wounded and they lost nearly all their vehicles.

The relief of Jerusalem became the first great test of the united Jewish

forces, now fighting under Haganah command, to overcome the staggering odds the Jews faced in an undeclared war that had begun as a defense
of partition, but in the face of mounting Arab aggression was developing
into a Battle for Israel. Early in April, light arms began arriving from
Czechoslovakia to enable the Haganah, with the help of the Irgun, to
launch a drive to reopen the Tel Aviv-Jerusalem highway. It only partly
succeeded, but some food convoys got through, enough to enable the city
to fight on.

An important link in the Arab encirclement of Jerusalem was Deir
Yassin, an agglomeration of brownish-pink stone houses mounted in tiers
on a terraced mountainside at about two thousand feet above sea level
and approximately two and a half miles southwest of the capital. Some of
its inhabitants normally worked as gardeners and domestics in the homes
of Jewish families in West Jerusalem, and the agricultural village as a
whole had always enjoyed good relations with the Jews who bought the
community's fruit and vegetables. Many villagers understood and spoke
Hebrew.

In war, journalists soon learn, truth is an early casualty, and truth was
violently dealt with throughout the Jewish struggle for independence by
nearly all concerned. At no point, however, was it more blatantly
mutilated than in the case of the battle for Deir Yassin. For years students
of the Arab-Israeli conflict, myself included, were gulled by "official"
Zionism's propagandists into believing that the Haganah had no hand in
the unhappy affair, that Deir Yassin itself had no strategic value and that,
broadly speaking, the attack on the "innocent village" was a dark episode
unworthy of Jewish valor which would not have occurred if a Jewish state
had been in being and capable of exercising effective control over all
armed forces operating in the area.

But time, as someone has said, is truth's best friend. Gradually, the
facts about Deir Yassin have emerged. The outcome of the battle was not,
perhaps, the "brilliant victory" the Irgunists have claimed. But war being
the ugly business we all know it to be, neither was it the heinous crime
depicted by Ben-Gurion at the time in an obsequiously apologetic letter to
his neighbor King Abdullah, whose friendship he had been secretly
wooing in hopes of not having to fight for Judea and Samaria after
establishment of the Jewish state in May 1948. Here then are the facts
about Deir Yassin as related to me in an interview with Mordechai
Raanan, the Irgun commander in Jerusalem at the time, and as corroborated by several other sources.

Apart from its strategic location, Deir Yassin was a transit depot for
Arab forces coming up from Bethlehem via Ein Kerem to the all-
important Kastel front from which they attacked Jewish convoys along the
road linking Jerusalem to Tel Aviv, the capital's lifeline. Deir Yassin was

not the "innocent village" it was painted; while not actually garrisoned, it was well-defended by a concrete pillbox at the entrance, and its houses sheltered many soldiers, including Iraqi transients. Lastly, an attack on the village was actually a part of the Haganah's overall plan for the relief of besieged Jerusalem in an operation code-named NAHSHON—in honor of the first Jew who walked into the Red Sea when Moses ordered the parting of the waters.

Although the Irgun was held mainly responsible for the bloody consequences of the assault on Deir Yassin, it was actually a joint operation with LEHI, whereof Shaltiel, the Haganah's regional commander in Jerusalem, was fully informed in accordance with the agreement that had reestablished unified resistance. Shaltiel himself confirmed this in a dispatch to Raanan, which the Irgun commander subsequently radioed to Menahem Begin in his headquarters in Tel Aviv. It said:

> I learn that you plan an attack on Dir (sic) Yassin. I wish to point out that *the capture of Dir Yassin and holding it is one stage in our general plan. I have no objection* to your carrying out the operation provided you are able to hold the village. If you are unable to do so I warn you against blowing up the village which will result in its inhabitants abandoning it, and its ruins and deserted houses being occupied by foreign forces. This situation will increase our difficulties in the general struggle. A second conquest of the place will involve us in heavy sacrifices. Furthermore, if foreign forces enter the place this will upset our *general plan for establishing an airfield.*

The attack was planned by Raanan and LEHI's Yehoshua Zettler. Of the 110 young men involved—few were over twenty; Raanan, the eldest, was twenty-four—the Irgun supplied seventy-five and LEHI the rest, with Ranaan in command. The troops were divided into three platoons: The two platoons were under Ben-Zion Cohen, and the LEHI group was under David Gottlieb. In addition, there were two auxiliary support units, one of eight men and one of five. Their total armament consisted of thirty-six rifles, mostly British; three Bren guns; fifteen Sten submachine guns and quantities of explosives and homemade grenades. Because the operation would start in the dark—and hopefully end at dawn—passwords were arranged. The challenge was "Achdut," and the countersign, "Lohamei." Zero hour was set for 4:30 A.M., when the villagers would be deep in sleep and presumably least inclined to offer resistance. The attackers counted on total surprise—after luck and superior firepower the most important element in battle—to capture Deir Yassin easily and quickly.

The plan was to attack Deir Yassin simultaneously from north, east and south, leaving the western approach free as an escape route for the villagers. The Irgunists moved toward their objective from Bet Hakerem, a Jewish suburb of West Jerusalem, and the LEHI group started from *kibbutz* Givat Shaul accompanied by a sound truck with which the population of Deir Yassin, numbering about six hundred, was to be warned to evacuate. It was also agreed that if for any reason shooting started on any one of the three fronts, the others were to open fire at once. The men moved toward their assigned positions over difficult, narrow trails between 1:30 and 2:00 A.M.

The Irgun's platoons were in place on time. The LEHI group, coming from the south, was late.

An Arab on guard duty heard movement in his vicinity. Believing the sounds were made by a colleague, he called to him: "Ahmed!" The hoarsely whispered "Ahmed!" sounded like "Achdut" to an Irgunist and he responded with the countersign: "Lohamei." The Arab recognized the response as Hebrew and scuttled up to the village to raise the alarm: "Yehud alain!"—Jews are coming.

By the time the sound truck lumbered up the element of surprise was lost and the shooting had started. To complicate matters further, the vehicle ran into a ditch in the darkness as it approached the entrance to the village. Precious minutes elapsed before the loudspeaker came to life and a voice shouted above the sounds of battle in Arabic:

You are being attacked by superior forces! Run for your lives! The road to Ein Karem is clear! Run immediately! Don't hesitate! We are advancing! Run toward Ein Karem!

About two hundred villagers apparently heard, took heed and escaped unscathed. But before the others could follow their example a full-scale battle was on. Machine gun and rifle fire poured from the pillbox guarding the entrance to the village and from several of the heavily shuttered stone houses facing the attackers, who were pinned down behind the stone walls of the terraced fields around the village. Daylight brought casualties among the assault troops: three dead and nineteen wounded. Apparently, every house was a stronghold and impenetrable by orthodox methods. Cohen asked Ranaan for permission to retreat.

Ranaan and Zettler held council with their lieutenants, and it was decided to revert to the tactics often used by the underground when faced with similar situations fighting the British. They would blow the houses apart one by one with dynamite. A small charge would be placed on the outer window ledge or doorstep of a house, then, ten seconds later, before the occupants could recover, a second much larger charge would be thrown into the building through the opening.

Under covering fire, single attackers placed the charges on window ledges or doorsteps and quickly took cover. Behind them came the men carrying the heavier charges with lighted fuses; they tossed in their deadly bundles and ran back to shelter. Eleven houses were thus treated. Between each attack, the sound truck blared its warning in Arabic to "Come out with your hands up or be blown up!" Each time, the reply was fire from rifles or automatic weapons from every window of every house. But the door of the twelfth house opened and out came thirty-odd Arabs—men, women and children—many in their underwear.

The shooting stopped and about two hundred Arabs from the remaining houses soon filled the village square. There they were loaded on four trucks brought up from Jerusalem, taken to East Jerusalem in the vicinity of Nablus Gate and freed. They disappeared into the Old City's souks and alleyways.

Between 1:30 and 2:00 P.M. Ranaan received a message from Shaltiel summoning him to Jerusalem. Shaltiel ordered Ranaan to occupy and hold Deir Yassin. The Irgun commander refused. His men were tired; they had been up all night and had been fighting for nearly nine hours.

Late that afternoon, Shaltiel sent a Haganah aide to Deir Yassin, by then largely a smoking ruin. What the officer found inside the blown houses horrified him, but after his inspection he hunched his shoulders and muttered, "War is war." He asked Raanan to have his men empty the houses and bury the bodies. The Irgun commander replied that his boys were not up to the grisly business of handling and burying shattered bodies of men, women and children, and requested that the Haganah send in men to help do the job. While the aide was on his way to report to Shaltiel, Ranaan's people began placing some of the bodies in a limestone quarry. Later, a Haganah unit arrived to take over and hold Deir Yassin; they completed the task of burying the dead.

Next morning, a Red Cross representative, Dr. Jacques de Reynier, found gruesome evidence of the fierceness of the Irgun-LEHI attack. Both underground organizations admitted there had been some indiscriminate shooting, but vigorously denied the wilder charges of murder, rape, looting and mutilation made by the survivors to British interrogators. The Irgun and LEHI insisted that their operation had been a straightforward attack that had met unexpectedly heavy resistance; it had resulted in forty percent casualties for the attackers. Their losses added up to four dead—among them Ben-Zion Cohen—and thirty-seven wounded, seven of them seriously. The Haganah buried the bodies of about two hundred fifty Arabs; some were partly burned in the limestone quarry.

The same day, April 10, Shaltiel issued a statement disavowing all responsibility and charging that the "dissidents" had not launched a military operation, but had "slaughtered men, women and children . . . in

a premeditated act which had as its intention only slaughter and murder."
Ranaan and Zettler countered by making public Shaltiel's dispatch,
leaving out, for security reasons, the words about ". . . establishing an
airfield." Ben-Gurion, in his apology to Abdullah called the latter "the
wise ruler who seeks the good of his people and this country," and
described Deir Yassin as the work of "dissidents." Abdullah rejected the
apology, declaring he did not believe in the existence of "dissidents" and
that he held *all* Jews responsible for what had happened.

But Deir Yassin had important military and psychological consequences. The much-needed Jerusalem airport was built. More impor-
tantly, panic spread among Palestine's Arabs. Kolonia, a village which
had previously repulsed repeated Haganah attacks, was evacuated overnight and fell without further fighting. Beit-Iksa also was evacuated. Both
places overlooked the Tel Aviv-Jerusalem highway and their fall made it
possible to keep this road open.

In the rest of the country, Arabs were fleeing in terror and after
Kaukji's forces were ambushed and defeated by the Palmach at Mishmar
Haemek, the gateway to the coastal plain, the Arab Liberation Army
retreated all the way back to Tubas, leaving the Jerusalem corridor clear.
For the Arab mercenaries fighting in Palestine, Deir Yassin was the
beginning of the end.

Nonetheless, the military situation remained grave. But Palestine's
Jewry charted its own course. Faced with full-scale war in an administrative vacuum being created by Britain's slow but steady withdrawal, the
Executive Committee of the Jewish Agency—headed by Ben-Gurion—
and the Vaad Leumi (Jewish National Council) acted to bring order out of
the increasing chaos. In a proclamation issued on March 23, the Jewish
authorities declared they would oppose any proposal preventing or
postponing establishment of a Jewish state, and rejected the scheme for a
United Nations trusteeship then being debated at Lake Success as an
alternative to partition. They asked that the United Nations Palestine
Commission proceed to Palestine without delay, recognize a Jewish
provisional government, and help establish authority where anarchy
reigned.

The proclamation announced that a Jewish provisional government
would begin functioning no later than May 16, in cooperation with United
Nations representatives, and would meanwhile try to minimize the
disruption caused by the British withdrawal. The Jews offered peace to
the Arab people, declaring their willingness to cooperate fully with
neighboring Arab states and made overtures to enter into permanent

treaty relations with them in the interests of peaceful development of all
the countries of the Middle East.

Meanwhile, the arrival of additional, and heavier, weapons from
Czechoslovakia—field pieces and armored vehicles—infused new strength
in the Jewish military effort. In Tel Aviv, a force of fifteen hundred handpicked men was assembled, many armed with rifles and machine guns still
greasy with the protective packing in which they had arrived. Scores of
vehicles were loaded with provisions. "Armored cars" were improvised
by sheathing trucks with heavy sheet metal, and the long forty-five mile
march to Jerusalem began. The Arabs still held the heights of Kastel,
whose guns dominated the road where it started its winding climb through
Abu Ghosh into the Judean hills. A Palmach unit operating out of
Jerusalem took the heights in a stubborn fight and killed Abdul Kader el
Husseini, the Arab commander of the Jerusalem front. The convoy from
Tel Aviv got through. Most convoys thereafter, used an improvised
"Burma Road" that was secretly built under the noses of the enemy.
Through months of continued ordeal there was no more talk of abandon-
ing the Holy City.

The disintegration of British authority in Palestine became increasingly
evident during the month of April as troops and police withdrew from
district after district, leaving behind them blockhouses, munitions dumps
and piles of smoldering documents and records. As army camps, police
forts or landing strips were evacuated they were seized by Jews or Arabs,
or bitterly fought over by them, each side now aware that decisive battles
lay ahead.

The Jewish military position improved steadily. In Haifa, where Arabs
earlier had massacred forty-one Jewish oil refinery workers, Syrian and
Iraqi irregulars massed for an attack on the Jewish quarter after British
troops under General Hugh C. Stockwell withdrew to the port area
preparatory to embarkation. That night, the Haganah and the Irgun
swooped down on the Arabs in a four-pronged attack from the heights of
Mount Carmel. The Arab commanders deserted, but their troops resisted.
Next morning, General Stockwell arranged a ceasefire and presided over
a meeting of Jewish and Arab leaders at which the Jews promised that the
city's Arab citizens would not be molested and could remain peacefully in
Haifa, provided they deposited their weapons. The General urged them to
accept the Jewish terms, but the Arabs left to consider the matter. On
their return, they said they had orders to evacuate the entire Arab
population into Lebanon, which was done with the help of British troop
carriers.

What the Arab leaders did not tell the meeting was that they had been
instructed to inform Haifa's Arab residents that they would be regarded as
renegades if they remained, and that when the British left, an attack in

force was planned to "drive the Jews into the sea." Of Haifa's sixty-two thousand Arab residents only about five thousand stayed behind. What was to become the highly publicized "Arab refugee problem," however, had already begun. Tens of thousands of monied Arabs had started leaving Palestine in December 1947.

Jerusalem, however, remained embattled in a siege within a siege. The city itself was cut off from the rest of the country, and the Jewish quarter in the Old City was isolated from the Jewish community in the New City. But convoys, sometimes of several hundred trucks, were getting through with food, medical supplies and ammunition, and the population bravely fought on. Elsewhere as the Mandate dragged to an end, the military situation underwent a sudden, almost spectacular transformation. What happened in Haifa also happened in Tiberias, Rosh Pinna and other key cities and towns. The Arab armies seemed to melt away, taking with them great numbers of civilians.

Now came the biggest Irgun operation of the undeclared war—the battle for Jaffa, Arab Jaffa, which Begin called "a pistol aimed at the head of Jewish Tel Aviv." It lay beyond the United Nations partition boundaries, and Begin had good reason to suspect that the large British garrison there was helping the Arabs organize a force to drive to Jerusalem, cutting off the Negev, dividing the territory into two parts and extinguishing Jewish hopes for a state in one last, desperate thrust.

The Haganah, now under the command of the tall, lean,. acutely intelligent scholar, Yigal Yadin, had been toying for some time with plans for an attack on Jaffa, hotbed of Arab nationalism, a major British stronghold and a constant threat to its sprawling Jewish neighbor to the south. Jaffa's Manshieh Quarter, surmounted by the Hassan Bek Mosque, formed a salient reaching into the northern outskirts of Tel Aviv, connected to the ancient town above it by a narrow strip of land between the hills and the sea. From Manshieh snipers and raiders had killed or wounded more than a thousand Jewish residents of Tel Aviv since the start of the Arabs' undeclared war on the Jews. Counter-raids and sallies by the Haganah had failed to eliminate the danger, and Yadin planned a major operation, scheduled to start on the first day of Passover, designed to end the threat to Tel Aviv and force Jaffa's capitulation when the British left. The Irgun knew of the Haganah's plans, but felt Yadin was not acting with sufficient urgency.

Begin decided the Irgun should attack Jaffa on its own to "put an end to the shameful and perilous situation."

On the evening of April 21, Begin and the Irgun's high command met at the home of Paglin's mother in Tel Aviv and drafted a plan for a Jaffa offensive. In Manshieh, the Arabs had built strong defenses—a succession of clever fortifications of the "hedgehog" type three, four, even five rows deep—manned by local Arab irregulars and imported Iraqis. Behind them, moreover, stood British troops with tanks and heavy guns positioned to prevent attackers from isolating Manshieh and reaching the sea. Tactically, the Irgun's plan was to do exactly that—cut Manshieh off from Jaffa and reach the shore. Strategically, its aim was to conquer Jaffa, a city of some seventy thousand Arab inhabitants, and permanently relieve Tel Aviv from Arab incursions. It would be a difficult operation, Begin knew, and for tough jobs like this one he invariably turned to one man to lead them: Amihai Paglin. This time, the Irgun did not inform the Haganah of its intentions.

During the next four days Paglin assembled the necessary forces: about six hundred men and more than one hundred vehicles, some "liberated" from the British, others rented or borrowed from sympathizers. Arms and munitions were no problem. Two recent raids—one against a British military camp at Pardess Hanna and another on a British ammunition train—had yielded tons of mortar shells, weapons and precious Piat armor-piercing shells. Men, vehicles and materiel were assembled near Ramat Gan at Camp Dov, named to honor the memory of the Dov Gruner whom the British had hanged.

At about 2:00 A.M. on the morning of April 25, the Irgun's troops formed a square. Into it walked a pale, slight man they had never seen before but whom they recognized instinctively as their leader, Menahem Begin. It was eight years since he had made a public speech, and for the first time in his life Begin experienced "stage fright," but only momentarily. When he spoke, his voice was steady, clear and strong. He said:

> Men of the Irgun! We are going out to conquer Jaffa. Know who is before you, and remember whom you are leaving behind you. Before you is a cruel enemy who has risen to destroy us. Behind you are parents, brothers, children. Smite the enemy hard. Aim true. Save your ammunition. In battle show no more mercy to the enemy than he shows mercy to our people. But spare women and children. Whoever raises his hands in surrender has saved his life. You will not harm him. You will be led in the attack by Lieutenant Gideon. You have only one direction—forward!

The men started moving out at about 3:00 A.M. on the morning of April 26, the first day of Passover. They went into battle singing Ashbel's "On the Barricades" in high spirits. It was nearly dawn before all had marched out as Begin watched from the window of the Irgun's temporary headquarters in the abandoned Alliance School building near Camp Dov.

Under his breath he muttered a prayer: "God protect them."

The battle started five hours later with a barrage of small-caliber mortar shells all over Jaffa, particularly on the narrow neck of land connecting the main part of the city to Manshieh. After several hours of shelling, the Irgunist infantry made a frontal attack westward in an attempt to cut the narrow, seemingly vulnerable land bridge between Manshieh and Jaffa. There, however, the Arabs were well dug in. Firing from concrete pillboxes at every crossroads and from shielded positions on rooftops, the defenders checked the Irgun's thrust. The attackers' Brens and Stens were no match for the Arabs' heavier Spandaus and Thompsons. Toward sundown the Irgunists withdrew, leaving behind a holding force and taking with them their first casualties: four dead and six wounded. The frontal assault had failed to do more than dent the Arabs' defenses, although the shower of mortar shells had sown panic in Jaffa. The city's Arab inhabitants were fleeing northward to Lebanon in cars and trucks, and by sea, in whatever boats they could find.

The tired troops reentered Camp Dov and slept—on the ground, in adjacent roadways, in backyards, in half-ruined buildings. Fresh soldiers arrived from Tel Aviv and Haifa, but the dawn brought newspapers and shocking reports.

"As we read them," said Begin, "everything went black." The Irgun's operation was described in the "official" press as "barren," "abortive" and "exhibitionistic." He saw the slurs as the work of the Haganah and the Jewish Agency; Ben-Gurion was playing politics again. What most disturbed Begin, however, was the report in one newspaper that the Irgun had drawn forces from all over the country for the Jaffa attack. "This, after all," cried Begin, "was giving information to the enemy." Which, of course, was true.

Begin probably was correct in assuming that the disparaging newspaper stories were "planted" by Jewish Agency propagandists, but wrong in assuming the Haganah had inspired the slanders. Yadin, for one, saw the Irgun attack in a different light. With his own Operation *Chametz* about to be launched, Yadin believed that at the very least the Irgun's action could usefully support the Haganah's impending offensive. Operation *Chametz,* meaning leaven—traditionally not eaten during Passover— awaited only final approval by Ben-Gurion who was reluctant to honor the March 8 Irgun-Haganah compact for joint operations against the Arabs and the British. In Yadin's view, it was more important for the Haganah to win battles than for the Irgun to be discredited.

Early the second day of the battle for Jaffa, Begin and Haim Landau were invited to meet with Yadin and Israel Galili, Ben-Gurion's Defense Minister. Yadin said the Haganah would approve the continuation of the Irgun's attack if the Irgun would agree to fight under the Haganah's command, provided the next twenty-four hours produced some measure of success. Begin agreed to Yadin's conditions, though inwardly he doubted ultimate success and actually was seriously considering scrubbing the Jaffa operation as too costly.

On his return to headquarters, Begin summoned his field commanders, reported on his meeting with Yadin and proposed to suspend the attack. He was for holding and defending whatever small gains had been made but wanted the bulk of the Irgun's troops withdrawn. A dead silence came over those present in the dimly lighted map room. Paglin listened, then turned and left without a word. The others followed, but were soon back, singly and in pairs, pleading with Begin for "one more chance." They flatly refused to quit the field. Begin was astonished and pleased, but he stuck to his decision. Frontal assault was proving too costly.

While Begin was arguing his case with yet another delegation of "mutineers," as he later jokingly called them, Paglin returned, breathless. He had been out surveying the front and had figured out a way through the Arab defenses. Begin agreed to resume the assault using the technique Paglin described: It was one that had served the Irgun well in the past against British strongpoints and at Deir Yassin—dynamite. The Irgun would blast a path through the houses and buildings that stood between the advancing forces and the sea, a distance of from fifteen hundred to two thousand yards, building protective sandbag walls for the men as they inched forward under the protective covering of machine gun and mortar fire. The men worked through the night, filling gunnysacks with sand from the nearby dunes and transporting them to where they would be needed.

Next day, the third day of the battle, the troops started dynamiting their way forward, yard by yard, blowing up pillboxes and constructing their sandbag walls under covering fire as they went, much like building a roofless tunnel above ground. At times, they were able to topple higher buildings onto Arab positions. It took them most of that day and all of the following night, but at nine o'clock on the morning of April 29, the forwardmost dynamiters reached the sea. The land bridge between Manshieh and Jaffa was cut.

When the Irgunists reached the shore they danced and sang and fired volley after volley into the air like so many jubilant Arabs. Paglin let them blow off steam for a while then reminded them there was still work to do. There were pockets of resistance to be cleared out here and there, and about twenty Arabs holed up in the Hassan Bek Mosque were still fighting like demons. By mid-morning, however, the Irgun's flag was flying from the Mosque's pock-marked minaret. Miraculously, the Mosque itself was not seriously damaged.

Simultaneously with the Irgun's victory, the Haganah launched Operation *Chametz*. It bogged down, and Yadin called on the Irgun's mortars for assistance which Paglin only too happily provided.

By noontime, April 30, the Irgun had the Manshieh Quarter under complete control, had taken the railway station at Jaffa and reinforced the roadblocks on the Jerusalem Road. The way into Jaffa lay open.

The Irgun's success took the British by surprise. In their Sarafand camp, they were prepared to evacuate and now, suddenly, came orders from London to "recapture Jaffa." Bevin was in a fury. The Jews were about to take an entirely Arab city beyond the partition boundaries; moreover, the conquerors were not just *any* Jews but the hated "terrorists" of the Irgun.

On the morning of April 30, General Sir Gordon MacMillan, British commander in Jaffa, sent a column of tanks from their lager in midtown Jaffa southward toward Manshieh. Paglin, however, had erected a block on the main road, and behind it stood a bazooka team with some of the Piat armor-piercing shells captured earlier in the Irgun's raid on the British ammunition train. The first British tank was hit squarely and burst into flames. A second lead tank of a column advancing on a lateral road was immobilized by an Irgun demolition team which dynamited a roadside building onto it.

Other demolition teams blew up the road behind the tanks and within two hours MacMillan's position was hopeless. His tanks could not advance and their withdrawal was imperiled. He ordered a retreat, but not before one of the tanks had knocked out an Irgun Bren carrier, killing its four crew members and wounding many more of Paglin's troops by hosing the area with bullets from the retreating tanks' rear machine guns.

The British retreat completed the panic generated in Jaffa by the Irgun's merciless mortar fire. Thousands of Arab civilians fled to the waterfront. Civil administration collapsed. There were no more Arab troops—they had been among the first to flee—and no police. There was rioting and looting and much settling of old scores with shootouts among the Arabs.

Having no other choice, MacMillan opened negotiations with the Irgun on ways to stabilize the situation. They requested the right to send tanks into the Manshieh Quarter to patrol it. Most of all they wanted the Manshieh police station as a base of operations. Begin responded that the Haganah could replace his Irgunists in Manshieh and allow the British in, if they wished, but he had other plans for the police station.

Paglin called a press conference to explain how Jaffa had been taken and discuss the details of the British proposal.

The correspondents gathered in the map room at Irgun Headquarters before 10:00 A.M. on the morning of April 31. Among other things, they wanted to know whether the Irgun would turn over the Manshieh police station to the British. Paglin looked at his watch. It was almost ten o'clock. He said nothing and waited. At exactly ten o'clock there was a tremendous explosion. Also, there was no more Manshieh police station. End of press conference.

The Haganah replaced the Irgun's men at the various sandbagged positions they had erected in Manshieh and the approaches to Jaffa. The transfer ceremony was brief with only one formality. The Irgun field officer in charge requested from his opposite number in the Haganah a "receipt." He got it. It was written on a page ripped from a notebook. It read: *Received from the Irgun Zvai Leumi: One Jaffa.*

The Irgun's contribution to the conquest of Jaffa was undoubtedly one of the seminal events of the subsequent birth of the state of Israel. It ended the first round of the Arab offensive, though at great cost. Of the nearly fifteen hundred Irgunists who participated in the battle, forty-two were killed and approximately four hundred were more or less seriously wounded.

With the fall of Jaffa, the Syrian trained "Army of Liberation" had failed in its main objective, that of seizing control of most of Palestine before the British departed. Transjordan's well-armed, British-trained and largely British-led Arab Legion, had wiped out the isolated Jewish settlements of the Etzion Bloc in an unpublicized "Deir Yassin" of their own, but the Legion's attempts to break through to the sea and cut Palestine in half had been frustrated.

Finally, the Arabs' undeclared war had cancelled the boundaries set by the United Nations partition resolution. At the same time, the Arab commanders, by encouraging mass departures of the Arab populations of cities, towns and villages—promising that a subsequent early victory would enable them to return and share in the spoils—contributed substantially to the creation of a "refugee problem" that would plague Arab-Jewish relations in the generation ahead.

Promptly at midnight, May 14, 1948, the British Mandate ended and early the following morning, in bright sunlight with a band playing "God Save the King," the British Commissioner left Palestine with the last of the British troops. In that moment—and as Egyptian bombs fell on Tel Aviv—the new state of Israel was formally proclaimed. It was immediately recognized *de facto* by the United States, whose example was quickly followed by most Western powers and the Soviet Union.

On the evening of May 15, every radio in Israel was tuned to the "Voice of Fighting Zion" to hear Menahem Begin, then, still a mysterious figure, a man wrapped in legend who had stirred the imagination of the people whether they were for or against the IZL's politics and activities. At precisely 8:30 P.M. there were a few bars of *Hatikvah*, then a brief announcement introducing the speaker.

Begin was nervous. It was the first time in nearly five years that he had spoken to a large radio audience in his own name. It was a poignant moment for him and for his listeners. As someone said later, he made "the speech of his life," telling his listeners that while one struggle had ended, another was about to commence. He addressed himself to Israel's mothers and sons, adjuring them to be of good heart and to finish the monumental task they had begun with the spirit with which they had started it. Lastly, Begin spoke to the future government of Israel, exhorting it to wisdom in dealing with other states, to be just and righteous in governing the people and to encourage the ingathering of the exiles of the Diaspora. Then he said:

> The Irgun Zvai Leumi is leaving the underground within the boundaries of the independent Hebrew state. We went down into the underground, we arose in the underground under the rule of oppression. Now, we have Hebrew rule in part of our Homeland. In this part there is no need for a Hebrew underground. In the State of Israel we shall be soldiers and builders. We shall respect its government, for it is our government.

The Irgun Zvai Leumi's cadres were soon incorporated into what became the Israel Defense Forces. Only in Jerusalem did the Irgun remain a military factor. The Holy City was not included in the partitioned Jewish state and remained in a sort of legal limbo. Begin strongly suspected that while Ben-Gurion might want the New City or West Jerusalem, he would not attempt to make the effort necessary to seize it all. Consequently, both the Irgun and LEHI maintained forces in the city, cooperating with each other and, whenever possible, with the always difficult Shaltiel and the Haganah.

Above all else, now, the people of Israel wanted peace with their neighbors—peace, and friendship. They would have neither.

Chapter 16

The *Altalena* Affair:
Myths and Realities

The British were gone. The long-awaited state of Israel was at last a
reality. The Jews had returned to sovereignty in their ancient homeland
after an absence of nearly two thousand years. As far as Menahem Begin
and the Irgun were concerned, the objectives for which they had fought
had been achieved. As Begin said in his May 15 radio speech to the
citizens of the newly risen Jewish republic, there was no longer any need
for an underground, and its dissolution was already under way. Except for
the small unit fighting in Jerusalem under Paglin, who took his orders
from the Haganah's Shaltiel, the Irgun's troops were fast being integrated
into what would become Zahal, the Israeli army.

The Jews had gained their longed-for independence, but now they had
to fight to keep it. The Arabs unleashed full-scale war to destroy Israel
less than six hours after it was born. Their declared objective was to
"drive the Jews into the sea" and the Zionist state with them. The armies
of Egypt, Transjordan, Syria, Lebanon, and Iraq—with contingents from
Saudi Arabia and Yemen—fell upon Israel from south, east and north
with twenty-five thousand regular troops supported by modern bombers
and fighters, artillery, tanks and armored cars.

It would be superfluous to recount in detail the progress of the Arabs'
first—and ultimately unsuccessful—attempt to destroy the Jewish state
aborning. Nevertheless, some knowledge of the military situation as it
developed during the first few weeks of the fighting is essential to an
understanding of the crisis that unfolded in the relations between
Menahem Begin and David Ben-Gurion during those critical early days in

the life of the fledgling nation, and that erupted in the notorious *Altalena* affair. Its bloody outcome late in June, while the fate of Jerusalem, indeed, of the state itself hung in the balance, would poison Israeli politics for a generation.

Officially, the commander-in-chief of the Arabs' assault was Transjordan's King Abdullah, whose military right hand was General John Bagot Glubb, honorary pasha and latter-day Lawrence who had created Transjordan's five-thousand-man Arab Legion, the best of the attackers' fighting units and by far the most successful. The Legion stormed the Old City of Jerusalem, laid siege to the New City and pushed northwestward toward Tel Aviv and the coast through Neve Yaakov and Latrun.

Meanwhile, the Egyptian army, with Saudi Arabian, Sudanese and Yemenite contingents, concentrated on the Palestine frontier with Sinai, one brigade group advancing along the coast toward Tel Aviv, while another pushed through Beersheba and Hebron to link up with Glubb Pasha's forces south of Jerusalem. The Syrians launched their main attack on Samakh, on the south shore of the Sea of Galilee, with a second thrust directed at Mishmar Hayarden, south of Lake Hula. The Lebanese forces attacked Malkiya,and an Arab pincer movement threatened all of Upper Galilee.

The Iraqi army comprised an armored brigade and eight infantry battalions, a total force of ten thousand men supported by three squadrons of aircraft. They established headquarters at Nablus, in Samaria, and occupied the whole Arab Triangle formed by Nablus-Jenin-Tulkarem, posing an additional grave threat to Israel's seacoast, only ten miles away. By the end of the first two weeks of fighting, the Egyptians had advanced as far as Ashdod, some twenty miles south of Tel Aviv and Bethlehem, almost near enough to Jerusalem to be called a suburb. They ultimately succeeded in cutting off the whole of the northern Negev by establishing themselves along the line from Migdal to Faluja.

In the meantime, the Arab Legion overran the Jewish Quarter of the Old City of Jerusalem, severed communications between Mount Scopus and the New City by capturing the heights at Sheikh Jarrah and cut Jerusalem from Tel Aviv by occupying Latrun. South of Jerusalem the Legion destroyed the Jewish *kibbutzim* of the Etzion Bloc—Revadim, Ein Tzurim, Masuot Yitzhak and Kfar Etzion. On the western shore of the Dead Sea, kibbutz Beit Arava was destroyed. Further north, the legion captured Atarot and Neve Yaakov, while the Lebanese took Malkiya.

The well-armed invaders had behind them the physical and human resources of some forty million people. Opposing them were at most fifteen thousand inadequately armed Israeli defenders of a scant seven hundred thousand Jews. The Arabs had good reason to anticipate victory, rich booty and a place in the Moslem heaven for having slain many thousands of "infidel Jews."

With weapons available for only one in every four of a possible fifty-four thousand fighters, the newly formed Israeli army, Zahal—into which several thousand men of the Irgun and LEHI had been integrated—could not as yet mount a counteroffensive. The Jews concentrated on holding a number of settlements in the enemy's rear while "mobile units"—actually mere jeep loads of daring young men who charged into action with Bren and Sten guns blazing—harassed the Arabs' flanks.

The Jews' biggest military losses, however, came at the hands of the Arab Legion, which conquered the Old City and occupied the territory within the Triangle, now known as the West Bank. The legion thereby established by conquest geographic "facts" that would endure until the Six Day War of 1967. And to this day Menahem Begin believes the legion's successes could have been averted, if only David Ben-Gurion, Prime Minister of the Provisional Government, had "listened to reason" and permitted the landing of the men and weapons aboard the Irgun's *Altalena*.

Over the years, Israeli historians have pointed to what became known as the *Altalena* Affair as evidence of Begin's determination to seize power in the Jewish republic. They have maintained that when the vessel arrived, Begin intended using the men and weapons aboard the *Altalena* to stage a right wing *putsch*. From Shmuel Katz, Eliahu Lankin, Eytan Livni and others whom I interviewed in the course of researching the life and times of Menahem Begin, however, I obtained an entirely different story. The saga of the *Altalena* as it emerged from a succession of interviews was as follows:

Back in December 1947, after publication of the United Nations' partition resolution and the British decision to leave Palestine by May 15, Begin anticipated a concerted Arab attack on the nascent Jewish state. He knew that the Haganah and the Irgun, even assuming an alliance such as was being negotiated at the time, could not offer any really effective resistance due to the critical shortage of weapons and ammunition. He was also aware of the fact that while the British remained in the country no appreciable quantities of arms would be allowed to enter Palestine's ports and that any ship suspected of gunrunning would be confiscated. Begin and his commanders planned, therefore, to bring in the *Altalena*, loaded with arms, ammunition and at least one thousand volunteers, at precisely one minute past midnight on May 15 when, legally, the British blockade would be lifted.

In France, however, Katz and Meridor ran into difficulties. Funds were scarce. The wealthy Jews of the United States and South Africa, both of which Katz visited, parted reluctantly with their money; they seemed incapable of understanding the urgency of the need. Accumulating materiel became a slow, painful process. Such funds as were available, went to support the steadily growing numbers of volunteer trainees.

On May 7, however, the French government indicated its willingness to provide the Irgun with substantial quantities of rifles, machine guns, ammunition, even a number of armored cars. But the transfer of the materiel to the Irgun had to be approved by the French cabinet. It soon became evident to Katz and Meridor that there would be bureaucratic delays and that the May 15 deadline could not be met.

The day Ben-Gurion proclaimed the establishment of the Jewish state, Katz and Meridor, who heard the news on the radio, chartered a DC-3 and flew to Tel Aviv—Lydda was in Arab hands—to explain to Begin what had happened and to make plans for the *Altalena*'s eventual arrival in Israel.

In the meantime, of course, the Arab attack had started. From Jerusalem, Paglin was begging Irgun headquarters for arms and ammunition. Another Irgun unit, fighting with the Haganah against the Arabs at Latrun, was also desperate for heavier weapons, mortar shells and .303 ammo for its machine guns. Late that same night, after making his radio speech, Begin decided to call on the Haganah for help.

Begin, accompanied by Landau, Meridor and Katz, met at Irgun headquarters in the Freud Hospital, on the outskirts of Tel Aviv, with Israel Galili, Ben-Gurion's Minister of Defense; Levi Shkolnik (later Eshkol) and David Cohen of the Haganah. Although the Irgun had more than $5 million invested in the *Altalena*, Begin offered to allow the Haganah to take over the vessel for a mere $250,000, the amount needed to equip the men waiting in France. The troops were to go directly into Zahal when the ship arrived. The Haganah representatives seemed well-disposed toward the idea and promised to report favorably to Ben-Gurion.

Two days later, on May 17, Galili informed Begin, through Landau, that Ben-Gurion had rejected the Irgun's offer. Begin was astonished. Katz and Landau were furious, and suggested the Irgun bring in the *Altalena* on its own as originally planned. Begin agreed, and Katz flew back to Paris from Haifa where the DC-3 that had brought him was making a return flight.

Awaiting Katz in Paris was Dr. Shmuel Ariel, the regular Irgun representative in the French capital, who had been negotiating with the government. Also in Paris at the time was Arieh Ben-Eliezer, who had escaped with Meridor from Gilgil in Kenya and joined the Irgun's overseas operations in Europe. They had good news. Through the intercession of Prime Minister Georges Bidault, a Zionist sympathizer, the *Quai D'Orsai* had agreed to supply the Irgun the required arms free of charge, pending approval by the Chief of Staff, General Rouen. The latter's endorsement came ten days later and shortly thereafter, on May 31, the French army set a delivery date: June 5.

By the end of May, several hundred volunteers had reported to IZL's Paris headquarters from Belgium, Holland, the United States, South Africa and North African countries. The IZL Paris staff checked their papers, and after being medically examined and given shots, they were sent to the Irgun's embarkation camp near Marseilles. There Eliahu Lankin, who would be the commander of troops aboard the *Altalena,* drilled them in the serious business of fighting, and possibly dying, for a cause. Youthful runaways and others who had joined up seeking romance and glamor were weeded out.

In Israel, meanwhile, the Haganah-Irgun negotiations for an alliance finally bore fruit. On June 1, Begin signed a treaty with the Haganah. However, remembering Ben-Gurion's negative response to the Irgun's offer to turn the *Altalena* over to the Provisional Government, Begin committed what was probably a serious error; he did not inform the Haganah of the French gift of weapons and ammunition, nor of the IZL's plans to bring in the ship. By then, Ben-Eliezer had arrived from Paris by air to make final arrangements for the vessel's arrival. A landing site, recognition signals and codes were decided.

In Paris, Katz and Ariel were in a fever to get the ship off as soon as possible in order to put its precious weapons in the hands of Jews who had been fighting tanks with Sten guns and homemade Molotov cocktails. Anxious to go, also, was the *Altalena*'s skipper, Monroe Fein, an American veteran of the war in the Pacific, who feared possible last-minute difficulties about clearances with the port authorities when it became known what the vessel would be hauling. Arms-smuggling was a dicey business.

Then came a serious complication. On May 29, the United Nations proposed a cease fire, and the Israeli government accepted it. Sooner or later, the Arabs would follow suit, and the terms of the truce undoubtedly would include an embargo against arms and immigrants of military age destined for Israeli ports. Katz and his confederates spent hours arguing the pros and cons of sailing under those circumstances but decided to go ahead with Operation Palest, come what may. The deciding factor was the dire need in Israel for weapons, a need as keenly felt by the Haganah as by the Irgun. It was not yet known in Paris what the attitude of the Israeli government would be, but it was agreed that the arms and the troops had to reach Israel's shores. It would then be up to the government to decide whether they should be landed or not.

There were other delays and contretemps, and intrigues enough to fill a suspense novel. Three days were lost, for instance, when the French police, ignorant of the Irgun's license to export arms, found a crate full of weapons that had mysteriously wound up in the passengers' baggage room of the railway station at Marseilles. The Irgunists who claimed the shipment were arrested, and a complicated diplomatic maneuver had to be mounted to get them released along with their "baggage." The matter was finally resolved, however, and a new delivery date was set: June 8.

On the appointed day, Katz and Ariel were at Sète awaiting the arrival of the weapons. They waited all day and most of the night, but nothing happened. On the dock, Katz and Ariel were joined in their vigil by the skipper, Fein, and Avraham Stavsky, the nominal owner of the *Altalena,* which had been purchased in his name. Having bought the ship, he was determined to see her through to the end of her mission.

The weapons arrived sometime before midnight. A French convoy unloaded 5000 rifles, 300 Bren guns, 150 Spandaus, five armored cars with caterpillar treads, four or five million rounds of ammunition, several thousand aerial and mortar bombs, 50 anti-tank guns and miscellaneous other equipment. There were weapons enough to equip ten battalions, turn the tide of battle at such sensitive points as Latrun and Jerusalem, and maybe even conquer the whole of Palestine west of the Jordan.

Loading started early the next day, June 9, but was delayed by an alarming incident. One of the cases marked "machinery" fell and broke open, spilling rifles all over the loading dock. The stevedores, among whom were many East Indian and North African Moslems, went on strike; they refused to load arms intended for use against their co-religionists in Palestine. The resultant panic, however, was short-lived. The volunteers themselves took over the unfamiliar, backbreaking job, making up with zeal and youthful energy their lack of experience. The work went on under a blazing Mediterranean sun, and as they worked the amateur dockers sang in a tongue strange to dockside loungers, even to many of the workers themselves; they were not all Jews.

The *Altalena* sailed with the feeble Mediterranean tide at 8:30 P.M. on the evening of June 11, just as a truce came into force between Israel and the invading Arab countries. None of the nine hundred troops on board could have imagined the dismal fate that awaited her and the Irgunist cause she represented.

Later that night, as the *Altalena* swung onto the southward leg of her course from Sète, the BBC reported from London the ship's departure and the details of the ceasefire ordered by the United Nations. As Katz had feared, the truce included a commitment by Israel and the Arab states to refrain from bringing additional arms into the area—a pledge both sides would honor in the breach.

In Israel, a longtime afficionado of BBC news broadcasts, Menahem Begin, heard the report. He was shocked. He had little faith that either side would respect the truce, but felt the Irgun should not bear the responsibility for the possible diplomatic consequences of a violation. After a hasty consultation with members of the high command, he drafted a cable for urgent transmission to the Irgun's Paris headquarters.

Katz received the message at his office the next morning, June 12, about twelve hours after the *Altalena* had sailed. Begin's cable said: DON'T SEND BOAT STOP AWAIT INSTRUCTIONS. Dismayed, Katz cabled back that it was too late and suggested that Begin establish radio contact with the vessel directly from Israel, as he had no ready means of communicating with her.

On receiving Katz's cablegram, Begin promptly radioed the *Altalena*: KEEP AWAY. AWAIT INSTRUCTIONS. He waited in vain for confirmation. He later would learn that the ship's radio equipment could receive but not transmit messages. Fearful that Ben-Gurion might prevent the vessel from landing as a breach of the truce, Begin late that same night—June 14—met again with Galili. Also present were Shkolnik, Cohen and another high-ranking security officer, one Pinhas Vaze. Oddly enough, the government men professed to have missed the BBC broadcast announcing the *Altalena*'s departure. They expressed shock on learning that the ship had sailed and probably would arrive in five days. They listened attentively, however, when Begin told them what the ship was carrying— weapons and men enough to tip the balance radically in favor of the Jews. Galili knew as well as anyone that the arms were desperately needed. In particular, there was an acute shortage of British .303 ammunition, for lack of which, many Haganah units were immobilized. Nine hundred volunteers, and arms enough for ten battalions might not win the war, as Begin enthusiastically claimed in arguing the case for bringing in the *Altalena,* but it was plain to Galili that they could make an important difference in the crucial days ahead.

According to Begin—and others with whom I discussed this particular point—Galili agreed that the ship should be brought in with all possible haste. They would settle later where the vessel should land (to avoid difficulties with United Nations observers), who would unload her and how the cargo should be distributed. Overjoyed, Begin radioed the *Altalena*: FULL SPEED AHEAD. He ordered Ben-Eliezer to return to Paris to inform Katz and liquidate the IZL's operations in Europe.

Although it was long past Ben-Gurion's bedtime, Galili telephoned the Prime Minister immediately after his three-hour session with Begin. Ben-Gurion was amazed and outraged by the magnitude of the Irgun's Operation Palest. Weapons valued at upwards of $5 million and nine hundred men! In a foul mood because Begin had not informed the Haganah about the *Altalena* and her cargo when the Irgun signed its June 1 alliance with the Provisional Government's security forces, Ben-Gurion decided that Begin was not bringing in the ship to help win the war against the Arabs, but to strengthen the Irgun and, perhaps, use the IZL to stage a *putsch*. Nevertheless, the *Altalena* carried a bonanza in modern weapons, and none knew better than Ben-Gurion how badly they were needed. He told Galili, who more than shared the Prime Minister's mistrust of Begin's intentions, to make the necessary arrangements for landing and unloading the ship.

Early the next morning, June 16, Begin met with Galili and his staff to discuss the details of the landing and unloading operations, and how the arms were to be distributed. At the suggestion of Pinhas Vaze, Begin agreed to change the scheduled landing site, originally designated as Tel Aviv, a preponderantly Irgunist area, to the beach off *kibbutz* Kfar Vitkin, a few miles further up the coast, near Natanya. Vaze said the change was necessary to avoid the attention of United Nations observers stationed in Tel Aviv. Actually, Kfar Vitkin was a Mapai stronghold and a Haganah base, but Begin, though fully aware of this, made no objection. After all, the Irgun and the Haganah were now allies; Begin and his organization had sworn allegiance to the Provisional Government, despite the fact that while Ben-Gurion had included in his Labor cabinet representatives of all other major parties, he had pointedly omitted the Revisionists.

The discussion then turned to the question of how the arms were to be divided. Begin proposed that one-fifth of the weapons be sent to the Irgun unit in Jerusalem, and the remainder distributed throughout the unified army among those battalions in which Irgun formations had already been integrated with the Haganah. Galili agreed that twenty percent should be sent to Jerusalem, but proposed that the balance be stored in government warehouses. Begin rejected the idea, and after some heated debate, the matter was left open, to be settled in further negotiations. Galili did not tell Begin that Ben-Gurion had decided that *all* the weapons were to go to Zahal, including those to be sent to Jerusalem.

Following the meeting, Begin radioed the *Altalena* instructions to land at Kfar Vitkin instead of Tel Aviv. The message was received aboardship with jubilation by Captain Fein and Commander Lankin.

"When we heard we were to land at Kfar Vitkin," Lankin told me over dinner at the King David in December, 1977, "we were delighted. I knew the *kibbutz* there to be Labor Party turf—Ben-Gurion territory. To me, the new destination meant only one thing—we had the government's cooperation. There were cheers when I paraded the troops that bright morning and told them the news. They were all in fine spirits and in excellent physical condition. I had put them through calisthenics twice every day from the time we sailed, and they were all bronzed and healthy and eager. But had I known what was in store for them, I think I would have ordered the *Altalena* back to Sète . . ."

At another meeting with Begin, this time at army headquarters in Ramat Gan, Pinhas Vaze again insisted that the *Altalena*'s weapons be stored in government warehouses. Begin sternly refused. There was no agreement as to how the arms were to be warehoused, which really meant a disagreement about how they were to be distributed.

Next day, Begin received a virtual ultimatum from Ben-Gurion via Galili. The essence of the Prime Minister's message was that unless Begin accepted the government's demands about how the weapons were to be divided and stored, the Irgun would have to bear the responsibility for the consequences. "And the responsibility," Ben-Gurion added, "would be heavy indeed. Unless you change your mind, we wash our hands of unloading the arms."

Begin, never a man to change his mind once he had decided he was in the right, was more relieved than angry. To him, Ben-Gurion's warning simply meant that the Irgun would unload the *Altalena*. So much the better; there would be no arguments over distribution or storage. It never occurred to him that Ben-Gurion would not allow the Irgun to discharge the *Altalena* or that the Prime Minister had no intention of permitting any of the weapons to fall into the hands of the Irgun. As far as Begin was concerned, the IZL had ceased to exist, except for the Jerusalem unit under Paglin, whom he had summoned to Tel Aviv to take charge of the twenty percent of the arms which Galili had agreed to allocate to the besieged city.

The rest of the story of the *Altalena*, as told to me by Lankin—and confirmed by what documentation survived the elaborate cover-up devised by Ben-Gurion and his Laborite lieutenants—does little honor to the party that would rule Israel for the next three decades. Ben-Gurion was indubitably a great leader, fully deserving of his reputation as "Israel's Churchill." But he was also a ruthless, power-hungry politician who tried to destroy aborning the only serious opposition he would have during his tenure, and very nearly succeeded.

"At daybreak on the morning of June 19," said Lankin, "the *Altalena* was about two hundred miles from Kfar Vitkin, and by nightfall we were within only forty or fifty yards from the shore. But the tide was out, and the water was too shallow to allow us to approach the pier. Besides, there was a strong offshore wind and the sea was too rough to land the troops. I was surprised to find there was no welcoming party, Irgun or otherwise. To make sure we were not spotted by United Nations observers, Fein and I decided to head back into open water. We sailed in circles all night about fifty miles off the coast . . ."

True, there was no "welcoming party" on the dock at Kfar Vitkin, but

Irgun watchers had seen the vessel. They had signaled her with flashlights, but Captain Fein had missed the signals. Realizing this, the signalers subsequently radioed the ship to return the following evening.

At 5:00 A.M. on the morning of June 20, the Irgun's Bezalel Amitzur met with David Cohen, Zahal's liaison officer, and informed him that the *Altalena* had arrived. Amitzur said the ship was due early that evening and asked whether the Haganah intended helping with the unloading. Cohen promised to cooperate, adding that he personally would mobilize the necessary vehicles. Either Cohen was dissembling, or he did not know that Galili was setting a trap for the Irgun.

The arrival of the *Altalena* had become a matter of high policy with the Provisional Government, and that same day the cabinet met to decide what to do about her. The Foreign Minister, Moshe Shertok—who had become Moshe Sharett in the mass Hebrewizing of surnames that began with the establishment of the Jewish state—sided with Galili in believing that the Irgun's Operation Palest posed a threat to the established government. Both conveniently forgot the danger of a truce violation if the arms were landed, regardless of whether they went to Zahal or the Irgun.

The debate was not altogether one-sided. Not all the members of the emergency cabinet—thirteen men of all parties drawn from the membership of the Provisional Council—felt as strongly as Sharett and Galili that the *Altalena* was a torpedo aimed at Ben-Gurion's authority as Prime Minister. The two members of the religious *Mizrachi* party and Yitzhak Gruenbaum, a so-called "Radical," felt that here was a gift from heaven, to be received in gratitude and not subjected to the morality dictated by a hypocritical world which had left the Jews to fend for themselves in desperate circumstances. For lack of weapons, the Jews had lost the Old City on May 28, and the New City itself was in grave peril. Latrun had fallen, and with it the Jerusalem corridor.

But the issue was not the immorality of breaking the truce which had been negotiated by the slender, elegant Count Folke Bernadotte of the Swedish Royal House. The real question was whether or not to use force to seize the weapons the *Altalena* had brought.

Yigal Yadin, commander of the newly formed Zahal was asked if he could spare the troops needed to do the job. Yadin responded that he had about six hundred men in the area, but he had serious doubts about using them to confiscate the *Altalena*'s cargo. He was not entirely certain his army would obey orders to fire on fellow Jews if force became necessary. Ben-Gurion was inclined to agree with Yadin, but Sharett and Galili carried the day. The cabinet voted to authorize Zahal to employ whatever measures might be required to prevent the arms from going to the Irgun. Ben-Gurion must have known that his government had just opted for civil war.

While the cabinet was making its momentous decision, Captain Fein maneuvered the *Altalena* into shallow water about forty yards from the beach at Kfar Vitkin.

"It was nearly sunset by the time she was moored," Lankin told me, "and Menahem came aboard. He looked like a kibbutznik in a conical cap, a khaki shirt with short sleeves and rumpled drill trousers when he joined Fein, Stavsky and me on the bridge. We quickly disembarked nearly all the volunteers and sent them off to camps. Those who remained—about forty-five or fifty—started unloading the ship."

The unloading was begun under the direction of Amihai Paglin. Lacking lightering barges and proper gear, the work went slowly. By daybreak only a small portion of the cargo had reached the beach in improvised rafts and rowboats. Shortly after sunrise, a small United Nations plane, white with blue markings, appeared overhead, circled the beach area and headed south toward Tel Aviv. Noting this, Begin ordered Paglin to expedite the unloading and to continue it through the daylight hours. Paglin quickened the pace as best he could, pressing into service even the *Altalena's* inflatable rubber life rafts, but very soon he received word that Zahal troops were advancing. They had formed a ring around the beach and had started setting up roadblocks. Alarmed by this show of force, Paglin signaled Begin on the ship, urging that the vessel be reloaded and moved to Tel Aviv.

Disturbed, Begin returned to the beach and an argument ensued between him and Paglin. The danger was not from Zahal, Begin insisted, but from the United Nations. Its observers had spotted the ship and would certainly take steps to impound the cargo. Paglin disagreed so vehemently that Begin relieved him of his duties and put Yaacov Meridor in charge of the unloading operation. Paglin went off in a huff to Natanya, and the work continued into early afternoon.

It was interrupted, however, with the arrival on the beach of a Zahal officer who handed Begin an ultimatum: Unless the arms were turned over to Zahal within ten minutes, the army would take them by force. Begin replied that such matters could not be settled in ten minutes, but the officer merely turned on his heel and left.

Meridor advised Begin to follow Paglin's suggestion, at least to the extent of moving the ship down to the originally scheduled landing site, the beach at the foot of Frishman Street in Tel Aviv, where there would be plenty of Irgunists to help unload the *Altalena* which still held nearly all the ammunition and three quarters of the remaining weapons and equipment. Begin was doubtful about "leaving the boys" surrounded as they were, but Meridor was insistent.

"Here you won't be able to do a thing for us," he said. "But in Tel Aviv you can get in touch with the government and straighten out this mess."

Meanwhile, Fein and Stavsky had come ashore in a rowboat and supported Meridor's proposal. If Zahal wants to start a civil war, they argued, it would be less likely to do so in a heavily populated Tel Aviv district. Begin reluctantly agreed. Captain Fein returned to his ship.

"Just as Fein reached the bridge," Lankin recalled, "all hell broke loose. There was machine gun and mortar fire, and it was directed at the beach. We could see men diving for cover, and Stavsky and a couple of crewmen dragging Begin away to the ship's launch. We couldn't hear him, but we could see he was yelling and kicking and trying to break loose. But Stavsky and the boys managed to get him into the launch, which headed for the ship.

"Fein had already started the diesels and the ship was backing off and turning slightly. This was lucky because, at that moment, a couple of government gunboats started shooting at the launch. Fein maneuvered the *Altalena* into position between the approaching launch and the gunboats, figuring they were trying to hit Begin, not the ship itself. Anyhow, Begin came aboard fighting mad and swearing in Yiddish. I'd never seen him in such a state."

Begin was angry because he had wanted to stay on the beach with his men. Leaving them, he felt, was "dishonorable." But Meridor would not allow any heroics. Begin's place was in Tel Aviv.

"You go," Meridor said. "I'm responsible here. You must go to Tel Aviv and get us out of this. If they start pumping shells into the *Altalena*, she'll explode. There's no time to lose. Go, damn it."

Ashore, Meridor and his men put up a brief resistance, then surrendered. Zahal gathered up the arms on the beach—roughly one fourth the total—and arrested the Irgunists, Meridor included. The Irgun lost six men and eighteen were wounded; Zahal lost two and six were wounded. But the civil war was not over.

"Captain Fein," said Lankin recalling what happened after leaving the beach, "headed the *Altalena* southward toward Tel Aviv. We hugged the shoreline as closely as possible, running at quarter-speed, feeling our way along and keeping out of range of the gunboats' cannon. It was nearly midnight when we felt—and heard—a terrible scraping on our bottom. We knew from the shore lights that we were close to where we should be, but in the pitch dark we couldn't tell exactly where we were, except that we had run up on a rocky reef several hundred yards out. The exhausted crew and the remaining volunteers bedded down to await daylight on a deck strewn with the personal baggage of those who had so hurriedly left the ship the night before. I was glad the boys were gone. There was no telling what morning might bring. Menahem catnapped in the bunk in the captain's quarters, but none of us got much sleep that night."

The saffron-tinted Mediterranean dawn found the *Altalena* beached like a helpless whale six or seven hundred yards from shore, almost directly opposite the Dan Hotel, where the United Nations observers were quartered, and diagonally across from the Ritz Hotel, further up the beach, where the Palmach's commander, Yigal Allon, and his deputy, Yitzhak Rabin, had their headquarters. From the seaward balconies of both beachfront hotels men with field glasses were watching every move being made aboard the stranded vessel. They saw a motor launch loaded with crates lowered from the ship's portside davits and followed its slow progress to shore. There, the crew quickly unloaded the boat. Watching from behind a jetty some thirty yards away was a platoon of Zahal troops armed with machine guns and grenades. The launch returned to the ship, leaving a few armed men behind to guard the weapons. Fein ordered the boat reloaded for a second run, noting through his glasses, meanwhile, that the area around the beach was filling up with Zahal's troops.

On hearing what had happened at Kfar Vitkin, Irgunists from the surrounding area started moving on Tel Aviv where the Irgun, as Allon and Rabin were well aware, outnumbered the Zahal. Advised of this, Ben-Gurion decided the "traitorous rebels" were to be severely punished. At an early morning meeting of the cabinet he was authorized to capture the *Altalena* for the government. He instructed Yigal Allon by telephone to do "what is necessary for the sake of Israel." He was certain beyond all reasonable doubt now that Begin and the Irgun planned a *coup d'etat*. In his long conversations with me, however, Lankin vigorously denied any such intention on Begin's part, and this view is largely accepted by most authorities.

"If we had wanted to stage a *putsch* as Ben-Gurion believed," Lankin said, "we would have behaved differently. For instance, we would have uncrated machine guns, rifles and grenades, and armed our men while we were still at sea so that when we arrived they could have gone into action immediately. But we didn't unpack so much as a single rifle. Besides, we wouldn't have landed at Kfar Vitkin, in Mapai country, but at Tel Aviv, where many of our people were concentrated. Anyhow, by noontime that day—the twenty-second—we had enough men in Tel Aviv to turn the situation around in our favor had we been so minded. I mean troops, not just citizen supporters."

Shortly after noon, Fein sent the second launch-load of cases toward the beach. Begin was beside him on the bridge with Stavsky and Lankin as the boat chugged toward the shore. When it was about twenty yards away, Zahal's machine guns opened up, sweeping the beach and the launch; its pilot was severely wounded, but he managed to steer his boat onto the beach. Over the ship's radio, which was repaired at sea enroute to Kfar Vitkin, Begin made contact with Landau at Irgun headquarters and asked him to try to persuade the government to order a ceasefire. Begin then rushed to a loudspeaker and bellowed at the troops to stop shooting. The reply was a burst of machine gun fire that swept the bridge, ripped the loudspeaker from its bracket and mortally wounded Stavsky. Bullets mowed down several men on the main deck, but the main target seemed to be Begin himself.

"There's no doubt about that," Lankin said. "Every time Menahem appeared on the bridge, the fire was intensified. Whenever he was out of sight, the firing was directed elsewhere. After about an hour, the shooting stopped as suddenly as it had begun. With a bullhorn, we told the Zahal commander we had many wounded on board and no doctor to help them. We asked him to send a boat to take them off. He said he would. We waited two hours. No boat came. Several wounded bled to death waiting for help. Suddenly, there was a sound overhead, half scream, half whistle. Fein recognized it instantly. 'Hell,' he said, 'that's a shell. They're shelling us. If they hit us amidships we're done for.' "

Lankin did not know at the time that Allon had requested, and received, Ben-Gurion's permission to use cannon and mortar fire to "warn" the ship, then sink her if necessary. Toward nightfall, when the "warnings" continued whistling overhead, Begin proposed that Captain Fein and his American lieutenants leave the ship; they had been engaged as sailors, not as soldiers in Israel's cause. But Fein refused. In the circumstances, there was only one thing to do: surrender. A direct hit on the ship would have blown her out of the water and some of Tel Aviv's waterfront along with her. Her hold was filled with aerial bombs and ammunition. Fein hoisted a white flag, but the shells kept coming closer; the gunners had bracketed the ship. With his bullhorn, Fein tried to get an explanation from the Palmach commander. After a pause, came the reply: "There is a general ceasefire, but the order has not yet reached all units."

Moments later, a shell penetrated the ship's belly and started a fire. Fein and his crew improvised rafts to take off the wounded. One by one they were lowered into the water. Meanwhile, with shells dropping all around the burning ship, smoke pouring from her hold, Fein opened the vessel's seacocks and gave the order to "Abandon ship!" The remaining volunteers started jumping overboard.

In the meantime, fighting had developed beyond the beach—confused, hysterical, uncontrolled fighting, factional fratricide. A small Irgun force broke through the Zahal cordon and raced to the beach. Using small boats, bathers' rubber rafts, even surfboards, they rowed and paddled toward the burning vessel to help the wounded and to pick up some of the volunteers who were swimming frantically shoreward.

Aboard the *Altalena,* the main deck was a sheet of flames. Lankin and Fein told Begin to jump, but he refused. At a signal from Fein, two husky seamen grabbed Begin and tossed him overboard in a lifejacket. They could hear him yelling and cursing all the way down to the water. When everyone else had gone over the side, Fein and Lankin also jumped. On shore, the firing had stopped but confusion reigned. The beach was strewn with wounded crying for help and with exhausted, half-drowned men. Lankin and the *Altalena*'s skipper managed to find Begin and took him away in the darkness. Behind them as they left the beach, the *Altalena* burned brightly, a Viking's funeral for the dead left on board. The Irgun lost sixteen men and seventy-two were wounded; Zahal counted only two dead and six wounded.

Although physically and spiritually exhausted, Begin went to the Irgun's radio transmitter that same evening and gave his version of the tragedy. To Israelis for whom every cartridge meant the difference between survival and disaster, he gave a shocking account of what had been lost in terms of ammunition, weapons and equipment. He told of his efforts to come to terms with the government over the disposal of the bonanza, and criticized those whom he held responsible for the debacle and the needless bloodshed. He was particularly bitter toward Sharett who, he charged, had been so hypocritical as to say the government had planned to turn the cargo over to Bernadotte and the United Nations.

"The Irgun's soldiers," he declared, "will not be a party to fratricidal warfare, but neither will they accept the discipline of Ben-Gurion's army any longer. Within the state area we shall continue our political activities. But our fighting strength we shall conserve for the enemy outside."

Oratorically, it was not one of Begin's best efforts. In one breath he was directing his followers to quit Zahal, and in another he said the Irgun would continue fighting the Arabs. If not within Zahal, then how? He did not say. Begin talked extemporaneously and far too long. At one point he did what political leaders must never do publicly: he wept. His voice broke and the tears flowed at the thought of men killed and wounded as Jew fought Jew on the beach at the foot of Frishman Street in Tel Aviv. Armchair patriots jeered at his "soft emotionalism." To them, he sounded incoherent, out of control. His excited speech helped to ensure the ascendancy of David Ben-Gurion, who throughout the nightmare had remained outwardly cool and firm.

Ben-Gurion had his problems, too. With the *Altalena* still flaring torchlike in the harbor, the Prime Minister next morning faced an angry meeting of the State Council. His men were rounding up Irgunists, and ugly charges of "dictatorship" and "Ben-Gurionism" were circulating among his political adversaries, even among some sharing office and responsibility with him. His strong-arm policy towards men whom the Jews preferred to consider patriots rather than rebels, brought to a boil the simmering conflict within his cabinet. Two ministers of the clerical wing resigned, alleging that Ben-Gurion, in a fury of vengeance, was seeking to resolve in a matter of days the problems of disbanding a resistance movement which, under similar conditions in 1945, had taken many months in countries like France and Belgium.

The official version of the *Altalena* incident came from Galili, who was politically affiliated with *Mapam*, the left wing of the Labor Party, and the power behind Palmach. He told a press conference that the crisis had resulted from the ship's arrival during the United Nations truce, without the government's knowledge, without being asked and in violation of the IZL's signed agreement with the Haganah. "Two or three days before the boat arrived," Galili said, "we were surprised in the dead of night by news that the boat was approaching our shores. Our demand that the boat be handed over unconditionally to the government and the army was rejected. They demanded that the arms be taken to the stores of the IZL and used primarily to arm IZL regiments."

The statement was so obviously a melange of half-truths and downright distortions that few of the foreign correspondents present were satisfied. Many of them had witnessed the tragic developments from the verandah and terraces of the Dan Hotel. They asked awkward questions. Why had the Palmach, which everyone knew enjoyed Galili's protection and patronage, opened fire first? Why had the Palmach's guns subsequently broken the ceasefire, then ignored the *Altalena's* white flag of surrender and bombarded the ship? Galili stuck to his story that the Irgun was to blame.

Galili probably did not know at the time that the wily Ben-Gurion was already planning to liquidate the Palmach. He wanted no private armies in Israel. He had become impatient with this *corps de'elite* of aggressive desert knights of left wing Socialism, who often behaved as though they were a law unto themselves. The Prime Minister plus a six-man committee devised an oath of allegiance which required all troops from the Chief of Staff down to the lowliest private to swear unconditional acceptance of Zahal discipline. The Palmach accepted it, not dreaming that the next step would be the corps' abolition and its absorption into the conscript army. Shortly afterward, Ben-Gurion also maneuvered Galili out of office, and the Palmach lost its protector within the Ministry of Defense.

To the jailed Irgunists, Ben-Gurion promised amnesty, if they consented to be bound by the new oath of allegiance. Hundreds did so, and before long they were back at their duties. Except for the unit fighting in Jerusalem under Mordechai Raanan, who had replaced Paglin, Menahem Begin's Irgun Zvai Leumi ceased to exist. With Zahal hot on his heels after his radio speech, Begin went into hiding in Jaffa.

Menahem Begin was a broken man after the *Altalena* affair. Friends had seen him occasionally worried and distracted, but never depressed and hopeless. It was a critical period in his life, during which he touched the depths of despair. However, his natural resilience and buoyancy soon asserted itself. Emerging from his Jafa hideout, he spent several days recuperating in the spacious Ramat Gan apartment of his close friend and adviser Shmuel Katz. There, in a series of conferences with the IZL's remaining commanders, plans were laid for the transformation of the Irgun into the political party that would become, in 1949, the *Herut.*

Katz told me in Jerusalem in December 1977 that after studying minutely every aspect of the *Altalena* incident, he was convinced Ben-Gurion personally had ordered the vessel sunk. "If Begin was killed in the process," Katz said, "well, so much the better from Ben-Gurion's point of view. A threat to Labor's domination of Israeli politics would have been eliminated." As Katz saw it, however, the real tragedy of the sinking of the *Altalena* lay in the fact that the event contributed greatly to the defeat of Shaltiel and the loss of the Old City on the Jerusalem front. "If the men and weapons of the *Altalena,*" Katz said, "had reached the Irgun fighters in time, the history of Israel might have been far different. The whole of Jerusalem would have been captured and the West Bank overrun."

More than a decade after the 1949 armistice and the contorted "non-frontiers" that ended Israel's War of Independence, Ben-Gurion claimed that a lack of good generals hampered the occupation of all of western Palestine in 1948. He was sharply taken to task for his charges by no less an authority than the Palmach's Yigal Allon. Writing in *Haboker*, in 1964, Allon said: "Mr. Ben-Gurion's words do not accord with the facts. They are a slur on the fighters in the War of Independence who longed to liberate the entire country and were not permitted to do so. When the then Prime Minister . . . ordered a halt to our advance we were at the height of our victories on all the decisive fronts, from the Litani River in the north to the heart of the Sinai desert. In a few days fighting we could have achieved the final destruction of the Arab invasion armies and the liberation of the whole country. The Army cannot be blamed for mistaken political decisions." As a result of those decisions, Allon charged, the country remained divided and the Old City of Jerusalem out of reach—a situation that endured until the Six Day War of 1967—not because of operations that failed but because of operations that were "disallowed and omissions that were forced on the Army by the political leadership headed by Ben-Gurion."

It was with the hope of correcting those past errors that Menahem Begin formed *Herut* and plunged into politics.

Book Five:

Israel 1948–1978

Chapter 17

The Political Begin
Emerges

The metamorphosis of Menahem Begin from revolutionary to politician was delayed several months by the resumption of Arab-Israeli hostilities. Both sides had used the United Nations June 11 truce to reinforce their respective armies, and four weeks latr, when the Arabs showed no eagerness to prolong the ceasefire, the Jews took the initiative.

New armored vehicles had arrived, along with a few planes and some artillery, and Zahal, considerably strengthened by the addition of seasoned Irgun units in its formations, easily took Ramleh and Lydda, plus several surrounding villages and Nazareth. They widened the Jerusalem corridor with the ejection of the enemy from every strongpoint except Latrun, where the Bible says Joshua commanded the sun to stand still to give him time to finish off the Canaanites, and where the Arabs would remain until they were beaten in the Six Day War of 1967.

Jewish planes, among them one piloted by Ezer Weizman, bombed Cairo, Damascus and Egyptian bases at Rafa and El Arish. Most of the Jewish population had no idea that they had acquired a mini-navy, and when a flotilla of gunboats materialized to bombard Tyre, in Lebanon, Israeli spirits soared. Armored columns broke the Egyptian line guarding the route to the Negev, and contact was restored with several beleaguered southern settlements. The Israelis soon found themselves holding nearly five thousand Arab prisoners and occupying a considerable portion of what the United Nations had proposed should become a Palestinian-Arab state. Kaukji's irregulars were routed, the Arab Legion was badly mauled and any pretense of coordination among the various Arab commands evaporated.

In only ten days, the offensive went so well that the Jews were confident
of their ability to recapture the Old City and make themselves masters of
the entire country west of the Jordan River within a month. Their hopes
for total victory were dashed, however, by Count Bernadotte, the Swedish
mediator. He had been away on a hurried mission to the Security Council,
but in mid-July he rushed back to Jerusalem to proclaim a second general
ceasefire.

Shortly after the truce went into effect, Menahem Begin made his first
official public appearance in Jerusalem. He was given a tremendous
welcome. Wherever he went—the hospitals to visit the wounded, the
religious quarter of Meah Shearim, the Sephardic communities in Mahne
Yehuda, even a Palmach training school—his car was surrounded by
cheering, applauding crowds.

In the late afternoon he addressed a huge mass meeting in the heart of
the city, Zion Square. Tens of thousands of people assembled to listen to
him. Some came out of curiosity to see what he looked like, as his
opponents maintained, but most came because he personified the struggle
against the British, and they were genuinely interested in what he had to
say. Among other things, he denounced Count Bernadotte as no impartial
mediator but as a puppet of the British, who were manipulating the strings
to win key territorial concessions for their Arab friends. He did not fail to
remind his audience that the King of Transjordan, their enemy on the
eastern front, was on the payroll of the British Foreign Office.

After the meeting, Begin's escorts literally had to fight their way
through the crowds to enable him to reach a nearby restaurant for dinner,
and the place had to be protected by armed guards to prevent the
enthusiastic mob from breaking in. Hundreds of well-wishers milled about
in the street waiting for Begin to emerge to receive a final cheer.

Next day, Begin performed the ceremonial function of handing the IZL
flag over to Raanan as Chief of Staff of the Jerusalem unit and thus of IZL
in toto; Menahem Begin was relinquishing field command of the Irgun
Zvai Leumi. The ceremony took place on a large sports field in Katamon,
an IZL parade ground. Rows of rifle-bearing men and women soldiers
stood at attention. There were mortars and Bren guns, a few armored cars
and jeeps, radio field equipment and first-aid detachments. It was a
strangely attired "army." Some troops looked more like booted partisans
than soldiers, and others were dressed in the swashbuckling Australian
manner. Most, however, wore the khaki shorts, shortsleeved shirts and
berets with vari-colored pompoms that had become the Irgunist uniform.

The climactic moment came when Begin handed Raanan the Irgun's
colors—the gleaming golden emblem of the hand grasping the rifle against

a background of white and blue silk. The newsreel and press photographers, foreign and domestic, had a field day. After days of uneventful truce-time inertia, punctuated only by the clashes and snipings which had lost their news value by their frequency, here was a "color story," a "photo-opportunity" par excellence, and the media made the most of it.

The day after the ceremonial parade, Begin left Jerusalem in a triumphal procession, cheered on his way by thousands of well-wishers. An IZL guard of honor complete with white-helmeted motorcyclists accompanied him back to Tel Aviv. The political career of Menahem Begin had begun, but his troubles were not yet over.

As the hot July wore on, the Jews worried that Bernadotte, in his anxiety to achieve a military and political settlement, would nullify their victories by forcing upon them a series of territorial rectifications before the existing frontlines could be transformed into borders. Their fears were not unfounded. The mediator was known to favor handing Jerusalem over to Transjordan, the absorption of the Jewish state into a hybrid Arab-Israeli confederation, restrictions on Jewish immigration and the return of some three hundred thousand Palestinian refugees to their original homes, with hardwon Haifa and Lydda becoming "free zones."

Bernadotte's solution, as originally proposed on June 27, could hardly commend itself to the Jews, who had given a convincing demonstration since the beginning of hostilities of their skill and tenacity in warfare. Nor did it meet the approval of the Arabs; Abdullah's allies were indignant that Transjordan should receive so rich a plum as Jerusalem as a result of a war into which all the Arabs had tossed their wealth, troops and martial reputations. Obviously, the mediator would have to reconsider his scheme for resolving the increasingly bloody conflict. To do so he flew off to the Island of Rhodes in one of the eighteen planes at his disposal, as part of his elaborate peacemaking set up which included: four ships, hundreds of vehicles and radio transmitters and technical personnel to move them, in addition to a staff of more than three hundred.

Bernadotte, a tall, vigorous extrovert in his late fifties, viewed the war in Palestine as a dramatic challenge to his credentials as a diplomat, and he was determined to transform the second ceasefire into a binding peace treaty. Visions of a Nobel Peace Prize danced in his head. As President of the Swedish Red Cross during World War II, he had negotiated with Heinrich Himmler in an eleventh-hour effort to rescue surviving prisoners in Nazi death camps. Although in the spring of 1945 many thousands of Jews were transferred to western Germany, where they were liberated by Anglo-American forces, the majority of the death camp inmates still alive in April had perished by the time the war ended in May. The Count, nevertheless, regarded his mission as a huge success. Rightly or wrongly, the Jews did not, and in Israel Bernadotte was generally looked upon as a pro-Arab pawn of the British.

By the time the mediator returned to Jerusalem in September, the Jews had won more defensible borders for themselves, and Bernadotte had decided to abandon his scheme for transferring Jerusalem to Arab sovereignty. In his final report to the Security Council, transmitted on September 16, Bernadotte also dropped his proposals for an Arab-Israeli union and for restricting Jewish immigration. He recommended giving the Negev to the Arabs, together with Lydda and Ramleh, and compensating the Jews territorially by awarding them Galilee. Lastly, he advocated a return to the idea of internationalization of Jerusalem under a United Nations trusteeship, rather than the city's outright cession to King Abdullah.

The Jews had no intention of yielding the Negev, much less of relinquishing their hold on Jerusalem, stoically held against almost hopeless odds. The Jews, not the United Nations, had saved the large Jewish population there. Bernadotte's proposal was interpreted by the Israelis in general, and by LEHI in particular, as Arab rule in Jerusalem disguised as internationalization—for its real ruler would be the King of Transjordan. Indeed, the Jews felt by now that whatever the shape into which the United Nations mediator cut the remnant of Palestine not occupied by them, the result would be the same: Britain, the power responsible for so much of their troubles, and who could have stayed Arab tanks and aircraft but had not done so, would still be there, on their very doorstep.

This in itself did not incur Ben-Gurion's wholehearted condemnation; he had often intimated his readiness to accept the existence of British influence over Israel's neighbors, which, as he saw it, would not necessarily be replaced by something better. But on the subject of Great Britain's continued presence in the area, he was practically a minority of one in Israel, even within his own Mapai party. To Nathan Yellin-Mor and the top brass of the LEHI, Bernadotte had become public enemy number one—another Lord Moyne.

Bernadotte's new proposals were spurned by both sides the same day they were presented. The following day, September 17, the Swedish mediator was gunned down in Jerusalem while on his way to an afternoon appointment with Dov Joseph, the city's military governor. His assassination provoked universal shock and revulsion. To the outside world it seemed a pointless killing, the murder in cold blood of a man of peace. In Israel, outrage mingled with concern that the deed would arouse an adverse international reaction, and the government moved promptly to demonstrate its disapproval.

Responsibility was claimed by a group dubbing itself the "Fatherland Front," a "cover-name" for an extremist faction within Yellin-Mor's LEHI, but suspicion was immediately directed toward Menahem Begin and the Irgun. Begin indignantly denied all complicity, and there was no doubt of the Irgun's innocence. Nevertheless, Begin received another ultimatum from Ben-Gurion: "Disband your organization, surrender your arms within twenty-four hours, and submit to the laws of Israel, or the army will move against you." This, of course, referred only to Jerusalem, since elsewhere in the land the Irgunists had already sworn allegiance to the government. Ben-Gurion's demand antagonized many of the Irgun's more hot-headed elements. Jealous of their organization's prestige, they were ready to take up the government's challenge. The IZL's position in Jerusalem was undoubtedly strong enough to have caused havoc in the ranks of the Haganah. The civil strife that had erupted briefly on the beach at Tel Aviv was renewed on a far larger scale. But Menahem Begin, strongly seconded by Shmuel Katz, would not be swayed from his decision to comply with Ben-Gurion's ultimatum.

On Monday, September 20, the Irgun Zvai Leumi ceased to exist as an independent military organization. The handing over of the Irgun's arms was carried out without incident, in spite of the fact that the military authorities tactlessly sent a unit of the Palmach, whose guns had fired on the *Altalena* only three months before, to receive the weapons. It was not the Palmach but the Haganah, however, that dismantled the Irgun's installations at Katamon, removed its wounded to government hospitals and began swearing in the individual members.

Bernadotte's assassins could not be found, but the LEHI was outlawed, and hundreds of known members were arrested, including their leader, Yellin-Mor. Many escaped from jail soon afterward and joined Zahal under assumed names. By the time Yellin-Mor was brought to trial early the following year and sentenced to a long prison term for "terrorist activities," the war was over, and Israel's first national elections were held. Elected to Parliament, Yellin-Mor was amnestied.

In the three months preceding the elections, there was more fighting, mainly with the Egyptians. Allon cleared the entire Negev of the enemy, and if Ben-Gurion had permitted it, the Palmach commander could have driven into Sinai and destroyed the Egyptian army. But the Prime Minister, heeding threatened intervention by Great Britain, Egypt's protector, stayed Allon's hand and the diplomats took over.

On January 6, 1949, the Egyptians agreed to send a delegation to Rhodes to discuss armistice terms with the new United Nations mediator, Ralph Bunche, Bernadotte's successor. Designed as *temporary* measures to be replaced rapidly by *permanent* peace treaties, a series of armistice agreements were concluded under United Nations auspices between January and July and signed by Egypt, Lebanon, Jordan and Syria. Iraq, whose armies had played so large a part in the invasion, declined to sign the treaty on the grounds that it had no common frontier with Israel.

Israel's boundaries became, not those envisioned by the Partition Resolution of November 1947, but those secured by the Israeli defense forces. Egypt retained the Gaza Strip, an economically unviable area crowded with refugees; the West Bank and the Old City of Jerusalem remained in Abdullah's hands and were eventually annexed by the newly created Hashemite Kingdom of Jordan. The virtual annexation of the Gaza Strip by Egypt and the formal annexation by Jordan of the West Bank, both earmarked as part of the designated Palestine-Arab state, was a crass violation of the 1947 Partition Resolution, but there were no objections from the preponderantly pro-Arab Western powers.

Territorially, the Israel that emerged from the armistice agreements represented only a fraction of the Israel envisioned in Revisionist Jabotinsky's dream of a Jewish state on the banks of the Jordan River and considerably less than his pupil, Menahem Begin, had hoped for when the *Altalena* sailed from France. Accordingly, Begin set out to achieve politically what he had failed to accomplish militarily as commander of the Irgun, the extension of Jewish sovereignty over the entire territory between the Jordan and the Mediterranean. In October, he recalled Shmuel Katz from Jerusalem to help him found the right wing Herut Party in preparation for the general elections, slated to be held the moment hostilities ceased. They took place on January 25, 1949.

Although the fighting had ended, it was a "khaki election," with virtually everyone still in uniform. If democracy can be measured quantitatively by the number of political parties vying for an electorate's favors, the Israel of 1949 was easily the world's most democratic country. Twenty-one parties contended for the votes of less than a million eligible voters, including Arabs who had accepted Israeli citizenship and were voting for the first time in their lives in a free society.

In the Israeli electoral system, any party obtaining one percent of the total votes cast receives representation in the 120-member Knesset. In 1949, nine parties fell short of the required minimum. The multiplicity of parties indicated an Israel rent even in infancy by internal cleavages— ethnic, social, religious, political and economic.

In addition to a Parliament, the Israelis also elected a President, in their country a purely honorific and ceremonial office. The winner, Chaim Weizmann, was disappointed at having been relegated to that status and once remarked to President Truman, "My handkerchief is the only thing I can stick my nose into; into everything else, it's Ben-Gurion's nose."

The results of the voting for the composition of the Knesset were not consoling to Ben-Gurion. His leftist-oriented Mapai party, which had dominated the politics of the Jewish community in Palestine for nearly a decade and a half before the state was founded, emerged with the largest representation. It won forty-six seats, a little more than one-third of the total, but far short of Ben-Gurion's hoped-for clear majority. Mapam, the party of the left wing socialists, won nineteen seats and an alliance of several religious parties followed with sixteen.

The next most important group, and the country's third largest single party, proved to be Menahem Begin's Herut. It established itself as a significant force, gaining eleven percent of the votes and fourteen seats. The General Zionists—Weizmann's party—won seven seats; the left-of-center Progressive party, five; the Communists, four; and the Arab lists, two. The remaining seven seats were scattered among several small parties.

Ben-Gurion was not repudiated in his country's first election, but neither was he clamorously acclaimed. He believed that he had earned the right to be accepted as national leader with power enough to run the Jewish state as he saw fit within, of course, a democratic framework. Instead, only the old guard of Mapai stood by him. To rule, he would require a coalition, but for unwavering loyalty he could rely only on his own comrades who drew their power in turn from the wide influence they exerted within the labor federation, the mighty Histadruth.

Ben-Gurion's strongest opposition came from the Herut. Begin campaigned strenuously on a nationalistic platform advocating Israel's expansion to its full "historical borders" on both sides of the Jordan, the adoption of a straightforward western orientation in foreign affairs as opposed to Ben-Gurion's advocacy of "non-alignment" and an actively capitalist approach in domestic policy instead of Mapai's "creeping Socialism." He also urged mass immigration and a written constitution to guarantee the nation's future stability, something which Israel does not have to this day.

Battle lines between Ben-Gurion and Begin were drawn early in the life of the new government from which, incidentally, the Prime Minister-designate had again excluded the leader of the Herut, vowing he would never form a cabinet with him and/or the Communists. On April 4, only four months after the elections, Begin called for a vote of non-confidence in Ben-Gurion's government for having signed an armistice with, and thereby having recognized, the Hashemite Kingdom of Transjordan. He charged the Premier with having given Abdullah, "the slave of the British . . . a vast area in the western part of the homeland," meaning the West

Bank. Referring to the mutual defense treaty between Britain and Abdullah, and heaping scorn on the government, Begin said, "We have achieved nothing through peaceful ways. You, who sit here have deluded yourselves into believing that if you agree to the partition of Eretz Israel, you will get the State of Israel peacefully . . . ."

Begin claimed partition would not ensure peace, and history would prove him right. "From the Arabs' point of view," he said, "there are two possibilities: Either they will want, and be able, to rise in arms against Jewish rule, or they will not. In the first case, they will fight, even against partition. In the second case they would not fight against Jewish rule even in the *whole* country." He returned to the theme in the foreign policy debate of June 15, 1949. "Peace," Begin said, "does not depend on signing peace treaties. Peace between us and the Arab state depends mainly, and perhaps only, on the military, economic, territorial and strategic power relations set up between us and them."

Thus, the Menahem Begin of the late 1970s was discernible in the Menahem Begin of the late 1940s, a politician for whom nationhood, sovereignty, the very existence of a nation are not a matter of mere empirical fact, but a reflection of ideas, of what he calls "the supremacy of moral forces," of historical rights, of sacred faith, of legal claim and, above all, of the proof of fire and steel. A nation exists, he would maintain throughout his career, insofar as it is willing and able to fight for its existence. Paraphrasing Descartes, he would say, "We fight, therefore we are."

Begin's outlook was, and has remained, that of the educated Polish Jew whom the anti-Semitism of his times goaded into Zionist rebellion. He belongs to the generation which saw the lofty ideals of Woodrow Wilson consumed in the flames of World War II. The collapse of Wilson's world left him with a Buchenwald complex: The world that emerged from the debacle is against the Jews, at best indifferent. Therefore, the very existence of the Jews is constantly endangered. Then, as now—and as would be dramatically demonstrated nearly thirty years later in the national elections of 1977—many Israelis shared Begin's catastrophic conception of Zionism. He believed then, and he believes now, that the world does not pity the slaughtered; it only respects "those who fight."

Initially, Herut's strength lay primarily among the East European middle class of Israel's larger cities. In the early 1950s, however, Begin concentrated increasingly on wooing the Oriental immigrants from Arab countries—the often darker-skinned Sephardic Jews who saw themselves closed out of the predominantly East European, Ashkenazic establishment, and who identified emotionally with Herut's nationalistic, hence anti-Arab, stance. Tough and uncompromising in its appeal to these diverse elements, Herut rapidly became the single most important reservoir of opposition to the Labor-controlled government.

However, Herut's—and Begin's—appeal fluctuated. In the 1951 elections, Begin's party lost strength, dropping back to eight seats in the Knesset and fifth place among the parties. The setback committed Begin to a policy of intensified militancy against the Labor regime. He needed an issue, and shortly after the elections the Prime Minister provided him with one.

The year before, Ben-Gurion had made an agonizing decision. The country was in desperate financial straits, and he sought help in the form of reparations from West Germany. The Bonn government expressed a willingness to talk and negotiations started—in Luxembourg, where Israelis and Germans could meet in a neutral atmosphere—for the payment by West Germany of compensation for the crimes committed during the Nazi regime against those few hundred thousands of Jewish survivors of the death camps who were now citizens of Israel. In recognition of Nazi culpability, the West Germans agreed to supply to Israel machinery and raw materials valued at $715 million over a period of fourteen years.

Although the government took pains to make clear that the reparations were to be regarded only as financial assistance to help the Jewish state absorb the survivors of the Nazi terror, the idea of taking "blood money" from Germany rocked Israeli public opinion. Too many Israelis had lost fathers and mothers, husbands or wives or children in the Holocaust. From the moment Ben-Gurion's intentions became known, the Jews became a community of mourners. Some Knesset members saw themselves again trudging through the snow in flight from Belsen and Buchenwald. The world had already largely forgotten the Nazi nightmare of the 1930s and 1940s, but not Israel's Jews, and, certainly, not Menahem Begin.

By December 1951, preliminary discussions with Bonn were concluded, and early the following year Parliament was summoned to approve broader negotiations. The ensuing debate was unprecedented in its violence. In so far as payment was possible, Ben-Gurion's Mapai, a few members of the religious parties and some non-Socialist Progressives favored making the Germans pay for their crimes. But bitter opposition was expressed by every shade of political opinion, including the conservative General Zionists, the ultra-Socialist Mapam, and the Communists. By far the most vociferous in their attack on the idea of any dealings with Germany, however, were Menahem Begin and the members of his Herut bloc. For Begin, German reparations signified "the ultimate abomination, the like of which 'we have not known since we became a nation."

In those days, the Knesset sat in a compact, narrow building with a curved stonework facade in King George V Avenue, only a few hundred yards from Zion Square where, on the morning of January 7, Menahem Begin was scheduled to make a speech. On his way there, he noted that the government, in anticipation of trouble, had ringed the Parliament building with barbed wire and mobilized hundreds of police, armed with shields, batons and gas-mask kits. They had erected roadblocks and diverted bus traffic. Begin was furious and in a highly emotional state when he addressed the crowd of some fifteen thousand Jerusalemites who had come to hear him.

"I am not here to inflame you," he shouted, "but the police have grenades containing tear gas manufactured in Germany. We shall suffer any torture they may think up for us to prevent a decision to deal with Germany! When they fired on us with their cannon (referring to the *Altalena* episode) I gave the order—No!—do not retaliate. Today I give the order—Yes! This will be a war of life or death."

Begin may not have intended to "inflame," but his speech was clearly a call to violence, and there was plenty of it later that day when several thousand demonstrators marched on the Knesset. Met with tear gas and smoke bombs, they responded with rocks and brickbats. Inside, the debate continued, though the building's windows were smashed and a few missiles barely missed the heads of some legislators. Smoke billowed through the chamber, and as fellow legislators buried their faces in handkerchiefs, Begin mounted the tribune. He denied the rioting had been stage-managed and read out a list of distinguished citizens who opposed reparations. Ben-Gurion, who had sat motionless until then, apparently unaffected by the choking atmosphere, rose and pointed to the broken windows.

"They"—meaning the names Begin had read out—"are not identified with your Fascist hooligans in the street," Ben-Gurion shouted.

"You are the Fascist hooligan," Begin hotly retorted.

The exchange caused an uproar. Begin refused to withdraw his unparliamentary remark, and to end the confusion, the Speaker ordered a recess.

Ben-Gurion went further; he called in the army to restore order. By then, the fighting had been going on for nearly four hours. Hundreds were arrested, filling the jails. About a hundred policemen were injured. Many of the demonstrators also were wounded, some of whom were taken by fellow Herutists to private first-aid stations, then spirited out of the city to avoid arrest.

When the Knesset reconvened later, Begin apologized for his personal attack on Ben-Gurion, but before leaving the dais, he hinted darkly at the possibility of civil war if the government persisted in its negotiations with Germany.

"There are things in life that are worse than death," he warned. "This is one of them. For this we will give our lives. We will leave our families. We will say goodbye to our children, but there will be no negotiations with Germany. Today you have arrested hundreds. Perhaps you will arrest thousands. We will sit together with them. If necessary we will die together with them, but there will be no reparations from Germany. Nations have gone to the barricades on less important issues."

Some legislators took this as a threat by Begin to reconstitute his Herut party as an underground movement to bring down the government. Begin underscored the threat by adding that he and his supporters no longer would promise to "respect the immunity of the members of the Parliament themselves."

Next day, Ben-Gurion, in a radio broadcast to the nation, denounced "the hand of evil" that had been "raised against the sovereignty of the Knesset." He reassured the country that all necessary steps had been taken to safeguard democratic institutions and a return to law and order. His speech had the desired effect. Begin called off further demonstrations.

The debate continued the following day, January 9, and the reparations issue was put to the vote. The result was closer than Ben-Gurion might have wished: Sixty-one to fifty, with five abstentions—authorizing the government to enter into direct negotiations with the West German government.

Eventually, the government's policy prevailed. Bonn agreed to a formula whereby money and goods were paid to Jews throughout the world as well as in Israel. Western governments and public opinion hailed the arrangement, but in Arab capitals it provoked such violent protest that ratification by the *Bundestag* was delayed until March 1953. The issue, however, was far from dead.

The pragmatic Ben-Gurion saw acceptance of German reparations as a practical solution to Israel's dire need for money and credits at a critical moment in its development. The idealistic Begin, on the other hand, sincerely believed the concept to be a violation of Old Testament ethics, morally reprehensible and a desecration of the memory of those Jews lost in the Holocaust. He saw reparations as blood money that gratuitously relieved the Germans of their collective guilt for the extermination of six million Jews during the Nazi hell.

Begin accepted without demurrer a Knesset resolution denying him his parliamentary seat for several months. The loss of his seat caused him to change his tactics, but not his attitude toward the government's policy. He remained faithful to the principle of non-contact with the postwar "New

Germany," where a host of former Nazi officers were being systematically "rehabilitated." Begin decided, however, to confine further agitation to the Knesset chamber. Begin the agitator became Begin the parliamentarian, and the government breathed more easily, but not for long.

On January 1, 1954, a historic trial opened in the Jerusalem district court. The defendant in what quickly became a *cause célèbre* was Malkiel Greenwald, a Hungarian-born Jew of seventy-two, accused of having committed criminal libel against Rudolf Kastner, a fellow Hungarian then employed as public relations director of the Israeli Ministry of Commerce and Industry. Greenwald, a professional pamphleteer, had emigrated to Palestine in 1938, where he joined the right wing Mizrachi party. He subsequently became the author of a newsletter that specialized in "inside" information about corruption in the Mapai leadership, and editorially agitated for "moral regeneration" in high places. Greenwald attacked Kastner, among others, as "a careerist who grew fat on Hitler's looting and murders." Because of Kastner's alleged "machinations and collaborations with the Nazis," Greenwald wrote, "I consider him implicated in the murder of our beloved brothers . . ." At this point, Dov Joseph, who had become the Laborite Minister of Commerce and Industry, instituted criminal proceedings against Greenwald.

A lawyer in his native Hungary, Kastner had served as chairman of the Jewish Rescue Committee in Budapest during World War II. On April 24, 1944, an associate, Joel Brand, was summoned to a meeting with the notorious Adolf Eichmann in Budapest's Majestic Hotel. The SS officer proposed trading eight hundred thousand Hungarian Jews for large quantities of Allied war material, mainly trucks. Brand was flown to Turkey on May 13 to transmit the proposal to Allied and Jewish Agency representatives. Meanwhile, Hungarian Jews were being deported at the rate of twelve thousand a day. Kastner bargained for a time while the matter was being considered, but to no avail. Finally, he came up with a proposal that Eichmann found acceptable. It was for Eichmann to allow a limited number of Jews to emigrate to Switzerland as a token of his "sincerity." Eichmann left it to Kastner to provide a list of two hundred families, and the latter came up with the names of 1,685 Jews. The German kept his word and arranged for the lucky ones to leave for Switzerland on two special trains, with permits allocated by Kastner. During the ensuing months, until the Red Army marched into Hungary, an additional 434,000 Jews were shipped to Auschwitz and murdered. Kastner, of course, was not among them.

Greenwald's defense was handled by Shmuel Tamir, one of the country's most brilliant legal minds and a fellow founder of Herut who was to play an important role in the party's political orientation in the decade ahead. Tamir cleverly turned the trial into an arraignment of Kastner's superiors in the Laborite leadership as participants in a "conspiracy of silence" surrounding the annihilation of Hungarian Jewry. During his interrogation by Tamir, Kastner admitted that at Nuremberg he had testified on behalf of one of the Nazi officials with whom he had dealt in the Budapest negotiations. Tamir's cross-examination from then on was fierce.

Determined now to place the onus for the tragedy of the Hungarian Jews squarely where he was convinced it belonged—on Kastner and his "allies," the Labor party officials who had directed the Jewish Agency during the war and who currently were running the government—Tamir went after Kastner with a vengeance. Why, he asked, had Hungarian Jews passively allowed themselves to be rounded up and deported to Auschwitz? Why had Kastner, knowing what was in store for them, not warned them so that they might have gone into hiding or escaped? Kastner replied somewhat lamely that he had feared jeopardizing his "negotiations" with Eichmann.

Then, documents in hand, Tamir revealed that of the 1,685 rescued Jews 388 came from Cluj, Kastner's hometown, and that every one of them was either his relative or friend. The government produced witnesses who sought to corroborate Kastner's testimony and who indicated that Kastner, far from having profited from his negotiations, had arrived in Palestine a virtual pauper. Tamir countered by accusing the prosecution's witnesses of protecting a government "clique" and of collaborating with Kastner in the "betrayal" of Hungary's Jews. Two witnesses—high-ranking Jewish Agency officials who had been in touch with Joel Brand in 1944—faltered and contradicted themselves on the witness stand. Tamir tore their testimony to shreds.

The unprecedented bitterness with which Tamir—widely respected for his patriotism, courage and integrity—and the Herut press attacked Kastner and the Labor party Jewish Agency leaders for their wartime roles had far-reaching political consequences. The trial lasted many months, well into August, months during which hundreds of thousands of survivors of the Holocaust wondered whether or not they had been betrayed by their own kind, by individuals who now occupied eminent positions in the Labor party and in the government. With general elections pending, the electorate was in a highly agitated state, aroused not only by the disclosures made during the sensational Kastner trial but by a renewal of Arab *fedayeen* terrorism on the borders, especially in the area of the Gaza Strip. All of this became grist for Menahem Begin's political mill.

Judge Benyamin Halevi issued his judgment on the Kastner case on

June 22, 1955, after deliberating nearly a year. His three-hundred-page opinion fell like a bombshell. Judge Halevi ruled that Kastner had in fact done nothing to alert Hungarian Jews to their impending danger, or to urge them to go into hiding, but instead had allowed tranquilizing rumors to circulate. It was therefore no mere coincidence that Kastner was able to save his relatives and friends in Cluj. When Kastner undertook to allocate permits for the two freedom trains, the judge said, he "sold his soul to the devil." Kastner's behavior was deemed "collaboration in the fullest sense of the word," and according to Jewish law a man who spares himself at the expense of others, "forfeits his right to life." Judge Halevi then declared the defendant, Greenwald, innocent of libel.

The verdict sent shock waves through the government. The following day, June 23, the cabinet met in emergency session and decided to appeal Judge Halevi's ruling to the Supreme Court. Four days later, in the Knesset, Begin's Herut bloc submitted a motion of non-confidence in the government, then headed by Ben-Gurion's successor, Moshe Sharett. The motion was defeated, but one of the main partners in the Labor-led coalition, the General Zionists, abstained, precipitating a parliamentary crisis. Sharett resigned, remaining only as a caretaker until new elections could be held in July.

On the hustings and in the press, Begin and his followers fully exploited the Kastner verdict as well as the government's seeming inability to put a stop to Arab terror raids. They charged that the establishment's willingness to employ Kastner was a decision "every bit as odious" as the acceptance of German reparations, and contended that the Laborites in power were "passively accepting fate" in dealing with Arab terrorism, just as a dozen years before they had allowed the Jews of Hungary to go to their doom like so many sheep.

The impact of this reasoning on the voting public was profound. In the elections held on July 26, 1955, Begin's Herut nearly doubled its Knesset membership, which rose from eight seats to fifteen, and thereby became the country's second-largest party.

Menahem Begin thereafter remained within the bounds of parliamentary responsibility. He assumed with evident relish the role of leader of the loyal opposition, and embarked on the long, slow and difficult course to power.

Chapter 18

The Road to Power— Part One

Despite his party's excellent showing in the 1955 elections, Begin was again excluded from participation in the new government formed by Ben-Gurion when the latter returned to power in succession to Sharett. Like all his Laborite successors, Ben-Gurion was always compelled to find coalition partners in order to obtain a working majority in the Parliament, but he had made it a rule—scrupulously followed by Laborite Prime Ministers for more than a decade—to accept all parties in their coalitions "except Herut and the Communists." Meanwhile, until the national emergency of the spring of 1967, Begin remained an outcast of Israeli politics, relegated to the role of perpetual critic of what he and his followers saw as corruption, sloth and "creeping Socialism" in a succession of Labor-dominated governments.

The exclusion was attributable purely and simply to the hostility which Ben-Gurion and the Labor party felt toward Begin and the Herut, as the political offspring of the Irgun and heirs to the ideology of Jabotinsky's Revisionist party. The animosity was reflected in a relentless ideological campaign of denigration of Revisionism as a dangerously revolutionary movement bent on destruction of Israel's social-democracy. The hostility began with the murder in 1935 of the Labor leader, Arlosoroff, a crime of which, it developed, the Revisionists were falsely accused. It deepened through such bitter episodes as "The Season," the *Altalena* affair, the Deir Yassin massacre and the Herutist demonstrators' march on the Knesset over German reparations.

It was a relatively simple matter for the propagandists of the Labor movement to equate Herut's Revisionism with Fascism and reaction. Herut and its leader were anathema to the pioneer generation who had drained Palestine's malarial swamps and built up the country's agriculture—and who had created industries, schools, hospitals and the nucleus of an army—while Jabotinsky's Betarim were marching about in Czechoslovakia and Poland wearing uniforms and singing nationalistic songs much like Mussolini's and Hitler's youth organizations. Those Israelis who uncritically accepted Labor's definition of Herut found it psychologically difficult to vote for Menahem Begin and his party's list of candidates at election time. Long after the War of Independence many Israelis continued to regard Begin as a revolutionary who conceivably might use force to overthrow the government and demolish its democratic institutions. The national *angst* on this score carried well into the 1950s.

Actually, Begin was deeply committed to democracy. As I have already indicated, one of the major planks in his party's platform called for a national constitution to safeguard individual rights and freedoms. Nevertheless, the Laborites persisted in seeing him as a genuinely dangerous individual, a rabble-rouser given to demagoguery and opportunism. Their distrust deepened during the 1955 elections, when Begin skillfully exploited the doubts and anxieties generated by the Kastner case and the Arab terrorist raids on the borders.

The nation's collective fear of Arab terrorism was dispelled in October 1956 when the government launched its militarily highly successful invasion of Sinai, Israel's first major armed reaction to years of Arab threats and harassment. In a brilliant campaign led by General Dayan, then Chief of Staff, Israeli troops astonished the world (and themselves) by reaching the Suez Canal within one hundred hours. Egypt's lengthening shadow over Israel was lifted, and Begin's charges in the Knesset that the Labor government was prepared to "submit passively to continued terrorist attacks" were effectively disproved. Having silenced the thunder from the right, Israel seemed headed for a period of internal peace, but a new crisis developed, and Begin was widely suspected of having created it.

Although Begin and the Irgun had renounced violence as an instrument of political action, other underground elements had not. Early in March 1957, while Israel was being pressed by the Great Powers in general—and in particular by the United States—to withdraw from Sinai and the Gaza Strip, the notorious Kastner was ambushed and mortally wounded outside his home in Tel Aviv. When captured, Kastner's three young assailants readily admitted being members of an extremist wing of the outlawed Freedom Fighters for Israel, the LEHI to which the killers of Lord Moyne had belonged. Searches subsequently disclosed large arms caches with which the criminals and their henchmen allegedly intended fulfilling a right wing vision of an "Israeli empire reaching from the Mediterranean to the Tigris and Euphrates."

Begin and the Herut, including most of the other non-Socialist leaders and parties, roundly denounced the threat to democracy. Begin, however, had led the attack on the government for yielding to external pressure and withdrawing from Sinai. He was particularly incensed that the government had agreed to retreat from the Gaza Strip, which had been a hyperactive Arab terrorist base ever since Israel's birth. Apart from the fact that he had helped to create the unsettled political atmosphere in which the young extremists had acted, their goal of a "greater Israel" sounded in Laborite ears remarkably like the maximalist territorial plank in the party platform of Begin's Herut. Although in the Knesset Begin castigated the murder of Kastner as "an assault on parliamentary democracy," his political opponents persisted in holding him responsible for having generated a climate conducive to violence by accusing the government, as he in fact had, in his usual inflammatory style, of "selling away Israel's security" by agreeing to withdraw from Sinai and the Gaza Strip.[1]

Here, however, I feel obliged to enter a brief parenthesis in Begin's defense. I was in Israel at the time and remember clearly the mood of the country. The feeling was widespread that by relinquishing the territory conquered from Egypt, Israel was returning to the uncertainties that had prevailed before the Sinai campaign was launched. Begin, it seems to me, was only voicing in the Parliament the doubts and fears about their country's future that in the winter of 1956-1957 anguished most Israelis.

So sharp were his critics' attacks that Begin felt constrained to deny any responsibility for the death of Kastner, and to make certain that journalists did not confuse the Irgun with any other underground force. I recall a press conference, held in Tel Aviv on March 23, in which Begin declared:

"There was only one bonafide underground in this country, and that was the Irgun Zvai Leumi, which drove the British out of Palestine. The term underground should not be desecrated by being applied to secret groups. Long before the establishment of the state, the Irgun resolved that it would never attempt to obtain power by force. Subversive activity would be dangerous because it would recreate the conditions of disunity which led to the destruction of the Jewish Commonwealth two thousand years ago."

In time, Begin dropped from the Herut's platform demands for a Jewish state on both sides of the Jordan. But his party's philosophy remained unmistakably ultra-nationalistic, animated by a romantic, highly idealistic dedication to the principle of nationhood, sacred in itself and justifying virtually anything done in its name. Ultimately, Begin fashioned a coalition of his own with which to contest Labor's monopoly over the government and its major institutions. But it was an uphill struggle all the way. To understand his difficulties, however, it is necessary to'see them in the context of Israel's complex society.

The Israeli electorate is not only strikingly heterogeneous, but its composition changes drastically from one election to the next. The 506,567 voters who chose the first Knesset in 1949 and gave Begin's Herut 14 seats were for the most part members of the Ashkenazic "pioneer" generation of Yiddish-speaking Jews from Eastern and Central Europe, who had played the main role in building the Jewish national homeland in Palestine. They still held the balance of power when the second Parliament was elected in 1951 and Herut dropped back to eight seats.

But by 1955, when Herut doubled the size of its representation in the Knesset, important demographic and generational changes had occurred in the composition of Israel's population. What before 1949 had been a mere trickle of immigrants from the Moslem countries of North Africa and the Middle East had become a veritable flood. It was composed of the Sephardic Jews who had lived as second and third class citizens in Morocco, Algeria, Tunisia, Libya, Egypt, Syria, Iraq and Yemen since the time of the Inquisition in 1492. In their countries of origin they had been tailors, cobblers, jewelers, mechanics, doctors, accountants, lawyers, shopkeepers and money-changers. Some had owned department stores and small factories, but all property had to be abandoned in return for exit permits. The total value of what the Jewish refugees from Arab countries left behind runs into the many billions of dollars, but nearly all arrived in Israel virtually penniless, with a few belongings carried in cheap fiber suitcases or tied up in pitiful bundles. It was among these newcomers—more than six hundred thousand who arrived between 1949 and 1955—that Menahem Begin found strong support for his political credo.

The new arrivals were Arabic-speaking Jews, deeply pious and wedded to distinctive, centuries-old traditions and communal customs. They had lived all their lives in the crowded Jewish quarters of cities like Casablanca and Algiers, Cairo and Damascus, and when they arrived in Israel, they preferred the already teeming slums of Tel Aviv and Haifa to the towns and villages of the open countryside. Consequently, established Ashkenazic Jews from Romania and Hungary found themselves packed tightly side by side with Sephardic immigrants from Morocco and Iraq, neither group able to speak the others' language or understand their mentality; few of the Sephardim knew enough Hebrew or Yiddish to make themselves understood. Most were unwilling or unfit to work with their hands in fields or factories, and soon there were two Israels: One consisting of the veteran Ashkenazim who understood the new society because they had built it and held the positions of power and influence; the other a bewildered horde of Sephardim—"strangers and afraid, in a world they never made."

Menahem Begin made himself the champion of the Sephardic Jews of the "other Israel." In the Knesset he became their voice for equal rights, better housing, and freedom of opportunity to pursue their traditional trades and businesses.

Although at the outset of his political career Begin's main strength lay with the urban middle class of European background, it was among the Oriental immigrants who felt excluded from the overwhelmingly Ashkenazic Labor establishment that he broadened his support. Gradually, as the Sephardim learned Hebrew and became aware of themselves as Israel's underprivileged proletariat, they looked increasingly to Begin as their leader. They were drawn to him by his oratory—whose message they could *feel* even when they did not fully *understand* it—by his tough, uncompromising line on how to deal with their despoilers and longtime tormentors, the Arabs, and by his piety.

Over the years, Begin developed a populist philosophy and an "image" much like that of an American politician of an earlier time, the bimetallist Ohio-born Democrat from Nebraska, "The Great Commoner," William Jennings Bryan. Both were devout parliamentarians and gifted debaters with a profound belief in their respective Bibles and the power of words. Begin, like Bryan, had the "common touch," a special capacity for assuming the role of "tribune of the people," unequaled in Israeli politics by anyone except Ben-Gurion; not even the immensely popular Golda Meir ever succeeded in establishing the rapport with the masses which Begin managed to achieve.

Begin realized, however, that although Herut's following was growing, his party would never be able to wrest control of the government from Labor on its own. After the 1955 elections, he cast about for allies among other right-of-center groups but without initial success. To extricate his group from its isolation, he modified his demands. His speeches in the Knesset and on other political platforms mellowed. He did not drop Herut's territorial claims, but he no longer asserted them with his old belligerency. He had learned at last that political extremism held little appeal for the Israeli "man in the street."

Meanwhile, the country's entire political structure, as unstable as a formula in the chemistry of hydrocarbons, was undergoing mergers and realignments. Mapai, the moderately socialist Labor party, which under Ben-Gurion's leadership had dominated the Zionist Organization and the Histadrut since the mid-1930s, had fallen into disarray, riven by ferocious internal squabbling over the infamous "Lavon affair," a labyrinthian dispute involving an undercover plot gone awry. This was an attempt in 1954 to blow up American and British information offices in Cairo and Alexandria in order to arouse Western public opinion against the Egyptians. The attempt fizzled, the plot was discovered and responsibility for the failure—and consequent loss of Israeli prestige—fell on Pinchas

Lavon, Ben-Gurion's protege and Minister of Defense at the time. Outraged when an investigation failed to clear Lavon, Ben-Gurion resigned in 1963, broke away from the Mapai party he had led for so long and formed the Rafi party with, among others, the charismatic Moshe Dayan and the stalwart Shimon Peres.

Sensing the time was ripe for a vigorous assault on Labor's traditional predominance in Israel's political life, the General Zionists and the Progressives merged to form the Liberal party. In the 1961 elections for the country's fifth Parliament, however, the new party won only seventeen seats, a number matched by Begin's Herut running alone. Begin might have made a better showing had he not chosen to do his campaigning in Tel Aviv's Hatikvah slum quarter in an open car, escorted by motorcycles with screaming sirens, an incongruous sight in Israeli national elections, offensive to Labor voters, who in the circumstances might have bolted the now shaky Mapai, and to Liberals displeased with the progressive tendency in their party.

Nevertheless, elements within both Herut and the Liberal party, heeding a call for unity from Menahem Begin, entered into negotiations for a merger early in 1964. A majority within both Herut and the Liberals approved of Begin's scheme to form a joint parliamentary bloc with a potential of thirty-four seats in the Knesset. But seven of the Liberals' seventeen Knesset members, mainly representing their party's progressive wing, declined to join the proposed new alignment; they balked at the Herut's still maximalist ideology, which they regarded as reactionary.

Yet the merger that Begin had envisioned was consummated. Undeterred by the defection of the seven, who formed a new Independent Liberal Party, the majority wing of the Liberals joined with Herut to constitute a parliamentary bloc known as Gahal. The new center-right grouping emerged from the bitterly contested 1965 elections for the sixth Parliament with an unspectacular twenty-six seats, considerably less than their previous combined strength and no threat to Labor's supremacy.

It was evident, however, that the Labor party was in deep trouble. Headed now by Levi Eshkol, Ben-Gurion's handpicked successor in the cabinet reshuffle of 1963, it managed to hold onto forty-five seats in the 1965 election, but only because it went to the polls in tandem with Mapam, the left wing Socialist group, headed by the prestigious Yigal Allon. Mapam had parted company with Mapai in 1948 but returned to the fold in 1965. Ben-Gurion himself, in a series of virulent attacks on his former protege, Eshkol, described the Labor establishment as "stale and sterile, a caucus of party hacks and job-seekers." Under Ben-Gurion's leadership, Rafi, promising all manner of reforms, elected only ten members to the new Parliament.

*   *   *

A dramatic turn in Begin's political fortunes came in the late spring and early summer of 1967, a watershed year in his own and Israel's history. It was a time of continued internal crisis and mounting external danger. The overtaxed national economy was beset by rising unemployment and shortages in food, housing and social services, while Israel's neighbors were arming to the eyeballs for "another round" of all-out warfare. From all sectors of the Israeli electorate came demands for a "wall-to-wall" coalition government capable of consolidating the country's resources and energies to solve the mounting domestic problems and meet the threat of invasion.

Menahem Begin now was no longer "the pariah of Israeli politics." The psychological barriers against his acceptance as a "respectable" political leader had begun to break down, partly as a result of the actions of successive Labor governments. Eshkol brought to Israel the remains of Vladimir Jabotinsky—something Ben-Gurion had sternly refused to do— and had them interred with full military honors on Mount Herzl, in Jerusalem, along with the other founding fathers of the Jewish state. The bodies of Eliahu Bet Zouri and Eliahu Hakim, the youthful terrorists who had killed Lord Moyne in Cairo, were obtained from Egypt and buried with honors in Israel. Furthermore, the government itself issued a booklet on Deir Yassin, long a symbol of Irgun's alleged brutality, which explained that the episode had not been "a wanton massacre." These gestures were symbolic, but they had an impact on party and public attitudes favorable to Begin and what he represented.

As war clouds gathered in May 1967, the National Religious Party demanded that Eshkol's governing coalition be broadened to include both main opposition groups—Begin's Gahal and Ben-Gurion's Rafi, whose parliamentary delegation also included two other nationally admired figures: Dayan and Shimon Peres. In addition, the NRP proposed that Premier Eshkol divest himself of the vital Defense Ministry. Although reputedly an expert in economic affairs, Eshkol was known to have little knowledge or understanding of military matters, and there was a growing consensus in the country that the right man for the post of Minister of Defense was General Dayan. Menahem Begin, however, had in mind an even more drastic change in the government. He believed the time had come for the return to power of his arch-enemy: David Ben-Gurion.

There was still no love lost between the two men. Their exchanges in the Knesset had been as acrimonious as ever. On one occasion, Begin had described the gulf between them as "a chasm filled with blood that no bridge can ever span." Nor had Begin forgotten that in a letter to a journalist Ben-Gurion had attacked him as "clearly a Hitlerist type, a racist willing to destroy all Arabs for the sake of the (geographic) completeness of the country, sanctifying all means for the sake of the sacred end—absolute rule."

Menahem Begin never easily forgave or forgot personal criticism. But in the face of the national emergency that began on May 18, 1967, when Egypt's President Nasser demanded and obtained withdrawal of the United Nations Emergency Force—which had been guarding the Egyptian-Israeli frontier since the end of the 1956 Sinai war—Begin, as he would often do in the future, was prepared to let bygones be bygones. He recognized the unifying strength which the Grand Old Man of Israeli politics could exert at a time of deepening crisis and political disunity. Begin felt that Eshkol should step aside in favor of Ben-Gurion. He realized that many Israelis, perhaps the overwhelming majority, yearned for the days of the Old Man's inspiring, if often controversial leadership.

Meanwhile, the Arab threat grew almost hourly. Egyptian and Syrian forces were massing on Israel's borders, and it became clear that Jordan would join them when war came. Other Arab states, displaying traditional solidarity against Israel, indicated their readiness to help Cairo and Damascus. Iraqi and Saudi Arabian troops joined Jordanian forces on the Israeli frontier, and Israel mobilized its citizens' army for a war on three fronts. As the month of May drew to a close, Israel's economy came to a virtual standstill. With four out of every five men in the country's army a civilian, shops and businesses were closed, factories were running at less than half capacity and some early crops were standing in the fields unharvested.

A sense of impending doom descended upon the Jewish state when, on May 23, Nasser announced that he was closing the Straits of Tiran—Israel's gateway to Africa and Asia—to Israeli shipping. Time was running out, and Begin acted. Having tested his idea with various highly placed politicians, including Rafi's Shimon Peres, Ben-Gurion's longtime aide and confidant, and having received a favorable response, Begin went to Eshkol and put it to him that in view of the mounting crisis, the Old Man should be brought into the government as Prime Minister.

"I suggest," said Begin, "that you hand over the premiership to him and continue as his deputy. From all that I have been able to gather in recent days, it seems to be the will of the people and the desire of many members of the Knesset, including some in your own party."

Eshkol was not unaware of what parliamentarians had been saying about him in the Knesset's cloakrooms and corridors, and over coffee and cigarettes in the Members' Snack Bar. Nevertheless, Eshkol—a big man physically, with an ego to match—was stung by Begin's suggestion and pondered it a long time before replying angrily that he did not believe he and Ben-Gurion could possibly work together. After a long and warm relationship, their friendship had soured over the Lavon affair and other matters; Ben-Gurion had never forgiven him, for instance, for bringing Jabotinsky's bones back to Israel in 1964 for burial on hallowed Mount

Herzl. Made aware of the enmity that had sprung up between the two men—an animosity comparable only to that which had long divided him from Ben-Gurion—Begin did not press his idea further. However, he kept his own options open: He pledged his and Gahal's full support in the critical days ahead. Eshkol and Begin parted friends.

Shortly after his unrewarding talk with Eshkol, Begin and several colleagues visited Ben-Gurion at the latter's home in Tel Aviv, a square, squat, two-storied stucco building on Keren Kayemet Street. The Old Man's dislike of Menahem Begin, incidentally, was not shared by Ben-Gurion's indomitable wife, Paula. She had always considered the former underground leader "a very nice man, so polite and courteous, a real Polish gentleman," and made him and his friends welcome in a house Begin had visited only once before—in 1956 when Ben-Gurion summoned political leaders to brief them on the Sinai crisis. Paula laid out fresh fruit, coffee, tea and cakes for the visitors.

Ben-Gurion held court in his spacious book-lined study on the second floor. Gathered about him in leather armchairs, Begin and his comrades heard the Old Man counsel against launching the preemptive war that Israel was contemplating. He saw it as a dangerous adventure that might turn the Western world against the Jewish state, unless the Arabs in general, and Egypt in particular, were clearly the aggressors. His downbeat analysis of the situation, to which Ben-Gurion added a few acerbic comments about Eshkol, his erstwhile friend and partner, made it clear he was not interested in resuming the premiership. He was eighty-one, tired and absorbed in writing his memoirs. Begin and the others left him convinced that Ben-Gurion was not the answer to Israel's problems after all.

Begin now urged Eshkol to resign his responsibilities as Defense Minister in favor of Moshe Dayan. In return, as he had assured the Premier in their previous conversation, Begin was prepared to lend Gahal's full support to the government. On May 28, while Eshkol took counsel with Golda Meir and other Laborite bigwigs, Nasser openly declared Egypt's aggressive intentions: "We intend to open a general assault against Israel. This will be total war. Our basic aim is the destruction of Israel." Next day, at a gathering of Labor party leaders, one speaker after another implored Eshkol to relinquish the Defense Ministry, if not to Ben-Gurion, then to Moshe Dayan. Apart from Golda Meir, the Prime Minister found himself with few defenders at the meeting.

Eshkol, though not overly bright about military matters, was nonetheless a shrewd politician. Bowing to pressures from within his own party and from the National Religious Party, whose members had threatened to resign from the cabinet unless Gahal and Rafi were co-opted—*and* the

Defense Ministry given to Dayan—Eshkol lost no time in forming a government of national emergency. On June 1, Eshkol formally proposed to offer the Defense Ministry to Dayan, as a representative of Rafi, and to include representatives of Gahal in a new government. By midnight that same day, the new cabinet was in session with Menahem Begin and Moshe Dayan in attendance, although they had not yet been sworn in at the Knesset.

Early the next morning, on his way to the swearing-in ceremony at the Knesset, Begin had his driver stop at Mount Herzl so that he could pay his respects at the grave of Vladimir Jabotinsky. The gesture was characteristic of Begin, whose emotions run deep. Before taking his oath of office, he wished to commune with the spirit of his mentor, the man he calls "my master." One imagines Begin informing the founder of Revisionism that his disciple had won acceptance as a minister of the government of Israel.

Begin stood at the foot of Jabotinsky's grave for a long moment, then saluted, turned smartly on his heel and left—a small, bespectacled figure in a dark suit, white shirt, with lightly starched collar, plain tie neatly knotted and black felt hat—the epitome of the respectability he had attained at last in the political life of his country.

The decision to go to war was taken at a final cabinet meeting that ran through the night of June 3. It sprang unanimously from an acute sense of Israel's vulnerability, shared by all the ministers, and the danger was real enough on all fronts: in the south, the east and the north.

In Sinai, Egypt had massed seven divisions and some nine hundred tanks. Egyptian armor was less than a half hour's drive from the port of Eilat—by moving across the southern Negev, enemy tanks could cut Eilat off from the rest of the country and deprive Israel of oil supplies from virtually its only source, Iran. From the Gaza Strip, Egyptian armor could reach populous, vulnerable Tel Aviv in less than two hours.

In the east, Jordanian artillery had both Jerusalem and Tel Aviv well within range. Here the threat was great indeed. The armies of Jordan and Iraq, possessing respectively three hundred and six hundred tanks, were deployed in close proximity to Israel. Jordanian tanks could cut the country in two in a fifteen-minute lunge to the Mediterranean across Israel's narrow, hourglass waist. The border ran through Jerusalem; Jordanian infantry positions were a mere twenty-minute quick march from Israel's Parliament.

In the north, Syrian artillery dominated the entire length of the Jordan Valley from the river's sources to the southern shores of the Sea of Galilee. A Syrian armored force of approximately five hundred and fifty tanks was deployed on the Israeli border within easy striking distance of Haifa.

The reality of Israel's susceptibility to grievous injury, perhaps even destruction at Arab hands engraved itself on Begin's brain during the war of nerves that preceded the actual fighting. He vowed to friends that if Israel survived the impending struggle—and none of the ministers was certain of the outcome as the cabinet voted in favor of a preemptive strike—he would do all in his power to prevent a recurrence of the dangers that prevailed on the eve of June 5, 1967.

Israel's fears were heightened by the reminders it received almost hourly from across the borders as to the fate awaiting the Jewish state. So great was the Arabs' sense of power at that time, so intense was their frenzy at the approaching hour of fulfillment, that most Arab leaders abandoned all restraint in depicting the shape of events to come. Typical and most explicit was the prognosis of Ahmed Shukairy, Yassir Arafat's predecessor as commander of the Palestine Liberation Organization. Asked in an interview on June 4, 1967, about the fate of native-born Israelis after the anticipated Arab victory, he said: "Those who survive will be allowed to remain in Palestine. But I estimate that not many will survive . . ."

To Israel's awareness of vulnerability was added a sense of being politically utterly alone. The arrangements which had brought about a decade of comparative quiet along Israel's borders had been mainly the work of the United States and were twice confirmed by President Eisenhower in 1957 after he had persuaded Ben-Gurion to withdraw from Sinai. In a speech on February 20 of that year, he said: "If, unhappily, Egypt does hereafter violate the armistice agreements or other international agreements, then this should be dealt with firmly by the society of nations." In a letter to Ben-Gurion dated March 2, 1957, he wrote: "I know that this decision (to withdraw from Sinai) was not an easy one. I believe, however, that Israel will have no cause to regret having thus confirmed the strong sentiment of the world community as expressed in various United Nations resolutions relating to withdrawal."

Yet, ten years later, the arrangements extolled by President Eisenhower collapsed. The United Nations Emergency Force, the supposed guardian of the peace, evacuated its positions along the Egyptian-Israeli border at the first sign of crisis. When Abba Eban went to Washington late in May 1967 to enlist American support, the State Department had trouble finding the documents relating to the 1957 arrangements which, among other things, had guaranteed "free and innocent passage of Israeli ships through international waterways." In response to Israel's plight as the Arabs bunched their military muscles, President Johnson lectured Eban on the limitations of presidential power. In short, the United States was unwilling to intervene on Israel's behalf.

The French reaction provided a further disappointment. President Charles de Gaulle, who, in the past, had called Israel "our friend and our ally," now turned his support abruptly to the Arabs. Speaking to Eban after Egypt had closed the Straits of Tiran, he warned Israel "not to fire the first round."

The Soviet Union, meanwhile, had actively contributed to the crisis by producing—before May 15—provably false reports about Israeli troop concentrations in the north for an attack against Syria. Russia subsequently did very little to restrain Nasser from escalating the crisis and, in all probability, shared with him an underestimation of Israeli military capabilities.

The Israelis struck at 7:10 A.M. on June 5, Six days later at 6:30 P.M. on June 10 it was all over. The Arabs had suffered catastrophic defeat on all fronts. The Israelis had removed the gathering threat and reversed what generals call the "strategic balance." Before the war, there were several Arab armies from within merely minutes to only two hours from Jerusalem and Tel Aviv. After the war, the Israeli forces were two hours from Cairo and an hour away from Amman and Damascus. Israel had gained a strategic depth which it had lacked before and which Menahem Begin, among others, was determined never to yield.

Israel's strategic depth would be put to the test six years later, in October 1973. The Yom Kippur War, which the Arabs started with almost total surprise, would be fought from start to finish far from Israel's urban centers. Had it begun on the old frontiers—the borders of June 5, 1967—there might not be an Israel today.

The climactic event of the Six Day War was the capture of the walled Old City of Jerusalem, an achievement for which Menahem Begin could take much credit. It was at his insistence, seconded by an old political foe—Yigal Allon—that troops were committed to the hazardous task of restoring the ancient City of David to Jewish sovereignty. The opportunity, however, was created by King Hussein.

The Israelis had hoped not to have to fight at all on the eastern front. The morning the war started, Prime Minister Eshkol sent King Hussein a message via United Nations commander General Odd Bull that read: "We shall not initiate any action whatsoever against Jordan. However, should Jordan open hostilities, we shall react with all our might . . ." But Hussein, gulled by false reports from Nasser of brilliant Egyptian ground and air victories, ignored Eshkol's warning; his artillery began bombarding West Jerusalem at 11 A.M.

When the bombardment started, Begin and Allon put their heads together. The former antagonists saw in the Jordanian attack an excuse to achieve what they had failed to accomplish in 1948-1949—the conquest and occupation of the West Bank and the Old City. At a cabinet meeting that afternoon, Dayan demurred, not relishing the probable cost of a frontal assault on the well-defended eastern half of Jerusalem; he had planned only to invest the surrounding area and ultimately choke off Arab resistance. But Begin and Allon pushed and prodded their reluctant fellow ministers for action, until finally, on the night of June 6, Dayan bowed to cabinet pressure and gave the order to attack the Old City. Word had come that a United Nations cease fire was imminent. If the Old City was to be taken, it would have to be seized before hostilities ended.

The resultant operation was carried out with almost surgical swiftness and precision. When the fighting stopped toward nightfall on Wednesday, June 7, Judaism's holiest of holies, the Western Wall of the Second Temple, as well as the Moslem holy places—the Dome of the Rock and the el-Aqsa Mosque—were in Israeli hands. So were other places sacred to Judaism, among them Jericho and Solomon's Pools, Rachel's Tomb and the Cave of the Patriarchs where, tradition has it, the remains of Abraham, Isaac and Jacob are buried. The Jews had regained the sites and shrines of their Biblical history and heritage, and thousands flocked to see them in the sudden outpouring of religious fervor released by the astounding victory.

But the war's crowning achievement, quite apart from terminating the Arab threat to Israel's existence, was the miracle of Jerusalem restored. The city had been divided for nearly twenty years, sawed apart into Jewish and Arab sectors. An entire generation of Jews had grown up unable to visit—or even see—their own most sacred relics in the Old City, because the Jordanians, in violation of the armistice agreements of 1949, would not allow them to enter.

Immediately after the war ended, there was a rush of Jerusalemites to the Western Wall. The first of Israel's dignitaries to reach it was Rabbi Shlomo Goren, chief chaplain of the Israeli army, who loosed a triumphant blast of the *shofar*, the ram's horn. Then came Dayan, helmeted and looking very martial. He stood before the venerable stones and enunciated what became the theme of Israeli policy regarding the captured territories: "We have returned to all that is holy in our land . . . never to be parted from it again."

In the euphoria of victory, while Dayan was still, in his own words, "waiting for a phone call from Nasser," Israel was prepared to hand back all of the approximately 28,000 square miles of conquered territory—except the Old City and a few strategic strongholds on the Golan Heights—in exchange for secure borders and a contractual peace. But the "phone call" never came, and after the Arab states decided at Khartoum on "no peace, no negotiations, no recognition," Israeli policy hardened in favor of standing on the existing cease fire lines and consolidating behind them.

The war demonstrated to even the most moderate Israelis that the prewar boundaries had been inadequate, and in its wake expansionist ideas flourished. They found expression in various ostensibly non-political organizations, the most important of which was the Land of Israel Movement, founded by an agglomeration of intellectuals, drawn from virtually every sector of the country's national life, and headed by Eliezer Livneh, a veteran Socialist and respected member of the Labor party whom I interviewed shortly after the Six Day War.

The Movement's manifesto, published in September, on the heels of the Arabs' Khartoum meeting, argued that no Israeli government had the "right" to hand back lands won in battle. It questioned the legality of Egyptian sovereignty over Sinai and of Jordanian sovereignty over the West Bank. It advocated largescale Jewish settlement in Judea and Samaria and intensive agricultural development of the wastelands of Sinai and the Golan Heights as in the days of King Solomon.

The elderly Livneh, I recall, was not motivated by historic or pietistic considerations but by a conviction, shared by the majority of Israelis at the time, that Israel's future security depended on the kind of territorial "defense in depth" attained in the June war. Nonetheless, the Movement's objectives appealed strongly to the Orthodox religious elements within Menahem Begin's Gahal faction, and the party's approach to territorial issues soon became indistinguishable from the one advocated by Livneh.

In the new situation created by the June war, Begin's territorial maximalism, which previously had seemed unrealistic and fanciful, suddenly assumed new validity and acceptability. The Israelis began seeing Begin in a new light—as a much-maligned patriot rather than as the dangerous extremist he had been painted. No one was surprised when he arrogated to himself the role of watchdog over the conquered territories and publicly demanded that Israeli sovereignty be extended "over all the lands liberated from unlawful foreign rule," particularly those "liberated" from their "unlawful ruler," the Hashemite King of Jordan.

Begin was opposed in the Knesset and at the cabinet table by Eshkol's able Finance Minister, Pinhas Sapir, and by his eloquent Foreign Minister, Abba Eban. Both understandably feared the demographic and political consequences of annexation. Joined to Israel's own Arab population, they argued, the Arabs of the occupied territories, who numbered about 1,100,000, would swell the country's non-Jewish population to approximately half its 2,600,000 Jewish inhabitants. Given an Arab birth rate incomparably higher than that of the Jews, the result would be an Arab majority, within a generation or less, and the end of Israel as a "Jewish" state.

Within the cabinet Begin found common ground, however, with the man whom he would eventually co-opt as his Foreign Minister: Moshe Dayan. As Eshkol's Minister of Defense and Military Governor of the occupied territories, Dayan favored expansion as opposed to outright annexation. He proposed that the government establish Jewish cities along the mountain ridge extending from Hebron to Nablus, creating in this manner Jewish islands in the Arab hinterland. He believed that by so doing, geographic and demographic frontiers between Arabs and Jews would become blurred. He called the process "creating facts while awaiting peace," but by any name his program was "creeping annexation."

Dayan bluntly declared that Israel should envisage its role in the occupied territories as that of "a permanent government, and plan and implement whatever can be done (in the way of economic integration of Arab and Jewish areas) without worrying about the day of peace, which might be far away." The government, he emphasized, "must create facts and not confine development programs to Israel proper. If the Arabs refuse to make peace, we cannot stand still. Denied their cooperation, let us act alone."

No single issue was as hotly debated in Israel as the future of the conquered territories. When Begin found little support within the cabinet for his baldly annexationist views, he backed Dayan's program, although he was well aware that of all Israel's leaders the former general was least influenced by religious or historical visions. Around the cabinet table, the two men formed the nucleus of a coalition of hawks that ignored party differences. Their main antagonists were Sapir and Eban.

Sapir, alarmed at Dayan's schemes for "establishing facts"—which really meant implanting Jewish settlements in the occupied Arab areas— forcefully objected to integration of the territories, or their inhabitants, into Israel's economy. Eban, meanwhile, warned that a brazenly expansionist program such as Dayan advocated would lose Israel friends abroad, particularly in the United States, Israel's main source of economic and military assistance.

The debate was suspended in February 1969 with the death of Premier Eshkol, who succumbed to a series of heart attacks induced by overwork, but it was resumed with renewed intensity after Golda Meir became Prime Minister of a caretaker government, pending national elections to be held later in the autumn. By the time Mrs. Meir took charge, however, the hawks in the cabinet had had their way. Arab East Jerusalem was annexed outright and reunited with Jewish West Jerusalem; the pre-state Jewish farm communities of the Etzion bloc were reestablished, and the government had approved a program for creating about thirty-five new Jewish settlements on the Golan Heights, in Sinai, and on the West Bank, with many more in prospect.

It was abundantly evident in the aftermath of the Six Day War that Israel had embarked on an expansionist program whose fruits would prove to be a millstone about the nation's neck, a standing provocation to the whole Arab world and an obstacle to peace in the Middle East. In the minds of many Israelis, territory came to be equated with national security, and the Messianic constant in Israeli politics flourished.

NOTES

1. Britain and France, it will be recalled, jointly, tardily and ineffectually attacked Egypt on the heels of the Israeli invasion in an effort to regain control of the Suez Canal, which President Nasser had appropriated through nationalization. Russia, Egypt's patron and armorer, threatened to hurl missiles at London and Paris, and to "flatten" Israel unless "the aggressors" withdrew immediately from Egyptian soil. Warned by the United States that America did not consider its NATO commitments binding in the Middle East, the Anglo-French attack was called off only hours short of total success—occupation of the Canal Zone and, very probably, Nasser's downfall. What decided Israel's retreat, however, was a sharp personal message from President Eisenhower to Premier Ben-Gurion, stating that unless Israel agreed to retreat from the Sinai peninsula, as the United Nations had demanded, the Jewish state could not expect any American help in the event of a Soviet attack. The Kremlin may have been bluffing, but Ben-Gurion had no desire to go down in history as the Jew who had started World War III.

Chapter 19

The Road to Power— Part Two

The Labor party's choice of the aging Golda Meir—she was seventy-one at the time—to succeed Eshkol aroused widespread speculation that the days of the government of national unity were numbered and political experts, never in short supply in Israel, freely predicted its imminent demise. Their gloomy forecasts were not ill-founded. Mrs. Meir personified her party's traditional dislike for Begin and his brand of politics; furthermore, she was known to disapprove most heartily of Moshe Dayan for having deserted the Laborite camp. Before the 1967 war, she had led the opposition to the formation of a coalition with Gahal and Rafi and had strenuously opposed Dayan's appointment as Defense Minister. It seemed a foregone conclusion that Mrs. Meir would jettison both Begin and Dayan, but the pundits were proved wrong.

While Mrs. Meir was unhappy at finding Begin and Dayan working in close harmony on the settlements matter, she was soon making common cause with them on this and other defense issues. She shared their view of the Arabs as implacably hostile to Israel—for nearly a year Egypt's Nasser had been waging his War of Attrition along the Suez Canal—and resisted appeals from dovish elements within the Alignment to placate the Arabs with conciliatory gestures. Pending national elections, due in October, Mrs. Meir made no startling changes in her caretaker cabinet and quickly proved to be every bit as much of a hawk as Begin or Dayan.

Recognizing in Mrs. Meir a more resolute figure than her predecessor, Begin defended her to Herutist critics as "a proud Jewess" worthy of their respect and cooperation. Charmed by his good manners, Mrs. Meir, in turn, was soon referring to Begin as "a perfect gentleman." She also admired his lawyer's talent for crossing "t's" and dotting "i's" in the formulation of policy statements, never one of her strong points. Although political opposites on domestic issues, the two developed a harmonious relationship in the area of foreign relations.

In the general elections that October, the Labor party went to the polls in a unified slate with the more leftish Mapam. The resultant Labor Alignment won easily as the party that had led the nation to victory in the Six Day War, returning 56 members to the Knesset, a gain of one, and Mrs. Meir to the Premiership. Begin's Gahal, with 26 seats, neither gained nor lost ground, but could congratulate itself that it had maintained its position as the country's second largest political grouping.

No longer considered "beyond the pale," Begin was invited to participate in a second coalition of national unity. The Foreign Ministry went to Abba Eban, Moshe Dayan was kept on as Minister of Defense and Begin was offered his choice of any one of several lesser posts but preferred to remain as Minister Without Portfolio. However, he would not be the only Herutist in the cabinet.

During the hectic forty-odd days of ministerial consultations and parliamentary horse-trading that attended the formation of the new government, Major General Ezer Weizman abruptly resigned from the army to join the Herut party. Tall, handsome and debonair and with a well-earned reputation for speaking his mind, Ezer had risen through the ranks in the air force to become its commanding general. In the 1967 war he had occupied the number two position as Head of Staff Branch in the General Staff and was generally credited with having engineered the air arm's stunning victory of June 5, when the Israelis swept the skies over Sinai and Egypt of enemy planes in the first twenty-four hours.

Since the 1967 war, generals had become Israel's new heroes. The objects of unrestrained adultation—Dayan was their prototype and outstanding example—they were readymade vote-catchers for the political parties, and often moved directly into politics without serving an interim apprenticeship. No one was surprised to see Ezer Weizman shed his uniform for civvies, but he caused a national sensation by joining Begin's Herut faction of Gahal. His uncle, Chaim Weizmann—spelled with two final n's, one of which Ezer dropped as though to underscore the political difference between him and his distinguished relative, Israel's first President—had been Revisionist Jabotinsky's bitterest enemy after Ben-Gurion and a frequent target of Begin's sharpest attacks.

Begin staged an enthusiastic, emotional, televised "welcome" for Ezer at Herut's party headquarters— "The Fortress" in Tel Aviv—embracing the newcomer to right wing Israeli politics as "my general, my dear brother," under Jabotinsky's portrait. With the threshold of violence lowering almost daily on the Suez front, Mrs. Meir agreed to add the general to her cabinet and made him Minister of Transport. But the addition of the flamboyant Weizman to the Herut hierarchy presaged trouble for Begin. Ezer was no "yes man" of the kind the party leader liked having around him, and fierce intramural battles lay ahead for the leadership of Herut and, eventually, the Likud.

Weizman's entry into politics was maneuvered by Herut's treasurer, Yosef Kremmerman, a millionaire businessman and a contemporary of Begin's, who believed the time had come for the party to emerge from its limited ideological environs by developing greater mass appeal. This he sought to accomplish by broadening Herut's anti-Socialist approach, and by recruiting young leaders with vote-catching potential. Weizman provided the ideal combination of hardnosed devotion to capitalistic freedom of enterprise and a highly charged personality that emanated magnetism.

But, despite Begin's recognition of Weizman's talents, the two men, while not complete opposites, were sufficiently far apart ideologically and in other more personal ways, to guarantee eventual conflict. Weizman was not one of the old Irgun "family," but a "loner" of independent opinions who was resented by the tightly knit coterie around Begin—Landau, Katz and Arieh Ben-Eliezer. They were piqued by Kremmerman's tactics; he had contrived Weizman's switch from a high post in the army to a seat at Mrs. Meir's cabinet table in twenty-four hours, without the Olympian Begin's clear consent. To make matters worse, such was Weizman's popularity that in addition to becoming Transport Minister, he was elected executive chairman of the Herut, a position that placed him second in command of the party. Although outwardly pleased, Begin was inwardly troubled at the turn of events. He sensed conflict ahead, and it was not long in coming.

The first open clash between Begin and Weizman occurred late in 1969, shortly after the two men—along with Haim Landau—had joined Mrs. Meir's new government of national unity. Dissension arose within the cabinet over how to respond to the War of Attrition that Egypt was waging in the south and that was bleeding Israel white, economically and militarily.

Actually, Israel had been fighting two wars since 1967—a "big war" against Egypt along the Canal and a "little war" against Arab guerrillas and terrorists on the Syrian and Jordanian borders. Both wars were taking a heavy toll in money—$ 3 million a day—and in the coin Israel treasures most: human life. Although by March 1969, Chief of Staff Haim Bar Lev had completed the hardened defenses along the eastern bank of the Canal that would bear his name, casualties among the defenders continued in alarming numbers. Hardly a day passed without the prominent display on the front pages of Israel's newspapers of photographs of the youthful faces of Jewish soldiers fallen under Egypt's incessant bombardment of Israel's "Bar-Lev Line."

In Israel, death never strikes anonymously. Every casualty is deeply felt, not only by the victim's family, but by the country as a whole. Even single casualties—the loss of a pilot or the death of a settler at the hands of terrorist invaders—assume sickening proportions. By July, the Israeli casualty rate had risen to seventy a month, and the nation clamored for retaliation.

In an attempt to reduce or reverse the heavy casualty trends, Israel launched a sustained air bombardment of Egyptian positions on the west bank of the Canal. For three months Israeli planes battered away at enemy emplacements and, gradually, the Egyptian guns along the waterway were silenced. Israeli losses dropped substantially. Further-more, the Israeli air offensive drove Egyptian civilians out of the population centers west of the Canal, and Nasser found himself faced with the serious problem of coping with several hundred thousand refugees of his own.

By the end of 1969, morale in the Egyptian armed forces had sunk to a new low, and discontent was spreading among the population. Egypt had lost virtually all of its air defenses and more than a third of its combat planes at the cost to Israel of only one Piper Cub shot down by Egyptian ground fire while on a spotter mission.

The political-military establishment in Israel concluded that the time had come to strike harder. It believed that by intensifying the air war and extending it to targets beyond the Canal, Nasser could be toppled or be persuaded to give up his War of Attrition and enter into peace negotiations. Accordingly, the cabinet was asked to consider a program of deep penetration raids against Egyptian industrial centers and defense installations located in and around Cairo itself. The 50 new F-5 Phantoms Israel had received from the United States would be used for the purpose.

Oddly, "superhawk" Begin opposed the idea at first, and urged careful consideration of the possible consequences before any final decision was reached. The cabinet was preparing to act on information being supplied by the Chief of Staff, Bar Lev, and by the head of the army's Intelligence Branch, General Aharon Yariv. Begin suggested further discussion with other generals and intelligence officers who might not agree that the proposed air offensive would produce the desired results. He also wanted to hear new, more imaginative strategic concepts for the conduct of the *blitz* against Egypt—ideas that went beyond simply dumping bombs on Egyptian targets. At least one former Israeli commander had been turning over in his mind plans for demolishing the Egyptian military establish-ment: the turbulent Ezer Weizman.

Ezer, longtime combat pilot and architect of "that wonderful madness called the Israeli air force" and the originator of Israeli air force doctrine, knew better than most what air power could and could not do. He was well aware that long-range bombing of "sensitive" targets—railway stations, fuel dumps, power stations, bridges and the like—would cause havoc in Egypt. But he was equally certain, from a knowledge of warfare painfully acquired over the years since the R.A.F. gave him his wings in 1945 at the age of twenty-one, that the proposed tactic would not "win" the War of Attrition. He told the cabinet that to achieve victory, "The Israeli army must be employed simultaneously in full and in overwhelming force, not only to put an end to the War of Attrition—important enough in itself—but also to check the Egyptians before they launched more dangerous offensives."

But his was a lonely voice. He did not even have the unqualified support of Menahem Begin, who was for a "show of force," but not for full-scale, all-out war. Since 1967, the Israeli military-political establishment had developed a defensive mentality.

Alternatively, Ezer urged his colleagues—both those around the cabinet table and those sitting on their duffs at Staff—to use the air force effectively, to strike such heavy blows at the Egyptians that they would cease to regard the War of Attrition as profitable. But here, too, he encountered opposition. For the first time in Israel's history, he dis-covered, air force commanders were making excuses. They responded that because of the Egyptians' Soviet SAM missile anti-aircraft system, they could not conduct successful operations unless the United States supplied them with the Shrike—an anti-radar missile pre-tuned to the radar band widths of the Russian SAM-2s and SAM-3s.

"Shrikes be damned," Ezer countered. "Go ahead and knock the hell out of those Russian missile barriers."

The government subsequently voted in favor of deep penetration raids into Egypt, a decision that Israel eventually would regret for the reason Weizman had foreseen. Airpower alone cannot win wars fought with conventional weapons, unless armor and infantry arrive in the wake of the bombs.

Israeli aircraft flew the first long-range missions into the Egyptian heartland early in January 1970, and enjoyed almost complete freedom of the skies. The few enemy interceptors that rose to meet the intruders were easily shot down; the Egyptians' Russian MIGs were no match for the highly maneuverable Phantoms. The bombings were both militarily damaging and politically humiliating to Egypt, but they also aroused Nasser's determination to continue the struggle.

On January 22, Nasser paid an urgent visit to Moscow. The Russians, who viewed Israel's military supremacy in the Middle East as an intolerable challenge to their own hegemony in the area, agreed to participate more actively in defending Egyptian military and civilian targets.

The Soviet Union had already provided Egypt with massive military assistance. After the Six Day War, the Russians increased Egypt's tank strength from 250 to 470, and added 400 excellent MIG-20s to the Egyptian air force. This dramatic reprovisionment was matched by a burgeoning Soviet physical presence in Egypt. By the end of 1969, some three thousand Russian military advisers were seconded to the Egyptian armed services.

With Egyptian and Russian prestige crumbling under the fierce Israeli bombardment, Nasser's January appeal for more help in 1970 fell on receptive ears in the Kremlin. By mid-February, less than three weeks after Nasser's visit, the Soviet airlift traffic to Egypt had more than quadrupled. Within six months the Russians had between ten thousand and fifteen thousand of their own "instructors" and "advisers" in Egypt, as well as an impressive fleet of 60 warships off the Egyptian coast—an armada that rivaled in tonnage and firepower the United States Sixth Fleet in the eastern Mediterranean.

The military results of Nasser's journey to Moscow soon became apparent. By early spring, Soviet pilots were flying late model MIG-J21s in air patrols over Egyptian territory. Russian officers and troops manned approximately 80 new SAM-3 anti-aircraft missile complexes. The strategic balance further shifted adversely against Israel with the subsequent introduction of literally hundreds of anti-aircraft missiles including many of the mobile SAM-4 and SAM-6 types.

Israeli attacks on these defenses rapidly approached the rhythm and scale of devastation of American raids in Vietnam, but with each Israeli bombing raid the Soviets expanded the area of their defensive responsibilities, and soon had created the densest electronic defense system in the world, except for the one that protected Moscow itself. Before the Russian missiles were detected on June 30, Soviet rockets shot down two Israeli Phantom jets. Early in July, they destroyed, in flight, an additional five, and the Israelis suspended their deep penetration raids as "too expensive." They recognized that they faced their gravest military crisis since the weeks preceding the 1967 war, for the battle on the west bank of the Suez Canal had become almost overnight a Soviet-Israeli confrontation.

Prime Minister Golda Meir expressed the anguished mood of her country when she declared on July 7 that "today, and I mean literally today, Israel is facing a struggle more critical than we have ever had to face before." Nonetheless, Israel was prepared to create a Vietnam in the Middle East if the Soviets wanted to risk it. On July 30, the Israelis intentionally baited Soviet pilots by feigning an attack on the Nile Valley, then ambushing the scrambled MIGs over the Gulf of Suez. Four Soviet planes were shot down and the rest peeled away from the duel; the Russians had no desire to become mired in a Vietnamization of the Arab-Israeli conflict.

As it happened, on June 19, 1970, Washington had proposed a "breathing space" for the Middle East. It took the form of a plan presented by Secretary of State William Rogers for a 90-day ceasefire, and calling upon Israel to enter into negotiations with Egypt and Jordan under the auspices of United Nations mediator Dr. Gunnar Jarring. The Swedish diplomat had been waiting in the wings for months, ever since failure of an earlier Rogers' proposal for a settlement. In New York representatives of the Big Four vainly tried to establish "guidelines" which he might use in seeking the "just and lasting peace" everyone talked about but only Israel and the Western powers really wanted.

The new Rogers proposals aimed at reaching agreement on mutual recognition of Israeli, Jordanian and Egyptian sovereignty, territorial integrity and political independence. They also insisted on an Israeli withdrawal from territories occupied in 1967 "in accordance with Resolution 242." In addition, there were strong hints from Washington that the continued supply of American weapons to Israel hinged on Jerusalem's acceptance of what came to be known as the Rogers Plan.

On June 29, Nasser flew to Moscow for another emergency conference, acknowledged the crippling effects of the War of Attrition on his military establishment and won Soviet support for his approval of the American proposals. Meanwhile, Jordan also approved, but Israel demurred.

In fact, it looked at first as if Israel would reject the Rogers Plan outright. Menahem Begin sat back and listened with evident relish as his Labor party colleagues attacked the idea at cabinet meetings. Nobody, except the most dovish of the doves in the government, was willing to return to the old borders. Yet, Israel could not afford to antagonize the United States, its only supplier of economic as well as military aid. Jerusalem, sparring for time, asked Washington for "clarification" of the Rogers proposals. Would Israel, for instance, be required to withdraw to the pre-1967 ceasefire lines?

The reply came from President Nixon himself in a note to Mrs. Meir on July 24. Nixon informed the Israeli Premier that in his interpretation of the Rogers initiative, Israel was to withdraw *not* to the pre-1967 frontiers, but to "secure and agreed borders." Furthermore, *no retreat would be demanded until a contractual, binding peace had been signed.*

The interpretation did not satisfy Begin. Withdrawal to new borders however minimal in extent meant relinquishing territory. In the cabinet and in the Knesset he represented not only the Herut faction of Gahal, but also the Land of Israel Movement, which expected him to insist on "no retreat" from territories that had been "occupied" or, as he put it, "liberated" in the Six Day War, particularly the West Bank and the Gaza Strip, regardless of inducements of any kind.

Tension developed between Begin and the Labor government's dovish faction headed by Abba Eban. The eloquent Foreign Minister argued that the risks of accepting the Rogers Plan were considerably less than the dangers of rejecting it. Rejection would mean continuation of the savage and increasingly costly war with Egypt, the prospect of involvement with the Soviet Union and erosion of American support for Israel. He saw no alternative to acceptance of the Rogers Plan and all its conditions: ceasefire, Resolution 242 and resumption of the Jarring Mission, a view eventually, though reluctantly, accepted by Golda Meir.

Begin and his supporters countered that the policy of Israel's government since 1967 had been—and still was as far as they were concerned— that the country's defense forces would remain on the ceasefire lines until peace was attained. Technically, Begin was right. However, the situation had changed, but Begin stubbornly refused to acknowledge it. The bombings-in-depth had been a tragic mistake; they had brought the Russians to Egypt's side in strength and had altered, in Egypt's favor, the strategic balance in the Middle East, an error for which Israel would pay dearly in October 1973. But in 1970, neither Begin nor anyone else except Weizman foresaw the Yom Kippur War. Begin was willing to accept the ceasefire portion of the Rogers plan, but declined to agree to any negotiations on the subject of withdrawal from the occupied territories until there was peace.

"But we won't have any ceasefire unless we also accept some of the less favorable conditions," the Prime Minister tried repeatedly to explain to Begin. "And what's more," she told him, "we won't get any arms from America." "What do you mean we won't get any arms?" Begin replied. "We'll *demand* them from the Americans."

Mrs. Meir was unable to persuade Begin that although the American commitment to Israel's survival was sincere, Israel needed the goodwill of President Nixon and Secretary Rogers much more than *they* needed Israel, and that Israel's policies could not be based entirely on Begin's assumption that the Jewish community in the United States either would or could oblige the President to adopt a position against his will or better judgment.

Begin, intoxicated by his own rhetoric, had convinced himself that all

Israel had to do was to go on telling the United States that it would not yield to pressure, and that if this was done long enough and loudly enough by its friends and supporters in America, the pressure from Washington would eventually vanish. Begin sincerely believed this, and there was no budging him. A movement developed within the Labor party to "dump Begin" before his hawkish ideas prevailed, although this might mean the end of the government of national unity.

Bowing to the government's majority view as outlined by Abba Eban, Golda Meir, in a long Knesset speech, proposed acceptance of the Rogers Plan, which envisioned withdrawal from the West Bank as well as the Gaza Strip and Sinai. At a meeting of the Gahal cabinet members to coordinate their positions for the impending debate of the government's position, Begin stressed that acceptance of the Rogers Plan, even with reservations, implied withdrawal to unacceptable borders, and Gahal, he said, would be obliged to quit the coalition. Begin was supported by his fellow Herutist, Haim Landau, but Liberal party colleagues suggested that Gahal remain in the cabinet to remain in a position to compel the government to maneuver away from total withdrawal. Begin talked the idea down as an unrealistic tactic.

"During all those years in opposition," he said, "my party and I believed we had a right to all of the Land of Israel, even when parts of it were not under our control. Do you really think that we can now agree to support the opposite of what we believe?"

It was the authentic Begin speaking—the hardnosed Jabotinskyite for whom the War of Independence had been "an incomplete job," with Old Jerusalem snatched from the state of Israel, the Gaza Strip in Arab hands and a thorn in Israel's side, and Judea and Samaria "stolen" by those Hashemite interlopers, the Jordanians. What had resulted from the war of 1948–1949 was in his view the Land of Israel without the Land of the Bible. It had become an article of faith with him that since those areas were now in Israel's possession, they could not be surrendered, certainly not as long as the Arabs held onto their vision of destroying the Jewish state.

Menahem Begin was not then the politician whose principles would yield to expediency, or the statesman who bends to reality out of recognition that compromise might be the way to pursue long-term objectives. For him, in the late summer of 1970, as the government pondered the Rogers Plan, the point was clear. He would not concur in any decision that returned "the estate of the forefathers" to Arab hands. At a Knesset caucus of Gahal members, he said: "I will cut off my right arm before signing approval of such a document." And he meant it.

Gahal's Liberals were not persuaded that their best interests would be served by leaving the government. The most vigorous opposition to

Begin's proposal that Gahal quit the cabinet, however, came not from the Liberals but from one of his own people: Ezer Weizman. He believed, correctly, that the Egyptians had accepted the ceasefire not because they could not withstand any longer the intensity of Israeli bombardment, but to gain time to fatten their anti-aircraft missile barrier and move it forward towards the Canal in preparation for "another round." No less a hardliner than Begin, he was opposed to acceptance of the American proposals, but was against leaving the government. Israel, he believed, faced far-reaching security decisions involving the war in the south and continued terrorist infiltration by the PLO from Jordanian bases. He saw this as reason enough for Gahal to stay in the government and try to influence policy rather than return to the opposition.

But Begin was immovable. He could not abide the thought that Gahal ministers would vote against the Rogers Plan, then remain members of a government that was about to agree to something contrary to his principles. He threatened to resign as leader of Gahal if the party decided not to support his view.

Early in August, the Israeli government unanimously decided to accept the Rogers proposal for a ceasefire along the Suez Canal, and accepted, by a majority vote, the Rogers peace initiative. On the second point, following Begin's lead, the Gahal ministers voted against. What Abba Eban later described as "a memorable period in Israeli history" was nearing its end.

Now it remained for the Gahal element to decide whether to remain in the government or withdraw. At a meeting of the central committees of the Herut and the Liberal parties the future of their Gahal coalition in government was decided. Begin threatened, cajoled and ruthlessly brought the faithful to heel, including that fledgling politician, Ezer Weizman. The majority of the Liberals were for staying, but the Herut members voted with Begin. The vote was extremely close—117 to 112— but Begin won. The Labor Alignment survived because it had, it will be recalled, a plurality of its own in the Knesset and could count on the support of the National Religious Party. But the government of national unity was a thing of the past. It had foundered on the rock of Begin's stubbornness. For Begin, there were no regrets.

"I swear to you," he told the meeting after the vote, with typical Beginesque hyperbole, "that in all my life I have never been more at peace with myself and my conscience than I am at the present moment."

Begin later related that he had come to the meeting with a distinct recollection of his mentor, Jabotinsky, leading his followers out of the World Zionist Organization in the mid-1930s because he disagreed with the WZO's policy.

There were, for Begin, lessons to be learned from the break. The narrow vote at the meeting increased his wariness of internal opposition, and thereafter he regarded Weizman with a jaundiced eye. It was the closest Begin had ever come to a defeat by his own supporters, and he inwardly blamed Weizman for it.

Within the anti-Labor opposition as a whole, the results of the meeting deepened the notion that their leader was really less interested in unifying the forces of the center-right than in remaining the undisputed spokesman for—and leader of—a permanent opposition. There seemed to be truth in this, for Begin was visibly a happier man as he walked the halls and corridors of the Knesset after resigning from the government than he was during the weeks of debate over the Rogers Plan. Previous hopes of a full merger between Herut and the Liberals to form a viable opposition to the Laborites subsided, then died away altogether, and most observers believed Begin was through as a leader. But they were wrong.

Chapter 20

The Road to Power— Part Three

Menahem Begin returned to the opposition benches in mid-August 1970, with his principles intact. He emerged from three years and two months of service as Minister Without Portfolio less inclined than ever, for instance, to give up the "territorial fruits" of the Six Day War of 1967. True, he no longer included the terrain east of the Jordan River in his public descriptions of the "historic Land of Israel," but his long exposure to other viewpoints in the give and take of cabinet politics had in no way moderated his own. He fitted perfectly Mr. Dooley's description of a fanatic as "a man that does what he thinks th' Lord wud do if He knew the facts iv th' case."

The "facts iv th' case," however, amply supported Begin's stand. Some were provided by the Egyptians. Shortly after the ceasefire ending the War of Attrition went into effect on August 7, they moved their missile bases forward to the edge of the Suez Canal under cover of the Rogers Plan and in express defiance of it, a violation quickly confirmed by Israeli and then—belatedly—by American intelligence. Other "facts" were supplied by PLO terrorists who occasionally penetrated Israel's West Bank defenses or shelled settlements from Jordanian bases. The incursions were rarely more than pin pricks, and the shelling did little damage, but the attacks helped to lend credibility to Begin's insistence on retention of the occupied territories.

Begin and his colleagues in Gahal, especially the farsighted Weizman, demanded an all-out assault to annihilate the Egyptians' missile system, but their pleas went unheeded, partly because the military-political leadership did not believe it could be done, but also because the country was in no mood to fight another full-scale war. The Israelis were grateful that there were no more bulletins listing dead and wounded fathers, brothers, husbands and sweethearts. Besides, an economic boom had started after the Six Day War, and the Israelis had settled back to enjoy their new-found prosperity, confident that the Arabs could never successfully attack "Fortress Israel," the new mini-power that since 1967 had risen on the eastern crescent of the Mediterranean.

There were other reasons for the government's reluctance to unleash another war. Jerusalem was loathe to impair the closer American-Israeli understanding that had developed in the wake of the influx of Soviet military equipment and "advisers" in Egypt. Washington shared the sense of betrayal and anxiety caused when the Egyptians advanced their missiles; then started shipping Israel substantial quantities of Phantoms, anti-missile missiles and other advanced weaponry. Assured of broadened American support, Premier Golda Meir's government evinced a new willingness to enter into peace negotiations with Egypt.

The Israelis were further influenced in this approach by the death on September 28, of their arch-enemy, President Gamal Abdul Nasser, the only man who had seemed capable of uniting the Arab world against them. The accession of his successor, Mohammed Anwar el-Sadat, allowed Jerusalem for the first time to anticipate a new and possibly more moderate Egyptian posture. At the time, however, their hopes were quickly dispelled.

In the inflexible Menahem Begin who quit Golda Meir's government mainly because it was willing to renounce large areas of the West Bank in exchange for peace with Jordan, the world had a preview of the Israeli Prime Minister of a later day. Similarly, the Anwar el-Sadat, who early in 1971 agreed to enter into indirect peace talks with Israel, foreshadowed the statesman of the momentous meeting of the two men in Jerusalem in 1977.

When the talks between Israel and Egypt started under Dr. Jarring's auspices, Sadat doomed them almost at the outset. Cairo expressed its willingness to enter into peace negotiations with Jerusalem, provided Israel committed itself *in advance* to a deadline for the ". . . withdrawal of its armed forces from Sinai and the Gaza Strip; achievement of a just settlement of the refugee problem in accordance with various United Nations resolutions; the establishment of demilitarized zones astride the borders in equal distances; the establishment of a United Nations peace-keeping force in which the four permanent members of the Security council (i.e., including the Russians) would participate; and (among other conditions) withdrawal . . . from *all* the territories occupied." It was much like the position Sadat would assume six years later.

The Egyptian terms were unacceptable to Premier Golda Meir and her advisers. The Israelis were prepared to compromise on territorial matters, now that Begin and his people were out of the government, but only on the understanding that their armed forces would withdraw to "secure, recognized and agreed boundaries to be established within the context of a peace agreement in accordance with Resolution 242." When the counteroffer proved not to Egypt's liking, the Jarring mission collapsed.

Events continued to favor Begin's position on the territories. In May 1971, Egypt and the Soviet Union signed a new, wide-ranging treaty under which the Russians agreed to train the Egyptian armed forces in the use of the new Soviet weapons. Egypt, in turn, undertook to coordinate its diplomatic moves and positions with the Soviet Union. One clause in the treaty defined Egypt as a country that had "set for itself the aim of reconstructing (its) society along Socialist lines."

Seeing no likelihood of displacing Soviet influence in Egypt in the foreseeable future, Washington limited its efforts in the Middle East to bolstering Israel's deterrent strength in hopes of foreclosing Sadat's war option. Early in 1972, an agreement was reached between Jerusalem and Washington ensuring a continued supply to Israel of Phantom jets and of other highly sophisticated electronic equipment. By the spring of the year, the Israeli air force was assured of superiority, not only over its Egyptian counterpart, but over the Egyptian-Soviet missile defenses.

Fearful of Israel's growing military power, Egypt urgently requested a Soviet commitment to help push the Israelis back from the Canal and to oblige them to accept Egyptian terms for a settlement. But while Moscow wanted to establish in Egypt a military base to be used for its own strategic purposes in the Mediterranean, it plainly was not interested in falling into what might easily become a Middle Eastern Vietnam, nor in provoking a confrontation with the United States. Angered that Egypt's relations with the Soviet Union had apparently become a one-way affair, Sadat retaliated in July 1972 by expelling the Russians.

Sadat's move both gratified and astonished Washington and Jerusalem. For the watchful Israelis, the split between Cairo and Moscow encouraged their determination to hold firm while resisting sporadic Egyptian bombardment of the Bar-Lev Line along the Canal. They came to regard Sadat's repeated warnings of large-scale conflict yet to come as the posturings of a dictator intent on bolstering his shaky regime with rhetoric and took his threats lightly. Actually, Sadat was psychologically preparing his forces—as he would later admit—for the Yom Kippur War of 1973.

Meanwhile, within Israel the debate over the occupied territories continued unabated. Although a minority still favored exchanging territories for peace, most Israelis took the occupied areas for granted, an idea which Menahem Begin encouraged in his public speeches and in his weekly articles for one of Tel Aviv's evening newspapers. His theme was always the same and as strident as a stuck whistle: "There is no separation between historic right, which is always actual, and the right to security, which is a daily affair. Were Judea and Samaria to be torn from us, the foundation of our security would be destroyed, and with it would collapse the chance for peace."

He organized an "Anti-Withdrawal Committee" that had the support of nearly forty Knesset members from the Labor party, as well as Gahal and the National Religious Party, and caused a map to be made and circulated showing what PLO terrorists could do to Israel if it ever gave up the West Bank. It was essentially the same map that Begin, after becoming Prime Minister in 1977, would take with him to Washington to demonstrate to President Carter Israel's vulnerability in the event an independent Palestine were created in Judea and Samaria. Such a "state" or "homeland" would undoubtedly be dominated by the PLO, Begin believes, and would constitute "a mortal danger" to the Jewish state.

That White House meeting—leaping ahead of chronology for a moment—took place in December 1977 after considerable friction had developed between Washington and Jerusalem over President Carter's frequent references to the need for recognition, in one form or another, of "Palestinian rights." Premier Begin was intent on giving the President a "lesson" in Israel's geography as a means of persuading him that he erred in upholding the Palestinian cause. The encounter revealed Begin's profound concern not only for the fate of the Jews of Israel but for the destiny of the Jewish people as a whole.

Pointing to the map he had brought with him, Begin showed the President that towns like Tulkarem and Jenin, which presumably would become PLO bases if a Palestinian state were erected on the West Bank, lay only about twelve miles from populous Tel Aviv. Two million Jews, Begin said, live in and around Israel's biggest city. The Premier went on to say that the possibility of that many Jews being destroyed by enemy action from the West Bank appalled him.

Begin then launched into an account of the tragedy that had overwhelmed European Jewry in Hitler's time—the memory of the Holocaust is ever-present in Begin's subconscious—and related how Europe's Jews were not merely "decimated" but "tertiated." At that point, Begin cried out, "Mr. President, I want to tell you that I have taken an oath in the name of the Jewish people that another such tragic episode in the history of the Jewish people will never happen again—never again."

And Menahem Begin, overwhelmed by his emotions, broke down. Tears welled in his eyes. President Carter looked away, and for ten or fifteen seconds there was absolute silence in the Oval Office.

Recovering, Begin resumed his exposition of what might happen to Israel if it were obliged to withdraw from the occupied territories. That evening, Begin was the President's guest at dinner at the White House—a kosher dinner, specially catered, the first ever served in the Presidential mansion, out of respect for the Prime Minister's Orthodoxy.

The oath to do everything in his power to prevent a possible Arab version of the Hitlerian Holocaust was taken by Begin publicly soon after leaving the government in 1970. In the Messianic spirit inculcated in him by, some say, his pious father, Begin saw himself as the divinely appointed defender of the rights of the Jewish people and the steward of their territorial bequest from the Almighty. He made "No reparceling of the Land of Israel" the central theme of the philosophy of a center-right coalition which he envisioned as an alternative to the dominant Labor Alignment and as the vehicle of his eventual rise to power.

Begin was aware that in accepting the Rogers Plan, the Labor government had returned to what Abba Eban would call "the partition logic." The Laborites did not believe that possession of the West Bank could be permanently reconciled with Israel's international best interests, the country's democratic nature or the basic Zionist concept of an Israel steeped in purely Jewish traditions and culture. The "partition logic" had been accepted by the Jewish Agency way back in 1947, when the ruling elements in the Jewish community acquiesced to the United Nations plan dividing Palestine west of the Jordan River into Jewish and Arab states.

Begin countered by advocating outright annexation of the West Bank. Although many Israelis still preferred exchanging territories for peace, Begin's proposal appealed strongly to centrist, rightist and religious elements who had begun taking the new borders for granted—as frontiers which the world at large, even the Arabs themselves, would eventually accept.

"There are those who claim that Hussein must get back Judea and Samaria," Begin declared. "Because of the twists and turnings of time and fashion, there are also those who argue that they should be transferred to a rule called 'Palestinian.' The moral and Zionist tragedy is that neither of these groups can conceive a third possibility: to maintain in the territories of the Land of Israel only a Jewish sovereignty."

Begin minimized the demographic consequences of annexation, which would mean the addition of upwards of one million Arabs to Israel's population. The answer to an increase in the number of the country's

Arab inhabitants, he said, lay in a massive Jewish immigration.

To those Israelis who objected to annexation on legal grounds, maintaining that Israel had no right to keep territories obtained in warfare, Begin responded that, under certain conditions, international law sanctioned changes in frontiers wrought by conquest. "Such changes," he insisted, "are always recognized if they are the result of a war fought in self-defense such as we fought in June of 1967." He cited as examples the recognition of postwar frontiers established in Europe after the First and Second World Wars.

Begin drew large crowds whenever he spoke in public and enjoyed a wide readership for his weekly pieces in *Yediot Aharonot*, one of Israel's biggest evening newspapers. Whether he was making headway politically, however, was not immediately apparent in an Israel suddenly beset by smugness and now in pursuit of materialistic rather than idealistic goals.

The country's borders were comparatively quiet after Hussein crushed the PLO in Jordan in 1970–1971, and Sadat expelled the Russians from Egypt in the summer of 1972. Peace reigned at last on the Suez Canal, in Sinai, the Gaza Strip, the West Bank and on the Golan Heights. Scores of new settlements were established in the occupied territories. Relations with the United States were stabilized, and the Labor Alignment could boast, not without reason, that it had accomplished all this.

When I visited Israel on a magazine assignment in mid-1972, businessmen told me they had "never had it so good." The country was in the midst of an unprecedented economic boom. Agricultural and industrial output had risen dramatically; upwards of one hundred thousand West Bank and Gaza Strip Arabs were being bused daily to and from well-paid jobs in Israel proper—mainly in the booming building trades—and, broadly speaking, the Israelis were disinclined to take Begin and Gahal seriously as an alternative to the Labor government. Another Labor victory in the national elections scheduled for the autumn of 1973 seemed a foregone conclusion.

What made another Labor Alignment electoral triumph predictable was the evident disarray in Gahal following its departure from the government. With few exceptions, the coalition's Liberal faction believed the break had been unnecessary and detrimental to Gahal's chances in the forthcoming elections; it could take no credit for the improvement in the country's overall prosperity and generally peaceful situation.

Worse still, Begin's own Herut was boiling with intramural dissension, and the heat came from an easily identifiable source: Ezer Weizman. The former Minister of Transport minced no words in describing Gahal's resignation from the seats of power as "a fatal mistake." He had acquiesced in the move "for the sake of party discipline," but knew the break had been an error, and as Chairman of the Executive Committee of

Herut said so loudly, clearly and often. He deeply resented having been bludgeoned by Begin into resigning his cabinet post.

Inevitably, antagonisms developed between the two men. They were poles apart in character, viewpoints and personal traits. The formalistic, Polish-born Begin was comfortable only when surrounded by the "yes-men" of his *mishpachat haloachim*, his "family of fighters" of Irgunist days. The informal, Israeli-born Weizman was a free spirit, a Sabra, given to speaking his mind, and definitely not a "yes man." Begin seemed content to run a small, closely knit opposition party loyal to his—and only his—views; Weizman, on the other hand, believed Herut needed new ideas and, above all, new blood.

In December 1972, after a heated Herut party convention during which the divergences between Begin and Weizman were thoroughly aired, the latter resigned his chairmanship. Emerging from the meeting, Weizman told an interviewer, "If you want to breathe fresh air, you can't do it in there. Everything revolves around Menahem Begin."

With national elections looming, Weizman started on a new career in business with his (and Begin's) old friend Yaacov Meridor, who had become something of a magnate in the field of transportation and largely shared Ezer's view of Begin as a virtual dictator intolerant of criticism. Ezer Weizman, it seemed, was through with politics. But events and an old colleague in arms, General Ariel (Arik) Sharon, intervened to return Weizman to the arena.

Mindful of the need to consolidate its position with an electorate that no longer regarded Begin and Gahal with antipathy, the Laborites early in 1973 evolved a program designed to take the wind out of the sails of the center-right parties. Devised by Israel Galili, a Minister Without Portfolio and Golda Meir's trusted confidant, the plan called for the integration of the country's economy with Arab agriculture and industry in the occupied territories. It provided for generous tax relief and government loans, similar to those offered to foreign investors in Israel itself, to business men who established industrial plants in the conquered areas.

The so-called Galili Plan also envisaged new Jewish settlements in the occupied territories as well as a Golan Heights industrial center, a regional commercial-industrial center in the Jordan Valley, a factory complex in northeastern Sinai near Rafa and new industrial zones in the vicinity of East Jerusalem, Nebi Samuel, Qalkilia and Tulkarem. For the first time, furthermore, Jews would be entitled to purchase Arab lands and property in the West Bank and Gaza. Under the Galili format, Labor's platform for the territories differed from Gahal's only to the extent that Gahal demanded outright annexation of the West Bank, the

Golan Heights, and part of Sinai. Otherwise, the Galili Plan was fully as "imperialistic" as Gahal's. Furthermore, it met the demands of the religious parties for preservation of the "historic Land of Israel." Labor had suffered small losses in both the 1965 and 1969 elections and assumed that the setbacks had resulted from the party's penchant for temporizing on the question of borders.

The Galili Plan faced Begin and Gahal with a dilemma. While the coalition had performed well enough in 1969, winning 26 seats, the number hardly threatened Labor's hegemony. It was evident to Begin that Gahal's best chance lay in arranging new marriages of convenience with other, smaller parties of the center and right: the Independent Liberals, the Free Center and the State List which between them held 10 seats in the Knesset. The addition of so small a number would not of itself overtake the Labor Alignment's 56 seats, but it might start a trend toward breaking the Laborites' monopoly.

A consolidation of Gahal with these other parties, however, would not be an easy task. Shmuel Tamir, leader of the Free Center—a splinter faction of the Labor party that had followed Ben-Gurion into political exile, then strayed further right—was a personal enemy of Menahem Begin's. The Independent Liberals were an agglomeration of "dovish" upper-middle-class gentlemen for whom Begin was too much of a hardliner. The State List, composed of dissident ex-Rafi members, leaned toward Labor. What was needed to bring together such strange political bedfellows was a dynamic personality. The missing element was supplied in the late summer of 1973 by General "Arik" Sharon, the burly paratroop commander who in the June war of 1967 had helped to silence the "Russian defenses" along the Suez Canal with a series of daring commando raids.

Sharon was the *enfant terrible* of the Israeli Defense Forces, idolized by his subordinates but highly unpopular with his superiors for his abrasive assertiveness, his impulsiveness and his critical public pronouncements. Informed that he would be passed over for appointment as Chief of Staff, Sharon angrily resigned from the army and called a press conference to announce that he intended entering politics as a member of the Liberal faction of Gahal. Friends were astonished. They doubted that "a wild one" like "Arik" would be welcome in a party composed of proper gentlemen interested mainly in corporative balance sheets.

Despite his difficulties with Weizman, Begin was delighted by Sharon's decision to join the Liberal party. The popular "Arik" would be a valuable asset as a member of Herut's ally in Gahal in the forthcoming elections, for Sharon's name was now as much a household word and potential vote-catcher as the names of Dayan and Weizman. But Sharon quickly found himself as unhappy in the Liberal party as Weizman had been in Begin's Herut. Shortly after announcing his plunge into politics, he caused another national sensation by calling a second press conference during which he issued a typically outrageous ultimatum: Unless all of the parties of the center and right wings coalesced into a force capable of contesting the imminent elections with the Labor Alignment, he personally would renounce a political career.

It was a formidable condition. Nevertheless, the chance to win the addition of this charismatic hero was highly compelling to the anti-Alignment factions. Moreover, the pressures from the rank and file, especially the younger generation, were too strong to be ignored. Begin, particularly, saw there was much truth in Sharon's argument that the only hope of unseating Labor lay in a fusion of all anti-Laborite forces. Meetings immediately started among their leaders, and by early September, after protracted negotiations, a new center-right bloc called Likud (Unity) was patched together. Only the Independent Liberals remained aloof from the new entity.

Fearing he might become a small fish in a large pond, Begin was unenthusiastic at first, but soon saw the potential advantages of the new coalition. Within it, all partners enjoyed a considerable degree of independence. Since Herut was the largest single component, Begin could wield the greatest influence, and he emerged as Likud's logical leader. Common policies, moreover, proved sufficiently close for even Tamir and Begin to come to terms on a modified Herut platform that could claim at last to be an alternative to the party that had dominated Israeli politics for a quarter of a century. Gahal and the other members of Likud would present a joint list for the impending elections that would contain nearly as many hawks and doves as the list of the Labor Alignment.

But the electoral test did not materialize as scheduled. At high noon on October 6, less than three weeks before the national elections, the armies of Egypt and Syria simultaneously attacked in force. The Yom Kippur War had begun, and the elections were postponed.

October 6, 1973, fell on a Saturday, the Hebrew Sabbath. Moreover, the date happened to coincide with Yom Kippur, the most sacred day on the Jewish religious calendar, a time of fasting, soul-searching and prayer for observant Jews everywhere, but especially in Israel. There, on this holiest of all days, public transport ceases, radios are silent, telephones do not ring, cinemas and stores and cafés are closed and the synagogues are filled.

When the war started, Menahem Begin was praying in the synagogue in Beit Jabotinsky, the Herut party headquarters within walking distance of his home in Tel Aviv. He had heard the sirens that announced a national emergency, but it was his daughter Leah who hurried to him to tell him what they meant: The government had summoned the nation to arms. Begin was bewildered. As a member of the Knesset Foreign Affairs and Security Committee, he was aware that the Egyptians had been holding maneuvers close to the Canal behind the ceasefire lines. But the Israelis had staged such maneuvers before without belligerent consequences, and he had accepted the Intelligence Branch's assurances that Sadat was merely making another "show of force" and that war was unlikely.

The Egyptians and the Syrians, attacking simultaneously and with overwhelming power, achieved almost total surprise, the element which, everything else being equal, is war's most powerful determinant of victory or defeat. As Ezer Weizman told me later, "the Arabs caught us with our pants down." Israel reacted slowly to the assault. Whereas the Israelis normally can mobilize to full strength in an emergency in twenty-four hours, this time it took them seventy-two. And the Israelis paid dearly for their unpreparedness. Israel came dangerously close to disaster.

Israel had emerged from its previous wars politically, economically and militarily stronger than ever. Not so in October 1973. The Jewish state survived the Arabs' latest attempt to erase it from the map of the Middle East only by the narrowest of margins. When the guns of October finally fell silent—not as a result of a clear-cut victory by either side but in response to a ceasefire imposed principally by the United States and the Soviet Union—an almost unrecognizable Israel emerged from the ugly debris of war; physically intact, but psychologically and in other ways deeply disturbed.

I was there at the time and found an Israel literally traumatized by the war. In a country where family ties are close-knit and cherished, the loss of almost three thousand men and the wounding of seventy-five hundred had plunged Israel into profound shock and grief. It was as though in approximately twenty days of fighting during the Vietnam War the United States, with roughly eighty times Israel's population, had two hundred and forty thousand killed and six hundred thousand wounded. The war, whose direct cost was calculated at more than $7.4 billion, roughly equal to the year's anticipated Gross National Product, also seriously undermined Israel's already overtaxed economy. Israelis asked themselves and each other how much longer they could endure this hemorrhage in lives and material resources.

To complicate matters further, the Yom Kippur War triggered an internal political upheaval, a struggle between right wing hawks and leftist doves which impaired the country's efforts to negotiate the "just and lasting peace" that the Jewish state long had recognized as essential to its survival. When the war ended, the hawks were in the ascendancy, with demands for a continued military posture that Israel could ill afford socially, politically or economically.

Moreover, the war immensely complicated East-West relations. The large-scale rival logistical operations whereby the Soviet Union replenished Arab losses in materiel and the United States did likewise for the Israelis, turned the Yom Kippur War into a superpower war by proxy. This was heavily emphasized when late in the hostilities Washington and Moscow found themselves in a military confrontation reminiscent in its awesome potentialities of the Cuban missile crisis of 1962.

Another of the war's byproducts was the politically effective Arab oil embargo that raised global crude prices by more than' four hundred percent and posed the world's industrialized nations, especially the United States, with a dilemma—support for Israel versus Arab oil. It was blackmail, and eventually, Washington would submit to it by substantially reversing its pro-Israel policy during the early part of Carter's administration.

Finally, the war wrought a drastic reexamination of Israel's self-image as an unbeatable military mini-power that was holding the eastern crescent of the Mediterranean in democracy's cause. Its course and its outcome opened the eyes of the Israelis to the incontestable fact that Arab soldiers, when properly trained and equipped—as the Russians had instructed and accoutered the Egyptians and the Syrians—could become, in time, a formidable, maybe even an insuperable enemy.

Nevertheless, the war again demonstrated Israel's qualitative superiority in manpower and in some categories of conventional weapons. The Israelis ultimately defeated the numerically superior Arab forces despite a much-criticized decision by Premier Golda Meir and Defense Minister Moshe Dayan not to secure the advantages of a preemptive strike when eleventh-hour intelligence reports—confirmed by our own Central Intelligence Agency—indicated an Arab attack was imminent. Although the Arabs enjoyed considerable initial successes during the first seventy-two hours of the fighting, Dayan took full charge of the military situation when the going got sticky, and it may fairly be said he had the last word.

There was plenty to criticize, however, in the way the war was conducted, at least in its early phases, but Menahem Begin held his tongue, voicing no public criticism of military or political mistakes. But he made it clear to Prime Minister Golda Meir that he would not remain silent when the battles ended. Afterwards, he led the chorus of protest from soldiers and officers who had witnessed the blunders that almost cost Israel its life.

The country seethed with resentment over the *mechdal* (culpable failure) of the military-political establishment in the October War. In the "heads must roll" atmosphere prevalent in the war's aftermath, most of the criticism was directed against Golda Meir and Moshe Dayan. At the time, Mrs. Meir was negotiating disengagement agreements with Egypt and Syria in the midst of the longest and deepest political deadlock Israel had ever experienced. Nevertheless, she was not immune to Begin's barbs. The Likud leader repeatedly demanded her resignation, but refrained from criticizing Dayan; the Defense Minister, in his opinion, was too valuable a "national resource" to be publicly beheaded politically for failures that could not be directly attributed to him.

Early in April, a Commission of Inquiry absolved Mrs. Meir, Dayan and the government of responsibility for Israel's poor showing in the early days of the Yom Kippur War. It blamed Israel's reverses on General David (Dado) Elazar, Chief of Staff at the time, and other top army officers and recommended their dismissal. The Commission's report precipitated a political storm. Begin charged the findings were unduly critical of the military and too lenient with the government leadership. He again demanded Mrs. Meir's resignation, and irate youngsters took to the streets en masse, shouting Likudist slogans.

Elazar resigned, complaining he had been treated "unfairly." A week later, on April 10, a weary Mrs. Meir decided that at seventy-six she had had enough of recriminations and also resigned. With her went Dayan, Eban, Sapir and others who personified the leadership that had carried the country through approximately a decade of storm and stress. Mrs. Meir was charged by her party's parliamentary group to head a caretaker government pending the emergence of a new leader, and the stage was set for the 1973 elections. Menahem Begin believed his time had come, but, for the time being, at least, he was wrong.

During the Yom Kippur War, Begin's Likud acquired a major political asset in the person of "Arik" Sharon. He had returned to the army the moment the fighting started, and as a reserve general back in active service commanded one of the three army corps that first blocked the Egyptian armored advance into Sinai, then counterattacked. He broke the enemy's defenses and crossed the Canal into Egypt, driving to within fifty miles of Cairo. I crossed in Sharon's wake over one of the two pontoon bridges he had flung across the Canal under heavy Egyptian fire and saw the havoc he had wrought in the deep salient between Ismailia and Suez. He was undoubtedly a brilliant commander of armor and the war's outstanding hero. His troops called him *"Arik, Melech Yisrael"*—Arik, King of Israel—and would have followed him to Cairo had he so ordered.

The Likud exploited to the fullest Sharon's potentialities as a vote-getter when he returned to civilian life and the political arena after the war. At Likud party rallies in Oriental neighborhoods, he was greeted ecstatically as *Melech Yisrael* but the quasi-disaster of the Yom Kippur War and its resultant resentments proved insufficient reason to alter substantially Israel's political balance. In the national elections for the eighth Knesset held at the end of December 1973, the Likud seated 39 members, a gain of 13 over Gahal's previous showing, but while Labor lost 4 seats, returning only 51 members instead of 55, it remained the largest grouping and held onto power. Obviously, the Israelis were not yet ready for a revolutionary change in their government.

But Israel was already in transition toward a new regime. An era had ended with the Yom Kippur War, and another had begun. In a sense, the threshold was crossed when, early in November, the eighty-seven-year-old widower, David Ben-Gurion, was stricken by a cerebral hemorrhage at Sde Boker in the Negev desert he loved so well. Taken to Hadassah hospital in Jerusalem, he died on December 1. The largest funeral in the nation's history evoked more than the passing of the widely beloved "Little Lion." At the graveside stood a tearful Menahem Begin.

Two days later, with the electoral campaign in full cry, the press published a letter drawn from Begin's files by his faithful aide and devoted longtime adviser, Yehiel Kadishai. The letter was written by Ben-Gurion to Menahem Begin while the latter was still a member of Mrs. Meir's cabinet. It said:

> Paula, my (late) wife, was for some reason an admirer of yours. I opposed your road, sometimes strongly—both before the State and after it arose—exactly as I would have opposed the road of Jabotinsky. I strongly objected to a number of your actions and opinions after statehood, and I do not regret my opposition. For, in my opinion, I was in the right; but personally I never harbored any grudge against you, and as I got to know you better over the recent years, my esteem for you grew and my Paula rejoiced in it.

The letter doubtlessly served to further enhance Begin's acceptability as a respectable member of Israel's political hierarchy. Nevertheless, the election results proved a disappointment to Begin. He could draw encouragement only from the (not surprising) fact that the vote in army polling stations had gone heavily in favor of his Likud. He was not invited to take part in the new Labor government.

The shift in the 1973 elections to younger Labor leadership in the person of Yitzhak Rabin was widely acclaimed. Rabin had covered himself with glory as Chief of Staff in the June war of 1967, and he was a Sabra, the first ever to become Prime Minister. After leaving the army, he had served as a Labor Minister in Mrs. Meir's government and had seen service as Israel's Ambassador to Washington, where he cultivated the friendship of President Nixon and Secretary Kissinger.

At the outset, Rabin demonstrated considerable political savoir-faire. He successfully resisted demands from those masters of political opportunism, the religionists, that he form a government of national emergency in tandem with the Likud, whose resistance to territorial concessions would have made negotiation of a final settlement with the Arabs extremely difficult if not impossible. It was to achieve peace, more than for any other reason, that Rabin had been given his mandate.

Rabin eventually formed a government which on June 3, 1974 won a 61 to 51 vote of confidence in the Knesset with 5 abstentions. The new cabinet's 15 holdovers were less noteworthy than the changes at the top. Shimon Peres replaced his friend Dayan as Defense Minister; Yigal Allon, in addition to retaining the office of Deputy Prime Minister displaced Abba Eban as Foreign Minister; and Yehoshua Rabinowitz, former Mayor of Tel Aviv, succeeded the one-time "kingmaker" of Labor politics, Pinhas Sapir, as Finance Minister. What everyone hoped was a "new era" in Israeli politics had begun.

The members of the new government and their known political leanings—as distinct from their actual party affiliations—caused Menahem Begin to remark, caustically, "We have not seen such a collection of doves since the days of Noah and his ark." Actually, however, Rabin's government was not as dovish as Begin indicated. It was irrevocably committed to "no return to the 1967 borders" and "no negotiation with the Palestine terrorists whose declared goal is the destruction of Israel," a position not too far removed from Begin's.

Rabin, however, inherited staggering problems, most of them economic. The October war had unleashed a costly Middle East arms race. Before 1973, Israel could hold its own, but the situation changed drastically when the Persian Gulf countries started making unprecedented sums of oil money available to Egypt and Syria, Israel's principal antagonists. In the first eighteen months after the Yom Kippur War, nearly $3 billion in Soviet and French weaponry flowed into the arsenals of Cairo and Damascus, most of it underwritten by Saudi Arabia, Kuwait, Qatar and the United Arab Emirates. Israel's defense budget leaped perforce from $1.5 billion in 1972 to $3.6 billion in 1974, representing about one-third of the nation's entire GNP. Moreover, most of Israel's weapons had to be purchased abroad in hard currencies, mainly dollars.

Imports of wheat, meat, fuel, sugar, seeds and other products also required payment in hard currencies, and all were soaring in price due to the inflationary effects of the exhorbitant rise in petroleum prices imposed by the Arab-dominated oil global monopoly. By the first quarter of 1974, Israel's foreign currency reserves had sunk to $1 billion, barely enough to cover imports for two months. The government borrowed heavily overseas, and by the autumn of 1974 was carrying a debt load of $5.5

billion, on which accumulated interest payments exceeded $1 billion, approximately half the value of the country's net exports. The cost of servicing the foreign debt, combined with shrinking reserves of foreign currencies, contributed to skyrocketing inflation. Prices jumped an unprecedented fifty-six percent during 1974 alone.

In an attempt to curb inflation, Rabin's government adopted the harshest fiscal measures in Israel's history. It raised taxes, already the Western world's highest, and imposed a huge compulsory loan. Then, it slashed subsidies on 14 items of public consumption ranging from gasoline to certain foodstuffs, a bitter decision for a Socialist regime. The prices of staples jumped anywhere from 50 to 100 percent. Meanwhile, the Israeli pound was devalued.

The following year, 1975, brought more of the same: higher taxes, another devaluation of the currency, still higher prices and a lowered standard of living. The resultant austerity was accompanied by social unrest which took the form of a series of crippling strikes in various sectors of the economy. At the same time, immigration—upon which Israel relied heavily to increase its reservoir of much-needed human resources—diminished sharply.

Altogether, though worse was yet to come, 1975 was a terrible year for Yitzhak Rabin. It witnessed a resurgence of bloody terrorist PLO activities on the West Bank and *Fatah* incursions from Lebanon. Israel's reactions to the terrorism—massive aerial bombings of Fatahland's guerrilla bases in southern Lebanon and repressive measures in Judea and Samaria—reduced the blood-letting, but did little to enhance Israel's "image" in the West. There the belief was widespread that the PLO's boss, Yassir Arafat, had moderated his stand and that his main interest now was creation of a Palestinian state on the West Bank. Once this new nation was established, the Palestine question would be "solved," peace would reign in the Middle East and the West's industrial nations would have all the oil they needed.

The full implications of Arafat's slogan, "a democratic, secular Palestinian state"—ventilated during his spectacular appearance before the United Nations General Assembly in October 1974—were curiously missed by the craven, oil-hungry countries of the industrialized world. They chose to see Arafat as a spokesman for refugees made homeless by Israel's emergence, as a "peacemaker" willing to live harmoniously with the Israelis, if only his people were given a home of their own on the West Bank and the Gaza Strip. What he sought, however, was what the PLO's charter clearly stated: The dismantling of the Jewish state to make way for another Arab country called Palestine. But Arafat's objectives were clearly discerned by Menahem Begin.

"Just listen to him," Begin implored. "Why won't anybody believe him? He wants to create an Arab nation on the ruins of Israel. He speaks of a 'democratic and secular' state. Where in the whole Arab world is there a democracy? And what Arab country is by any definition 'secular' in character?"

In the third year of Rabin's premiership, tensions developed within his cabinet, mainly between him and his rival, Shimon Peres, and between the latter and Yigal Allon. Soon the Labor party's intramural rivalries overshadowed the more important issues and filled the newspapers with sensational copy as the country moved toward new elections in 1977.

The conflicts rose to a climax when Peres announced his candidacy for the Labor party's nomination for its leadership, meaning the premiership. It was an unprecedented challenge to an incumbent, and both men—Rabin and Peres—uninhibitedly attacked each other in their efforts to win the support of Labor's rank and file. Meanwhile, government came to a virtual standstill.

Rabin finally won his party's nomination, but only by the narrowest of margins. However, thanks to an alert Israeli press, his victory would be short-lived.

After the Yom Kippur War, Israel's newspapers were in a muck-raking mood. Since early in the year, they had been reveling in a series of scandals involving highly placed Labor party bigwigs.

On January 3, 1977, Housing Minister Avraham Ofer, who had been linked in the press to a police probe of corruption in his ministry, shot himself to death in Tel Aviv. In a suicide note proclaiming his innocence, Ofer said he had been driven to taking his own life by the innuendos that had been leveled at him for months.

The newspapers had been saying that Ofer was the principal target of a police investigation into allegations of financial irregularities involving *Shikun Ovdim*, a construction company which he had headed before joining Rabin's cabinet. The firm was owned by the Histadrut and the investigation, confirmed by the police on January 3, was said to have involved the sale of government-subsidized apartments to unauthorized tenants, illegal discounts for housing sales to journalists and other public figures, and illicit land transactions.

At a state funeral for Ofer on January 5, Rabin said he believed the minister was not guilty of any wrongdoing. Shortly afterwards, the Israeli cabinet accepted Attorney General Aharon Barak's recommendation that the police investigation into Ofer's affairs be dropped and that the late minister be considered legally innocent because he could no longer be proved guilty in a courtroom.

Begin's Likud, however, demanded in parliament that the investigation of Ofer be resumed despite the cabinet's decision to drop the probe.

On the heels of the Ofer tragedy, came the scandal involving Asher Yadlin, a prominent Labor party figure. On February 22, Yadlin was sentenced to five years in prison and fined the equivalent of about twenty-eight thousand dollars following his conviction on four counts of bribery and one of tax evasion. Yadlin, who had been nominated to head the Bank of Israel just prior to his arrest in October 1976, had pleaded guilty to the charges on February 14.

Yadlin admitted that some of the illegal kickback money he had received in real estate deals had been channeled to the Labor party to cover its 1973 election campaign expenses. According to his own testimony, he had kept five thousand dollars for himself and turned nine thousand dollars over to the party. Again, the deals in question had been made through the Histadrut during Yadlin's tenure as head of the labor confederation's health fund in the early 1970s.

The press then started hounding Rabin himself. On March 15, one of Israel's leading dailies, *Haaretz*, published a report stating that the Prime Minister's wife, Leah, maintained a dollar bank account in Washington in violation of Israel's currency laws. This evoked from Mrs. Rabin an acknowledgement that the account existed, but that it contained only two thousand dollars.

On April 8, however, the newspaper *Maariv* reported from Washington that the Rabins actually had two bank accounts, with deposits totaling twenty thousand dollars, when they left Washington in 1973. That ten thousand dollars remained was a fact discovered by an enterprising Israeli reporter. Israeli currency laws (since rescinded by Begin's government) required the disclosure of foreign accounts within six months of an Israeli citizen's repatriation.

When *Maariv* hit the newstands that day, Rabin promptly resigned as the Labor party's candidate for a second term, with the elections only five weeks away. He announced his decision after admitting that he and his wife had lied about the amount they had kept in their bank accounts in Washington, which represented moneys earned by both on the lecture circuit. In submitting his resignation, Rabin also sought to step down as Prime Minister. Israeli law, however, required that he remain at his post until after the elections, because he headed a caretaker regime which had been in office since the dissolution of his coalition majority in December 1976. Rabin, it will be recalled, had dismissed the ministers of the National Religious Party after they had accused him of having desecrated the Sabbath by receiving a flight of Phantoms from the United States on a Saturday.

On April 10, the Labor party nominated Defense Minister Shimon Peres as its standard bearer in the forthcoming elections.

Accusations also were made against Abba Eban over bank accounts held abroad. Although police investigations never came up with anything that might incriminate the former Foreign Minister, the row raised by the newspapers further damaged the Labor party's image.

The divided, scandal-ridden Labor party that went to the polls in the early summer of 1977 was no match for Menahem Begin and his Likud.

Chapter 21

The Revolution of 1977

The national elections of 1977 which projected Menahem Begin into the premiership were likened by oldtime Laborite observers to an "earthquake," a "deluge," an "electoral storm." Actually, however, the ruling Labor Alignment had been in steady decline for many years, and the results of the elections were predictable enough. Nevertheless, they evoked almost as much shock and surprise in Israel, and abroad, as a cataclysm, whereas what happened was merely a voters' revolution whereby the Israeli electorate achieved with ballots what neighboring Arab countries, indeed, most nations in the Afro-Asian world, normally achieve with bullets.

Oddly, it was Ezer Weizman, not one of the Irgun's "fighting family" but the maverick of the Herut faction of Likud, who sensed that the time was ripe for an all-out effort to unseat the Laborites and largely engineered the "revolution." Born with a self-confessed "tremendous desire to succeed" at whatever he undertakes, the tall, handsome paladin of right wing Israeli politics demanded of Menahem Begin—and was granted—complete control of the Likud's electoral campaign.

It was an unprecedented concession on Begin's part. In the past, he had always run a one-man show, personally drafting the Herut's position papers, writing his own speeches and arranging even the minutest details of his party's campaigns. But he had failed eight times to achieve power, never, in fact, coming even close to success. Realizing, perhaps, that at sixty-three, his ninth chance might be his last, Begin agreed to stand aside and allowed Weizman, ten years his junior, to take charge. The former

general, who would become Begin's Minister of Defense and his main
emissary in negotiations with Egypt's President Sadat, gave the Likud and
its hardnosed leader a "new look" that reflected the nationalistic
aspirations of a rising generation of native-born Israelis eager for change
in the dramatis personae of government and a "realistic" approach to
peace with the Arabs.

Weizman undertook no easy task. He had to "sell" Menahem Begin to
an electorate schooled to think of the former commander of the Irgunist
underground as a leader more apt to turn Israel into another Masada
rather than into an Israel capable of living in peace with its Arab
neighbors. From the outset, with the help of paid professionals in the field
of public relations, Weizman presented Begin to the voters as a family
man, a doting grandfather, a patriot, and an incorruptible politician who,
unlike some of his Laborite opponents, lived frugally within his limited
means. The image of Begin which Weizman projected was close enough
to the truth to make it acceptable, even convincing.

From a purely political or ideological standpoint, as I have already
indicated, Weizman's job was not very difficult. For some time the Labor
party had been talking to the people with two voices, one stressing the
Alignment's willingness to accept territorial compromises in order to
arrive at an accommodation with the Arabs, the other emphasizing
Labor's reluctance to give up the occupied territories. In its attempt to
straddle the territorial issue, Labor befuddled the electorate with complicated arguments.

Moreover, dovish elements that might have been attracted to Labor
were turned off by the number of hawkish candidates on its parliamentary
list, and, conversely, hawkish voters were dismayed by the number of
dovish Laborites seeking office. Furthermore, the Rabin government had
opposed the workers' insistent demands for higher wages. The resultant
strikes had seriously eroded Labor's image as the "Socialist friend of the
working class."

Weizman, on the other hand, could present Begin and the Likudists
running with him in their true light. Moreover, Begin and his followers,
unlike the Laborites, could not be accused of the military unpreparedness
that had caused the near-debacle of October 1973, and that still rankled in
Israeli hearts.

Campaigning in his usual forceful style, Menahem Begin blasted the
Labor government for having signed the Israeli-Egyptian Sinai disengagement agreement mediated by the energetic Henry Kissinger in September
1975. The accord obliged the Israelis to yield the vital Gidi and Mitla
passes, and to surrender the Abu Rodeis oil fields, which since 1967 had
supplied Israel with a substantial portion of its petroleum requirements.
Although the Sinai passes were placed under the protection of a United

Nations force within a buffer zone separating limited Egyptian and Israeli forces, Begin criticized the agreement as a unilateral withdrawal for which Israel received in return only unfulfilled promises of freedom of passage through the Suez Canal.

Begin repeatedly condemned the agreement as "one-sided" and detrimental to Israel's security. "We gave up important strategic advantages for nothing," he declared. "We presented Egypt with our most essential security positions in Sinai without getting anything in return. Such withdrawals could only bring the enemy to our very doorstep." He accused the Labor leadership of having "acted recklessly," and solemnly promised never to behave in similar fashion.

Begin's arguments struck home. What had happened in the Yom Kippur War was still fresh in Israeli memories, and every Israeli knew the map of the Sinai Peninsula well enough to know the importance of the Gidi and Mitla passes. Whichever side controlled them, dominated the vast, desert peninsula itself. And in Egyptian hands, the passes would be the gateways to an Israel vulnerable from the south. Begin played on Israeli fears that the Laborites' readiness for territorial compromise in Sinai might lead to similar concessions in the West Bank. An invasion from Sinai, far from Israeli population centers, presumably could be contained in time, but the western borders of Judea and Samaria are only a few miles from the Mediterranean coast, and territorial concessions there could lead to the positioning of Arab guns within firing range of Israel's main cities and towns. Begin made this point over and over again to good effect.

The Likud leader's territorial posture appealed to his preponderantly Sephardic constituency, and particularly to the religionists. The latter had long since developed a proprietary attitude toward the West Bank and the Gaza Strip as integral, inseparable parts of the "historic homeland," and in their view the areas were "not negotiable." With Begin's blessing, though without his personal participation, religious groups staged huge, noisy demonstrations against the Sinai withdrawal agreement and planned new settlements to be implanted in the occupied territories, especially in Judea and Samaria.

However, even more popular than Begin with the ultra-Orthodox Gush Emunim, a small but extremist religious sect, was the Yom Kippur War hero, General Sharon. Although instrumental in informing the Likud, Sharon now seemed hellbent on undermining it. No happier among the stuffed shirts of the Liberal party hierarchy than Weizman had been in the Herut's briar patch of Begin's idolaters, Sharon bolted to form his own party, denouncing the Labor party as "anachronistic" and the Likud as "too weak."

Earlier, in 1975, Sharon had taken a most unusual step; he had agreed to serve as an advisor on security matters to his old army friend, Premier Rabin. The country as a whole was astonished, and Likud wrote him off as a turncoat. It was widely assumed that Sharon had made the move in an effort to capitalize on his brilliant war record, and return to a high command in the army with Rabin's help.

Meanwhile, however, the Labor government had started falling apart, and Sharon found himself cooling his heels in the Prime Minister's office oftener than he liked. When Rabin signed the withdrawal accord with Egypt, the tempestuous general resigned and retired to his farm in the south in the regal manner of an unappreciated statesman.

But Sharon quickly terminated his self-imposed exile. He was soon back in the political arena at the head of a minuscule party called Shlomzion after the Queen of Hordus, King of Israel in the time of the Second Temple, a period in Jewish history also known as the Second Common- wealth. The arrogant Sharon's yearnings to create a Third Commonwealth are well known. When the 1977 electoral campaign got under way, Sharon submitted his own list of candidates for seats in the ninth Knesset.

Begin, meanwhile, in accordance with Weizman's plans, lost no opportunity to maintain close personal contact with his constituents. He enhanced his reputation for modest living by holding weekly "open house" meetings in the unpretentious three-room flat on the ground floor of Number One Rosenbaum Street, in north Tel Aviv. It was the same apartment that Begin had owned for three decades, and where he and Aliza had raised their three children. When their son and two girls were growing up, Begin and his wife slept in the living room on a con- vertible couch. Visitors could see for themselves Begin's almost spartan quarters and lifestyle, and mentally make comparisons with the far more luxurious manner in which some Laborite ministers were known to be living.

Visitors were impressed, also by the obvious warmth and harmony that prevailed between Menahem and Aliza, now a matronly lady in her mid- fifties, with a quick smile and manners as charming as her husband's. When female guests sized her up as the wife of a potential Prime Minister, they saw a woman much like themselves, simple and direct in speech, attentive to her spouse's needs and an efficient housewife, with a talent for making ends meet on the small family income, which at the time was about five hundred dollars a month before taxes and less than half that amount after taxes and compulsory social security deductions at the source.

Unlike other politicians' wives, Mrs. Begin took good care over the years to remain "a very private person," even after her husband emerged from the underground to enter politics. But during the 1977 campaign, Aliza Begin gradually emerged as a cultured lady fluent in English, French and German as well as Hebrew, of course, and Polish. A Latinist, she and

Menahem like reading Virgil aloud to each other "to keep in practice." A lover of classical music, she reads mystery stories for relaxation at bedtime.

Given their close relationship, it is presumable that Menahem Begin discusses policy decisions with Aliza, but it is highly doubtful that she wields any great influence in matters of state. Mrs. Begin's only outside interests are the Weizmann Institute, for which she has helped to raise funds for scientific research, and an organization that helps women with over-large families, for which she acts as a volunteer counsellor.

In Menahem Begin, weekend visitors to the flat in Rosenbaum Street found a relaxed paterfamilias, fond of playing in the garden with one or more of his eight grandchildren. Laborite opponents were provoked to scorn when a campaign photo showed Begin holding a grandson during the traditional circumcision ceremony. "The Likud's admen have discovered," they mocked, "that Menahem Begin is a human being." It was precisely the image Weizman's underlings had meant to project, and it remained unchallenged.

Throughout the campaign, Begin deviated little from a long-established daily routine which he would take into the premiership. In Tel Aviv, as later in Jerusalem, his day started at the crack of dawn, about 5:00 A.M., with a thorough reading of the daily newspapers, paying particular attention to the editorials and the pages carrying letters-to-the-editor. Incidentally, he has a phenomenal memory, of the kind often described as "photographic," and remembers everything he has read. For years Begin subscribed to the *Manchester Guardian, Le Monde,* and *Pravda.*

It was Begin's habit—and it still is—to lie abed, reading, until about 6:30 A.M.. Then, over a simple breakfast—fruit juice, tea sweetened with saccharine (he is mildly diabetic) and toast—he listens to the radio news broadcasts of Kol Israel and London's BBC. In the evenings, before he became Prime Minister, Begin liked to read for pleasure, mostly biographies and historical works. Books, he says, "expand my horizons— and provide me with quotable material for my speeches and articles."

Until his accession to the premiership, Begin wrote a weekly column of political commentary for *Maariv*, an important evening newspaper. His aide, Kadishai, confided to me that Begin's pieces, written in longhand, were invariably "wordy," running to four thousand words or more. "It would take him about a thousand words just to get started," Kadishai chuckled, remembering telephoned pleas from editors to persuade his boss to limit himself to two thousand words or less. "In the end," Kadishai said, "the editors prevailed." It was probably one of the rare times that Begin yielded to force majeur. He needed the "platform" *Maariv* supplied *and* the small, but welcome, extra income.

*   *   *

Although Weizman's handling of the Likud's campaign was masterful, worthy of a politician with far greater experience, he was undeniably aided by a favorable political climate. Under Rabin, great progress had been made in the reconstruction of Israel's defense potential; the country had reasserted itself as the ranking military power in the Middle East. This was dramatically illustrated by the daring and highly successful rescue of 101 Israeli hostages in the commando raid on Entebbe, on July 3–4, 1975.

Incidentally, it should be noted in passing, Rabin informed Begin about the ultra-secret operation before the Israeli paratroopers left on their hazardous mission, and Weizman saw to it that the Likud leader's comment to the Prime Minister on that occasion was made known during the campaign. "This operation," Begin was reported to have said, "is as courageous as anything we have ever attempted. I pray for its success. But I want you to know that, if it should fail, I will back you up. No one will ever be able to claim that we of the Likud opposed it, and we will never use a setback as political ammunition." Among the first to greet the returning heroes of Entebbe was Menahem Begin, riding the shoulders of cheering Likudniks. Rabin subsequently praised Begin for having demonstrated "a sense of real national responsibility."

But Entebbe was not enough to save Rabin and the Labor coalition. The raid's success raised national morale, but the big problems of the economy and international relations remained. In fact, they had grown in size and complexity, as had the failure in labor relations, in civic conduct, and, particularly, in the social structure of the country. Rabin's term in office was plagued not only by strikes, a decline in civic morality, and disunity within his government, but also by a growing balance of payments deficit, uncertainties about relations between Jerusalem and Washington, and the ever-present problems of achieving co-existence with hostile neighbors.

It was in this atmosphere, replete with Laborite shortcomings, that the tall, lean, former Chief of Staff and widely respected archaeologist, Yidal Yadin, emerged as a potential leader of a new party dedicated to restoring democratic morality in government. Jerusalem-born, Yadin owned impressive credentials. He had joined the Haganah in his early twenties, and in 1947, when he turned thirty, was appointed its Chief of Operations and Planning, in which capacity he played a central role during the War of Independence. With Ben-Gurion, he established the Israel Defense Forces (IDF) and planned the successful Negev campaign against Egypt. As Chief of Staff after the war, 1949–1952, Yadin introduced order and discipline in the armed forces, welding into a single service the units of the Haganah, the Palmach and the Irgun. Then, returning to academic life in

1952, he conducted the excavations that uncovered the splendors of Hazor and Masada, and was instrumental in Israel's acquisition of the Dead Sea Scrolls, all confirming irrefutably Judaism's claims to the Holy Land.

On the eve of the 1977 elections, Yadin, now sixty, tentatively "tested the waters" for an entry into political life. In a lecture and subsequent television interview, he called on his fellow countrymen to give highest consideration to the internal crisis developing in Israel rather than to questions of war and peace. He implied a willingness to enter the fray in support of a program of "moral regeneration" of the democratic process, which he considered more important than matters of international diplomacy or a search for an accommodation with Israel's neighbors.

Although the initial reception to Yadin's moralistic approach seemed barely lukewarm, there was sufficient evidence that he had struck a responsive chord to cause him to organize the Democratic Movement for Change (DMC), known in Israel as DASH. Its platform emphasized domestic reform rather than foreign policy, and addressed itself to the immediate needs of the Israeli society. It was in effect an "Israel First" program that would have wide appeal, enough to make serious inroads into Labor's following and enhance the Likud's chances.

In the meantime, the Likud's prospects were being further improved by the news that was coming out of Washington. The newly installed President Carter held a succession of press conferences that completely disoriented the Israelis. The President formulated new ideas and reiterated old ones in a way unfamiliar to the Israelis. The partial and sometimes garbled texts in the Israeli media gave the impression that the United States was backtracking on its commitments to Israel.

While the implications of Carter's widely publicized remarks about a future peace settlement that would allow Israel to establish "defensible borders" beyond the existing frontiers were being debated by the candidates, Carter added yet another discomfitting formulation. Replying to a question posed by a reporter at a town meeting in Clinton, Massachusetts, on March 16, Carter said that, while the Palestinians must be prepared to recognize Israel, "there has to be a homeland provided for the Palestinian refugees who had suffered so many, many years." The phrase would haunt United States-Israeli diplomatic relations, not only throughout Israel's election campaign, but for a long time afterwards. It did at least as much to improve the Likud's chances of victory as the Labor party's failures. It certainly helped to produce in Israel what some observers have characterized as a "hemorrhage to the right." The territorial maximalists were bound to profit from Jimmy Carter's implied, and subsequently confirmed, advocacy of "a homeland for the Palestinians."

*   *   *

However, the campaign was not all smooth sailing for Menahem Begin. In March, with the electioneering at its height, the physically fragile Begin collapsed. Stricken by a heart attack, he was taken, more dead than alive, to a Tel Aviv hospital near his home. "It was a near thing," a mutual friend later confided. "Menahem was only a few heartbeats away from death."

But Begin recovered. The faithful Aliza put it this way: "Menahem didn't like the next world and decided to come back to us."

Fully restored, though still pale and haggard-looking, Begin returned to the hustings some weeks later to hear his uninhibited Labor opponents openly question whether "a man with a bad heart could really function as Prime Minister."

Weizman determined to put an end to such talk. Shortly before the electorate went to the polls, he staged a television confrontation between Begin and his main opponent, Shimon Peres, much in the manner of the debate between the late John F. Kennedy and Richard Nixon in the campaign for the 1960 elections in which the visual medium played a major, if not decisive role in determining who should be President of the United States.

Peres, whom I have known for many years as an able and magnetic politician, lost the debate even before it began. To start with, he arrived at the studio in his official car, escorted by motorcycle police and a large retinue of government functionaries. Begin came in a small private car, accompanied only by Kadishai and members of his immediate family, a contrast in styles, documented by the media, that was not lost on the electorate.

Begin looked rather tired and pale on Israel's TV screens, but this worked to his advantage; his appearance belied his hawkish reputation. Moreover, he was courteous, gentlemanly, and his neat, almost formal attire contrasted sharply with Peres' open-shirted informality. In short, Begin looked like a statesman, Peres like just another Israeli politician, although he is, as everyone knows, considerably more.

It was in the political exchanges, however, that Begin scored heavily. By the time the program ended, Peres seemed to the viewers every bit as hawkish as Begin on territorial matters, and Begin just as eager for peace as Peres. The hawk-dove dissimilarities between the contenders became blurred, and Begin emerged as a staunch defender of parliamentary democracy.

The TV debate was the climactic event of Weizman's campaign to transform Menahem Begin's image from rambunctious rebel to solid statesman. Laborite propagandists tried hard to recall to public mind the "old Begin." In TV spots they used grainy photos from Begin's early election campaigns, showing him being escorted to party rallies by

motorcycle outriders, or haranguing the mob of rowdy Herutniks who
marched on the Knesset and hurled stones during the crucial debate on
German reparations. But it was all ancient history to the viewers,
particularly those in their twenties and thirties, whose eyes were turned to
the future.

Begin had no "image problem" with the members of the younger
generation. Few of them were even born when he had led the Irgun's
revolt against the British, hence had no memories of "The Season," Deir
Yassin or the *Altalena* affair. They saw him only as a patriot dedicated to
guarding the security of the state for which many of them had fought in
1967 and 1973. In the previous national election, the youngsters in the
army had voted overwhelmingly for the Likud candidates, and they would
do so again.

Among the oldsters, Weizman's slick admen were less successful,
perhaps, but here the desire for change was sufficiently pervasive to cause
many to accept Begin as the "responsible politician" who in 1967 had
helped to form a government of national unity on the eve of the Six Day
War, and who left the cabinet in 1970 rather than accept Labor policies
that he opposed. Ergo, a man of principle and integrity—and tough. But
wasn't toughness a desirable quality in the face of rumblings from
Washington about a "Palestinian homeland" and continued PLO talk
about creating a "secular, democratic Palestinian state" on the ruins of an
Eretz Yisrael erected over the years at almost unimaginable cost in human
and material resources?

Begin's main appeal was to those who believed, as he did, that the
"Land of Israel" between the sea and the River Jordan should never again
be partitioned, and that, if possible, Israeli sovereignty should be
extended over the whole of the West Bank and the Gaza Strip. If this
meant another war, so be it; the Israelis had learned to live with war.
They craved peace, but not at the price of losing the Israel they had so
painstakingly built.

Begin also talked of peace. Early in the campaign, at a party
convention, he told his followers that if the Likud was asked to form the
next government, its first concern would be "to prevent war." "A Likud
government," he said, "will undertake a number of peace initiatives. We
will ask a friendly country, which maintains diplomatic relations with
Israel and her neighbors, to convey to them our proposal to open
negotiations for the signing of peace treaties. Such negotiations, however,
must be direct, without prior conditions, and free of any imposed solution
from the outside." In addition, Begin promised he would pay "special
attention to Israel's relations with the United States" and make every
effort to normalize relations with the Soviet Union and France. It was the
kind of talk most Israelis wanted to hear.

In the area of domestic policy, Begin also said what many Israelis were prepared to support. He promised the electorate that the Likud would liberalize the Socialist economy by removing foreign currency controls, abolishing food subsidies and encouraging private enterprise. He would do his utmost, Begin said, to halt government intervention in industry and agriculture and to give free play to capitalism.

In the early hours of May 18, computer predictions indicating a Likudist victory were broadcast from Jerusalem. The election's results amply bore out the computer's forecast; the Labor Party, which had ruled Israel since its establishment, had lost.

The results were as follows (seats in the previous Knesset in parentheses): Likud 43 (39); Labor Alignment 32 (51); Yadin's Democratic Movement for Change (DMC) 15 (none); National Religious Party 12 (10); Torah Front 5 (5); Sharon's Shlomzion 2 (none); and Shmuel Flatto-Sharon 1(none). These last three supported Likud.[1]

Moshe Dayan subsequently resigned from the Labor Alignment and remained in the Knesset as an independent member supporting the Likud government.

The Knesset approved the new government by 63 to 53 on June 21. Begin was the new Prime Minister; Simha Ehrlich, the Minister of Finance; Ezer Weizman, Defense; and Moshe Dayan, Foreign Minister.

On October 24, following the decision of the DMC to join the coalition, the Knesset approved the appointment of four DMC ministers, of whom Yadin was named Deputy Prime Minister.

The main question to which both Israeli and American experts addressed themselves after the election was, "Who won?" Behind the question lay the belief that the Likud had achieved its plurality by inadvertence. This view had surface plausibility. Labor lost 21 seats and 17 of them could be accounted for without reference to the Likud. Two seats lost by the United Arab list, which is federated with Labor, went to Rakah, the Communist party, and 15 seats were won by Yadin's DMC. Therefore, analysts theorized, the entry of the DMC was mainly responsible for the Likud's victory.

"Wrong," says my friend Kadishai, pointing out that the DMC took three seats from the Independent Liberals, two from another small party, and ten from the Labor Alignment. "Ergo," reasons Kadishai, "Likud won on its own merits, mainly by encroaching on Labor's strength in the big cities and towns."

The interpretation of the elections as simply involving the repudiation of Labor had greater currency in the United States than in Israel, where Labor's weaknesses became obvious in early analyses of voting patterns. All who voted for Yadin and his DMC were not previous Labor voters. According to the Labor Alignment's own monthly, *Migvan*, the majority of the DMC's 15 seats cannot be explained by voter defection from Labor. According to this study, admittedly biased, only 6 of the new party's seats came from former Labor voter, the others came from various non-Labor elements in the electorate. At least 4, the survey indicated, came from former Likud voters.

The Likud, therefore, no less than Labor, had to make up for the losses it suffered to the DMC in order to emerge as the dominant political grouping. This it did by cutting sharply into Labor constituencies in the development towns and in the cooperative villages, as well as in major population centers. It also did extremely well with new and young voters, most particularly in the army where, with its concentration of youthful voters, the Likud won 44 percent of the vote, more than Labor and the DMC combined.

My own impression is that the Israelis voted for "something new" in both domestic and foreign policy. The Likud has set itself major economic and social targets; it hopes to revise radically the ideologically grounded institutional structures which have controlled the economy since before the Jewish state was created. But how successful Menahem Begin will be in putting into operation the Likud's domestic programs probably will remain unclear for some time. Unquestionably, however, the right wing domestic policies of the Likud offer a distinct alternative to the socialistic programs of Labor.

The question of the territories was another matter. It was by no means clear when Menahem Begin became Prime Minister that the policies which the Likud would follow would be substantially different from those which a Labor government would have pursued. In practical terms, the difference between a Likud and a Labor government in decision-making over the future of the territories may be the smallest difference between them.

With civil war raging in Lebanon, the northern border was on constant alert due to Israel's declared interest that the Christian villages near the border remain unmolested and that PLO or Syrian Army units remain north of the Litani River. Because of this the focus of attention remained on the Begin government's standing in Washington. When he arrived in mid-July for his initial meeting with Carter, Begin had to overcome two preconceptions about himself: that of the Arab-hating Jewish "terrorist," widely publicized by a pro-Arab lobby, and that of the all-wise, kindly,

Jewish father-figure, somewhat oversold by Begin's supporters and by Begin himself. Nevertheless, Begin disarmed all but the most skeptical critics. He agreed with Carter on the objectives of the then much-discussed Geneva peace conference, without unduly dwelling on the means of getting there. This was to be left to discussions between U.S. Secretary of State Cyrus Vance and Dayan, and between Vance and the Arab foreign ministers when they met in New York in September for the United Nations General Assembly.

Within twenty-four hours of his return from Washington, however, Begin authorized the legalization of three Jewish settlements on the West Bank of the Jordan River. Suddenly, everything changed. On August 4, the *Jerusalem Post* headlined its defense correspondent's account, "War more likely than Geneva," and on August 10, it reflected the general impression of American intentions with a bold headline: "U.S. closes gap with Arabs in attempt to isolate Israel."

On August 14, the Israeli government decided to extend current Israeli social services and privileges to the occupied West Bank and Gaza, a move which again produced inexplicably adverse comments from Washington and other Western capitals.

A few days later, Begin visited Romania. In November, President Sadat invited himself to Jerusalem and the negotiating process began. There was a feeling at the time, borne out by subsequent events, that the Middle East would never be the same again.

NOTES

1. In all, 1,771,726 votes were cast, representing 79.2 percent of the electorate. Likud received 33.4 percent of the vote; Labor 24.6 percent (as against 40 percent in the previous election), and the DMC 11.6 percent. The combined vote of the religious parties accounted for 14 percent of the votes cast.

Chapter 22

The Peace Process: Deadlock to Denouement

Israel's thirtieth birthday celebration in mid-May 1978, six months after President Sadat's spectacular visit to Jerusalem and his initial encounter with Prime Minister Begin, found the country's three million Jewish inhabitants in a mood of foreboding and anxiety. They had good cause for dejection; the Jewish state had crossed the threshold into maturity, but it still had failed to achieve its paramount lifelong objective: peace with its Arab neighbors.

The "peace process" that had begun in Jerusalem on the nineteenth and twentieth days of the previous November had generated high hopes of a final settlement of their long-standing conflict with the Arabs. But the expectations of peace begot by the historic meeting between the Egyptian President and the Israeli Premier remained unrealized. Visions of peace all but vanished shortly after Sadat and Begin met at Ismailia on Christmas Day 1977, when the Prime Minister presented to Sadat his proposals for a final settlement of the Arab-Israeli dispute.

Shortly afterward, on January 18, 1978, President Sadat had abruptly terminated the negotiations, claiming that neither in Jerusalem nor at Ismailia had Begin been sufficiently "forthcoming," as he put it, in Israel's response to the Egyptian "peace initiative." Oddly, many Israelis, as well as most foreign observers and commentators, agreed with Sadat, who had been touted as a candidate for a Nobel Peace Prize and at one point was characterized by President Carter as "the world's foremost peacemaker."

"I have given the Israelis everything . . . everything," Sadat declared after having rudely interrupted the peace negotiations, "and they have given me nothing. They have haggled, created new settlements, and refused to share my vision of peace."

There were grains of truth in Sadat's charges. It was true enough that the legalistic Begin had "haggled" over many points, among them the applicability to the West Bank and the Gaza Strip of Resolution 242. It was also true that Begin sanctioned the creation of new Jewish settlements in disputed territory.

But it was patently untrue that Begin had offered Sadat "nothing" at Ismailia at Christmas time following the televised hoopla in Jerusalem. Although in Jerusalem Begin, in his reply to Sadat' speech, had relied on a boring old script that offered the Egyptian little in the way of compensation for his beau geste, at Ismailia the Prime Minister presented generous terms for peace with Egypt. They had been checked beforehand with President Carter who had found them indicative of a "constructive approach."

Begin was so "forthcoming" at Ismailia, in fact, that he was subsequently severely criticized by former Prime Minister Golda Meir for being overly generous. She particularly objected to Begin's proposed solution for the knotty problem of the future status of the West Bank. Begin's proposal that eventually, within five years, the Palestinian Arabs residing in the area be granted civil authority, Mrs. Meir asserted, could easily lead to the creation of a "Palestinian state" with dangerous consequences to Israel's security. "Some people," she declared, "give too little too late. Begin has given too much too soon."

In a matter of weeks after Sadat broke off negotiations, Begin's popularity plummeted at home and abroad. The interruption in the "peace process" depressed the Israelis. Their spirits were weighed down by a new sense of loneliness, a feeling of increasing isolation in a hostile setting engendered by a growing conviction that during the stalemate they had lost their one true friend and ally, the United States. The feeling was general in Israel that President Carter, despite frequent avowals to the contrary, seemed to be yielding to Arab pressures to "squeeze Israel"— Sadat's own inelegant phrase—in order to oblige Begin to accept the Egyptian's terms for peace much as he had outlined them in his speech to the Israeli parliament on the previous November.

Over the years there have been highs and lows in relations between Jerusalem and Washington, but in the spring and early summer of 1978 these relations were at the lowest point since Secretary of State Dulles, in President Eisenhower's time, threatened to impose sanctions against Israel unless it withdrew completely from Sinai after its swift victory over the Egyptians in 1956.

Coupled with the diplomatic friction between Israel and the United States, came a well-orchestrated campaign in the media—visual and printed—to discredit Israel and put it on the defensive. Whereas in 1967 the media praised Israel lavishly for a victory of immense strategic value to the United States—the June War of that year was as much a defeat for Soviet imperialism as it was a setback to Pan-Arabism—now the media, with few exceptions, could only find fault with Israel's conduct of the "peace process" and with Menahem Begin himself.

Few journalists bothered to analyze the events and the negotiating positions of the participants. Most accepted dubious arguments without objective challenge. Saudi Arabia, for example, was invariably depicted as a "moderate" Arab power, meaning, presumably, that it supported Sadat's courageous "peace initiative" and its own intentions toward Israel were peaceful. Personally, I recall no statement from Riyadh indicating Saudi "moderation." On the contrary, when the PLO staged its slaughter of the innocents along the Tel Aviv-Haifa highway in March last year, the terrorist organization received hearty congratulations from the Saudi capital.

Correspondents also generally faulted Premier Begin's handling of the peace negotiations, from his reply to Sadat in the exchange of speeches in the Knesset that memorable November afternoon onward. By and large they were right about Begin's response to Sadat in Jerusalem; his speech contained nothing new or heart-lifting. But he could not really be blamed for this. Like the rest of us, he was taken completely by surprise, for in the ground rules governing the meeting between him and Sadat, Begin had advised his visitor-to-be that Israel "categorically and absolutely" rejected the conditions which Sadat had stipulated. And Sadat came anyway.

But the critical attitude of the foreign press, painful though it was for the sensitive Begin to bear, disturbed him far less than the opposition he was encountering at home. Some three hundred young men from all over the country organized a highly vocal "Peace Now" movement. Most were combat officers in the reserves, army men who presumably had helped give Begin the majority that had propelled him into the premiership. Now they addressed a letter to him condemning his policies and imploring him to make "substantial concessions" for a permanent peace. Begin was deeply wounded by their action. He replied that whereas the petitioners represented only "mere hundreds," he had been elected by "many hundreds of thousands" of Israelis who had given him and his cabinet a mandate to act on their behalf.

Abroad, meanwhile, Begin continued to be criticized as "obstinate, adamant, inflexible," and disinclined to make peace. They blamed him, not Sadat, for the breakdown in the negotiations, some going so far as to question Begin's sincerity.

Menahem Begin is undoubtedly an "obstinate" man by nature and "adamant" about making only the kind of peace that he feels would ensure his country's security and the physical safety of its inhabitants. He is also unquestionably "inflexible" in his commitment to the beliefs, principles, basic values, and political concepts that have been the hallmarks of his career, first as commander of the Irgun's bloody revolt against British rule in Palestine in 1944-1948, then as leader of the nation's right wing parliamentary opposition, and now as Israel's Prime Minister. But to doubt Begin's sincerity in his pursuit of a peaceful settlement of Israel's quarrel with its Arab enemies is like doubting that the world is round or that the earth revolves around the sun.

The moment has arrived, in this account of the life and times of this extraordinary man, to examine in detail Sadat's original offer of peace and Begin's subsequent reply in order to clarify where the responsibility lay for the long hiatus in the "peace process" that lasted from January 1978 until President Carter invited the principals to Camp David for the momentous Summit Conference of last September.

To begin with, it is not generally realized even now, months after the event, that when Sadat came to Jerusalem he offered *only* recognition of Israel's "right to exist," a privilege already granted to the Jewish state by the world at large as represented by the United Nations in their Partition Resolution of November 1947. Nonetheless, a readiness to concede Israel's sovereignty foretold a major change in Arab-Israeli relations. It was a welcome 180-degree turn in Arab attitudes toward the Jewish state to which the Israelis, as already noted, responded with unbridled, quasi-hysterical joy.

Begin's critics, however, seemed prone to overlook the fact that the "concession" came not from the Arabs as a whole, but from only one Arab: the princely Sadat, and, therefore, had limited validity. It was a purely unilateral gesture in which Sadat's Arab League allies, notably Syria, Iraq, and Jordan, or so-called confrontation states—not to mention Yassir Arafat's Palestine Liberation Organization—refused to join. Instead, they publicly vowed eternal hostility to Israel and in the case of the PLO swore to assassinate the Egyptian "peacemaker" for his infidelity to the Arab cause.

The rest of Sadat's "offer" as outlined in his speech to the Israeli parliament, where he made hearts quicken with a ringing promise of "no more wars"—a pledge subsequently muted in "conditions"—was really a reiteration of routine Arab demands: total Israeli withdrawal from all Arab territories occupied in the 1967 War, the creation of a Palestinian Arab state on the West Bank and in the Gaza Strip, and, for good measure, the reamputation of Jerusalem. Sadat made no mention of the "secure and recognized" boundaries for Israel called for in the United Nations Security Council Resolution 242 of 1967 or its sequel, Resolution

338, adopted in 1973, neither of which required Israel to return to the vulnerable frontiers that prevailed before the Six Day War.

After Sadat returned to Cairo and a tumultuous reception from his followers, the question was not whether Begin *would* come forward with peace proposals acceptable to Egypt and to the other "confrontation states," but whether he *could*. Observers familiar with the history of the Arab-Israeli conflict asked themselves whether a man with Begin's Revisionist background could find within himself the resilience or adaptability required for a radically new approach to the problem of peace between Israel and its Arab neighbors which the unique circumstances created by Sadat demanded.

In all honesty, I was among those who concluded at the time that a man forged in the fires of the Holocaust and his country's bitter struggle for independence, and tempered to political hardness by thirty years in Israel's parliamentary opposition, would find it extremely difficult, if not impossible, to be sufficiently flexible to ensure a successful outcome of the peace negotiations, certainly not on the basis Sadat had originally offered. The situation as it developed following Sadat's visit to Jerusalem clearly required a high level of statesmanship, and in November 1978 Begin the Statesman had not yet emerged from the silky cocoon that held Begin the Politician.

But at Ismailia—to the amazement of longtime students of the Arab-Israeli conflict, and to the astonishment of everyone familiar with Menahem Begin's background—the Prime Minister produced a peace plan which offered the Arabs considerably more than they had ever been offered before. When the plan was shown to him in mid-December during Begin's visit to the White House, President Carter not only called it "constructive" and a "notable contribution" toward an overall settlement, but immediately telephoned Sadat to indicate that the Israeli proposals warranted another meeting between him and Begin. The result was the Ismailia conference.

Congressional reaction in Washington was even more positive than Carter's. Senators who lunched with Menahem Begin at Blair House and were thoroughly briefed on the plan's admittedly intricate details described it as "an offer the Arabs couldn't refuse." Secretary of State Vance also endorsed the Begin plan as indicative of "understanding and statesmanship." Similarly warm praise came from National Security Adviser Brzezinski, former President Gerald Ford, and former Secretary of State Henry Kissinger. Begin, in a joyous mood, generously credited them all with having helped to create the psychological climate in which progress would be possible.

Ten days before the Ismailia meeting, the atmosphere for the forthcoming talks between Sadat and Begin was further improved by President

Carter. At a December 15 press conference he declared that "the PLO have been completely negative. They have rejected United Nations Resolutions 242 and 338, refused to make a public acknowledgement that Israel has a right to exist, and [thus have] removed themselves from any participation in a peace discussion."

The Administration's realization of the true nature of PLO intransigeance was long overdue, and the Israelis were immensely grateful. In high spirits, Menahem Begin proceeded to Ismailia with his "offer the Arabs couldn't refuse."

The two leaders' choice of a date for their meeting at the balmy Suez Canal city—Christmas Day 1977—was undoubtedly purely a matter of mutual convenience, but its symbolism could not be missed in the Christian world. Hopes rose anew everywhere that the birthday of the Prince of Peace would produce a settlement at long last of the vexing Arab-Israeli conflict.

Sadat waited for his guest in the garden of his villa, one of several which he uses for rest and relaxation; the one at Ismailia has a splendid view of the Canal.

The two men met alone for about twenty minutes, then were joined by their aides for the full meeting at which Begin, maps and papers at hand, submitted the Israeli plan. Begin was accompanied by Dayan and Weizman, and Sadat was flanked by his Vice President, Husni Mubarak, his War Minister, General Mohammed Ghany el Gamasy, and his Foreign Minister, Ibrahim Kamel.

Begin's plan contained twenty-six points. Its major provisions were:

—Israel would abolish its military administration in the occupied territories and Arab administrative units would take their place.

—Arab residents would elect an 11-member administrative council that would serve a four-year term and oversee the needs of the Arab inhabitants.

—Israeli forces would remain in the West Bank and Gaza Strip to maintain security and public order.

—Arabs in both territories would have a choice of Israeli or Jordanian citizenship.

—Israelis would be permitted to purchase land and settle in the Arab territories, while the Arabs who chose Israeli citizenship would be allowed to buy land in Israel and settle there.

—Arrangements would be made for Palestinian immigration to the West Bank and the Gaza Strip.

—The overall accord would be subject to review after a five-year period.

While Israel maintained its claim to sovereignty over the West Bank and the Gaza Strip, Begin proposed that "in the knowledge that other claims exist," and "for the sake of agreement and peace, the question of sovereignty in these areas" would be "left open." As for the status of Jerusalem, another major sticking point from the Egyptian point of view, Begin said freedom of access to holy shrines would be guaranteed for members of the Moslem, Christian and Jewish faiths.

Furthermore, Begin proposed restoration of Egyptian sovereignty over the Israeli-occupied Sinai peninsula, with the following *temporary* safeguards: (a) the area east of the Gidi and Mitla passes would be demilitarized, and the forces between the Suez Canal and the line of the passes would be administered by Israel and protected by Israeli forces; (b) Israeli forces would remain on a defense line in central Sinai "for a number of years," and air bases and early-warning systems would also remain during that period "until the ultimate withdrawal of Israeli forces to the international boundary."

In addition, Begin proposed that freedom of navigation in the Straits of Tiran, leading to the Gulf of Aqaba, be guaranteed "either by a United Nations force which cannot be withdrawn except with the agreement of both countries and by a unanimous decision of the United Nations Security Council," or by a joint Egyptian-Israeli patrol. This guarantee would assure Israel's shipping lanes to its southern port of Elath, Israel's gateway to the Orient and a vital oil port.

The two delegations then split, and the Egyptians and Israelis conferred separately. All the participants showed signs of strain. The first serious peace negotiations ever conducted by Arab and Israeli leaders were taking their toll of the conferees' stamina.

At 7:00 P.M. both delegations went into an unscheduled evening session that lasted several hours. On the Israeli side of the table sat Menahem Begin, looking frail and drawn, between Dayan and Weizman. Opposite him sat Sadat, perspiring freely as always, flanked by Kamel and General Gamasy. Several times, Begin and Sadat left the conference room to talk privately. Matters seemed to be progressing smoothly enough, but there were indications that Sadat's advisers were nit-picking; evidently the Israeli plan had fallen short of their expectations.

However, there were some hopeful signs. It was decided, for instance, that the on-going Cairo conference, which had begun earlier at the "technical level" at the Mena House, in the shadow of the Giza pyramids, should be upgraded to ministerial rank. It was also agreed to create Egyptian-Israeli "standing committees," a Military Committee headed by the countries' Defense Ministers to handle military matters and a Political Committee headed by the two Foreign Ministers to deal with political issues. The Military Committee would meet in Cairo and the Political Committee in Jerusalem.

Late Christmas night, after many hours of discussion, Dayan and Kamel, sitting as a "sub-committee of two," had their first serious disagreements. They clashed over the future of the West Bank and the Gaza Strip, the thorniest of the issues that would ensnarl the "peace process" thereafter. The Egyptians, invoking the principle of the "inadmissibility of conquest of territory by force," demanded *total* Israeli withdrawal from the territories to make way for an independent Palestinian state. The Israelis, arguing correctly that Resolution 242 did not require *total* withdrawal, refused. By 9:00 P.M. the negotiations were deadlocked. Both sides, however, seemed determined to continue their efforts to arrive at an accommodation, leaving the details to the two Standing Committees.

The talks were formally recessed the following day. Significantly, and contrary to an announcement made the night before, the parties did not issue a promised "joint declaration of principles." Instead, Sadat and Begin separately issued statements which merely confirmed that little progress, if any, had been made.

Sadat's short communique clearly defined the major roadblock to peace— "the Palestinian problem." It said: "The position of Egypt is that on the West Bank and the Gaza Strip a Palestinian state should be established. The position of Israel is that Palestinian Arabs in Judea, Samaria, the West Bank of Jordan and the Gaza Strip should enjoy self-rule." Although he had no mandate from either the Jordanians or the Palestinians, Sadat evidently had made himself their spokesman.

In his even briefer communique, Begin made no mention of the "Palestinian problem," but stressed that the two days of negotiations had been "very good days for Egypt, Israel and for peace." He and Sadat, he said, had talked as "friends" who wanted to "establish real peace."

Having largely drafted it himself, with Dayan's help, Begin was convinced that his peace plan was the best of all possible solutions for settlement of Israel's differences with its neighbors, and that eventually it would prevail. This became apparent at the joint news conference held at the Suez Canal Authority's research center, prior to Begin's departure. Although Sadat's replies to journalists' questions indicated that only minimal progress had been made during the two-day "summit" conference, Begin, ever the optimist, insisted that he was leaving Ismailia "a happy man." He admitted, however, that a long and difficult negotiating process lay ahead. While Sadat spoke of "weeks," Begin mentioned "months."

On his way home, Begin fulfilled a long-cherished desire to see the great pyramids of Giza, one of the Seven Wonders of the World, erected between 2613 and 2494 B.C. with slave labor, much of it Jewish. Flying in an Israeli commercial airliner chartered for the trip—unlike Sadat, Begin has no special plane and refuses to have one set aside for his personal use—the Prime Minister got a fine bird's eye view. With Sadat's permission, Begin's plane flew west from Ismailia, then north, and circled low over the pyramids before flying east toward home. Arriving at Ben-Gurion Airport about two hours later, Begin mused on the experience at a news conference.

"The pyramids are phenomenal," he said. "It is very difficult to understand how Egypt's rulers of that distant time came to the idea of eternizing themselves. Cheops (the greatest of the three pyramids) is constructed of three million stones. And how they schlepped those massive stones in those days it is very difficult to understand. From time to time we shall visit them again . . ."

Begin then read a statement that exuded optimism about the eventual outcome of the negotiations. He spoke of "continuing momentum" and of the "warm atmosphere" that had prevailed at Ismailia, whereas actually there had been little of either. He admitted there had been "differences," but believed that "the mutual desire to overcome them" would result in "peace, real peace."

Menahem Begin apparently remained oblivious to the fact, implicit in everything Mohammed Anwar el-Sadat said, that Egypt's leader had no intention—or so it seemed at the time—of modifying his territorial demands any more than he, Menahem Begin, intended yielding the occupied territories of the West Bank and the Gaza Strip.

A few days later, Egypt's terms for an overall settlement were made public in Cairo by Foreign Minister Kamel. He declared that Israel must accept the principle of full Israeli withdrawal from the West Bank and the Gaza Strip and recognize the "inalienable rights of the Palestinians to self-determination," a phrase, incidentally, President Carter had used earlier in one of his innumerable—and often ill-timed and ill-conceived—comments on the Middle East crisis.

Those two principles, Kamel insisted, were not open to negotiation. Once they were accepted by the Israelis, he said, the negotiations should focus on the issue of security for both parties, following which the negotiators could proceed to set a time-table for the withdrawal of Israeli troops and the creation of "an independent Palestinian State."

Clearly, the conquered were dictating to the victors the terms of peace even before the Standing Committees encharged with responsibility for conducting the negotiations had formally met. Equally clearly, however, the "peace process" had come to a full stop, but no one was ready as yet to admit it, and the charade continued.

The weeks between the Ismailia Conference and the opening discussions in Cairo of the Military Committee on January 11 were a period of polarization of the two countries' respective positions. Both in Egypt and in Israel, the leaders focused on their own constituencies, stressing the less flexible elements in their plans, thus provoking from the other side equally strong declarations. Sadat continued to adhere to his two basic demands: total Israeli withdrawal from all the territories and self-determination for the Palestinians, including the right to establish a state. Begin, meanwhile, stood firmly on his "peace plan," declaring it would eventually serve as the basis for negotiating an overall Middle East settlement, implying there was no other. Obviously, he had no monopoly on "inflexibility."

As for the Political Committee, scheduled to convene in Jerusalem on January 16, Sadat disclosed he expected it to formulate a "declaration of intentions" based on a statement upon which he and President Carter had agreed on January 4, 1978 at Aswan. Carter had interrupted a nine-day, seven-country tour to confer with Sadat at the latter's request, after having visited Saudi Arabia's King Khalid and Crown Prince Fahd in Riyadh the day before.

Several days earlier, on December 28, Carter had said he did not favor the establishment of a "radical new independent Palestinian state" on the West Bank and Gaza Strip. Sadat was "surprised and embarrassed" by Carter's remarks and wanted them clarified. He further declared that if the statement truly reflected Carter's position, it would "create severe difficulties in the negotiations." "If true," he said, "President Carter has created for me an obstacle that will need great efforts to overcome." The Egyptian seemed to be so upset that Carter interrupted his world tour to mollify him.

In a statement issued after his forty-five-minute visit with Sadat, Carter redefined for the umpteenth time his stand on the Palestinian question. Its resolution, he said, "must recognize the legitimate rights of the Palestinian people and enable the Palestinians to participate in the determination of their own future." Sadat was satisfied. "Our views were identical," he said after his talk with Carter, and he let it be known that he had urged the American President to press Israel for concessions, "particularly regarding the Palestinian question."

In Jerusalem, Begin seethed. He criticized Sadat for having urged Carter to apply pressure on Israel. "I call upon him (Sadat) not to issue calls for the imposition of pressure on Israel. I never asked the Government of the United States to exert such pressures on Egypt. We, the representatives of Egypt and Israel, are in a phase of serious negotiations for peace—a comprehensive peace in the Middle East leading to signed peace treaties. We must conduct the negotiations . . . as free men. We have no need for pressures of any kind from the outside—not on Israel and not on Egypt."

Begin expressed satisfaction that neither Carter nor Sadat had used the words "Palestinian *state*" during their brief meeting, but noted, after talking by radio telephone with Carter—who was aboard Air Force One en route from Aswan to Paris—that self-determination for the Palestinian Arabs as urged by Sadat and agreed to by Carter was tantamount to a "Palestinian state."

"We don't beat about the bush," Begin said, "we shall not agree to such a mortal danger to Israel."

Begin reiterated that in his view the PLO would take over such a state in no time, and would turn it into a Soviet base, whereupon Israel's civilian population would be within range of Soviet-supplied Arab artillery. He said the Arab people already had "self-determination" in twenty-one sovereign countries, and disputed their right to an additional state. "There are now several million American Mexicans in the U.S.," he said. "They don't ask for the creation of a Mexican state on the border between Mexico and the United States."

But new obstacles were rising along the road to peace. Two days after the Carter-Sadat Aswan talks, Israel acknowledged it was expanding its settlements in the occupied areas of the Sinai Peninsula, territory which it had offered to restore to Egypt in a peace settlement. Begin's office said that the groundbreaking for new farms in northeast Sinai was consistent with the peace proposals which stipulated that Israeli settlements should remain in the area of the "Rafah approaches," a well as along the western, Egyptian shore of the Gulf of Aqaba.

Sadat, reacting to press reports about the settlements, said the Israelis should "burn" them once a treaty was agreed upon. Begin, speaking to a meeting of Likud's Herut faction, retorted, "We should leave the monopoly on burning to Nero."

Secretary Vance arrived in Jerusalem on January 16 and went straight into informal talks with Begin and Dayan in preparation for the opening the next day of a new round of peace talks. The Political Committee meeting was delayed a day, however, because the two sides were unable to agree on the wording of the agenda. Vance forced a compromise formulation, vague enough not to offend either side, with the Arabic version subtly different from the Hebrew version. In the section setting forth the guidelines relating to the issue of the territories captured by Israel during the 1967 war, for instance, the Egyptian version referred to "the West Bank and Gaza," while the Hebrew version specified "Judea, Samaria and Gaza."

Then, suddenly, came another of Sadat's surprises. He had succeeded in totally surprising the world in general, and the United States in particular, in November 1977 when he went to Jerusalem. In mid-January

1978, he surprised everyone once more by abruptly breaking off the political talks in the Israeli capital two days after they had begun. The second occasion was embarrassing to all concerned, but especially to Washington, since by calling off the Jerusalem meetings, Sadat made Secretary Vance's trip to Jerusalem—decided on in Washington on the strength of preliminary exchanges with both sides—look like a rather pointless exercise in accumulating transatlantic flying time.

Vance went to Cairo on January 20 to find out exactly why Sadat had elected to discontinue the talks. He then left the problem in the hands of Assistant Secretary Alfred Atherton who, avoiding publicity as best he could, continued to try to salvage the half-finished Egyptian-Israeli "declaration of principles" and to induce Jordan to join the negotiating process.

Both Vance and President Carter, in their statements immediately after the suspension of the Jerusalem talks, stuck to generalities and endeavored to maintain a low profile. In his annual State of the Union address, Carter made only a brief and rather noncommittal reference to Middle East issues. Yet it is in the nature of the Arab-Israeli conflict that the United States' role grows in direct proportion to the differences between the sides. When the latter seem on the road to understanding, the American role is diminished; when serious obstacles emerge, mediation by Washington is in immediate demand.

The swift change—within ten days—from Vance's last inconclusive visit to Cairo to planning Sadat's "crucially important" visit to Washington on February 3 was a case in point. Those of us who felt back in November that the ultimate purpose of Sadat's dramatic gesture was to oblige the United States to exercise maximum pressure on Israel for a settlement along Egyptian lines, were proved right. Sadat's demand—made publicly on January 21—that the United States arm Egypt on a quantitative and qualitative scale comparable to the US-Israeli arms relationship, seemed to support this view. His argument that Egypt needed the weapons to properly fulfill its "responsibility" as a power on the *African* continent was primarily a public relations ploy to ease Congressional approval of Egypt's extensive arms shopping list.

Indications from Washington were that Sadat was making progress in drawing the United States to his side in pressuring for further Israeli concessions. Some quarters in Washington favored supplying Egypt with a few dozen "Tiger" F-5E fighter bombers. This was a significant departure from the declared United States policy of supplying only "non-lethal" military equipment. These same quarters simultaneously advocated a "revision" of United States' plans for arms supplies to Israel—which would thus be caught in a situation in which Egypt's military stance was being enhanced by the United States, as well as by the Western European countries, usually with financing by the Arab oil states, while its own was being limited—with all the implications such a "tilt" would have on the relative negotiating strength of both.

Another indication was the publication by the CIA (half-heartedly explained away afterwards as an "administrative error") of a report saying that Israel was in possession of "a number of atomic bombs." The timing of the report's release on January 25 implied that Israel did not really need the conventional weapons it had requested from the United States. In addition, the report could be used to argue that Israel's demands for territorial security had now become irrelevant.

Sadat, however, evidently failed to convince the United States on one vital point: his contention that Israeli foot-dragging and haggling had made the suspension of the Jerusalem talks inevitable. On the contrary, the impression that Sadat had acted rashly or even deliberately, and without fully considering the consequences, persisted in the United States. American admonitions to move from diplomacy by mass media to quieter, less visible and less audible means of promoting the negotiating process were addressed to Egypt at least as much as to Israel.

Sadat's subsequent weekend meeting with Carter at Camp David and his sojourn in Washington to meet Congress—and gain valuable exposure to the American mass media—provided the opportunity for them to sort out the many, and in some ways contradictory, strands of Egyptian-American relations.

Various explanations have been put forward by Western and Israeli observers for President Sadat's decision, announced on January 18, to call the Egyptian delegation back to Cairo from the Political Committee meeting in Jerusalem. None was fully satisfactory.

Then, during the first two months of 1978 American and Soviet policy in the Middle East became involved in a complex interplay of forces extending far beyond the immediate confines of the Arab-Israeli dispute. The Horn of Africa, and to some extent the Sahara conflict, became an integral part of the Middle East picture. The interdependence of these issues, from the standpoint of the Great Powers, was first brought home by the massive Soviet airlift to Ethiopia in December. President Carter's New Year's visits with the leaders of Iran, Saudi Arabia and Egypt were taken up as much by the conflict on the Horn of Africa as by the Israeli-Egyptian peace negotiations. Not surprisingly, then, while Sadat's visit to the United States took center stage during the first half of February, even *his* presentation of the Middle East picture was sharply colored by his African concerns, real or imaginary.

Sadat's "shock treatment" of the United States involved, in effect, a return to his earlier theory that the key to a Middle East settlement was in American hands—a theory he had shelved when he initiated his November journey to Jerusalem. In his trip to the United States he sought to achieve three interrelated strategic goals:

1. Persuading the Carter Administration to exert more pressure on Israel for territorial and other concessions in the peace negotiations. This effort was concentrated in the discreet, private talks held at Camp David on February 3–5. An official United States statement gave some indication of the measure of Sadat's success in this regard—the United States registered its commitment to Israeli withdrawal on "all fronts of the conflict" and its opposition to the Israeli settlement policy both on legal and political grounds. Initially, the Administration sought to balance these demands by noting the necessity of protracted negotiations, the reaffirmation of America's commitment to Israel's security, and the decision to dispatch Assistant Secretary of State Atherton to the area to complete a "Declaration of Principles," so that Egypt and Israel could resume negotiations, with possible Jordanian participation.

However, the Administration's repeatedly expressed strong objections to Israel's settlement policy—most significantly Secretary Vance's February 11 statement that the settlements "shouldn't exist"—together with its effort to again push the notion of a "Palestine homeland" linked with Jordan, created the impression that Sadat had succeeded in eroding the United States' image of "honest broker" and transforming it into that of an "arbiter," with well-defined views and preferences of its own, ominously similar, in Israel's view, to Sadat's "non-negotiable" positions.

2. Wooing the American press and public, including the American Jewish community, to adopt the Egyptian viewpoint regarding negotiations with Israel. Here Sadat, who had already proved his mastery at "media magic," made definite inroads. One indication of his own assessment of his success in this regard was reflected in his repetition of a frequently voiced threat, at the conclusion of his visit—while passing through London on his way to Germany—to resign if negotiations with Israel failed.

3. Lobbying Congress—the Carter Administration had already voiced at least partial support—to approve a new status for Egypt, equal to that of Israel, as a recipient of sophisticated United States' weaponry. Sadat's purpose in this regard appeared to be twofold. On the one hand, Egypt was asking for American weapons, including fighter planes, in order to counter growing Soviet and radical threats in Africa—on Egypt's flanks in Libya; in Ethiopia, source of the Blue Nile and a neighbor of Egypt's ally, the Sudan; and in the Sahara conflict. President Sadat plainly enjoyed President Carter's sympathy in this regard, and probably persuaded a number of Congressmen to support an Egyptian role as "a pro-Western

policeman in Africa," particularly in light of America's self-enforced passivity there.

Sadat's second objective was to try to neutralize American arms support for Israel, by demanding *parity* with Israel. He did so by seeking such sophisticated American weaponry as F-16 aircraft and M-60 tanks, which are virtually unobtainable elsewhere.

President Sadat's stay in Washington appeared to have been fruitful enough to persuade him to continue to pursue the option of negotiations with Israel. The resumption of Atherton's efforts, coupled with Sadat's agreement to meet with Israel's opposition leader Peres, and possibly again with Prime Minister Begin, along with Sadat's apparent acceptance of Carter's "Aswan formula" for mere Palestinian "participation in determining their future," added weight to this assumption.

However, it was not altogether clear to what extent the Washington visit fulfilled Sadat's declared desire to impart new momentum to his peace initiative. On arriving in Washington he stated: "We are now at a crossroads." Upon departing, the element of threat and ultimatum had still not disappeared from his rhetoric.

Evidence mounted rapidly thereafter that American policy was tilting sharply toward the Arabs. The tilt became visible to all but the most myopic observers when the Administration in Washington announced on February 14 that it planned to sell jet warplanes to Saudi Arabia and Egypt in a "package deal" that included Israel. Involved in the proposed sale, worth $4.8 billion to the suppliers, were 60 F-15 Eagle aircraft for Saudi Arabia, 50 F-5 fighters for Egypt and 15 F-15 jets for Israel. Jerusalem was astonished and dismayed for two reasons:

First, the proposal marked another sharp reversal in Administration policy. In May 1977, President Carter had vowed that the United States would not be "the first supplier to introduce into a region newly developed, advanced weapons which could create a new or significantly higher combat capability." This was interpreted by most observers as meaning that the United States would refrain from altering the balance of power in the Middle East or anywhere else in the world.

Second, the F-15 Eagle is the world's most sophisticated combat aircraft. It is incredibly fast—capable of speeds in excess of Mach 2.54 (1,676 miles per hour)—and at combat weight, with half its fuel load, it can climb faster and turn more sharply than any other aircraft. Finally, it carries the Hughes AN/APG-63 fire control radar, which has a phenomenal target range of upwards of one hundred miles. Air Force General John Vogt has described this system as "a decade ahead of anything else" now flying.

Obviously, Carter had gone back on his word, and intended to introduce an advanced weapon in two regions—the Middle East and the Persian Gulf. Until then, Israel had been the sole recipient in the Middle East of advanced American weaponry. The sale to the Saudis of the 60 F-15s definitely would alter the balance of forces in the area.

In Jerusalem, Menahem Begin warned that the sale would turn Saudi Arabia overnight into a "confrontation state," and called on Washington to "reappraise" its decision. Speaking in the Knesset, he claimed that Cairo was now threatening war unless Israel complied with its terms for peace, and he pointed out that "the supply of offensive weapons (to Cairo and Riyadh) . . . could only nourish that threat." Begin knew whereof he spoke: Egypt's army was in a state of "high alert" at the time.

In the national furor that ensued in the United States, supporters of the proposed deal argued that the supply of lethal weapons to Egypt—Cairo also was slated to receive unspecified numbers of armored personnel carriers—was vital to enable it to withstand the threat of the Soviets and their Ethiopian, Libyan and other clients in the region. Moreover, it was said, an American refusal to replace the Soviet Union as Egypt's armorer would be detrimental to Washington's "credibility and prestige." Finally, the argument ran, pressure to send arms to Egypt was being exerted by the Saudis, whom oil-hungry America could not afford to offend.

The pro-Israeli school contended, on the other hand, that the strengthening of the Egyptian armed forces might undermine Sadat's search for peace rather than invigorate it. An enhanced Egyptian military capability might encourage militant Egyptian elements to reconsider the military option and to pressure Sadat to withdraw his "peace initiative."

What most worried the Israelis themselves was that the arms in question would substantially tip the scales of military power in the Middle East in the Arabs' favor. In another war, Israel probably would have to face not Egypt alone, but the cumulative might of all Arab armies—whether they were supplied by the United States or the Soviet Union.

The Soviet threat to Egypt, which proponents of the arms deal used to justify it, was quite remote compared to the direct threat to Israel's security. For geographic and other reasons, there was little the Soviets and their local allies could do to injure Egypt. The chances were infinitely greater that Moscow's Arab allies would ultimately seek to combine with Egypt in another *jihad*—holy war—against Israel than that they would utilize their forces in an attack on Egypt.

Finally, Egypt's need for additional armaments was not nearly as acute as everyone had been led to believe. Egypt has been steadily purchasing— mainly with hard currencies supplied by Saudi Arabia and the oil shiekhdoms of the Persian Gulf—sophisticated military equipment from West European countries. Contrary to published reports, its Soviet-made arsenal has by no means become paralyzed for lack of spare parts, which are obtained by Egypt from Romania, Yugoslavia and other countries. In a time of crisis, furthermore, Egypt would have available to it the arsenals of its Arab neighbors—not to mention the ever-present possibility of a renewal of direct Soviet replenishment.

The debate raged for some time, but Carter and Vance had their way. Arguing in support of the sale of the F-15s to Saudi Arabia, Secretary Vance said the country was of "immense importance in promoting a course of moderation . . . with respect to peace-making and other regional initiatives, and more broadly in world affairs, *as in petroleum and financial policy.*" (Italics mine—F.G.)

Two of the less believable statements in the Administration's efforts to sway the Senate were Vance's insistence that "Saudi Arabia strongly supports a negotiated settlement for the Middle East conflict," and Defense Secretary Harold Brown's testimony that "Saudi Arabia has never been a confrontation state in the Arab-Israeli conflict." The Saudis had never openly endorsed Sadat's "peace initiative" or publicly acknowledged even Israel's right to exist, whereas they have quite openly subsidized the PLO to the tune of $40 million yearly, and they praised the PLO terrorist raid on Israel in March 1978. *Some of the PLO weapons recovered after the raid were American-made with Saudi army markings.* Brown's definition of "confrontation state" ignored Saudi Arabia's combat role against Israel in 1948 and 1973.

In advocating the "package deal," the Administration relied heavily on "written assurances" from the Saudis that the F-15s would not be used against Israel or transferred to some other state. The "assurances" contradicted public statements by Saudi Crown Prince Fahd, the real power in Riyadh, that "Saudi Arabia allocates all its forces and strength to bring about a victory of Arab rights. This means that the task entrusted to our army is not only to protect the kingdom, but that it would intervene anywhere that our national duty commands." Earlier, Prince Sultan, the Saudi Defense Minister, said, "All we own is at the disposal of the Arab nation and will be used in battle against the common enemy."

Obviously, however, our need for oil balanced or surpassed our concern for the future safety of small, faraway, democratic Israel, and on May 15, by a 54–44 vote, the United States Senate approved the Administration's "package deal." To ensure Senate approval, Vance informed members of the Senate Foreign Relations Committee beforehand that Israel would be allowed to buy twenty additional F-15s later. After the vote, President Carter said he was "deeply gratified" and stoutly reaffirmed America's "historic and unshakeable commitment to the security of Israel."

*   *   *

A few little-publicized but highly authoritative statistics about the extent of the Arab arms buildup in the Middle East may illuminate the enormity of the danger that Israel might face unless there is a negotiated peace in the Middle East. By 1980, the Arab states will have more artillery than the United States, almost as many tanks and double the airpower of NATO itself.

The ominous question—ominous not only for Israel but for the world at large—is why is this monumental increment in Arab armaments taking place? It is axiomatic that while nations invariably insist they arm for peace, oftener than not their weapons are used to make war.

Orders placed by Arab states since 1977 for arms to be supplied by 1980 amount of $35 billion so far, of which $24 billion already has been expended by Saudi Arabia alone. The volume of Saudi military orders since 1977, not including the purchase of F-15s from the United States, exceeds the total volume of all American arms sales to Israel since 1949. Projected Saudi arms orders through 1980 could supply the armies of the entire African continent, as well as a majority of the NATO forces in France, West Germany, Belgium, Denmark, Norway and the Netherlands.

In addition to American super-jets, Saudi Arabia is buying huge amounts of armaments, including late-model Mystères and Mirages, from the French. The purchases represent a ten-fold expansion of Saudi military capability since 1972 and make that country, with a population of approximately six million, the largest single arms buyer in the world. The facts contradict the picture of "a defenseless Saudi Arabia" that worries about thirty-six antiquated MIG-19s in the hands of Communist-oriented Southern Yemen, its neighbor to the south.

The Arab states, furthermore, have half a million more men under arms, three thousand more tanks and several hundred more combat aircraft than NATO. One cannot escape the conclusion that Washington and the world's other armorers are consciously ignoring a situation fraught with the gravest dangers for mankind, even if, as seemed likely at this writing, Egypt concluded a separate peace with Israel.

Meanwhile, Israel remained under pressure from Washington to be less "intransigeant" in its search for peace and make substantial "concessions" to the other side. The situation seemed to call for patience on Washington's part rather than for additional "arm-twisting." On the Panama Canal issue, the United States negotiated for thirteen years before arriving at a solution, and with Vietnam it was approximately four years before America could extricate itself from a civil war that was probably none of its business. The problems of an Arab-Israeli conflict that had endured for three decades were far too complex to be speedily resolved. Until midsummer, there had been less than twenty-four hours of substantive negotiations between the parties to the Arab-Israeli dispute.

No peace between warring parties is possible without concessions on both sides, and for months after the Ismailia meeting none were forthcoming from Cairo. Egypt had not agreed to concede an inch of territory. One might or might not like the proposals put forward in December 1977 by Menahem Begin, but until Sadat finally responded, Begin's were the only terms extant for negotiating peace in the Middle East. Sadat had flatly rejected the "offer the Arabs couldn't refuse."

Then, toward the end of May 1978, at a press conference in Cairo, Sadat vaguely hinted that he would spring a "big surprise" come July 23. The "surprise" arrived earlier, in fact, on July 5, in the form of his own peace plan for the Middle East, and it turned out to be not very "surprising." It was virtually a restatement of the conditions he had laid down in his speech to the Israeli parliament the previous November, with a few tougher provisions. One called for *total* Israeli withdrawal from the occupied territories, *including* East Jerusalem, as a precondition for negotiations. Sadat's second initiative, so called, was the result of pressure from the United States for a resumption of the long-dormant "peace process."

Earlier, sometime in the spring of 1978, Sadat had proposed the return of the Gaza Strip to Egypt and the West Bank to Jordan as "interim steps" for a five-year period, at the end of which the status of those areas would be finally determined in accordance with the "principle of self-determination," a formulation that caused hackles to rise in Jerusalem. Sadat's proposal was intended to break the deadlock in the negotiations, but it was hardly a new approach to the problem. Transmitted to Washington in response to Carter's importunings to come up with a plan of his own, the Administration found Sadat's demands much too rigid to convey to the Israelis.

Actually, Sadat had said much the same thing as far back as January, following his peremptory recall of his delegation from the Political Committee meetings in Jerusalem, and he had conveyed the text of his proposal to Ezer Weizman in their March meeting. Thus it was difficult to see how he hoped to open new avenues for negotiation with a call for an immediate return to Israel's pre-1967 geographic situation, which Sadat knew was unacceptable to Menahem Begin.

Sadat's curious behavior was probably best explained as an attempt to recruit the support of Jordan and Saudi Arabia for maintaining the momentum of his dramatic "peace initiative." In mid-May, Sadat sent Vice President Mubarak to Riyadh and Amman to present his latest ideas, and a week later Foreign Minister Kamel journeyed to Riyadh to continue those efforts. At the same time, Sadat held talks in Cairo with visiting Saudi dignitaries and the ex-Speaker of the Jordanian parliament, Arif Al-Faiz.

Public statements by Egyptian officials at the time indicated that Sadat was taking a tough stand with the Jordanians, while handling with kid gloves the Saudis, controllers of the exchequer that supplies Egypt with the funds it requires for economic survival and arms purchases—for example, the acquisition of those controversial fifty F-5E's from the United States in the summer of 1978.

Officially inspired Cairo dispatches accused Jordan's King Hussein of an "ambiguous and erratic approach" to the issue of participation in the "peace process." There were strong implications that if Hussein did not go along with the latest Egyptian initiative, *Sadat might proceed without him*. This was the first hint that Sadat might be contemplating a separate peace with Israel, but it went unnoticed at the time.

In spite of Sadat's proposal that the West Bank be returned by Israel to Jordanian sovereignty, King Hussein was not responsive. He let it be known that Jordan would not take part in the Egyptian-Israeli peace talks "unless all parties to the conflict participate," meaning, presumably, the Saudis, the Iraqis, the Syrians and the PLO, as well as the two Super Powers. Obviously, the visit to Amman of Egyptian Vice President Mubarak had failed.

Logically, Jordan should have been pleased with Sadat's proposal. After all, it was Egypt, more than any other Arab country, that endorsed Jordan's oft-expressed view that a "special link" existed between the West Bank and Jordan. Why, then, Hussein's diffidence toward Sadat's "peace" plan? There were—and there continue to be—several possible reasons, but the most pertinent is one rarely mentioned: Hussein knows better than anyone else that the much-talked-about "Palestinian state"— one of the major objectives of Egyptian diplomacy until the Summit Conference at Camp David—already exists, only it is called "Jordan."

Hussein could help solve the Middle East dilemma overnight simply by changing the name of his country back to what it was in 1921 when Winston Churchill arbitrarily carved it out of the Palestine Mandate to create Transjordan— "territory across the Jordan"—that became the Hashemite Kingdom which Hussein now rules.

Ever since Sadat's visit to Jerusalem, Hussein has been playing a complicated game. Sitting on the diplomatic fence, he has coldly pursued a "heads I win, tails you lose" policy. On the one hand, he whispers to Western journalists that deep in his heart he supports Sadat's "peace initiative," and on the other hand he has consistently sabotaged peace by avoiding any overt commitment to it. Jordan and Saudi Arabia both have hindered rather than helped an Arab peace with Israel.

Sadat's new formula—the one trumpeted as his "second initiative"—called for Israel to retreat from the West Bank and the Gaza Strip during a five-year period, meanwhile investing Jordan and Egypt, respectively, with transitional sovereignty over these areas. At the end of the five years, Sadat proposed, the approximately one million Egyptian inhabitants of the two areas would be allowed to decide their own future. All this, of course, as "preconditions" for the resumption of negotiations.

In essence, the "Sadat plan" had been published by Cairo newspapers about ten days before its official announcement—as a trial balloon—and the Israelis had promptly shot it down. I recall the rather smug smile on Carter's face at a televised press conference as he criticized the Israelis for having "rejected" the "Egyptian peace plan" before having received it. In Jerusalem, Premier Begin patiently explained that Israel had dismissed only Sadat's "*preconditions*, not the plan itself." In fact, the plan was not too far removed from Begin's own solution for the future of the West Bank—Judea and Samaria, in his political dictionary—and the Gaza Strip as outlined by him at Ismailia.

But the ultimate obstacle to Israeli acceptance of Sadat's proposals was the Egyptian's insistence on Israeli abandonment of East Jerusalem. Whatever else might be "negotiable," the future status of Jerusalem, Judaism's holy of holies, was not.

The issue rose again at Camp David in September last year, and nearly wrecked what was otherwise the most successful attempt at settlement of the Arab-Israeli conflict in more than three decades. In the cool, clean air of what the late Franklin Delano Roosevelt called "Shangri La," in the bosom of the Catoctin Mountains, Moslem Anwar Sadat and Jewish Menahem Begin—under the watchful eye of that "born-again" Christian, Jimmy Carter—agreed to make peace between their respective countries, a peace that may make the larger dream of a peaceful and prosperous Middle East come true.

The principals came down from President Carter's mountain-top hideaway with two agreements. One, and for all practical purposes the most important, provided for the rapid conclusion of a formal peace treaty between Egypt and Israel. The other accord sketched out the framework of an overall, "comprehensive" settlement of the Arab-Israeli conflict. It envisioned bilateral treaties on the Egyptian-Israeli model between the Jewish state and each of its Arab neighbors. These treaties, however, may be long in coming—years, perhaps, instead of mere months.

The accords were a victory for the counsels of moderation and pragmatism over the strident voices of dogmatism and fanaticism rather than victories or defeats for the participants. There were honors enough at Camp David for all concerned—for host Jimmy Carter as well as for his often fretful guests. It seems fair to say, however, that during those hectic thirteen days in President Carter's "pressure cooker" in Maryland, Menahem Begin rose to heights of statesmanship which not even his most worshipful followers imagined he possessed. For he successfully translated the ideas of security, honor and dignity from abstractions into concrete acts of accommodation with Israel's most populous and most powerful enemy, even risking his political future by agreeing to dismantle Israel's settlements in the Sinai Peninsula, something he had vowed never to do. Begin the idealist evidently had learned to compromise with the political; realities of high public office.

Epilogue

By the time this reaches readers early in 1979, they and the world probably will have witnessed yet another stirring episode in the great Middle East peacemaking drama which began unfolding back in November 1977 when Sadat visited Jerusalem: the conclusion of a peace treaty between Egypt and Israel. Of course, nothing is ever certain in the Middle East, an area renowned for political instability, hence the precautionary adverb. Only someone possessing the prophetic vision of Jeremiah would dare forecast with total assurance the course of events in a region historically riven by internecine quarrels, intramural struggles and fratricidal wars.

Peace between Egypt and Israel was clearly envisioned in one of the two accords negotiated by Sadat and Begin at Camp David last September. In the document in question the Egyptian and Israeli leaders—as unlikely a pair of peacemakers as ever sat across a conference table—solemnly pledged themselves to negotiate a peace treaty between them "within three months" after they had signed the Camp David agreements. By late October of 1978, the evidence was overwhelming that an Egyptian-Israeli peace eventually would become an accomplished fact although serious obstacles to final agreement remained.

The enabling instrument was the one entitled "Framework for the Conclusion of a Peace Treaty between Egypt and Israel." In it, the Egyptian leader fully achieved his main goal—the restoration of the entire Sinai Peninsula to Egyptian sovereignty—without conceding even an inch of land to accommodate Israel's demands for "secure borders." The

357

Israeli negotiators—Premier Begin, Foreign Minister Dayan and Defense Minister Weizman—were obliged to commit themselves to several painful concessions, among them the evacuation of strategic Israeli air bases in Sinai.

Particularly painful, however, was their pledge to remove Israeli settlements at Sharm El-Sheik and in the so-called Rafia salient in northeastern Sinai guarding the approaches to Israel from the south. The removal of these colonies ran counter to Zionist principles, Laborite or Revisionist. It meant uprooting several thousand settlers, an action which required the approval of the Israeli parliament. Begin obtained it, and overwhelmingly, but only after a long and bitter battle in the Knesset which shattered the unity of his own party, the Herut, and threatened the solidarity of his ruling Likud coalition.

At first glance, in fact, it would seem that at Camp David President Sadat obtained what he and his predecessor, Gamal Abdul Nasser, had repeatedly failed to obtain by war. In effect, it was probably the first time in history that the vanquished successfully dictated peace terms to the victors.

These achievements, however, were gained at a price. In return for withdrawal from Sinai, Egypt agreed to full normalization of relations between Cairo and Jerusalem, meaning the establishment between the two countries of diplomatic, economic and cultural relations, including an end to boycotts and to barriers to the free movement of goods and people across their common frontier as well as mutual protection of each other's citizens.

The Egyptian concessions were in clear contradiction to past declarations by President Sadat that "normalization" of relations between the two countries would take place only as the result of a long, gradual process, and certainly not before "the last Israeli soldier leaves Egyptian territory." By the terms of the Camp David accord, the process was scheduled to start when the first stage of Israel's withdrawal from Sinai is completed no later than nine months after the parties signed a peace treaty. Barring the unforeseeable, therefore, Egypt and Israel should be exchanging diplomatic representatives sometime in the summer of 1979. Not too long ago Sadat was saying that "normal relations" with Israel would be "something for another generation to conclude."

In return for evacuating the Sinai Peninsula—its oil fields as well as the air bases and settlements—Begin and his aides also obtained Egypt's commitment to a number of important provisions designed to ensure Israel's military security. The abandoned airfields, for instance, are to revert to strictly civilian use by Egypt and possibly other nations, including Israel. In addition, Israel was guaranteed the right of free passage through the Gulf of Suez and the Suez Canal in accordance with the Constantinople Convention of 1888 which had been abrogated by

Nasser. Furthermore, vessels flying the Israeli flag would have unimpeded and unsuspendable freedom of navigation in the Staits of Tiran and the Gulf of Aqaba. Finally, the Sinai Peninsula was to be for all practical purposes demilitarized; the Egyptians' military strength in the area would be limited to only one division, mechanized or infantry, and highly sophisticated early warning stations were to be erected enabling each side to check on the military movements of the other.

According to the blueprint for an Egyptian-Israeli peace, the burden of peacekeeping in Sinai would be entrusted to United Nations troops. UN forces are to be stationed in the Rafiah salient, where most of the Israeli settlements are located, and in the vicinity of Sharm El-Sheik overlooking the vital Straits of Tiran. In contrast to the 1957 armistice agreement that followed the Suez War of the previous year, these troops could be removed only by a unanimous vote of the United Nations Security Council where, with its veto power, the United States could prevent unilateral removal of the UN forces by Egypt as Nasser did in May 1967, thereby precipitating the Six Day War.

Despite the many concessions to Israel's security needs which he was obliged to make, however, Anwar Sadat could not be dissatisfied with his achievements at Camp David. The resultant peace would enable him to devote a larger share of his country's limited resources to national development and progress, both in short supply in Egypt. Sadat clearly hoped to free Egypt from the heavy economic burden of conflict with Israel in order to channel resources thus saved into more useful pursuits.

For Sadat the alternatives to a settlement with Israel were far less palatable than making at least some concessions to Israel's security needs. They would have compelled him to admit failure, to humble himself before his opponents in the Arabs' vociferous "rejectionist camp," and to give up cooperation with the United States, a major element of his overall policy. Collapse of the Camp David negotiations might have led him to seek a rapprochement with the Soviet Union, thereby exposing Egypt to the risks of another devastating war—and no one knows better than Sadat that the Kremlin never makes friends in the Middle East to "wage peace."

It was not surprising, therefore, that on the issues of the overall Arab-Israeli peace outlined in the Camp David document entitled "The Framework of Peace in the Middle East" Egypt's achievements were less unequivocal, although in many ways they went considerably beyond the broad "declaration of principles" originally demanded by Sadat at the beginning of his "peace initiative." Israel, for instance, committed itself to negotiate peace with its other neighbors on the basis of Resolution 242 and recognized the need to solve the Palestinian problem "in all its aspects" including recognition of the "legitimate rights of the Palestinians," conditions long spurned by Israel.

Moreover, Israel agreed to terminate its military government and civilian administration in the West Bank and the Gaza Strip to make way for a locally raised civil authority which would govern the areas during a five-year interim period. Egypt, Jordan and representatives of the Palestinian inhabitants were recognized by Israel as "partners" in determining the composition of the new civil government.

But in the West Bank and Gaza, Egypt failed to obtain a clearcut Israeli commitment to transfer the territories to Arab sovereignty at the end of the interim period; the principle of self-determination for the Palestinian Arabs was not set down; the controversial Israeli settlements were not even mentioned and the final withdrawal of Israeli military forces was not specified. On the contrary, they were to remain, though "confined to certain areas."

Lastly, the thorny question of the future status of Jerusalem was dealt with only in an accompanying exchange of letters in which Israel made no substantial concession while Sadat recognized that the city would not again be divided.

Above all, no formal "linkage" was established between the two "frameworks": the Egyptian-Israeli agreement and the agreement designed to produce a settlement in the West Bank and the Gaza Strip. This exposed Egypt to the accusation that at Camp David it had made, in effect, a separate peace with Israel.

Consequently, in spite of all its achievements, the Camp David accords met with a cool reception in the Arab world. This time not only the "rejectionists" opposed Sadat's decisions but even the more moderate states expressed reservations, and Egypt was confronted with the prospect of isolation in an Arab world.

At first, Sadat treated the howls and threats from the rejectionist front with studied indifference. To interviewers he said he was accustomed to such waves of criticism and reaffirmed his determination to proceed with fulfillment of the Camp David accords even if none of the other Arab states joined him. Sadat's confidence was based on the fact that the radical rejectionists would have rejected *any* agreement with Israel. The diffidence of the conservative regimes was, however, a more serious matter.

Sadat's initial confidence was nourished by extensive support at home. The resignation of his new Foreign Minister, Kamel, caused some embarrassment, but it contrasted sharply with the flood of messages of support from various key figures in his administration, trade union leaders, professional organizations, student associations and private citizens. Such professions of loyalty are a matter of routine in Egypt's regime, but in this case there were many indications that they were genuine. Similarly, the enthusiasm of the multitudes who cheered Sadat upon his return to Cairo from Camp David simply could not be attributed to regimentation. The Cairenes, like the overwhelming majority of all Egyptians—and Israelis—wanted peace.

As time passed, however, Sadat proved himself far more susceptible to pressures from the rejectionist camp than he publicly admitted. Early in November, the Arab League concluded a four-day summit meeting in Baghdad with the issuance of a communique calling on Egypt to refrain from signing a peace treaty with Israel. The meeting was attended by twenty of the League's twenty-one members: Egypt was not invited. The membership denounced the Camp David Accords as an infringement of the rights of the Palestinian people and other Arabs. It reaffirmed the right of the Palestinians to return to their "homeland" and reconfirmed the PLO's role as their *sole* representative.

Moreover, secret resolutions were adopted by the rejectionists providing for political and economic sanctions against Egypt if it concluded a peace treaty with Israel. League representatives also established a ten year, $3.5-billion annual fund to "counter the effects" of an Egyptian-Israeli rapprochement. It was by any name a war chest for the continuation of hostilities against Israel. The funds were pledged by that highly touted "moderate," Saudi Arabia ($1 billion), Iraq and Libya ($500 million each) and the rest by the Persian Gulf states on behalf of Syria, Jordan and the PLO.

Although publicly Sadat shrugged off the implications of the results of the Baghdad summit, he suddenly began making new demands for modification of the peace treaty which had been negotiated at Blair House, in Washington, by Egyptian and Israeli diplomats. He now required a formal "linkage" between the proposed Egyptian-Israeli treaty and negotiations for settlement of the future of the West Bank and Gaza, as well as a definite "timetable" for elections in those areas and the beginning of Palestinian self-rule.

Rightly or wrongly, Israel rejected Sadat's demands for modification of the proposed treaty. As I've already indicated, no formal "linkage" was established at Camp David between the two accords which Sadat had accepted. Indeed, he seemed anxious at the time to go his own way regardless of opposition from the rejectionists. His change of heart came after the Baghdad meeting and in the wake of reliable reports of large sums offered him—the amounts ranged from $5 billion to $10 billion—to induce him to abandon his "peace initiative."

At this writing, the question of linkage between an agreement over Sinai and settlement of the dispute on other territories—particularly the West Bank and Gaza—constituted one of the most serious obstacles to peace. From Cairo's point of view, separation of the two issues would undermine Egypt's argument that it was not signing a separate peace treaty. The fact that Israel has agreed to return the whole of Sinai both highlights the inconclusive nature of the agreement on the West Bank and Gaza and exposes Egypt to the charge that it has sold Arab rights to regain its own territory.

Linkage is not a simple matter for the Israelis, either. Egypt cannot be considered Israel's partner for an agreement on the West Bank and Gaza. Anything agreed with Egypt would still have to be negotiated with Jordan, the Palestinians, or both, with no certainty about the outcome. If the two Camp David accords were linked and progress toward settlement became stalmated—as well it might given the complexity of the problems involved (Jerusalem, refugees, Palestinian rights, settlements, Israeli historical claims, border)—the Israelis could find themselves in a situation where, after having completed their troop withdrawals, their treaty with Egypt was nullified and they were left with neither peace nor Sinai.

It would be dangerous for Israel, therefore, to set any hard and fast deadline for proceeding with the settlement of the future of the West Bank and Gaza. For, if the timetable was not kept, Egypt could refuse to live up to the terms of its peace treaty with Israel on the grounds that Jerusalem had failed to meet the established deadline for Palestinian autonomy—even if that failure was due to obstructive elements in the occupied territories and even if Israel had already withdrawn its troops from the Sinai Peninsula.

As the first anniversary of Sadat's mission to Jerusalem—November 19—came and went, it was Egypt, not Israel, that was obstructing completion of the peacemaking process which the Egyptian President had begun.

Meanwhile, Menahem Begin could congratulate himself that the basic elements contained in the Camp David "framework" dealing with the future of the West Bank and Gaza remained roughly those which he had proposed at Ismailia and which Sadat had rejected. However, he too faced trouble at home but of a different kind. The political storm that was brewing in Israel—a nation of roughly three million Jewish citizens and as many would-be prime ministers—seemed to be gathering strength enough to blow him out of office when he returned to ask the Knesset's approval of the Camp David accords.

Shortly after he descended from the Catoctin heights, the Prime Minister received me briefly in his well-guarded suite in the Regency Hotel in midtown New York prior to his departure for Israel. Physically, he looked fit, in far better shape than when I had seen him in Jerusalem in November 1977, or in London the following month. He was lightly tanned from his frequent walks in the summery Maryland sunlight and evidently had dined well on the excellent kosher food served at Carter's hideaway, for he had obviously gained weight—"about ten pounds," his personal physician confided.

But the Prime Minister was not the ebullient Begin I had expected to find. The godhead of Israeli conservatism had come away from the

Summit Conference with something which none of his Laborite predecessors had ever been able to achieve: signed documents paving the way
to peace between Israel and its Arab neighbors. Yet, it was not a
triumphant but a visibly worried Begin who shook my hand warmly and
said—feelingly, I thought—"I hope I will still be Prime Minister when
your book is published!" Begin might merely have given voice to a passing
thought, but I sensed genuine concern about what might happen in the
Knesset where, according to reports, a fearsome opposition was building
up. He left later that afternoon to do battle with his opponents in
Jerusalem. . . .

The great debate on the Camp David "frameworks" started in the
Israeli parliament at about 10:30 A.M. on Wednesday, September 20.
Begin opened the session with a televised speech to the nation from the
crowded chamber's rostrum in which he explained and defended the
agreements. He assured the parliament and the country at large that
national security would not be jeopardized by the removal of the military
airfields in Sinai and the peninsula's reversion to Egyptian sovereignty.
"Our experts on security assert and confirm," he said, "that we have
attained sufficient and satisfactory security conditions."

Begin stressed the similarities between his plan for "limited autonomy"
in the West Bank and Gaza areas as he had presented it at Ismailia and
the Camp David "framework" for peace in the Middle East, and added a
number of points: (1) When the five-year trial autonomy ends, Israel
would assert its right of sovereignty over the West Bank and the Gaza
Strip; (2) There would be no plebiscite among the residents of Judea,
Samaria and Gaza; (3) Under no conditions "or in any circumstances"
would there ever be a Palestinian state in those territories.

Begin admitted, however, that his commitment to remove the Jewish
settlers from Sharm El-Sheik and the settlements in northeastern Sinai
was a "most painful matter." "Without hiding my pain," he said, "I must
tell you we are faced with the following choice: either we accept [Egypt's
demands that the settlements be evacuated] or the negotiations on a peace
treaty will not even begin and all the accords reached at Camp David will
have come to naught. Thus, I shall ask this House to authorize the
government to withdraw the Israeli settlers from Sinai and resettle them
elsewhere."

In the great square outside the heavily guarded Knesset, pro-settler
demonstrators were shouting "Traitor!" and demanding Begin's resignation. Inside the chamber itself, the Prime Minister was constantly heckled
and interrupted by members of his own party, notably Geula Cohen who
finally had to be escorted from the House.

But the majority of the members of the Knesset apparently believed
with Begin that Israel had arrived at "a historic moment when it could,

with very great sacrifice, sign a peace treaty with an Arab nation of forty million people and afterwards with Israel's other neighbors." Most of the parliament's 120 members—free to vote their beliefs rather than in accordance with party discipline—seemed to agree that the Camp David accords represented the beginning of a new era in Arab-Israeli relations.

After a marathon session that ended at 3:30 A.M. on Thursday September 21, the Knesset approved the Camp David accords by 84 votes to 19, with 17 abstentions, most of them members of Begin's own government coalition. Ten members of the Likud actually voted against, among them Moshe Arens, chairman of the Knesset's Committee for Foreign Affairs and Defense. The abstentions included Industry Minister Hurvitz and Education Minister Hammer.

With the Knesset's approval of the Camp David agreements, the way was cleared for an Egyptian-Israeli peace treaty. But Begin's Herut, indeed, the Likud itself, lay in ruins. To the Prime Minister, however, it seemed a small price to pay for peace with Israel's most formidable enemy. Whatever might follow, Menahem Begin had proved himself as adept at statesmanship as he had been at revolution.

Statesmanship, someone has written, is the art of transforming nations from what they were into what they ought to be. Even longtime Laborite opponents were obliged to admit that the Camp David accords, if fully implemented, would transform Israel and Egypt—and, one could hope— the entire Middle East from embattled belligerents into what they ought to be, namely, partners in a system of fruitful coexistence as envisioned in the preamble to the agreements:

> After four wars during 30 years . . . the Middle East, which is the cradle of civilization and the birthplace of three religions, does not yet enjoy the blessings of peace. The people of the Middle East yearn for peace, so that the vast human and natural resources of the region can be turned to the pursuits of peace and so that this area can become a model for coexistence and cooperation among nations.

Whether those objectives will ever be reached, only time can tell. The obvious flaw in the Camp David accords was that they did not solve the vexatious Palestinian problem. It should be noted, however, that if any attempt had been made at "solving" that one, there would have been no agreements at Camp David. The larger solution lies down the road— probably far down—but its direction was mapped up there at President Carter's hideaway in the Catoctins.

In the meantine, the Nobel Committee of the Norwegian Parliament awarded the Nobel Peace Prize jointly to President Sadat and Premier

Begin. Perhaps more than at any time in previous years, the 1978 prize was intended less as a reward for past deeds on behalf of peace than as an incentive to future action.

"The Nobel Committee," the official announcement said, "wishes not only to honor actions already performed in the service of peace, but to encourage further efforts to work out practical solutions which can give reality to those hopes of a lasting peace."

With such encouragement and with the continued if sometimes inept proddings of President Carter—whose efforts were rewarded by the Nobel Committee with an honorable mention—it seemed fairly certain that Sadat and Begin would sooner or later sign an Egyptian-Israeli peace treaty. The "comprehensive peace" desired by President Carter remained a laudable goal but that distant objective should not be allowed to slow down the progress toward a bilateral peace between Cairo and Jerusalem. Far from wrecking the chances of an overall settlement, an Egyptian-Israeli peace would enormously enhance them.

Bibliography

Aldington, Richard. *Lawrence of Arabia, A Biographical Enquiry*. New York: Regnery, 1955.

Arberry, A.J., and Landau, Rom (Eds.). *Islam Today*. London: Faber and Faber, 1943.

Begin, Menachem. *The Revolt*. English version edited by Ivan Greenberg. Trs. by Samuel Katz. Jerusalem, Tel Aviv, Haifa: Steimatzky's Agency, n.d.

———— *White Nights, the Story of a Prisoner in Russia*. (Trs. from the Hebrew by Katie Kaplan.) Jerusalem, Tel Aviv, Haifa: Steimatzky's Agency, 1957.

Bein, Alexander. *Theodor Herzl: A Biography*. Philadelphia: Jewish Publication Society, 1941.

Bell, J. Bowyer. *Terror Out of Zion, Irgun Zvai Leumi, LEHI, and the Palestine Underground, 1929–1949*. New York: St. Martin's, 1977.

Ben-Gurion, David. *Rebirth and Destiny of Israel*. Ed. and trs. from the Hebrew under superv. of Mordekhai Murock. New York: Philosophical Library, 1954.

Bilby, Kenneth W. *New Star in the Near East*. New York: Doubleday, 1950.

Bonné, Alfred. *State and Economics in the Middle East, A Society in Transition*. Rev. ed., London: Routledge & Kegan Paul, 1955.

Burckhardt, Jacob. *Force and Freedom, Reflections on History*. New York: Pantheon, 1964.

Cahn, Zvi. *The Philosophy of Judaism*. New York: Macmillan, 1962.

367

Crum, Bartley C. *Behind the Silken Curtain, A Personal Account of Anglo-American Diplomacy in Palestine and the Middle East.* New York: Simon and Schuster, 1947.

Dayan, Moshe. *Diary of the Sinai Campaign.* New York: Harper and Row, 1965.

Dimont, Max I. *Jews, God and History.* New York: New American Library, 1964.

Dolav, Aharon, "White Nights and Tempestuous Days in the Life of Menahem Begin." *Ma'ariv.* Tel Aviv: June 10, 1977.

Eban, Abba. *Voice of Israel.* New York: Horizon Press, 1957.

Elath, Eliahu. *Israel and her Neighbors: Lectures Delivered at Brandeis University.* Cleveland: World Publishing Co., 1957.

Esco Foundation for Palestine, Inc. *Palestine: A Study of Jewish, Arab and British Policies.* 2 vols. New Haven: Yale University, 1942.

Eytan, Walter. *The First Ten Years: A Diplomatic History of Israel.* New York: Simon and Schuster, 1958.

Frank, Gerold. *The Deed.* New York: Simon and Schuster, 1963.

Freud, Sigmund. *Moses and Monotheism.* New York: Knopf, 1939.

García-Granados, Jorge. *The Birth of Israel: The Drama as I Saw It.* New York: Knopf, 1948.

Gervasi, Frank. *The Case For Israel.* New York: Viking Press, 1967.

——— *Thunder Over the Mediterranean.* New York: David McKay, 1975.

Gitlin, Jan. *Conquest of Acre Prison.* Tel Aviv: Hadar, 1962.

Government of Palestine. *Survey of Palestine 1946.* Jerusalem: Government Printer, 1947.

Hecht, Ben. *A Child of the Century.* New York: Simon and Schuster, 1954.

Henriques, R. *One Hundred Hours to Suez.* New York: Viking, 1957.

Horowitz, David. *State in the Making.* Trs. by Julian Meltzer. New York: Knopf, 1953.

Institute of Jewish Affairs. *Jews in Moslem Lands.* New York: World Jewish Congress, 1959.

Isaac, Erich and Rael Jean. *Middle East Review.* Vol. X, no. 1 (Fall, 1977).

Katz, Doris. *The Lady Was a Terrorist* (During Israel's War of Liberation). New York: Shiloni, 1953.

Katz, Samuel. *Days of Fire.* London: W.H. Allen, 1968.

Kimche, Jon. *There Could Have Been Peace.* Dial Press, 1973.

Kurzman, Dan. *Genesis 1948.* New York: World, 1970.

Litvinoff, Barnet. *Ben-Gurion of Israel.* New York: Praeger, 1954.

Lowdermilk, Walter Clay. *Palestine, Land of Promise.* New York: Harper and Brothers, 1944.

Ludwig, Emil. *The Mediterranean, Saga of a Sea.* New York: McGraw-Hill, 1942.

Marshall, S.L.A. *Sinai Victory*. New York: William Morrow, 1957.

Meridor, Ya'acov. *Long is the Road to Freedom*. Tr. from Hebrew. Johannesburg, South Africa: Newzo Press. 1955.

Merlin, Samuel, "Menahem Begin: Orator, Commander, Statesman." *The National Jewish Monthly* (July–August, 1977).

Nathan, Robert R., Gass, Oscar, and Creamer, Daniel. *Palestine: Problem and Promise*. Washington, D.C.: Public Affairs Press of the American Council on Public Affairs, 1946.

O'Ballance, Edgar. *The Arab-Israeli War 1948*. New York: Praeger, 1957.

Owen, George Frederick. *Abraham to the Middle East Crisis*. 4th ed. Grand Rapids, Mich.: Eerdmans, 1957.

Patai, Raphael. *Israel Between East and West: A Study in Human Relations*. Philadelphia: Jewish Publication Society, 1953.

"Peace in an International Framework." *Foreign Policy* 19 (Summer, 1975).

Pearlman, Moshe. *The Army of Israel*. New York: Philosphical Library, 1950.

Royal Institute of International Affairs. *Great Britain and Palestine*. New York: Oxford University Press, 1939.

Sachar, Howard M. *A History of Israel, From the Rise of Zionism to Our Time*. New York: Knopf, 1976.

Simmel, Ernst (ed.). *Anti-Semitism, A Social Disease*. New York: International Universities Press, 1946.

Speiser, E. A. *The United States and the Near East*. Cambridge: Harvard University, 1950.

Toynbee, Arnold J. *A Study of History*. London: Oxford University Press, 1947.

Tritton, A. S. *Islam: Belief and Practice*. London: Hutchinson's University Library, 1954.

Uris, Leon. *Exodus*. New York: Doubleday, 1959.

Voss, Carl Hermann. *The Palestine Problem Today: Israel and Its Neighbors*. Boston: Beacon Press, 1953.

Wavell, A. P. *The Palestine Campaigns*. 3rd ed. London: Constable and Co., 1938.

Weizmann, Chaim. *Trial and Error: The Autobiography of Chaim Weizmann*. Philadelphia: Jewish Publication Society, 1949.

Wolf, Leonard. *The Passion of Israel*. Interviews taken and edited in collaboration with Deborah Wolf. Boston: Little, Brown, 1970.

Ziff, William B. *The Rape of Palestine*. New York: Longmans, Green, 1938.

Index